The Second Gates of Paradise

THE SECOND GATES *of* PARADISE

The Anthology of Erotic Short Fiction

ALBERTO MANGUEL

Macfarlane Walter & Ross

Toronto

MACFARLANE WALTER & ROSS
37 A Hazelton Avenue
Toronto, Canada M5R 2E3

Canadian Cataloguing in Publication Data

Main entry under title:
The Second gates of paradise: volume II of
the anthology of erotic short fiction

ISBN 0-921912-77-3

1. Erotic stories
1. Manguel, Alberto, 1948-
PN6120.95.E7843 1994   808.83'93538   C94-932286-5

The publisher gratefully acknowledges the support
of the Ontario Arts Council

Printed and bound in Canada

To Susan Swan, to Ana Becciu

Then I said to these exquisite women:
"How you will remember when you are old
the glorious things we did in our youth!

We did many wonderful, beautiful things.
And every time we take leave of one another
the sharp pain of love circles my heart."

— SAPPHO

And in these second mansions
there are even more riches than in the first.

    – ST THERESA DE JESUS,
    The Castle of the Soul

Oh, guardian, what a paradise of joy
Have I passed over!

    – JOHN FORD,
    Tis Pity She's A Whore

Not at all, have hope: Venus, who closes
the gates, can also open them.

    – FERNANDO DE ROJAS,
    La Celestina

The happiest lovers have no hope except
on starry nights, beyond the gates,
in the apple orchards of Paradise.

    – MARINA TSVETAYEVA,
    Collected Poems

Contents

Introduction

This happened far away and long ago.

About a thirty-minute bus ride from my house in Buenos Aires was the elevated bridge of the Pan-American Highway which supposedly (I say "supposedly" because somewhere in Brazil the builders ran out of money) stretched from the tip of the toe of Tierra del Fuego to the stiff icy fingers of Alaska. I was thirteen or fourteen years old and the vast travelling road that spanned the continent from south to north appealed enormously to my dreams of adventure. To travel along that road was my deepest wish, which I knew was then impossible, and I had to console myself with simply watching the cars and trucks speed along on their way to darkest North America. But under the bridge, between the grey cement pillars that lifted the desired highway, there was another thrill which was, I discovered, available to me. There, beneath the rumbling traffic, newspaper vendors had set up little kiosks to sell candy, small plastic toys, combs, paper handkerchiefs, cold drinks. And specialized magazines.

I can't remember now how I discovered those sepia-coloured magazines seemingly devoted to artistic photography and bodybuilding. The artistic ones showed languid women in serious underwear revealing shaved armpits, tempting breasts and huge, gleaming buttocks. The bodybuilding magazines sported bulging men flexing their muscles at the camera, posing in a blank landscape or reclining on a rock. Slightly bawdy stories and *risqué* cartoons accompanied the first; earnest exhortations to breathe deeply and eat raw vegetables beefed up the second. I was enthralled by all this vaguely naked flesh and I pictured myself among the boudoir beauties and the hunky bathers. The longed-for adventures on the transcontinental road were wonderful, but equally wonderful were my encounters on those grubby pages with beautiful and sensuous people who looked me straight in the eye as if my lust were reciprocated.

For all I knew, these men and women were now old, or puritanically buttoned-up, or dead: I didn't care. There, on the pages of magazines with names such as *Tutti-Frutti, All Night Long, Corpore Sano, Muscle and Steel,* and *Baby Doll,* their erotic offerings were all mine. Later, in my father's library, I read these magazines, hiding them between the covers of the respectable *Espasa-Calpe Encyclopedia.* I wonder what astonished reader will discover them one day while looking up information on Euclid or the Battle of Lepanto.

It didn't take me long to learn, in those distant days, that looking at erotic pictures, like reading erotic literature, is a generous experience, both private and communal. Erotic literature, like few others, offers a shared experience to the armchair traveller who, by merely opening a book, becomes a voyeur, a lover, a loved one. Every erotic text is a *ménage à trois.*

Samuel Pepys, the celebrated English diarist, jotted down,

one day in 1668, his impressions of just such a *ménage*. He had bought the notorious bawdy novel *L'Ecole des Filles* and resolved, as soon as he had read it, "to burn it, that it may not stand in the list of books, nor among them, to disgrace them if it should be found." But soon he realized that the erotic adventures of the licentious heroines enthralled him no end. In a mingling of English, Spanish and French, in order to keep his writing secret, Pepys confessed that "it did *hazer* (make) my prick *para* (to) stand all the while, and *una vez* (once) to *decharger* (come)."

I believe that it was not by chance that my early intimations of sex happened in the vicinity of the Pan-American Highway. So close is the erotic experience to that of exploring foreign places, of going beyond accustomed boundaries, that travel and erotic literature share a certain common vocabulary. Voyagers have long known the urge to set down in writing their experiences of a place, to capture in watercolours or on film a granted vision. This act of recording is not merely an act of witnessing but also provides us, the indiscreet readers of someone else's business, with the vicarious pleasure of being there too, in Arcadia. The early Greek love novels of Chariton, Xenophon, Iambilichus, Heliodorus and other ancient precursors of John Updike and Colette were set in a bucolic landscape that reflected dale by dale and brook by brook the inner world of their fictional lovers.

"Everything was filled with the beauty of spring," wrote Longus in his second-century *Daphnis and Chloe*. "Tender young creatures that they were, the two lovers imitated what they saw and heard. They heard the birds singing and they sang; they saw the lambs skipping and they took little jumps; they imitated the bees and gathered flowers." And when Chloe asks Daphnis whether there's anything more to love than "kissing, embracing and lying together upon the ground," Daphnis finds his answer in their exemplary landscape. "We'll follow the sweet practise," he says, "of what the rams do to the ewes and the he-goats to the she's." Into this happy place the reader is invited and is made welcome to take part in the frolic.

Not only the act of love itself, but the lovers' bodies are geographies to be discovered and mapped out.

> *Woman's body, white hills, white thighs,*
> *You resemble the world in your generous offering*

writes Pablo Neruda, echoing John Donne, for whom the hair is a forest, the brow a sea, the cheeks the Fortunate Isles and the lips a harbour

> *To which when wee are come,*
> *We anchor there, and think our selves at home.*

For the lover, the loved one's body is earth, water, jungle, mountains, cities. In this geography, everything, from weather to politics, acquires a new sense. In one of his love poems, Stephen Spender describes the erotic encounter as a country. "Here you may wonder," he says, "how it was that works, money, interest, building, could ever hide/The palpable and obvious love of man for man."

Travel writing is not only about the description of a place;

erotic literature is not only about the moment of pleasure. The erotic landscape, which so many times is an idealized theatrical set of painted trees and mechanical birds, becomes all too often a nightmarish place loud with the sound of storm and battle, as in this love poem by James Joyce:

> *I hear an army charging upon the land,*
> *And the thunder of horses plunging, foam about their knees:*
> *Arrogant, in black armour, behind them stand,*
> *Disdaining the reins, with fluttering whips, the charioteers.*
>
> *They cry unto the night their battle-name:*
> *I moan in sleep when I hear afar their whirling laughter.*
> *They cleave the gloom of dreams, a blinding flame,*
> *Clanging, clanging upon the heart as upon an anvil.*
>
> *They come shaking in triumph their long, green hair:*
> *They come out of the sea and run shouting by the shore.*
> *My heart, have you no wisdom thus to despair?*
> *My love, my love, my love, why have you left me alone?*

In that other, anguished reality, both the presence and the absence of the lover delineate a precise physical space, a clear cartography of the erotic encounter. One of the love sonnets of Jorge Luis Borges begins:

> *And the city, now, is like an open map*
> *Of all my humiliations and my pain;*
> *From this door I've seen the evening fall*
> *And by this marble I've long waited in vain.*

Something violent and dark enters at times the erotic chronicle, as if the writer, trying to bring to life once more the fleeting moment, suddenly felt the allegorical shadow of those other companions of Eros: Fear, Disappointment, Despair, even Revulsion.

Love has pitched her mansion in the place of
Excrement

laments W. B. Yeats, recalling his reading of St Augustine, who had observed: "We are born between feces and urine."

"I fell in her dark, primordial sea," wrote the Danish novelist Jens Jacobsen, describing a scene of lovemaking in one of his stories, "where I knew blind sea-creatures would rip my flesh to shreds." And Sylvia Plath, in *The Bell Jar*, looking for the first time at a man's penis, says: "The only thing I could think of was turkey neck and turkey gizzards, and I felt very depressed."

For Baudelaire, the very island of the goddess of love, Cythera, becomes a mirror of the darkest aspects of the sensual body:

On your island, oh Venus, I found only the symbol
Of a gallow from which my own image hung ...
Oh Lord, my Lord, grant me the strength and the courage
To look without disgust at my heart and my body!

Donne, however, affects upon the erotic imagination one final metamorphosis. Love is a voyage, and the chronicle of that voyage, bound in a volume, becomes in turn the universe itself. The circle is completed, and the creation of the world has taken place once more through the power of the erotic act.

> *This Booke, as long-liv'd as the elements,*
>   *Or as the worlds forme, this all-graved tome*
>   *In cypher writ, or new made Idiome,*
> *Wee for loves clergie only are instruments:*
>   *When this booke is made thus,*
>   *Should againe the ravenous*
>   *Vandals and Goths inundate us,*
>   *Learning were safe; in this our Universe*
> *Schooles might learn Sciences, Spheares Musick, Angels Verse.*

Just as every book has its reader, every book has its censor. When I was in high school, where my friends and I conducted feverish and comprehensive searches for anything that might be considered, however vaguely, erotic, I was astonished to find that the sensuous but fairly tame poems of Garcia Lorca were considered indecent by one of my teachers who nevertheless thought highly of Verlaine. Perhaps she had never come across the poem which he and Rimbaud lovingly composed in praise of the asshole and which I and my friends discovered one morning among the dusty volumes of the school library:

> *Wrinkled and dark like a purple carnation*
> *It breathes, meekly hidden away in the froth,*
> *Damp still with love from the soft sloping thighs*
> *Running all the way down to the rim of its seam.*

The history of erotic literature runs parallel to the history of censorship, and the reading of both varies curiously. As we prove again and again, something that seems serious and proper to one eye appears lewd and debauched to another.

When the intricate Temple of Kandarya-Mahadeva was built in Khajuraho, in central India, between the tenth and the eleventh century, its multitudinous friezes of loving couples intertwined in a frenzy of erotic postures elicited (as far as we can tell) nothing but praise from the community's religious leaders who considered the stones' voluptuousness to be sternly didactic. At the same time, however, His Eminence the Cardinal of Mainz, in Germany, ordered his painters to "cover decently the private parts of those figures necessarily depicted naked, so that Adam's shame be hidden from our eyes and as well as that of Eve."

Centuries later, when the English courts infamously banned D. H. Lawrence's *Lady Chatterly's Lover*, a book in which they saw nothing but "gutter filth," a certain Ed Zern reviewed the book in *Field and Stream* and found in it much to please his audience: "This fictional account of the day-by-day life of an English gamekeeper is of considerable interest to outdoor-minded readers, as it contains many passages on pheasant-raising, the apprehending of poachers, ways to control vermin, and other chores and duties of the professional gamekeeper. Unfortunately," Mr Zern conscientiously added, "one is obliged to wade through many pages of extraneous material in order to discover and savour these sidelights on the management of a Midland shooting estate, and in this reviewer's opinion this book cannot take the place of J. R. Miller's *Practical Gamekeeping*."

According to Professor Eric Partridge, one of the probable ety-mologies of the word "obscene" derives from that which, in the theatre, lies off-stage. There, in the wings, huddle the danger-ous props, the unconventional backdrops, the actors for whom the featured play has no part, the playwrights whose work no one dares put on. As fashion changes, so do the inhabitants of this shadowy corner. They are the officially unwanted, the publicly scorned, the secretly desired, and their aspect and their nature varies from age to age and from land to land.

In the ancient world, an erotic text might have been found offensive only if it touched upon the persons in authority. King Ptolemy II, for instance, had the Cretan poet Sotades drowned for having composed a poem describing in unflattering terms the royal wedding night. And the Emperor Augustus banished Ovid from Rome not because of the lewdness of his book *The Art of Love,* but because in some secret way the poet's words undermined Augustus's imperial power.

After the delight with which the Italian Renaissance discov-ered Greek and Roman sculpture, the Counter-Reformation decreed the body itself to be obscene. To conceal or temper it, the statues' impudent parts were chiselled away, fig-leaves were devised to cover the offensive scars and the Vatican amassed, in the course of a few decades, the world's largest collection of marble penises, now arranged in neat rows and displayed in shallow cases that are only pulled out for the perusal of selected visitors.

In nineteenth-century China, the disturbance created by an erotic text lay not in the story, but in the vocabulary. Therefore the members of the Golden Lotus Society, dedicated to the idea that love was "the highest form of art," wrote intricate erotic descriptions but replaced the sexual terms with coded numbers: "I will kiss you from my lips to your 4571 and then tenderly on 93270," wrote a lascivious Golden Lotus lady. "Oh, for you to tell me of 0001 and 0002 and to keep whispering such wickedness – that is sweet to hear while I make your tea."

And in our time, it is the context that seems to provide the occasion for offense. The novels of Marguerite Duras, the stories of David Leavitt, a biography of Oscar Wilde can be purchased with no trouble at almost any Canadian bookstore; but those same books, sent by their publishers to one of the gay and lesbian bookstores of Toronto or Vancouver, are detained by Canada Customs at the border. What offends the official sensibility in this case is not the text itself but the implicit reader for whom the text has been created.

———

Creating life is one of the exclusive prerogatives of God; for that reason, certain religions – Judaism, Islam, the Oogro cult of northern Brazil – expressly forbid the depiction of living things. Sometime in the sixteenth century, Rabbi Judah Loew ben Bezabel of Prague made a Golem, a living man out of clay, to help him out in the synagogue. To punish the rabbi for his temerity, God caused the Golem to wreak havoc in the ghetto so that all should witness the consequences of disobeying His sacred rules.

And yet the urge to mould in clay, to set on canvas or paper the images of the world around and within us, is greater than this fear of *lèse majesté*. The ancient and full-fleshed venuses dating from tens of thousands of years ago, the immemorial priapic giant cut into the earth of an English hillside, the coupling beasts painted on the cavern walls of the Tessali Plateau in the days when the Sahara was green testify to this persistent obsession. It is an obsession not only to record the vision of eyes long turned to dust, but to recreate, across the centuries, a certain experience of all the senses, something which the body learned one afternoon and would have otherwise quickly forgotten.

The Latin dictum regarding the shortness of life and the perseverance of art speaks of a valiant hope: that, against all odds, the brief pleasures of our present can live on in something more durable than mere flesh; that the experience may outlast the body that experienced it; that, like tentative gods, we can bring to life in words or clay a semblance of what we continually lose. Perhaps that is why we carve the name of our loved one on school benches and on the trunks of trees, why we keep a paper napkin from the coffeeshop of our first date, why we recognize in tearjerkers and great dramas our own intimate experiences. I remember once realizing that a stone I had carried around for a number of years was meant to remind me of a person and a place and a time that no longer existed (the place had been torn down and the person had disappeared from my life) except in what I could or would allow myself to conjure up.

Alas, like Rabbi Loew, we are not only poor magicians; we are also fickle and unreliable magicians.

In the second part of Goethe's *Faust*, the student Wagner is in his laboratory, making, he says, "a man." Mephistopheles ironically inquires if Wagner has locked a pair of lovers up the chimney. "The old method of doing it," Wagner answers, "is now unfashionable and absurd. The tender shoot of a new life,

the sweet energy forcing its way out, giving and taking, impos-
ing its pattern, enfolding what is close, then what is far – all
that is discredited. Animals may still take their pleasure in it,
but human beings with their great gifts must have a higher,
purer source from here onwards." Wagner is creating an artificial man, a homunculus (unlike the clay Golem, a homunculus
is said to be made from human sperm). Wagner is also putting
forward a theory popular in Goethe's eighteenth century: that
intellectual creations are nobler than the creations of nature,
that art is superior to biology, that what is artificial improves
on what is natural. Even eighteenth-century gardening exem-
plifies this conviction, with its symmetrical layouts and fantastical topiaries which lend a pleasing order to the bewildering
chaos of Nature's behaviour. According to Goethe's Wagner,
Nature must learn to imitate Art.

To achieve erotic pleasure without the sexual act, to be able
to reproduce artificially the mysteries of nature, to create the
sensations of reality without the labours of intimacy, without
the presence of another, without sweat and without tears: in
these endeavours the alchemist resembles the dreamer of erotic
dreams, and the kabbalist approaches the author of erotic tales.
Something beyond lust, something that has to do with a wish
for immortality, for the endurance of the moment of pleasure,
kindles both the fantasies of the dreamer and the fantasies of
the writer – which at times are confused in one. Readers, by
and large, seek in the text confirmation of a transitory experience or intuition, the grounding of the senses in words of
memory or desire. The erotic text grants both.

———

"If it had been possible to build the Tower of Babel without ascending it," wrote Kafka in 1919, "the work would have been permitted." Something true, something live, something that speaks of ascent and victory runs through the best erotic literature, like an electric wire. The God of Rabbi Loew and His representatives on earth today – censor boards, political and religious leaders, customs officials, educators terrified of education and librarians afraid of books – attempt again and again to deny us that building adventure, telling us that the Golem will destroy us and that the wages of pleasure are darkness and the gaping grave.

I don't believe them. Like all our human encounters, the erotic act is fraught with dangers and no small part of the thrill of erotic literature is that it offers us a glimpse of something so obscurely intimate and mysterious that we have refused it a vocabulary.

The visionary William Blake argued that the Gates of Paradise were for the sexes. Inside God's garden, the distinction between the sexes vanishes and humanity wanders eternally in dreams of bliss and sensual enjoyment, having learned that body and soul are indistinct. That is our realm. But Paradise is an ever-changing place, and the first gates we cross in our earliest erotic experience are certainly not the last. Beyond those gates rise another set of gates, and these too we must cross, because every true erotic encounter is a new one, as dangerous and unforeseeable as the first, and – please the stars – as full of magic.

Alberto Manguel
Toronto, July 1994

DOROTHY ALLISON

MONKEYBITES

In Greece and in Rome it was one of the signs of a well-educated person to know all of Sappho's poems by heart. Born sometime in the seventh or sixth century B.C., her poems, mostly addressed to her women lovers, earned her the title of "tenth muse." Until late in the eleventh century, her work was copied and translated; then, in 1075, Pope Gregory VIII condemned Sappho's poems as obscene and had all copies of her books burnt in Rome and Constantinople. Sappho survives today in a handful of fragments and in one word, "lesbian," coined from the name of her island of birth.

Literature depicts realities from which certain readers are excluded. For the longest time, lesbian readers found no identifiable images in fiction. Then, in 1928, The Well of Loneliness, *a somewhat turgid novel by the English writer Radclyffe Hall, achieved huge notoriety after an obscenity trial which resulted in its being banned in England "for its unabashed depiction of female homosexuality." As censors have obviously not yet learned, banning books is an efficient way of promoting them.* The Well of Loneliness *sparked hundreds of novels with lesbian themes, as well as the recognition of a literary past that had remained up to that point largely undetected.*

But much of that new-found lesbian literature was didactic. Dorothy Allison belongs to a new tradition of writers who no longer feel that their mission is to teach the reader. "I do not think that my purpose in life is to explain, particularly to explain to straight people, what lesbian lives are like," says Dorothy Allison. Nothing in her fiction is instructive. Instead, her stories – such as "Monkeybites" – are about the redemptive powers of sex, both liberatory and healing. But, "to get to healing," Allison argues, "you have to break your heart first. You have to crack the scar. That's what good writing is about."

———————

IN COLLEGE I contemplated a career in biology for one long year, and rats – fat grey ones with minuscule wires in their skulls or slender white ones trailing coloured threads to mark the buried electrodes. The animal labs were in a cinder-block building set away from the campus. I went there like a pilgrim to stare into the cages and finger the plush on a monkey's neck, the monkey bent to a frame that kept his razor teeth from my flesh. After a while the teeth were gone with the larynx, and he only spat when I came to see him.

It hurt me that he could not bite; the rats at least kept their teeth. I told myself that the security of a career in science demanded sacrifice. I would have to get used to rats with wires and monkeys without teeth. But it was hard, hard. I hated the white-washed walls and the raw, shrinking creatures under my hands as much as the implacable mechanical motions of the professors in rubber gloves. After I got the job of cleaning up the lab, my dreams were full of monkeys' teeth and the sibilant scratches of rats' nails on formica counters. On those rare nights when Toni and I could sleep over at a friend's house in the city, I would wake shuddering, feeling her arms around me like the wires that trussed the monkeys.

"You are one restless woman," Toni would tell me in the morning, showing me the scratches I'd made on her arms and back. "Can't lie still to save your life." More out of guilt than desire, I'd kiss her shoulders and slide down between her legs to ease with my tongue what I could not cure with words. I felt about oral sex with Toni the way my roommate in the dorm felt about transcendental meditation. At the point at which my neck began to ache and my fingers spasmed on her thighs, I would begin to feel righteous. The longer it took to get her off, and the greater the ache in my neck and back, the farther away I would go in my mind until finally it was as if I were not making love to Toni, but to myself. I became a point of concentration, icy and hot at the same time. When she began to babble those love words that meant she was just about to come, my own thighs would shake sympathetically. I rarely came making love to Toni, but nothing made me feel so balanced as an hour or two pushing my tongue between her swollen labia. It was expiation and penance. It was redemption.

But for Toni, sex was a matter of commitment; making love was a bond itself. She had her own cage, her own need for expiation, and she hated the way I could go away into my own head, the distance between us that she could not cross. She wanted a bridge across my nerves, a connection I could not break at will. Hanging out in the lab with me, she'd tease and flirt, laughing at the other lab assistants and the carefully serious expressions with which they'd clean rat shit off their fingers. The truth was Toni loved the lab, the perfectly square cinder-block rooms, the walls of cages, and the irritable way I'd stalk around with my broom and dustpan. She loved to follow me over in the evening to watch me sweep up the little grey turds and chopped-up computer printouts that lined the bottoms of the cages. Sipping from her omnipresent thermos of vodka and orange juice, she'd throw cashews at the bald-headed monkeys and tease me about how my ass moved when I bent over with my pan.

Once I'd gotten so angry I'd grabbed her thermos and threatened to kick her out of "my" lab.

"Oh sweetheart, you don't want me to go," she'd told me, and tried to coax me up on one of the big empty lab tables beside her.

"Have a sip. Have a little smoke. Tell me how you always wanted to find somebody like me to tease you, and love you, and suck on your nipples till you howling at the moon."

"Oh yeah. Uh huh. I just always knew some black-eyed woman was gonna come along dying to fuck me silly in front of a bunch of toothless monkeys."

"Prescient. That's what you are."

"Desperate, maybe. That's what I was when I let you talk me into bringing you over here."

"Oh, girl." She held a joint in her left hand and using her right hand only, she pulled out a match, struck it against the pack, lit the joint, took a puff, and then held it out to me.

"Have a smoke and lighten up. I'm the one on your side, you know."

Her mouth was wide and soft; the right side turned up a little in that way made my hips feel loose. Above that mouth her black eyes were shining and bright. Sometimes when I wanted to make her feel good, I would make my own eyes widen, intensify my gaze, and give her the look of love she was giving me at that moment. For me it was lust; only in her eyes did it become love. But she *was* on my side, I knew that. Toni was old school. For all that she was my age and just another scholarship student in a blue-jean jacket, she was and knew herself to be, a bar dyke with a bar dyke's studied moves, the low and sauntering strut of a great fighter and a better lover. She had, too, a bar dyke's rough and ready talent for getting me angry and then charming me out of it. Every time she played that game and made those moves, all the anger went out of me.

"Yeah," I told her, looking into her soft eyes. "You're on my side."

She drew the smoke deep into her lungs and smiled drunkenly. "Girl, girl. You act like butter wouldn't melt in your mouth. Keeping your eyes down and your voice so soft. Wearing those silly-assed sandals and damn-fool embroidered denim blouses. Always telling those drawling lies about all your cousins, and granddaddies, and uncles …"

"They ain't lies."

"Then they should be."

"And you." She was making me angry again. "Who do you think you are?"

She pulled her legs up, ran one hand down her heavily muscled thigh, arched her back to stretch, and gave me another of her slow wandering looks, her eyes sliding up from my crotch to my face, heating my skin as she went.

"Me?" she drawled. "Me? Why, I'm just the daughter of the man with the smallest used car lot in Pinellas County and a mama who ain't been sober since the day I was conceived. They wanted me to go to college and make something of myself, so here I am. Trouble is they ain't got the first notion that all I really want is to be the sun and the moon and the stars to some butter-tongued girl in silly-assed sandals and an embroidered denim blouse."

"You say."

"I do indeed."

I'd laughed, not believing her, but enjoying her anyway – maybe because I didn't believe her. It was so much easier if she was not too serious, if I didn't have to think about what might happen if what was going on between us was love – love the way people talked about it, real love, dangerous and scary and not to be trusted at all. I pulled open the top snap on my blouse and trailed my fingernails up from my breasts to my throat.

"You the butter-tongued one it seems to me."

I leaned forward until my face was close to hers. She turned the joint around, tucked the lit end in her mouth, and kissed me so that the smoke shotgunned into my lungs. I melted into her ribs, pushing my hips against her thighs. She kept pushing smoke into me until the room seemed to rock unsteadily and my hands started to roam over her bunched and shaking shoulders.

Toni hadn't seemed to draw a breath through all that long speech, but when I slid into her arms she was breathless, and so was I.

"Do me." The words came out in a grating whisper. "Do me right."

"Oh, girl!" Her voice was hoarse. Her teeth raked my neck, and her fingernails tore at my ribs. My hands started shaking so bad, I couldn't get my jeans unzipped. She grabbed my wrists and pulled my hands behind my back, holding them there with one hand while she used the other to rip the snaps of my blouse open and unzip my jeans slowly. I wanted to scream "hurry," but clamped my teeth instead. If I said a word, she would just slow down and tease me more ruthlessly. I heard my sobs like they were echoes in a wind tunnel. She inched my jeans down over my butt until I was whining like a monkey strapped to a metal table.

"Oh, fuck me. Goddamn it! Fuck me!" I begged. Toni slid me to the edge of the table until my head hung off and my hair swept the floor. When her fingers opened my cunt and her teeth found my breast, I started to scream and the monkeys in the wall cages screamed with me. I jerked and pushed against her, wanting to fight, wanting to give in, wanting the world to stop and wait while I did it all. When I finally started to come, I swung my head until the cages blurred and the monkeys became red and brown shimmering cartoons. Toni climbed over me and put her naked belly against mine, and I began to cry the deepest aching sobs. It felt as if my skin itself were trying to absorb her, soak up the peace and silence inside her. I wanted to stuff myself with her until I was all cotton-battened, dark and still.

"Love," Toni whispered.

"Sex," I told myself, inside my vast quiet open body. "Sex, sex, just sex."

———

I was bitten as a child by a monkey – a dirty-furred, grey-faced creature kept caged by the lake where my stepfather would go on Sunday to try for a catfish dinner. That monkey was so mean she was famous for it. She had an old red collar with a bell on it, and I always wondered how anyone got close enough to her to put it on. When we'd tried to feed her sugar water from my sister's baby bottle, she'd jumped for the wire mesh walls of her cage and shrieked into my sister's terrified face. Then she'd grabbed the nipple off the bottle before any of us could pull it away, chewed it into little pieces and spit them out, swung down and grabbed handfuls of sand and fish scales from the bottom of the cage and thrown them at us. In stunned slow motion, my little sister started to blink and cry, and the monkey came up like an avenging angel to catch her long blonde hair and try to pull her through the wire mesh.

It happened so fast, I couldn't think. I put one hand flat against the cage, grabbed my sister's hair close to her scalp and set myself to fight the monkey for her. But the monkey was faster – faster and smarter. She dropped the air and sprung against the mesh, curled little monkey claws around my wrist, and began to happily chew off my little finger while grinning up into my eyes. The man who managed the fishing camp ran over with a string of dead fish and used them to beat the monkey off. I got my hand back with a web of fine toothy slices ridging my knuckles and wrist.

The curious thing was after that, I loved that monkey. When we'd go back to the fishing camp, I'd show off my gouged and dented fingers to the other kids and boast.

"See. She ate a piece of me."

All the kids in the camp would come to see, then go over to toss fish heads and stones into her cage. They were awed and fascinated, and more than a little scared, too. The monkey, with her gnat-eaten neck and mad red eyes, shrieked and shrieked. Eventually, too many parents complained about the noise and the stink. They dropped the monkey, cage and all, into the centre of the lake.

———

Toni loved my story of the fishing camp, said it made her Southern literature class come alive when she re-read the books in my drawl. "Trailer parks and fishing camps – that's where we growing our storytellers these days. You got possibilities, girl, as a true storyteller. Put a little work into it and you could be famous."

"Right, make a living at it, no doubt."

"Of a kind. Make some people happy anyway. You think about what a queer sort you are, girl, you and your finger-eating monkey. You Southern dirt-country types are all alike. Faulkner would have put that stuff to use, made it a literary detail. Faulkner would have had you in here spouting soliloquies to the monkeys."

Toni pulled a library book out of her backpack and tossed it in my direction. "Or Flannery O'Connor. This one's just like you, honey. She'd have given you a vision of Jesus with monkey's blood. She'd have had you chop off your own fingers and feed them to the monkeys." Toni hugged her pack to her ribs and rocked with giggles.

"Shit girl, it's just too much, too Southern Gothic – catfish and monkeys and chewed-off fingers. Throw in a little red dirt and chicken feathers, a little incest and shotgun shells, and you could join the literary tradition."

I caught her shoulder with my hand and shook her, suddenly outrageously angry. "Shit and nonsense!" I cursed, but Toni just rolled in my grip and went on laughing.

"God damn, honey. It's all nonsense, like sexual obsession – nothing to do with reality no how." She pushed my hands away and pulled her pack on.

"Remember, I'm the literature major around here. You just the anthropologist."

"Biologist. I told you I'm gonna switch over and become a biologist."

Toni shook her head indulgently. "Sure, then you're gonna settle down, marry some sweet boy, and raise mean-assed daughters to please your mama. I'll believe that when I see it."

When I didn't say anything, Toni's face took on a mock-serious expression. She reached out to the rack of cages against the wall and put her fingers to the trembling crossed wrists of a scared young monkey.

"You know," she began, "if you were to work your stories well enough, someone would be sure to conclude they had something to do with your inverted proclivities, your les-bi-an-ism. Something like you constantly re-enacting the rescue of your little sister. Hell, you could make some psychiatrist just piss his britches with excitement."

I felt my lips pull tight with anger. The monkeys chittered in their cages. "But what about you, huh? What do you believe, Miss Literary Analyst?"

"Oh, honey," she stretched her drawl, almost laughing at me. "It's got nothing to do with what I believe. I'm talking about the world, everyone outside the circle of you and me – all those professors you tell your cute little stories to and the women who come 'round to hear your lies – all those lies you don't have to tell me."

"I don't lie to you."

"Don't you?" Her laugh this time wasn't funny. "Well, never mind then. Tell me the story 'bout the fishing camp again. Tell me about that poor sad monkey you got so fond of."

Toni scratched the fur on the soft-eyed monkey in her cage, tracing a line above red-lined patient eyes. "How 'bout this one over here? Your monkey look like this one?"

"I don't remember. That was a long time ago."

"Only a moment in the mind, girl. Think about it. All those details you produce on prompting, the feel of the mesh, the stink of the fish, all that story stuff that rolls out of you so easily when you got an audience around. Bet you got that monkey in your mind all the time."

"You jealous?"

"More like you're guilty? Guilty 'bout how you play up to any and everybody, but got so little time for the folks who really care about you?"

"You, huh? You want me to believe you just live for me, huh?"

"Hell, me and the monkeys, girl. Me and the monkeys." She was teasing and she wasn't. It was the end of the semester, and for weeks she'd been trying to talk me into moving out of the dorm and into an apartment with her for the beginning of the next term.

"Think about it. We'd have a door we could lock against the world."

I thought about it. I thought about never being alone when I wanted to be, about Toni keeping track of where I went and what I did, of her sudden angers and drunken tirades. But I also thought about all those Sunday mornings lying against Toni's thigh out in front of the dormitory, reading the paper and swapping nasty stories until we were both squirming in our jeans with nowhere to go to have sex. Then I thought about making love any time I wanted until I would get to needing it, having to have it, and only Toni to provide it. I thought about getting to where I trusted her and what she might do then. A kind of terror came up from my belly and strangled me. I'd never trusted anybody in my life. How could I trust Toni?

"No," I told her. "I don't want to move in with you."

Toni's black eyes narrowed, and her left hand slapped the monkey cage, sending its captive into shrieking hysterics. "Shit, bitch. You just want your stuff taken care of and never having to trade nothing for it. You tell yourself it's just sex, and sex ain't nothing but itch-scratching. You tell yourself lies, girl. You live your life on lies."

She grabbed my wrists and pulled me close to her. I pulled back, and we both almost fell. For a moment we stood close, trembling, then she threw my hands down.

"Even monkeys take mating seriously." Her anger and hurt and outrage seemed to vibrate right through me. My own anger came rolling back.

"What do you know about monkeys? What do you know about anything?"

"More than your stories, girl. More than your stories tell anyone. I know who I am. I know what I want. And I know what ain't worth my trouble, what ain't worth another minute of my time."

I thought she was going to slap me. I wanted her to slap me. If she slapped me, she would be the bad guy. I would be the heroine, the victim. I'd be able to stare her down and hate her forever. But she didn't touch me. She shook her hands like she was throwing off dust, turned around and walked away. It was a good move. It was the perfect dismissive bar dyke move.

———

I worked in the labs over the holidays, slept on a lab table, and went back to the nearly empty dorm only to shower and change my clothes. I lived on peanut butter sandwiches and Pabst Blue Ribbon beer from the cases the other lab assistants had hidden behind the furnace. The warm beer gave me gas, and I'd sit up on one of the tables and entertain the monkeys with rock-and-roll punctuated with burps. I sang the love songs the loudest, emphasizing the female pronouns by slapping the table.

The monkeys were remarkably quiet, only getting noisy if I beat the table too long. They stared at me out of infinitely wise and patient faces. I poured them all a little beer and smeared peanut butter on their feed trays. They loved the peanut butter and chewed with great wide-smacking sounds. I knew I could trust them. They wouldn't tell my secrets to anybody.

"The problem is …" I told them, checking first to be sure the door was locked. "The problem is I don't love her. I want to love her. I want to love somebody. I want to go crazy with love, eat myself up with love. Starve myself, strangle and die with love, like everybody else. Like the rest of the whole goddamned world. I want to be like the rest of the world."

I went up and put my hands flat against one of the cages. The monkey inside, old and hunched and grey, watched me with eyes that seemed to be all whites.

"But I'm not," I whispered. I was drunk, but I was telling the truth. "I'm not like anyone else in the whole wide world. And all I want of Toni is just a little piece now and then. A little controlled piece that she won't mind giving me, that she wants to give me. You understand? I don't want nothing too serious. I don't want to need her too much. I don't want to need her at all."

Those wide blank eyes looked back at me. I could see myself in the black centres, my hair wild and uncombed around my face, my own eyes as wide as the monkey's, as blank, the pupils as black and empty as night. My mouth worked, and in the blackness I saw my own teeth – clenching, shining, grinding. My teeth scared me right down into my soul. I stole all the dimes from the petty cash drawer and called Toni from the pay phone in the dorm. She listened to me babble and made soft soothing noises into my ears.

"It's all right, baby. I understand. Don't none of us want to be too alone if we can help it, now and then."

I put the phone tight to my teeth and sobbed until she yelled to make me stop.

"If now and then's all you got to offer, then we'll see about now and then."

———

The last Sunday before we all went away for the summer, Toni borrowed a few hours time from a friend with an apartment in town. I'd quit my job in the lab and taken another in the post office, signed up for computer classes, and was trying to stop dreaming about plush-faced monkeys and wild red rats. Toni and I made love until we were too sore to move and then lay naked, sweating into each other's hips. Toni held my hands, fingering the two scars that remained on my right little finger. After a few minutes she sucked my fingers into her mouth and bit down gently.

"Tell me about that fishing camp again." I could barely understand her, and didn't want to talk anyway.

"No."

"That monkey left her mark on you, didn't she?"

"Only one that ever did." I looked into her eyes when I said it, knowing what I was saying as much as she did.

"Only one, huh? You think that's just?"

I shrugged, my eyes never leaving hers.

"There is no justice," I told her, meaning it, meaning it absolutely.

Toni sighed and rolled over. She took a long pull from the half-empty glass of beer she'd left on the floor, and then looked up at me from under her eyebrows.

"Tell you what," she whispered, "I want you to put me in one of your stories sometime."

I took the glass away from her, took a drink myself. "What in the world for?"

She took the glass back and turned away from me. "I want to be there," she said over her shoulder. "I just want to be there, right in there with the monkeys. Me, you understand – raw and drunk and hairy. Me, the way I am. You put me in there, huh? You just put me in there."

J. G.
BALLARD

LOVE IN A COLDER CLIMATE

*"I quite consciously rely on my obsessions in all my work,"
says J. G. Ballard. "I deliberately set up an obsessional state
of mind." One of the most inventive science-fiction writers
in the English language, Ballard's obsessive settings are
often in the future or on faraway worlds beyond the stars,
worlds uncomfortably similar to our own. "The only alien
planet is the Earth," he once wrote.*

*The advantage of imagining the future is that it can
serve as an experimental stage, a place where we can, with
almost complete impunity, play at "what if." In such a
world, sex has often undergone a change and in its muta-
tions we, the readers, can learn vicariously about our own
sexuality. In 1952, Philip Jose Farmer examined the possibilities of erotic encounters between different species in a
short story called "The Lovers"; a few years later, Theodore
Sturgeon redefined sex roles in* Venus Plus X; *in 1969,
Ursula K. LeGuin attributed to all beings the fluidity of
both sexes in* The Left Hand of Darkness. *But these sexual*

utopians had their precursors, mainly in the French eighteenth century: Restif de la Bretonne's The Pornographer, Alexis Piron, Y or The Crotch, the reverend Godard de Beauchamps' History of Prince Apprius in the Land of Sedire (Sedire is an acronym for desire). In all these, the possibilities of the erotic seem even more varied than in our varied world.

Ballard, whose imaginary places include a concrete island in the Los Angeles freeway and a vast underwater realm, explores erotic variations throughout his fictions. In some of them, as in "Love In a Colder Climate," the future reverses our conventions. Ballard's narrator, remembering what might be our lot, says: "Marriage or any monogamous relationship was taboo during the period of one's patriotic duty, the desired aim being an open promiscuity and the greatest possible stirring of the gene pool." In this forced freedom, Eros cannot thrive and, as in the constraints of strict puritanism, it must find devious methods of survival. Eros, Ballard seems to say, must always be subversive.

ANYONE reading this confession in 1989, the year when I was born, would have been amazed to find me complaining about a state of affairs that must in every respect have resembled paradise. However, yesterday's heaven all too easily becomes today's hell. The greatest voluptuary dream of mankind, which has lifted the spirits of poets and painters, presidents and peasants, has turned only twenty-two years later into a living nightmare. For young men of my own generation (the word provokes a shudder in the heart, if nowhere else), the situation has become so desperate that any escape seems justified. The price that I have paid for my freedom may seem excessive, but I am happy to have made this savage, if curious, bargain.

Soon after I reached my twenty-first birthday I was ordered to enlist for my two years of national service, and I remember thinking how much my father and grandfather would have envied me. On a pleasant summer evening in 2010, after a tiring day at the medical school, I was ringing the doorbell of an apartment owned by an attractive young woman whose name I had been given. I had never met her, but I was confident that she would greet me in the friendliest way – so friendly that within a few minutes we would be lying naked together in bed. Needless to say, no money would change hands, and neither she nor I would play our parts for less than the most patriotic motives. Yet both of us would loathe the sight and touch of the other and would be only too relieved when we parted an hour later.

Sure enough, the door opened to reveal a confident young brunette with a welcoming, if brave, smile. According to my assignment card, she was Victoria Hale, a financial journalist on a weekly news magazine. Her eyes glanced at my face and costume in the shrewd way she might have scanned a worthy but dull company prospectus.

"David Bradley?" She read my name from her own assignment card, trying hard to muster a show of enthusiasm. "You're a medical student ... How fascinating."

"It's wonderful to meet you, Victoria," I riposted. "I've always wanted to know about ... financial journalism."

I stood awkwardly in the centre of her apartment, my legs turning to lead. These lines of dialogue, like those that followed, had seemed preposterous when I first uttered them. But my supervisor had wisely insisted that I stick to the script, and already, after only three months of national service, I was aware that the formalized dialogue, like our absurd costumes, provided a screen behind which we could hide our real feelings.

I was wearing the standard-issue Prince Valiant suit, which a careful survey of the TV programmes of the 1960s had confirmed to be the most sexually attractive costume for the predatory male. In a suit like this Elvis Presley had roused the Las Vegas matrons to an ecstasy of abandon, though I found its tassels, gold braid and tight crotch as comfortable as the decorations on a Christmas tree.

Victoria Hale, for her part, was wearing a classic Playboy bunny outfit of the same period. As she served me a minute measure of vodka her breasts managed to be both concealed and exposed in a way that an earlier generation must have found irresistibly fascinating, like the rabbit tail that bounced above her contorted buttocks, a furry metronome which already had me glancing at my wristwatch.

"Mr. Bradley, we can get it over with now," she remarked briskly. She had departed from the script but quickly added: "Now tell me about your work, David. I can see that you're such an interesting man."

She was as bored with me as I was uneasy with her, but in a few minutes we would be lying together in bed. With luck my hormonal and nervous systems would come to my rescue and bring our meeting to a climax. We would initial each other's assignment cards and make a thankful return to our ordinary lives. Yet the very next evening another young man in a Prince Valiant suit would ring the doorbell of the apartment, and this thoughtful journalist would greet him in her grotesque costume. And I, in turn, at eight o'clock would put aside my anatomy textbooks and set out through the weary streets to an arranged meeting in an unknown apartment, where some pleasant young woman – student, waitress or librarian – would welcome me with the same formal smile and stoically take me to bed.

To understand this strange world where sex has become compulsory, one must look back to the ravages brought about in the last decade of the 20th century by the scourge of AIDS and the pandemic of associated diseases clustered around its endlessly mutating virus. By the mid-1990s this ferocious plague had begun to threaten more than the millions of individual lives. The institutions of marriage and the family, ideals of parenthood, and the social contract between the sexes, even the physical relationship between man and woman, had been corrupted by this cruel disease. Terrified of infection, people learnt to abstain from every kind of physical or sexual contact. From puberty onward, an almost visible cordon divided the sexes. In offices, factories, schools and universities the young men and women kept their distance. My own parents in the 1980s were among the last generation to marry without any fear of what their union might produce. By the 1990s, too often, courtship and marriage would be followed by a series of mysterious ailments, anxious visits to a test clinic, a positive diagnosis and the terminal hospice.

Faced with a plunging birth rate and with a nation composed almost entirely of solitary celibates, the government could resort only to its traditional instruments – legislation and compulsion. Urged on by the full authority of the Protestant and Catholic churches, the Third Millennium was greeted with the momentous announcement that thenceforth sex would be compulsory. All fertile, healthy and HIV-negative young men and women were required to register for their patriotic duty. On reaching their twenty-first birthdays they were assigned a personal supervisor (usually a local clergyman, the priesthood alone having the moral qualifications for such a delicate task), who drew up a list of possible mates and arranged a programme of sexual liaisons. Within a year, it was hoped, the birth rate would soar, and marriage and the family would be re-established.

At first, only one assignation each week was required, but the birth rate stubbornly refused to respond, possibly as a result of the sexual ineptness of these celibate young men and women. By the year 2005 the number of compulsory assignations was raised to three each week. Since clearly nothing could be left to nature, the participants were issued with costumes designed to enhance their attractiveness. In addition to the Prince Valiant and the Bunny Girl, there were the Castilian Waiter and the Gypsy Brigand for men and the Cheerleader and the Miss America swimsuit for women.

Even so, the earliest participants would often sit tongue-tied for hours, unable to approach each other, let alone hold hands. From then on they were carefully coached in the amatory arts by their clergymen-supervisors, who would screen erotic videos for the young recruits in their church halls, by now substantial warehouses of pornographic films and magazines.

As could be expected, the threat of two years of enforced sexual activity was deeply resented by the conscripted young men and women. Draft-dodging was carried to extreme lengths, of which vasectomy was the most popular, any perpetrators being sentenced to a testicular transplant. To prevent the young people from failing to perform their sexual duties, a network of undercover inspectors (usually novice priests and nuns, since only they possessed the necessary spirit of self-sacrifice) posed as the participants and would exact fierce on-the-spot fines for any slackening-off or lack of zeal.

All this at last had its effect on the birth rate, which began its reluctant ascent. The news was little consolation to those like myself, who every evening were obliged to leave our homes and trudge the streets on the way to yet another hour of loveless sex. How I longed for June 2012, when I would complete my period of patriotic duty and begin my real sex life of eternal celibacy.

———

Those dreams, though, came to an abrupt end in the spring of 2011, when I called upon Lucille McCabe. After meeting her I woke to discover a lost world of passion and the affections whose existence I had never suspected, and to fulfil my life's ambition in a way I had not foreseen.

Lucille McCabe, my assignment for the evening, lived in the Spanish quarter of the city, and to avoid any catcalls – those of us doing our patriotic duty were figures of fun, not envy – I had dressed in my Castilian Waiter costume. The apartment was in a nondescript building kept on its feet by an armature of crumbling fire escapes. An elevator surely booked into a museum of industrial archaeology carried me grudgingly to the seventh floor. The bell hung by a single exposed wire, and I had to tap several times on the door. The silence made me hope that Miss McCabe, a lecturer in English literature, had been called away for the evening.

But the door opened with a jerk, revealing a small, white-faced young woman with spiky black hair, dressed in a polka-dot leotard like a punk circus clown.

"Miss McCabe…?" I began. "Are you –"

"Ready to order?" She gazed with mock wide eyes at my waiter's costume. "Yes, I'll have a paella with a side dish of gambas. And don't forget the Tabasco."

"Tabasco? Look, I'm David Bradley, your partner for –"

"Relax, Mr. Bradley." She closed the door and snatched the keys from the lock, which she jingled in my face. "It was a joke. Remember those?"

"Only just." Clearly I was in the presence of a maverick, one of those wayward young women who affected an antic air as a way of rising above the occasion. "Well, it's wonderful to see you, Lucille. I've always wanted to know about English literature."

"Forget it. How long have you been doing this? You don't look totally numbed." She stood with her back to me by the crowded bookshelf, fingers drumming along the titles as if hunting for some manual that would provide a solution to the problem posed by my arrival. For all the bravado, her shoulders were shaking. "Is this where I fix you a drink? I can't remember that awful script."

"Skip the drink. We can get straight on with it if you're in a hurry."

"I'm not in a hurry at all." She walked stiffly into the bedroom and sat like a moody teenager on the unmade divan. Nothing in my church hall, had prepared me for all this – the non-regulation costume, the tousled sheets, the absence of flattering chitchat. Was she a new kind of undercover inspector, an *agent provocateur* targeted at those potential subversives like myself? Already I saw my work norm increased to seven evenings a week. Beyond that lay the fearsome threat of a testicular booster ...

Then I noticed her torn assignment card on the carpet at her feet. No inspector, however devious, would ever maltreat an assignment card.

Wondering how to console her, I stepped forward. But as I crossed the threshold a small, strong hand shot up.

"Stay there!" She gazed at me with the desperate look of a child about to be assaulted, and I realized that for all her fierceness she was a novice recruit, probably on her first assignment. The spiked tips of her hair were trembling like the eye feathers of a trapped peafowl.

"All right, you can come in. Do you want something to eat? I can guarantee the best scrambled egg in town, my hands are shaking so much. How do you put up with all this?"

"I don't think about it any more."

"I don't think about anything else. Look, Mr. Bradley – David, or whatever you're called – I can't go through with this. I don't want to fight with you ..."

"Don't worry." I raised my hands, already thinking about the now free evening. "I'm on my way. The rules forbid all use of force, no fumbling hands or wrestling."

"How sensible. And how different from my grandmother's

day." She smiled bleakly, as if visualizing the courtship that had led to the conception of her own mother. With a nervous shrug, she followed me to the door. "Tell me, what happens next? I know you have to report me."

"Well … there's nothing too serious." I hesitated to describe the long counselling sessions that lay ahead, the weeks of being harangued by relays of nuns brandishing their videos. After all the talk there was chemotherapy, when she would be so sedated that nothing mattered, and she would close her eyes and think of her patriotic duty and the next generation, the playgrounds full of laughing tots, one of them her own … "I shouldn't worry. They're very civilized. At least you'll get a better apartment."

"Oh, thanks. Once, you must have been rather sweet. But they get you in the end …"

I took the latchkey from her hand, wondering how to reassure her. They dye had run down her powdered forehead, a battle line redrawn across her brain. She stood with her back against the bookshelves, a woad-streaked Boadicea facing the Roman legions. Despite her distress, I had the curious sense that she was as concerned for me as for herself and even now was trying to work out some strategy that would save us both.

"No …" I closed the door and locked it again. "They won't get you. Not necessarily …"

———

My love affair with Lucille McCabe began that evening, but the details of our life together belong to the private domain. Not that there is anything salacious to reveal. As it happens, our relationship was never consummated in the physical sense, but this did not in any way diminish my deep infatuation with this remarkable young woman. The long months of my national service notwithstanding, the hundreds of reluctant Rebeccas and stoical Susans, I soon felt that Lucille McCabe was the only woman I had ever really known. During the six months of our clandestine affair I discovered a wealth of emotion and affection that made me envy all earlier generations.

At the start, my only aim was to save Lucille. I forged signatures, hoodwinked a distracted supervisor confused by the derelict apartment building, begged or bribed my friends to swap shifts, and Lucille feigned a pregnancy with the aid of a venal laboratory technician. Marriage or any monogamous relationship was taboo during the period of one's patriotic duty, the desired aim being an open promiscuity and the greatest possible stirring of the gene pool. Nonetheless, I was able to spend almost all my spare time with Lucille, acting as lover, night watchman, spymaster and bodyguard. She, in turn, made sure that my medical studies were not neglected. Once I had qualified and she herself was free to marry, we would legally become man and wife.

Inevitably we were discovered by a suspicious supervisor with an over-sensitive computer. I had already realized that we would be exposed, and during these last months I became more and more protective of Lucille, even feeling the first pangs of jealousy. I would attend her lectures, sitting in the back row and resenting any student who asked an over-elaborate question. At my insistence she abandoned her punk hairstyle for something less provocative and modestly lowered her eyes whenever a man passed her in the street.

All this tension was to explode when the supervisor arrived

at Lucille's apartment. The sight of this dark-eyed young Jesuit in his Gypsy Brigand costume, mouthing his smooth amatory patter as he expertly steered Lucille toward her bedroom, proved too much for me. I gave way to a paroxysm of violence, hurling the fellow from the apartment.

From the moment the ambulance and police were called, our scheme was over. Lucille was assigned to a rehabilitation centre, once a church home for fallen mothers, and I was brought before a national service tribunal.

In vain I protested that I wished to marry Lucille and father her child. I had merely behaved like a male of old and was passionately dedicated to my future wife and family.

But this, I was told, was a selfish aberration. I was found guilty of the romantic fallacy and convicted of having an exalted and idealized vision of woman. I was sentenced to a further three years of patriotic duty.

If I rejected this, I would face the ultimate sanction.

Aware that by choosing the latter I would be able to see Lucille, I made my decision. The tribunal despaired of me, but as a generous concession to a former student of medicine, they allowed me to select my own surgeon.

FREDERICK BARTHELME

CUT GLASS

"Barthelme's male protagonists," writes Margaret Atwood, *"are in a direct line of descent from Fred Astaire, who, when actual copulation loomed, preferred to dance on the ceiling or make love to a hat-stand." His heroes – like the anonymous philanderer in "Cut Glass" – explore the fringes of lovemaking and find erotic sense in all sorts of small activities. They are uneasy fetishists, uncomfortable masochists, reluctant voyeurs, shy exhibitionists. All they have in common is the need for adventure.*

Because our world is organized and forseeable, because our work is routine and our leisure time carefully scheduled, we long for adventure. Accidents, sicknesses, and betrayals chequer our existence, but we still believe that we are creatures of habit, and dream of nothing so strongly as of the unexpected. We are fascinated by other lives we imagine we might have lived, and every night die heroic deaths in the arms of strange and extraordinary lovers. It may be that Ulysses never left home, and that Troy and the encounters with the sirens and the sorceress and the one-eyed giant were merely the fruits of wishful thinking, which Penelope patiently endured.

High seas and magic islands are no longer possible as places of adventure, and we have had to seek in everyday sites for occasions in which we can, for a moment at least, be like heroes. Our Aegeans are bleak: singles bars, business-trip motels, early-morning cafeterias present us – we believe – with little bursts of exultation sprung from a look, a word, a chance encounter. In these instants of anonymity we become, all of a sudden, legendary lovers. The elevators of corporate hotels are full of Abelards and Heloises, and every cocktail lounge has its scattering of domestic Mata Haris and inexperienced Casanovas – such as Barthelme's hero.

A MAN IN A ROOM in a hotel in a city which is strange to him, a dark room, although it is night: he stands at the window looking out at the lights of the city. He is happy to be alone, although he can imagine being unhappy for the same reason. He loves the carpet in the room, the dresser, the coat hangers, the wallpaper, the padded headboard of each double bed. He has not seen the city except from the window; he has avoided every sight pictured in the hotel's *Guide to Chicago*; he will leave knowing the city no better than when he came.

He will do what he is doing: stand naked in the darkened,

rented room and look out the window in peace and quiet and in pleasure.

Now he pushes away from the glass, dials Cold on the climate control, slips into the large bed, and pulls the yellow sheet and the thick spread to a point just below his nostrils.

Watching the local news on television he recalls visiting the city as a young man, recalls walking past a barber shop in which a barber was fighting with a customer. The barber knocked the customer down. Remembering this makes the man want to leave Chicago. He is uneasy. He closes the curtain and returns to bed but cannot sleep, so sits up and stares at himself in the mirror mounted on the opposite wall.

———————

A blond woman says hello to him in the hallway. Her voice is cracked and slow, her breath is sweet, and when they stand together at the window in his room he marvels at her suppleness. Having noticed the dark pleasant scent of her breath he becomes worried about his own, and the conversation that is carried on is carried on with both of their faces near the glass, their breathing apparent on the pane. When he turns, finally, to brush his lips against her forehead he does not breathe, but she restrains him there, his lips on her skin, and he is forced to exhale into her hair, which smells heavenly.

She laughs then and pulls away, moving toward the dresser to make herself a drink. He watches her back as she skirts the corner of the bed; he admires her; the dress she is wearing is stylish and light, and it moves as if caught by wind as she walks.

"I want to undress now," he says.

"I don't mind."

He starts to unbutton his shirt, wondering if she has told him the truth. When the shirt is open and out of his pants he feels strongly that she has not, that it is the wrong thing to do, that undressing will reduce the moment if not the whole experience, and he decides not to continue. She asks why he has stopped.

"I'm not used to this. Ordinarily I am alone here."

Light is coming from the bathroom door, which is slightly ajar, coming from behind the woman, and he sees that she is lovely in her own shadow.

"Do I make you nervous?"

"Anyone would," he says. Then, thinking that this answer might offend her, he adds: "Yes. You in particular."

"I am nervous too. But it's pleasant, don't you agree? I'll go if you like."

"No. Well – not yet, not yet."

She goes into the bathroom. The man switches the television off and on several times, quickly, then undresses and gets into the bed nearest the window, stretching his legs and feet toward the corners of the mattress.

"Usually I'm here alone," he shouts into the darkness, toward the bathroom.

When she is into the second bed he says, "Usually I'm alone," then feels foolish for having repeated himself and pushes his hand out in the direction of the bed she is in. It is an uncomfortable moment because when his hand first reaches her bed she does not know that it is there and he has to pat the mattress to get her attention. Then, after a time, in the darkness of that hotel room in a city with which he is by choice unfamiliar, he feels cool wetness between his fingers and feels her blond hair softly fallen on his wrist, and he realizes that she is kissing his hand with her tongue, and laughing.

In the morning at the newsstand she says: "This is as far as you go."

"Yes. But I fly a lot. All over. I have a friend to meet today, upstairs."

"A friend?"

"Not a woman."

She leaves and he buys copies of *Domus* and *Abitare* from the clerk and returns to his room, to the chair by the window. He studies the magazines carefully, taking pleasure in the lovely homes on mountainsides, in canyons, homes of very modern design, homes in which plainness is elevated to unbearable beauty.

The woman calls the hotel from her office. He has opened the window and there is the smell of spice, of cinnamon, in the room.

"I'm coming back tonight."

"Good."

"Do you know who is dead? Sartre."

"I know."

"I think it's very curious that Sartre is dead, don't you?"

"I suppose he should be. Dead, I mean."

"Exactly."

He takes a long bath and goes back to the window with a towel around his waist, a towel draped on his shoulders, and a towel over his head. There are people walking in the street and along the waterfront, brightly coloured people, and the wind has shifted, and he can no longer smell the spice.

————————

When she returns they shake hands and then she laughs and pulls him into an embrace, kisses the still wet hair behind his ears.

"Hello," she finally says.

He notices that she looks tired, that her dark skin is rougher than he remembers, that her hair is more brown than blond and less well cut than he thought.

"You're marvellous," he says.

She turns from the window. "Thank you."

"My friend," he says, looking past her toward the Hancock silhouette against the closing sky, "my friend is not my friend anymore. He has gone crazy, I think."

She says: "Do you have a cigarette?" and he imagines that she sounds like a wonderful movie actress.

"In my jacket." He is pleased that she will leave her scent in the pocket of his coat.

She stays at the window with both hands in the waistband of her jeans.

"I want to smell your hands," he says.

Smiling, she pulls her hands out of her waistband and walks to him holding her hands out palms upward. He takes the hands in his and bends his face to them, smelling the palms, backs, wrists, each in turn, inhaling deeply, slowly, each in turn, until she moves both hands up against his eyes. She holds them there, pressed tight, and he is made acutely aware of the shape of his face, of his cheekbones and the bones over his eyes, and of her hands, slight, almost skeletal, hard.

"I like this very much," he says.

————

He tells the woman that he has decided to stay in Chicago, that he wants her to stay with him, at the hotel.

"Can I do that?"

"Don't pretend to be silly."

The night is deeply hazed; lights out the window are ringed with glares in which they can see small rainbows. The man and the woman sit on the two beds, talking little; he does not drink so much as he did the first night, she does not drink at all. They sit watching the mist tighten on the glass.

She brings two suitcases and a tote and fills the bathroom with her scents, her perfumes and soaps. The following day, while she is at work, he goes through her things as if they were pieces in a treasure, touching them softly, turning bottles against light, savouring, gently tracing outlines of objects with his fingers.

————

He is in the bathroom when she returns.

"What's going on?"

"Just a minute," he says through the locked door.

She drops her coat on the chair and her attention is drawn to the view: the day is crisp, even cold, and looking out the window she realizes that from that vantage it is not possible to tell exactly what the weather is, that it could as well be warm and overcast, or humid, or even bitterly cold, much colder than it actually is. What is most curious to her about this is that something so obvious should have gone unnoticed.

The man comes out of the bathroom with her beige dress.

"Playing with my dress?"

"I want you to wear it again." He drops the dress on the bed behind her.

Automatically unbuttoning her blouse and tugging it loose from her pants, she hands it to him as one might hand a shirt in need of ironing to a valet. "I suppose you'll want this right away."

He stretches out on her bed and drops the blouse over his face. "It looks funny through this," he says. "You're vague-looking."

"Swell. I called at half-past three."

"Many magical things happened."

"The message lamp is still blinking."

"Let it blink all night, I like it."

"Why do you stay here? It gets on my nerves, it already gets on my nerves. It doesn't work like this, people don't do things this way."

"They would if they could."

"You can't even tell what the weather's like."

"Sure I can; it's cold. I felt the glass."

"It's not just the weather, for God's sake."

They sit in silence. He watches the goose bumps appear on her naked shoulders, then disappear, then appear again; she looks out the window at the greying sky.

————

When he wakes up the next morning she is packing.

"I don't understand," he says.

"You understand."

"Right, I understand. But I think you're wrong."

He sits up in bed and sniffs the air, twists his head back and forth. "The smell, the scent – is that you?"

"Who else?"

"No, I mean it's new, isn't it?"

"Yes."

"Where'd you get it? Was it here?"

"Bought it yesterday, downstairs."

"It's wonderful," he says. "Everything we need right in the building."

She kisses him softly on the cheek and he holds her, puts his arms around her.

"This is awkward," he says.

She pulls free of him and walks to the door. He looks at the window, stares at it, at its whiteness and the way it seems to push itself into the room.

"It's very pretty," he says. "To see it close like this is very pretty."

She lines her cases at the door and takes a last look at the room. It is snowing. Flat spots of white slip down and across the window. The buildings of the city are obscured by the dense snow and the glass has the look of a wall. She dials room service, then sits beside the man on the bed, and they wait, and the bellman comes, and she gives him bills, and he takes the bags away.

SAUL BELLOW

SOMETHING TO
REMEMBER ME BY

In Argentina, when I was an adolescent, it was considered proper for a middle-class boy to be initiated by an experienced whore. The father of a friend of mine had introduced his son to one such expert – her name was Margaret, like the former British Prime Minister – and she had proven such a success that my friend suggested that I too take advantage of Margaret's skills. Very nervously I phoned her and she told me to meet her outside a small hotel of the kind that rents rooms by the hour. Margaret was dark and tall; she looked down at me and sighed and then told me that it might be better if we entered the hotel through the side door. Later, in the room which smelled of bleach, she explained to me, as she undressed, how she was putting her little boy through school and that she was planning to take him on a holiday to the sea. Whatever I learned that afternoon, it was tinged with a horrible sadness.

Perhaps every first sexual experience is a failure. Sometimes memory eases the clumsiness, the awkward manoeuvres, the fumbling, the mistakes, but at the time of the first crossing we are usually vastly uninformed and unprepared. Greek society held itself responsible for the sexual education of its young. In Athens, young boys were initiated by older men and – to a much lesser degree – young girls by older women. The temples of Aphrodite lodged sacred prostitutes who furthered the boys' erotic skills, though there were no similar services provided for the girls. Other societies have not been that fortunate and have had to rely on inspired amateurs. Colette's Ripening Seed, *Charles R. Webb's* The Graduate *and Saul Bellow's "Something to Remember Me By" are in their own way homages to the ancient pedagogues.*

WHEN there is too much going on, more than you can bear, you may choose to assume that nothing in particular is happening, that your life is going round and round like a turntable. Then one day you are aware that what you took to be a turntable, smooth, flat, and even, was in fact a whirlpool, a vortex. My first knowledge of the hidden work of uneventful days goes back to February 1933. The exact date won't matter much to you. I like to think, however, that you, my only child, will want to hear about this hidden work. When you were a small boy you were keen on family history. You will quickly understand that I couldn't tell a child what I am about to tell you now. You don't talk about deaths and vortices to a kid, not nowadays. In my time my parents didn't hesitate to speak of death and the dying. What they seldom mentioned was sex. We've got it the other way around.

My mother died when I was an adolescent. I've often told you that. What I didn't tell you was that I knew she was dying and didn't allow myself to think about it – there's your turntable.

The month was February, as I've said, adding that the exact date wouldn't matter to you. I should confess that I myself avoid fixing it.

Chicago in winter, armoured in grey ice, the sky low, the going heavy.

I was a high school senior, an indifferent student, generally unpopular, a background figure in the school. It was only as a high jumper that I performed in public. I had no form at all, a curious last-minute spring or convulsion put me over the bar. But this was what the school turned out to see.

Unwilling to study, I was bookish nevertheless. I was secretive about my family life. The truth is that I didn't want to talk about my mother. Besides, I had no language as yet for the oddity of my peculiar interests.

But let me get on with that significant day in the early part of February.

It began like any other winter school day in Chicago – grimly ordinary. The temperature a few degrees above zero, botanical frost shapes on the windowpane, the snow swept up in heaps, the ice gritty and the streets, block after block, bound together by the iron of the sky. A breakfast of porridge, toast, and tea. Late as usual, I stopped for a moment to look into my mother's sickroom. I bent near and said, "It's Louie, going to school." She seemed to nod. Her eyelids were brown, her face much lighter. I hurried off with my books on a strap over my shoulder.

When I came to the boulevard on the edge of the park, two small men rushed out of a doorway with rifles, wheeled around aiming upward, and fired at pigeons near the rooftop. Several birds fell straight down, and the men scooped up the soft bodies and ran indoors, dark little guys in fluttering white shirts. Depression hunters and their city game. Moments before, the police car had loafed by at ten miles an hour. The men had waited it out.

This had nothing to do with me. I mention it merely because it happened. I stepped around the blood spots and crossed into the park.

To the right of the path, behind the winter lilacs, the crust of the snow was broken. In the dead black night Stephanie and I had necked there, petted, my hands under her raccoon coat, under her sweater, under her skirt, adolescents kissing without restraint. Her coonskin cap had slipped to the back of her head. She opened the musky coat to me to have me closer.

I had to run to reach the school doors before the last bell. I was on notice from the family – no trouble with teachers, no summons from the principal at a time like this. And I did observe the rules, although I despised classwork. But I spent all the money I could lay hands on at Hammersmark's Bookstore. I read *Manhattan Transfer*, *The Enormous Room*, and *A Portrait of the Artist*. I belonged to the Cercle Français and the Senior Discussion Club. The club's topic for this afternoon was Von

Hindenburg's choice of Hitler to form a new government. But I couldn't go to meetings now, I had an after-school job. My father had insisted that I find one.

After classes, on my way to work, I stopped at home to cut myself a slice of bread and a wedge of Wisconsin cheese, and to see whether my mother might be awake. During her last days she was heavily sedated and rarely said anything. The tall, square-shouldered bottle at her bedside was filled with clear red Nembutal. The colour of this fluid was always the same, as if it could tolerate no shadow. Now that she could no longer sit up to have it washed, my mother's hair was cut short. This made her face more slender, and her lips were sober. Her breathing was dry and hard, obstructed. The window shade was halfway up. It was scalloped at the bottom and had white fringes. The street ice was dark grey. Snow was piled against the trees. Their trunks had a mineral-black look. Waiting out the winter in their alligator armour they gathered coal soot.

Even when she was awake, my mother couldn't find the breath to speak. She sometimes made signs. Except for the nurse, there was nobody in the house. My father was at business, my sister had a downtown job, my brothers hustled. The eldest, Albert, clerked for a lawyer in the Loop. My brother Len had put me onto a job on the Northwestern commuter trains, and for a while I was a candy butcher, selling chocolate bars and evening papers. When my mother put a stop to this because it kept me too late, I found other work. Just now I was delivering flowers for a shop on North Avenue and riding the streetcars carrying wreaths and bouquets to all parts of the city. Behrens the florist paid me fifty cents for an afternoon; with tips I could earn as much as a dollar. That gave me time to prepare my trigonometry lesson, and, very late at night, after I had seen Stephanie, to read my books. I sat in the kitchen when everyone was sleeping, in deep silence, snowdrifts under the windows, and below, the janitor's shovel rasping on the cement and clanging on the furnace door. I read banned books circulated by my classmates, political pamphlets, read *Prufrock* and *Mauberly*. I also studied arcane books too far out to discuss with anyone.

I read on the streetcars (called trolleys elsewhere). Reading shut out the sights. In fact there *were* no sights – more of the same and then more of the same. Shop fronts, garages, warehouses, narrow brick bungalows.

The city was laid out on a colossal grid, eight blocks to the mile, every fourth street a car line. The days short, the streetlights weak, the soiled snowbanks toward evening became a source of light. I carried my carfare in my mitten, where the coins mixed with lint worn away from the lining. Today I was delivering lilies to an uptown address. They were wrapped and pinned in heavy paper. Behrens, spelling out my errand for me, was pale, a narrow-faced man who wore nose glasses. Amid the flowers, he alone had no colour – something like the price he paid for being human. He wasted no words: "This delivery will take an hour each way in this traffic, so it'll be your only one. I carry these people on the books, but make sure you get a signature on the bill."

I couldn't say why it was such a relief to get out of the shop, the damp, warm-earth smell, the dense mosses, the prickling cactuses, the glass iceboxes with orchids, gardenias, and sickbed roses. I preferred the brick boredom of the street, the paving stones and steel rails. I drew down the three peaks of my racing-skater's cap and hauled the clumsy package to Robey Street. When the car came panting up there was room for me on the long seat next to the door. Passengers didn't undo their buttons. They were chilled, guarded, muffled, miserable. I had reading matter with me – the remains of a book, the cover gone, the pages held together by binder's thread and flakes of glue. I carried these fifty or sixty pages in the pocket of my short sheepskin. With the one hand I had free I couldn't manage this mutilated book. And on the Broadway-Clark car, reading was out of the question. I had to protect my lilies from the balancing straphangers and people pushing toward the front.

I got down at Ainslie Street holding high the package, which had the shape of a padded kite. The apartment house I was looking for had a courtyard with iron palings. The usual lobby: a floor sinking in the middle, kernels of tile, gaps stuffed with dirt, and a panel of brass mailboxes with earpiece-mouthpieces. No voice came down when I pushed the button; instead, the lock buzzed, jarred, rattled, and I went from the cold of the outer lobby to the overheated mustiness of the inner one. On the second floor one of the two doors on the landing was open, and overshoes and galoshes and rubbers were heaped along the wall. At once I found myself in a crowd of drinkers. All the lights in the house were on, although it was a good hour before dark. Coats were piled on chairs and sofas. All whiskey in those days was bootleg, of course. Holding the flowers high, I parted the mourners. I was quasiofficial. The message went out, "Let the kid through. Go right on, buddy."

The long passageway was full, too, but the dining room was entirely empty. There, a dead girl lay in her coffin. Over her a cut-glass lustre was hanging from a taped, deformed artery of wire pulled through the broken plaster. I hadn't expected to find myself looking down into a coffin.

You saw her as she was, without undertaker's makeup, a girl older than Stephanie, not so plump, thin, fair, her straight hair arranged on her dead shoulders. All buoyancy gone, a weight that counted totally on support, not so much lying as sunk in this grey rectangle. I saw what I took to be the pressure mark of fingers on her cheek. Whether she had been pretty or not was no consideration.

A stout woman (certainly the mother), wearing black, opened the swing door from the kitchen and saw me standing over the corpse. I thought she was displeased when she made a fist signal to come forward and pulled both fists against her bosom as I passed her. She said to put the flowers on the sink, and then she pulled the pins and crackled back the paper. Big arms, thick calves, a bun of hair, her short nose thin and red. It was Behrens's practice to tie the stalks to slender green sticks. There was never any damage.

On the drainboard of the sink was a baked ham with sliced bread around the platter, a jar of French's mustard and wooden tongue depressors to spread it. I saw and I saw and I saw.

I was on my most discreet and polite behaviour with the woman. I looked at the floor to spare her my commiserating face. But why should she care at all about my discreteness; how did I come into this except as a messenger and menial? If she wouldn't observe my behaviour, whom was I behaving for? All she wanted was to settle the bill and send me on my way. She picked up her purse, holding it to her body as she had held her fists. "What do I owe Behrens?" she asked me.

"He said you could sign for this."

However, she wasn't going to deal in kindness. She said, "No." She said, "I don't want debts following me later on." She gave me a five-dollar bill, she added a tip of fifty cents, and it was I who signed the receipt, as well as I could on the enamelled grooves of the sink. I folded the bill small and felt under the sheepskin coat for my watch pocket, ashamed to take money from her within sight of her dead daughter. I wasn't the object of the woman's severity, but her face somewhat frightened me. She levelled the same look at the walls, the door. I didn't figure here, however; this was no death of mine.

As if to take another reading of the girl's plain face, I looked again into the coffin on my way out. And then on the staircase I began to extract the pages from my sheepskin pocket, and in the lobby I hunted for the sentences I had read last night. Yes, here they were:

Nature cannot suffer the human form within her system of laws. When given to her charge, the human being before us is reduced to dust. Ours is the most perfect form to be found on earth. The visible world sustains us until life leaves, and then it must utterly destroy us. Where, then, is the world from which the human form comes?

If you swallowed some food and then died, that morsel of food that would have nourished you in life would hasten your disintegration in death.

This meant that nature didn't make life, it only housed it.

In those days I read many such books. But the one I had read the night before went deeper than the rest. You, my only child, are only too familiar with my lifelong absorption in or craze for further worlds. I used to bore you when I spoke of spirit, or pneuma, and of a continuum between spirit and nature. You were too well educated, respectably rational, to take stock in them. I might add, citing a famous scholar, that what is plausible can do without proof. I am not about to pursue this. However, there would be a gap in what I have to tell if I were to leave out my significant book, and this after all is a narrative, not an argument.

Anyway, I returned my pages to the pocket of my sheep-skin, and then I didn't know quite what to do. At 4:00, with no more errands, I was somehow not ready to go home. So I walked through the snow to Argyle Street, where my brother-in-law practised dentistry, thinking that we might travel home together. I prepared an explanation for turning up at his office. "I was on the North Side delivering flowers, saw a dead girl laid out, realized how close I was, and came here." Why did I need to account for my innocent behaviour when it *was* innocent? Perhaps because I was always contemplating illicit things. Because I was always being accused. Because I ran a little truck farm of deceits – but self-examination, once so fascinating to me, has become tiresome.

My brother-in-law's office was a high, second-floor walk-up: PHILIP HADDIS D.D.S. Three bay windows at the rounded corner of the building gave you a full view of the street and of the lake, due east – the jagged flats of ice floating. The office door was open, and when I came through the tiny blind (win-dowless) waiting room and didn't see Philip at the big, back-tilted dentist's chair, I thought that he might have stepped into his lab. He was a good technician and did most of his own work, which was a big saving. Philip wasn't tall, but he was very big, a burly man. The sleeves of his white coat fitted tightly on his bare, thick forearms. The strength of his arms counted when it came to pulling teeth. Lots of patients were referred to him for extractions.

When he had nothing in particular to do he would sit in the chair himself, studying the *Racing Form* between the bent mantis leg of the drill, the gas flame, and the water spurting round and round in the green glass spit-sink. The cigar smell was always thick. Standing in the centre of the dental cabinet was a clock under a glass bell. Four gilt weights rotated at its base. This was a gift from my mother. The view from the middle window was divided by a chain that couldn't have been much smaller than the one that stopped the British fleet on the Hudson. This held the weight of the druggist's sign – a mortar and pestle outlined in electric bulbs. There wasn't much daylight left. At noon it was poured out; by 4:00 it had drained away. From one side the banked snow was growing blue, from the other the shops were shining warmth on it.

The dentist's lab was in a cupboard. Easygoing Philip peed in the sink sometimes. It was a long trek to the toilet at the far end of the building, and the hallway was nothing but two walls – a plaster tunnel and a carpet runner edged with brass tape. Philip hated going to the end of the hall.

There was nobody in the lab, either. Philip might have been taking a cup of coffee at the soda fountain in the drugstore below. It was possible also that he was passing the time with Marchek, the doctor with whom he shared the suite of offices. The connecting door was never locked, and I had occasionally sat in Marchek's swivel chair with a gynecology book, studying the coloured illustrations and storing up the Latin names.

Marchek's starred glass pane was dark, and I assumed his office to be empty, but when I went in I saw a naked woman lying on the examining table. She wasn't asleep, she seemed to be resting. Becoming aware that I was there, she stirred, and then without haste, disturbing herself as little as possible, she reached for her clothing heaped on Dr. Marchek's desk. Picking out her slip, she put it on her belly – she didn't spread it. Was she dazed, drugged? No, she simply took her sweet time about everything, she behaved with exciting lassitude. Wires connected her nice wrists to a piece of medical apparatus on a wheeled stand.

The right thing would have been to withdraw, but it was already too late for that. Besides, the woman gave no sign that she cared one way or another. She didn't draw the slip over her breasts, she didn't even bring her thighs together. The covering hairs were parted. There were salt, acid, dark, sweet odours. These were immediately effective; I was strongly excited. There was a gloss on her forehead, an exhausted look about the eyes. I believed that I had guessed what she had been doing, but then the room was half dark, and I preferred to avoid any definite thought. Doubt seemed much better, or equivocation.

I remembered that Philip, in his offhand, lazy way, had mentioned a "research project" going on next door. Dr. Marchek was measuring the reactions of partners in the sexual act. "He takes people from the street, he hooks them up and pretends he's collecting graphs. This is for kicks, the science part is horseshit."

The naked woman, then, was an experimental subject.

I had prepared myself to tell Philip about the dead girl on Ainslie Street, but the coffin, the kitchen, the ham, the flowers were as distant from me now as the ice floes on the lake and the killing cold of the water.

"Where did you come from?" the woman said to me.

"From next door – the dentist's office."

"The doctor was about to unstrap me, and I need to get loose. Maybe you can figure out these wires."

If Marchek should be in the inner room, he wouldn't come in now that he heard voices. As the woman raised both her arms so that I could undo the buckles, her breasts swayed, and when I bent over her the odour of her upper body made me think of the frilled brown papers in a box after the chocolates had been eaten – a sweet after-smell and acrid cardboard mixed. Although I tried hard to stop it, my mother's chest mutilated by cancer surgery passed through my mind. Its gnarled scar tissue. I also called in Stephanie's closed eyes and kissing face – anything to spoil the attraction of this naked young woman. It occurred to me as I undid the clasps that instead of disconnecting her I was hooking myself. We were alone in the darkening office, and I wanted her to reach under the sheepskin and undo my belt for me.

But when her hands were free she wiped the jelly from her wrists and began to dress. She started with her bra, several times lowering her breasts into the cups, and when her arms went backward to fasten the snaps she bent far forward, as if she were passing under a low bough. The cells of my body were like bees, drunker and drunker on sexual honey (I expect that this will change the figure of Grandfather Louie, the old man remembered as this or that but never as a hive of erotic bees).

But I couldn't be blind to the woman's behaviour even now. It was very broad, she laid it on. I saw her face in profile, and although it was turned downward there was no mistaking her smile. To use an expression from the Thirties, she was giving me the works. She knew I was about to fall on my face. She buttoned every small button with deliberate slowness, and her blouse had at least twenty such buttons, yet she was still bare from the waist down. Though we were so minor, she and I, a schoolboy and a floozy, we had such major instruments to play. And if we were to go further, whatever happened would never get beyond this room. It would be between the two of us and nobody would ever hear of it. Still, Marchek, that pseudoexperimenter, was probably biding his time in the next room. An old family doctor, he must have been embarrassed and angry. And at any moment, moreover, my brother-in-law Philip might come back.

When the woman slipped down from the leather table she gripped her leg and said she had pulled a muscle. She lifted one heel onto a chair and rubbed her leg, swearing under her breath and looking everywhere with swimming eyes. And then, after she had put on her skirt and fastened her stockings to the garter belt, she pushed her feet into her pumps and limped around the chair, holding it by the arm. She said, "Will you please reach me my coat? Just put it over my shoulders."

She, too, wore a raccoon. As I took it from the hook I wished it had been something else. But Stephanie's coat was newer than this one and twice as heavy. The pelts had dried out, and the fur was thin. The woman was already on her way out, and stopped as I laid the coat over her back. Marchek's office had its own exit to the corridor.

At the top of the staircase, the woman asked me to help her down. I said that I would, of course, but I wanted to look once more for my brother-in-law. As she tied the woollen head scarf under her chin she smiled at me, with an Oriental wrinkling of her eyes.

Not to check in with Philip wouldn't have been right. My hope was that he would be returning, walking down the narrow corridor in his burly, sauntering, careless way. You won't remember your Uncle Philip. He had played college football, and he still had the look of a tackle, with his swelling, compact forearms. (At Soldier Field today he'd be physically insignificant; in his time, however, he was something of a strong man.)

But there was the long strip of carpet down the middle of the wall-valley, and no one was coming to rescue me. I turned back to his office. If only a patient were sitting in the chair and I could see Philip looking into his mouth, I'd be on track again, excused from taking the woman's challenge. One alternative was to tell her that Philip expected me to ride back with him to the Northwest Side. In the empty office I considered this lie, bending my head so that I wouldn't confront the clock with its soundless measured weights revolving. Then I wrote on Philip's memo pad: "Louie, passing by." I left it on the seat of the chair.

The woman had put her arms through the sleeves of the collegiate, rah-rah raccoon and was resting her fur-bundled rear on the banister. She was passing her compact mirror back and forth, and when I came out she gave the compact a snap and dropped it into her purse.

"Still the charley horse?"

"My lower back, too."

We descended, very slow, both feet on each tread. I wondered what she would do if I were to kiss her. Laugh at me, probably. We were no longer between the four walls, where anything might have happened. In the street, space was unlimited. I had no idea how far we were going, how far I would be able to go. Although she was the one claiming to be in pain, it was I who felt sick. She asked me to support her lower back with my hand, and there I discovered what an extraordinary action her hips could perform. At a party I had overheard an older woman saying to another lady, "I know how to make them burn." Hearing this was enough for me.

No special art was necessary with a boy of seventeen, not even so much as being invited to support her with my hand – to feel that intricate, erotic working of her back. I had already *seen* the woman on Marchek's examining table and had also felt the full weight of her when she leaned – when she laid her female substance on me. Moreover, she fully knew my mind. She was the thing I was thinking continually, and how often does thought find its object in circumstances like these – the object *knowing* that it has been found? The woman knew my expectations. She *was*, in the flesh, those expectations. I couldn't have sworn that she was a hooker, a tramp. She might have been an ordinary family girl with a taste for trampishness, acting loose, amusing herself with me, doing a comic sex turn as in those days people sometimes did.

"Where are we headed?"

"If you have to go, I can make it on my own," she said. "It's just Winona Street, the other side of Sheridan Road."

"No, no. I'll walk you there."

She asked whether I was still at school, pointing to the printed pages in my coat pocket.

I observed when we were passing a fruit shop (a boy of my

own age emptying bushels of oranges into the lighted window) that, despite the woman's thick-cream colour, her eyes were Far Eastern, black.

"You should be about seventeen," she said.

"Just."

She was wearing pumps in the snow and placed each step with care.

"What are you going to be, have you picked your profession?"

I had no use for professions. Utterly none. There were accountants and engineers in the soup lines. In the world slump, professions were useless. You were free, therefore, to make something extraordinary of yourself. I might have said, if I hadn't been excited to the point of sickness, that I didn't ride around the city on the cars to make a buck or to be useful to the family, but to take a reading of this boring, depressed, ugly, endless, rotting city. I couldn't have thought it then, but I now understand that my purpose was to interpret this place. Its power was tremendous. But so was mine. I refused absolutely to believe for a moment that people here were doing what they thought they were doing. Beneath the apparent life of these streets was their real life, beneath each face the real face, beneath each voice and its words the true tone and the real message. Of course, I wasn't about to say such things. It was beyond me at that time to say them. I was, however, a high-toned kid, "La-di-dah," my critical, satirical brother Albert called me. A high purpose in adolescence will expose you to that.

At the moment, a glamorous, sexual girl had me in tow. I couldn't guess where I was being led, nor how far, nor what she would surprise me with, nor the consequences.

"So the dentist is your brother?"

"In-law – my sister's husband. They live with us. You're asking what he's like? He's a good guy. He likes to lock his office on Friday and go to the races. He takes me to the fights. Also, at the back of the drugstore there's a poker game…."

"*He* doesn't go around with books in his pocket."

"Well, no, he doesn't. He says, 'What's the use? There's too much to keep up or catch up with. You could never in a thousand years do it, so why knock yourself out?' My sister wants him to open a Loop office but that would be too much of a strain. I guess he's for inertia. He's not ready to do more than he's already doing."

"So what are you reading – what's it about?"

I didn't propose to discuss anything with her. I wasn't capable of it now. What I had in mind just then was entirely different.

But suppose I had been able to try. One does have a responsibility to answer genuine questions: "You see, miss, this is the visible world. We live in it, we breathe its air and eat its substance. When we die, however, matter goes to matter and then we're annihilated. Now, which world do we really belong to, this world of matter or another world from which matter takes its orders?"

Not many people were willing to talk about such notions. They made even Stephanie impatient. "When you die, that's it. Dead is dead," she would say. She loved a good time. And when I wouldn't take her downtown to the Oriental Theatre she didn't deny herself the company of other boys. She brought back off-colour vaudeville jokes. I think the Oriental was part of a national entertainment circuit. Jimmy Savo, Lou Holtz, and Sophie Tucker played there. I was sometimes too solemn for Stephanie. When she gave imitations of Jimmy Savo singing "River, Stay Away from My Door," bringing her knees together and holding herself tight, she didn't break me up, and she was disappointed.

You would have thought that the book or book fragment in my pocket was a talisman from a fairy tale to open castle gates or carry me to mountaintops. Yet when the woman asked me what it was, I was too scattered to tell her. Remember, I still kept my hand as instructed on her lower back, tormented by that sexual grind of her movements. I was discovering what the lady at the party had meant by saying, "I know how to make them burn." So of course I was in no condition to talk to this girl about the Ego and the Will, or about the secrets of the blood. Yes, I believed that higher knowledge was shared out among all human beings. What else was there to hold us together but this force hidden behind daily consciousness? But to be coherent about it now was absolutely out of the question.

"Can't you tell me?" she said.

"I bought this for a nickel from a bargain table."

"That's how you spend your money?"

I assumed her to mean that I didn't spend it on girls.

"And the dentist is a good-natured, lazy guy," she went on. "What has he got to tell you?"

I tried to review the mental record. What did Phil Haddis say? He said that a stiff prick has no conscience. At the moment it was all I could think of. It amused Philip to talk to me. He was a chum. Where Philip was indulgent, my brother Albert, your late uncle, was harsh. He might have taught me something if he had trusted me. He was then a night-school law student clerking for Rowland, the racketeer congressman. He was Rowland's bagman, and Rowland didn't hire him to read law but to make collections. Philip suspected that Albert was skimming, for he dressed sharply. He wore a derby (called, in those days, a Baltimore heater) and a camel's hair and sharp, pointed, mafioso shoes. Toward me, Albert was scornful. He said, "You don't understand fuck-all. You never will."

We were approaching Winona Street, and when we got to her building she'd have no further use for me and send me away. I'd see no more than the flash of the glass and then stare as she let herself in. She was already feeling in her purse for the keys. I was no longer supporting her back, preparing instead to mutter "bye-bye," when she surprised me with a sideward nod, inviting me to enter. I think I had hoped (with sex-polluted hope) that she would leave me in the street. I followed her through another tile lobby and through the inner door. The staircase was fiercely heated by coal-fuelled radiators, the skylight was wavering, and the wallpaper had come unstuck and was curling and bulging. I swallowed my breath. I couldn't draw this heat into my lungs.

This had been a deluxe apartment house once, built for bankers, brokers, and well-to-do professionals. Now it was occupied by transients. In the big front room with its French windows there was a crap game. In the next room people were drinking or drowsing on the old chesterfields. The woman led me through what had once been a private bar – some of the fittings were still in place. Then I followed her through the kitchen – I would have gone anywhere, no questions asked. In the kitchen there were no signs of cooking, neither pots nor dishes. The linoleum was shredding, brown fibres standing like hairs. She led me into a narrower corridor, parallel to the main one. "I have what used to be a maid's room," she said. "It's got a nice view of the alley but there is a private bathroom."

And here we were – the place wasn't much to look at. So this was how whores operated – assuming that she was a whore: a bare floor, a narrow cot, a chair by the window, a lopsided clothespress against the wall. I stopped under the light fixture while she passed behind, as if to observe me. Then she gave me a hug and a small kiss on the cheek, more promissory than actual. Her face powder, or perhaps it was her lipstick, had a sort of green-banana fragrance. My heart had never beaten as hard as this.

She said, "Why don't I go into the bathroom awhile and get ready while you undress and lie down in bed. You look like you were brought up neat, so lay your clothes on the chair. You don't want to drop them on the floor."

Shivering (this seemed the one cold room in the house), I began to pull off my things, beginning with the winter-wrinkled boots. The sheepskin I hung over the back of the chair. I pushed my socks into the boots and then my bare feet recoiled from the grit of the floor. I took off everything, as if to disassociate my shirt, my underthings from whatever it was that was about to happen, so that only my body could be guilty. The one thing that couldn't be expected. When I pulled back the cover and got in I was thinking that the beds in the Bridewell would be like this. There was no pillowcase, my head lay on the ticking. What I saw of the outside was only the utility wires hung between the poles like lines on music paper, only sagging, and the glass insulators like clumps of notes. The woman had said nothing about money. Because she liked me. I couldn't believe my luck – luck with a hint of disaster. I blinded myself to the Bridewell metal cot, not meant for two. I felt also that I couldn't hold out if she kept me waiting long. And what feminine thing was she doing in there – undressing, washing, perfuming, changing?

Abruptly, she came out. She had been waiting, nothing else. She still wore the raccoon coat, even the gloves. Without looking at me she walked very quickly, almost running, and opened the window. As soon as the window shot up it let in a blast of cold air, and I stood up on the bed but it was too late to stop her. She took my clothes from the back of the chair and heaved them out. They fell into the alley. I shouted, "What are you doing!" She still refused to turn her head. As she ran away she was tying the head scarf under her chin and left the door open. I could hear her pumps beating double time in the hallway.

I couldn't run after her, could I, and show myself naked to the people in the flat? She had banked on this. When we came in, she must have given the high sign to the man she worked with, and he had been waiting in the alley. When I ran to look out, my things had already been gathered up. All I saw was the back of somebody with a bundle under his arm hurrying in the walkway between two garages. I might have picked up my boots – those she had left me – and jumped from the first-floor window, but I couldn't chase the man very far, and in a few minutes I would have wound up on Sheridan Road naked and freezing.

I had seen a drunk in his union suit, bleeding from the head after he had been rolled and beaten, staggering and yelling in the street. I didn't even have a shirt and drawers. I was as naked as the woman herself had been in the doctor's office, stripped of everything, including the five dollars I had collected for the flowers. And the sheepskin my mother had bought for me last year. Plus the book, the fragment of an untitled book, author unknown. This may have been the most serious loss of all.

Now I could think on my own about the world I really belonged to, whether it was this one or another.

I pulled down the window, and then I went to shut the door. The room didn't seem lived in, but suppose it had a tenant, and what if he were to storm in now and rough me up? Luckily there was a bolt to the door. I pushed it into its loop and then I ran around the room to see what I could find to wear. In the lopsided clothespress, nothing but wire hangers, and in the bathroom, only a cotton hand towel. I tore the blanket off the bed; if I were to slit it I might pull it over my head like a serape, but it was too thin to do me much good in freezing weather. When I pulled the chair over to the clothes-press and stood on it, I found a woman's dress behind the moulding, and a quilted bed jacket. In a brown paper bag there was a knitted brown tam. I had to put these things on, I had no choice.

It was now, I reckoned, about 5:00. Philip had no fixed schedule. He didn't hang around the office on the off chance that somebody might turn up with a toothache. After his last appointment he locked up and left. He didn't necessarily set out for home; he was not too keen to return to the house. If I wanted to catch him I'd have to run. In boots, dress, tam, and jacket, I made my way out of the apartment. Nobody took the slightest interest in me. More people (Philip would have called them transients) had crowded in – it was even likely that the man who had snatched up my clothes in the alley had returned, was among them. The heat in the staircase now was stifling, and the wallpaper smelled scorched, as if it were on the point of catching fire. In the street I was struck by a north wind straight from the Pole and the dress and sateen jacket counted for nothing. I was running, though, and had no time to feel it.

Philip would say, "Who was this floozy? Where did she pick you up?" Philip was unexcitable, always mild, amused by me. Anna would badger him with the example of her ambitious brothers – they hustled, they read books. You couldn't fault Philip for being pleased. I anticipated what he'd say – "Did you get in? Then at least you're not going to catch the clap." I depended on Philip now, for I had nothing, not even seven cents for carfare. I could be certain, however, that he wouldn't moralize at me, he'd set about dressing me, he'd scrounge a sweater among his neighbourhood acquaintances or take me to the Salvation Army shop on Broadway if that should still be open. He'd go about this in his slow-moving, thick-necked, deliberate way. Not even dancing would speed him up, he spaced out the music to suit him when he did the fox-trot and pressed his cheek to Anna's. He wore a long, calm grin. My private term for this particular expression was Pussy-Veleerum. I saw Philip as fat but strong, strong but cozy, purring but inserting a joking comment. He gave a little suck at the corner of the mouth when he was about to make a swipe at you, and it was then that he was Pussy-Veleerum. A name it never occurred to me to speak aloud.

I sprinted past the windows of the fruit store, the delicatessen, the tailor's shop. I could count on help from Philip. My father, however, was an intolerant, hasty man. Slighter than his sons, handsome, with muscles of white marble (so they seemed to me), laying down the law. It would put him in a rage to see me like this. And it was true that I had failed to consider: my mother dying, the ground frozen, a funeral coming, the dug grave, the packet of sand from the Holy Land to be scattered on the shroud. If I were to turn up in this filthy dress, the old man, breaking under his burdens, would come down on me in a blind, Old Testament rage. I never thought of this as cruelty but as archaic right everlasting. Even Albert, who was already a Loop lawyer, had to put up with these blows – outraged, his eyes swollen and maddened, but he took it. It never occurred to us that my father was cruel, only that we had gone over the limit.

There were no lights in Philip's D.D.S. office. When I jumped up the stairs the door with its blank starred glass was locked. Frosted panes were still rare. What we had was this star-marred product for toilets and other private windows. Marchek – whom nowadays we would call a voyeur – was also, angrily, gone. I had screwed up his experiment. I tried the doors, thinking that I could spend the night on the leather examining table where the beautiful nude had lain. There also I could make telephone calls. I did have a few friends, although there were none who might help me. I couldn't have known how to explain my predicament to them. They'd think I was putting them on, that it was a practical joke – "This is Louie. A whore robbed me of my clothes and I'm stuck on the North Side without carfare. I'm wearing a dress. I lost my house keys. I can't get home."

I ran down to the drugstore to look for Philip there. He sometimes played five or six hands of poker in the druggist's back room, trying his luck before getting on the streetcar. I knew Kiyar, the druggist, by sight. He had no recollection of me – why should he have? He said, "What can I do for you, young lady?"

Did he really take me for a girl, or a tramp off the street, or a gypsy from one of the storefront fortune-teller camps? Those were now all over town. But not even a gypsy would wear this blue sateen quilted boudoir jacket instead of a coat.

"I wonder, is Phil Haddis the dentist in the back?"

"What do you want with Dr. Haddis, have you got a toothache, or what?"

"I need to see him."

The druggist was a compact little guy, and his full round bald head was painfully sensitive looking. It could pick up any degree of disturbance, I thought. Yet there was a canny glitter coming through his specs, and Kiyar had the mark of a man whose mind never would change once he had made it up. Oddly enough, he had a small mouth, baby lips. He had been on the street – how long? Forty years? In forty years you've seen it all and nobody can tell you a single thing.

"Did Dr. Haddis have an appointment with you? Are you a patient?"

He knew this was a private connection. I was no patient. "No. But if I was out here he'd want to know it. Can I talk to him one minute?"

"He isn't here."

Kiyar had walked behind the grille of the prescription counter. I mustn't lose him. If he went, what would I do next? I said, "This is important, Mr. Kiyar." He waited for me to declare myself. I wasn't about to embarrass Philip by setting off rumours. Kiyar said nothing. He may have been waiting for me to speak up. Declare myself. I assume he took pride in running a tight operation, and gave nothing away. To cut through to the man I said, "I'm in a spot. I left Dr. Haddis a note, before, but when I came back I missed him."

At once I recognized my mistake. Druggists were always being appealed to. All these pills, remedy bottles, bright lights, medicine ads drew wandering screwballs and moochers. They all said they were in bad trouble.

"You can go to the Foster Avenue station."

"The police, you mean."

I had thought of that too. I could always tell them my hard-luck story and they'd keep me until they checked it out and someone would come to fetch me. That would probably be Albert. Albert would love that. He'd say to me, "Well, aren't you the horny little bastard." He'd play up to the cops too, and amuse them.

"I'd freeze before I got to Foster Avenue," was my answer to Kiyar.

"There's always the squad car."

"Well, if Phil Haddis isn't in the back maybe he's still in the neighbourhood. He doesn't always go straight home."

"Sometimes he goes over to the fights at Johnny Coulon's. It's a little early for that. You could try the speakeasy down the street, on Kenmore. It's an English basement, side entrance. You'll see a light by the fence. The guy at the slot is called Moose."

He didn't so much as offer a dime from his till. If I had said that I was in a scrape and that Phil was my sister's husband he'd probably have given me carfare. But I hadn't confessed, and there was a penalty for that.

Going out, I crossed my arms over the bed jacket and

opened the door with my shoulder. I might as well have been wearing nothing at all. The wind cut at my legs, and I ran. Luckily I didn't have far to go. The iron pipe with the bulb at the end of it was halfway down the block. I saw it as soon as I crossed the street. These illegal drinking parlours were easy to find, they were meant to be. The steps were cement, four or five of them bringing me down to the door. The slot came open even before I knocked and instead of the doorkeeper's eyes I saw his teeth.

"You Moose?"

"Yah. Who?"

"Kiyar sent me."

"Come on."

I felt as though I were falling into a big, warm, paved cellar. There was little to see, almost nothing. A sort of bar was set up, a few hanging fixtures, some tables from an ice cream parlour, wire-backed chairs. If you looked through the window of an English basement your eyes were at ground level. Here the glass was tarred over. There would have been nothing to see anyway: a yard, a wooden porch, a clothesline, wires, a back alley with ash heaps.

"Where did you come from, sister?" said Moose.

But Moose was a nobody here. The bartender, the one who counted, called me over and said, "What is it, sweetheart? You got a message for somebody?"

"Not exactly."

"Oh? You needed a drink so bad that you jumped out of bed and ran straight over – you couldn't stop to dress?"

"No, sir. I'm looking for somebody – Phil Haddis? The dentist?"

"There's only one customer. Is that him?"

It wasn't. My heart sank into river mud.

"It's not a drunk you're looking for?"

"No."

The drunk was on a high stool, thin legs hanging down, arms forward, and his head lay sidewise on the bar. Bottles, glasses, a beer barrel. Behind the barkeeper was a sideboard pried from the wall of an apartment. It had a long mirror – an oval laid on its side. Paper streamers curled down from the pipes.

"Do you know the dentist I'm talking about?"

"I might. Might not," said the barkeeper. He was a sloppy, long-faced giant – something of a kangaroo look about him. That was the long face in combination with the belly. He told me, "This is not a busy time. It's dinner, you know, and we're just a neighbourhood speak."

It was no more than a cellar, just as the barman was no more than a Greek, huge and bored. Just as I myself, Louie, was no more than a naked male in a woman's dress. When you had named objects in this elementary way, hardly anything remained in them. The barman, on whom everything now depended, held his bare arms out at full reach and braced on his spread hands. The place smelled of yeast sprinkled with booze. He said, "You live around here?"

"No, about an hour on the streetcar."

"Say more."

"Humboldt Park is my neighbourhood."

"Then you got to be a Uke, a Polack, a Scandihoof, or a Jew."

"Jew."

"I know my Chicago. And you didn't set out dressed like

that. You'da frozen to death inside of ten minutes. It's for the boudoir, not winter wear. You don't have the shape of a woman, neither. The hips aren't there. Are you covering a pair of knockers? I bet not. So what's the story, are you a morphadite? Let me tell you, you got to give this Depression credit. Without it you'd never find out what kind of funny stuff is going on. But one thing I'll never believe is that you're a young girl and still got her cherry."

"You're right as far as that goes, but the rest of it is that I haven't got a cent, and I need carfare."

"Who took you, a woman?"

"Up in her room when I undressed, she grabbed my things and threw them out the window."

"Left you naked so you couldn't chase her … I would have grabbed her and threw her on the bed. I bet you didn't even get in."

Not even, I repeated to myself. Why didn't I push her down while she was still in her coat, as soon as we entered the room – pull up her clothes, as he would have done? Because he was born to, while I was not. I wasn't intended for it.

"So that's what happened. You got taken by a team of pros. She set you up. You were the mark. Jewish fellows aren't supposed to keep company with those bad cunts. But when you get out of your house, into the world, you want action like anybody else. So. And where did you dig up this dress with the fancy big roses? I guess you were standing with your sticker sticking out and were lucky to find anything to put on. Was she a good looker?"

Her breasts, as she lay there, kept their shape. They didn't slip sideward. The inward lines of her legs, thigh swelling toward thigh. The black crumpled hairs. Yes, a beauty, I would say.

Like the druggist, the barman saw the fun of the thing – an adolescent in a fix, the soiled dress, the rayon or sateen bed jacket. It was a lucky thing for me that business was at a standstill. If he had had customers, the barman wouldn't have given me the time of day. "In short, you got mixed up with a whore and she gave you the works."

For that matter, I had no sympathy for myself. I confessed that I had this coming, a high-minded Jewish high school boy, too high-and-mighty to be orthodox and with his eye on a special destiny. Inside the house, an archaic rule; outside, the facts of life. The facts of life were having their turn. Their first effect was ridicule. To throw my duds into the alley was the woman's joke on me. The druggist with his pain-sensitive head was all irony. And now the barman was going to get his fun out of my trouble before he, maybe, gave me the seven cents for carfare. Then I could have a full hour of shame on the streetcar. My mother, with whom I might never speak again, used to say that I had a line of pride straight down the bridge of my nose, a foolish stripe that she could see.

I had no way of anticipating what her death would signify.

The barman, having me in place, was giving me the business. And Moose ("Moosey," the Greek called him) had come away from the door so as not to miss the entertainment. The Greek's kangaroo mouth turned up at the corners. Presently his hand went up to his head and he rubbed his scalp under the black, spiky hair. Some said they drank olive oil by the glass to keep their hair so rich. "Now, give it to me again, about the dentist," said the barman.

"I came looking for him, but by now he's well on his way home."

He was then on the Broadway-Clark car, reading the Peach edition of the *Evening American*, a broad man with an innocent pout to his face, checking the race results. Anna had him dressed up as a professional man but he let the fittings – shirt, tie, buttons – go their own way. His instep was fat and swelled inside the narrow shoe she picked for him. He wore the fedora correctly. Toward the rest he admitted no obligation.

Anna cooked dinner after work, and when Philip came in my father would begin to ask, "Where's Louie?" "Oh, he's out delivering flowers," they'd tell him. But the old man was nervous about his children after dark, and if they were late he waited up for them, walking – no, trotting – up and down the long apartment. When you tried to slip in he caught you and twisted you tight by the neckband. He was small, neat, slender, a gentleman, but abrupt, not unworldly – he wasn't ignorant of vices, he had lived in Odessa and even longer in St. Petersburg – but he had no patience. The least thing might craze him. Seeing me in this dress, he'd lose his head at once. *I* lost *mine* when that woman showed me her snatch with all the pink layers, when she raised up her arm and asked me to disconnect the wires, when I felt her skin and her fragrance came upward.

"What's your family, what does your dad do?" asked the barman.

"His business is wood fuel for bakers' ovens. It comes by freight car from northern Michigan. Also from Birnamwood, Wisconsin. He has a yard off Lake Street, east of Halsted."

I made an effort to give the particulars. I couldn't afford to be suspected of invention now.

"I know where that is. Now that's a neighbourhood just full

of hookers and cathouses. You think you can tell your old man what happened to you, that you got picked up by a cutie and she stole your clothes off you?"

The effect of this question was to make me tight in the face, dim in the ears. The whole cellar grew small and distant, toylike but not for play.

"How's your old man to deal with – tough?"

"Hard," I said.

"Slaps the kids around? This time you've got it coming. What's under the dress, a pair of bloomers?"

I shook my head.

"Your behind is bare? Now you know how it feels to go around like a woman."

The Greek's great muscles were dough-coloured. You wouldn't have wanted him to take a headlock on you. That's the kind of man the Organization hired, the Capone people were in charge by now. The customers would be like celluloid Kewpie dolls to him. He looked like one of those boxing kangaroos in the movies, and he could do a standing jump over the bar. Yet he enjoyed playing zany. He could curve his long mouth up at the corners like the happy face in a cartoon.

"What were you doing on the North Side?"

"Delivering flowers."

"Hustling after school but with ramming on your brain. You got a lot to learn, buddy boy. Well, enough of that. Now, Moosey, take this flashlight and see if you can scrounge up a sweater or something in the back basement for this down-on-his-luck kid. I'd be surprised if the old janitor hasn't picked the stuff over pretty good. If mice have nested in it, shake out the turds. It'll help on the trip home."

I followed Moose into the hotter half of the cellar. His flashlight picked out the laundry tubs with the hand-operated wringers mounted on them, the padlocked wooden storage bins. "Turn over some of these cardboard boxes. Mostly rags, is my guess. Dump 'em out, that's the easiest."

I emptied a couple of big cartons. Moose passed the light back and forth over the heaps. "Nothing much, like I said."

"Here's a flannel shirt," I said. I wanted to get out. The smell of heated burlap was hard to take. This was the only wearable article. I could have used a pullover or a pair of pants. We returned to the bar. As I was putting on the shirt, which revolted me (I come of finicky people whose fetish is cleanliness), the barman said, "I tell you what, you take this drunk home – this is about time for him, isn't it, Moosey? – he gets plastered here every night. See he gets home and it'll be worth half a buck to you."

"I'll do it," I said. "It all depends how far away he lives. If it's far, I'll be frozen before I get there."

"It isn't far. Winona, west of Sheridan isn't far. I'll give you the directions. This guy is a city-hall payroller. He has no special job, he works direct for the ward committeeman. He's a lush with two little girls to bring up. If he's sober enough he cooks their dinner. Probably they take more care of him than he does of them."

"I'll walk him home, if he can walk."

"First I'll take charge of his money," said the barman. "I don't want my buddy here to be rolled. I don't say you would do it, but I owe this to a customer."

Bristle-faced Moose began to empty the man's pockets – his wallet, some keys, crushed cigarettes, a red bandanna that looked foul, matchbooks, greenbacks, and change. All these were laid out on the bar.

When I look back at past moments I carry with me an apperceptive mass that ripens and perhaps distorts, mixing what is memorable with what may not be worth mentioning. Thus I see the barman with one big hand gathering in the valuables as if they were his winnings, the pot in a poker game. And then I think that if the kangaroo giant had taken this drunk on his back he might have bounded home with him in less time than it would have taken me to support him as far as the corner. But what the barman actually said was, "I got a nice escort for you, Jim."

Moose led the man back and forth to make sure his feet were operating. His swollen eyes now opened and then closed again. "McKern," Moose said, briefing me. "Southwest corner of Winona and Sheridan, the second building on the south side of the street, and it's the second floor."

"You'll be paid when you get back," said the barman.

The freeze was now so hard that the snow underfoot sounded like metal foil. Though McKern may have sobered up in the frozen street, he couldn't move very fast. Since I had to hold on to him I borrowed his gloves. He had a coat with pockets to put his hands in. I tried to keep behind him and get some shelter from the wind. That didn't work. He wasn't up to walking. I had to hold him. Instead of a desirable woman, I had a drunkard in my arms. This disgrace, you see, while my mother was surrendering to death. At about this hour, upstairs neighbours came down and relatives arrived and filled the kitchen and the dining room – a deathwatch. I should have been there, not on the far North Side. When I had earned the carfare, I'd still be an hour from home on a streetcar making four stops to the mile.

Toward the last, I was dragging McKern. I kept the street door open with my back while I pulled him into the dim lobby by the arms.

The little girls had been waiting and came down at once. They held the inner door open while I brought their daddy upstairs with a fireman's carry and laid him on his bed. The children had had plenty of practice at this. They undressed him down to the long johns and then stood silent on either side of the room. This, for them, was how things were. They took deep oddities calmly, as children generally will. I had spread his winter coat over him.

I had little sympathy for McKern, in the circumstances. I believe I can tell you why: He had passed out many times before, and he would pass out again, dozens of times before he died. Drunkenness was common and familiar, and therefore accepted, and drunks could count on acceptance and support and relied on it. Whereas if your troubles were uncommon, unfamiliar, you could count on nothing. There was a convention about drunkenness established in part by drunkards. The founding proposition was that consciousness is terrible. Its lower, impoverished forms are perhaps the worst. Flesh and blood are poor and weak, susceptible to human shock. Here my descendant will hear the voice of Grandfather Louie giving one of his sermons on higher consciousness and interrupting the story he promised to tell. You will hold him to his word, as you have every right to do.

The older girl now spoke to me. She said, "The fellow phoned and said a man was bringing Daddy home, and you'd help with supper if Daddy couldn't cook it."

"Yes. Well?…"

"Only you're not a man, you've got a dress on."

"It looks like it, doesn't it. Don't you worry, I'll come to the kitchen with you."

"Are you a lady?"

"What do you mean – what does it look like? All right, I'm a lady."

"You can eat with us."

"Then show me where the kitchen is."

I followed them down the corridor, narrowed by the clutter – boxes of canned groceries, soda biscuits, sardines, pop bottles. When I passed the bathroom, I slipped in for quick relief. The door had neither a hook nor a bolt, the string of the ceiling fixture had snapped off. A tiny night-light was plugged into the baseboard. I thanked God it was so dim. I put up the board while raising my skirt, and when I had begun I heard one of the children behind me. Over my shoulder I saw that it was the younger one, and as I turned my back (*everything* was happening today) I said, "Don't come in here." But she squeezed past and sat on he edge of the tub. She grinned at me. She was expecting her second teeth. Today all females were making sexual fun of me, and even the infants were looking lewd. I stopped, letting the dress fall, and said to her, "What are you laughing about?"

"If you were a girl, you'd of sat down."

The kid wanted me to understand that she knew what she had seen. She pressed her fingers over her mouth, and I turned and went to the kitchen.

There the older girl was lifting the black cast-iron skillet with both hands. On dripping paper, the pork chops were laid out – nearby, a mason jar of grease. I was competent enough at the gas range, which shone with old filth. Loath to touch the pork with my fingers, I forked the meat into the spitting fat. The chops turned my stomach. My thought was, "I'm into it now, up to the ears." The drunk in his bed, the dim secret toilet, the glaring tungsten twist over the gas range, the sputtering droplets stinging the hands. The older girl said, "There's plenty for you. Daddy won't be eating dinner."

"No, not me. I'm not hungry," I said.

All that my upbringing held in horror geysered up, my throat filling with it, my guts griping.

The children sat at the table, an enamel rectangle. Thick plates and glasses, a waxed package of sliced white bread, a milk bottle, a stick of butter, the burning fat clouding the room. The girls sat beneath the smoke, slicing their meat. I brought salt and pepper back from the range. They ate without conversation. My chore (my duty) done, there was nothing to keep me. I said, "I have to go."

I looked in at McKern, who had thrown down the coat and taken off his drawers. The parboiled face, the short nose pointed sharply, the life signs in the throat, the broken look of his neck, the black hair of his belly, the short cylinder between his legs ending in a spiral of loose skin, the white shine of the shins, the tragic expression of his feet. There was a stack of pennies on his bedside table. I helped myself to carfare but had no pocket for the coins. I opened the hall closet feeling quickly for a coat I might borrow, a pair of slacks. Whatever I took, Philip could return to the Greek barman tomorrow. I pulled a trench coat from a hanger, and a pair of trousers. For the third time I put on strangers' clothing – this is no time to mention stripes or checks or make exquisite notations. Escaping, desperate, I struggled into the pants on the landing, tucking in the dress, and pulled on the coat as I jumped down the stairs, knotting tight the belt and sticking the pennies, a fistful of them, into my pocket.

But still I went back to the alley under the woman's window to see if her light was on, and also to look for pages. The thief or pimp perhaps had chucked them away, or maybe they had dropped out when he snatched the sheepskin. The windows were dark. I found nothing on the ground. You may think this obsessive crankiness, a crazy dependency on words, on printed matter. But remember, there were no redeemers in the streets, no guides, no confessors, comforters, enlighteners, communicants to turn to. You had to take teaching wherever you could find it. Under the library dome downtown, in mosaic letters, there was a message from Milton, so moving but perhaps of no utility, perhaps aggravating difficulties: A GOOD BOOK, it said, IS THE PRECIOUS LIFE'S BLOOD OF A MASTER SPIRIT.

These are the plain facts, they have to be uttered. This, remember, is the New World, and here one of its mysterious cities. I should have hurried directly, to catch a car. Instead, I was in a back alley hunting pages that would in any case have blown away.

I went back to Broadway – it was very broad – and waited on a safety island. Then the car came clanging, red, swaying on its trucks, a piece of Iron Age technology, double cane seats framed in brass. Rush hour was long past. I sat by a window, homebound, with flashes of thought like tracer bullets slanting into distant darkness. Like London in wartime. What story would I tell? I wouldn't tell any. I never did. It was assumed anyway that I was lying. While I believed in honour, I did often lie. Is a life without lying conceivable? It was easier to lie than to explain myself. My father had one set of assumptions, I had another. Corresponding premises were not to be found.

I owed five dollars to Behrens. But I knew where my mother secretly hid her savings. Because I looked into all books, I had found the money in her Mahzor, the prayer book for the High Holidays, the days of awe. As yet I hadn't taken anything. She had hoped until this final illness to buy passage to Europe to see her mother and her sister. When she died I would turn the money over to my father, except for ten dollars, five for the florist and the rest of Von Hugel's *Eternal Life* and *The World as Will and Idea*.

The after-dinner neighbours and cousins would be gone when I reached home. My father would be on the lookout for me. It was the rear porch door that was locked after dark. The kitchen door was off the latch. I could climb over the wooden partition. I often did that. Once you got your foot on the door-knob you could pull yourself over the top and drop to the porch without noise. Then I could see into the kitchen and slip in as soon as my patrolling father had left it. The bedroom shared by all three brothers was just off the kitchen. I could borrow my brother Len's cast-off winter coat tomorrow. I knew which closet it hung in. If my father should catch me I could expect hard blows on the top of my head, on my face, on my shoulders. But if my mother had, tonight, just died, he wouldn't hit me.

This was when the measured, reassuring, sleep-inducing turntable of days became a whirlpool, a vortex darkening toward the bottom. I had had only the anonymous pages in the pocket of my sheepskin to interpret it to me. They told me that the truth of the universe was inscribed into our very bones. That the human skeleton was itself a hieroglyph. That every-thing we had ever known on earth was shown to us in the first days after death. That our experience of the world was desired by the cosmos, and needed by it for its own renewal.

I do not think that these pages, if I hadn't lost them, would have persuaded me forever or made the life I led a different one.

I am writing this account, or statement, in response to an eccentric urge swelling toward me from the earth itself.

Failed my mother! That may mean, will mean, little or nothing to you, my only child, reading this document.

I myself know the power of nonpathos, in these low, devious days.

On the streetcar, heading home, I braced myself, but all my preparations caved in like sand diggings. I got down at the North Avenue stop, avoiding my reflection in the shop windows. After a death, mirrors were immediately covered. I can't say what this pious superstition means. Will the soul of your dead be reflected in a looking glass, or is this custom a check to the vanity of the living?

I ran home, approached by the back alley, made no noise on the wooden backstairs, reached for the top of the partition, placed my foot on the white porcelain doorknob, went over the top without noise, and dropped down on our porch. I didn't follow the plan I had laid for avoiding my father. There were people sitting at the kitchen table. I went straight in. My father rose from his chair and hurried toward me. His fist was ready. I took off my tam or woollen beret and when he hit me on the head the blow filled me with gratitude. If my mother had already died, he would have embraced me instead.

Well, they're all gone now, and I have made my preparations. I haven't left a large estate, and this is why I have written this memoir, a sort of addition to your legacy.

BONNIE BURNARD

NIPPLE MAN

There is a legend, profusely illustrated in Western art, of the Roman matrons who, during a siege, fed the soldiers on the milk from their breasts. This episode, known under the title of "Roman Charity," served for centuries to justify the depiction of an older man suckling at the breast of a woman; the woman's nipple, from which usually a shower of milk could be seen gushing, became symbolic of generous plenty. In Burnard's story, it is the terrible absence of that breast that becomes erotic, against all conventional notions of love and of beauty.

In 1988, Bonnie Burnard published a collection of short stories called Women of Influence in which she explored, patiently and compassionately, the labours and tactics of women in and out of love. Her next collection, Casino, where "Nipple Man" appears, broaches a similar territory but the characters seem older, less surprised by injustice and, in a strange way, more contented – even when they face misfortune.

Love between men and women past middle age seems to require excuses in art and literature. Most fictional amorous couples are traditionally shown in or barely past their teens — Romeo and Juliet, Paolo and Francesca — while old male lechers and randy elderly matrons are the staples of bawdy stories. Throughout the Middle Ages and the Renaissance, the meeting of Sarah and Abraham or some such biblical tale was needed for the artist to justify the depiction of more mature flesh. In our time, it was with a sigh of relief that audiences watched Jack Nicholson's paunch meet Shirley MacLaine's sagging breasts in Terms of Endearment. *In this new tradition, Burnard makes no apologies for celebrating the love of a couple no longer young.*

JOHN MCLARTY'S FURNITURE, in his office in the History building, his old teak desk and the two extra chairs and the filing cabinets and the book shelves and the potted plants, had been rearranged over the years into every conceivable configuration. And he'd replaced the drapes, at his own expense, twice. He believed there was a perfect arrangement, something conducive to clear thought and to an overall peace of mind for himself and everyone who entered his office. He'd had some help, initially from his reluctant wife, and then from two or three of the others, and recently even his daughter had spared him a Sunday afternoon. They'd shared a bottle of wine as they hauled things around and argued amicably about what looked best where.

His window, which he liked directly in front of him when he sat at his desk, overlooked the largest expanse of grass left on the campus since the building program of the seventies. The grass, a dozen shades of green on any day of the week from April through October, was usually spotted with the small bodies of students wandering purposefully from one lecture to another. A narrow sidewalk connected John's building to Talbot, further up the hill, where the economics people plied their trade. He'd never been there. Seventeen years on this campus and he'd never even thought to walk over. Everything he needed was on his own floor and the floors beneath him, colleagues, support staff, archives. He did, of course, use the main library at the base of the hill but none of the other faculties overlapped his own. Except socially, for those who could endure it. He wasn't one of those who could endure it.

They'd given their share of dinner parties when they'd first arrived, or Carol had, he'd simply been there to pour the scotch, and they'd continued for a few years to make appearances at the gatherings orchestrated by his fellows in the history department. And then they'd eased out. Carol had eased them out. She'd said, one spring evening, standing in her panty hose and camisole at the bathroom mirror applying her blush, sucking in her tummy, that she couldn't go. He thought she might be sick, or premenstrual, or maybe just exhausted from the kids, who were all at the age when they had to be lifted and carried and fed and buckled up and wiped clean and tucked in, but she said no, she was fine, everybody else was sick. And she paraphrased some of the dirty, cynical gossip she'd heard exchanged by warm little groups in kitchens and she told him about the clammy hands tracing her rear end when they were crowded around pianos in living rooms, supposedly singing, and about the rigorous, nerve wracking effort needed to keep the whole thing in perspective. And the clincher, which had been a whispered longing expressed in their own back yard by a dull-witted Yank who had long since departed for greener academic pastures, to see her nipples. She said she'd wanted to strip off her blouse and bra right there at the barbeque and say there you go darlin', and aren't they as plain as plain can be, and you will notice they are not erect under your gaze and there's not a snowball's chance in hell they ever will be, and now will you please just pass me that jar of mustard.

John was astonished, but he knew better than to accuse her of exaggeration. The thought occurred to him that maybe she wasn't exaggerating at all. You didn't say that, he said, plugging in his shaver. What did you really say? Nothing, she said. "I said nothing. Nothing at all. I walked over to you and Jenny and interrupted some inane discussion you were having about a cactus."

They'd skipped the dinner party. They'd gone instead to a dismal Bergman film and seen Liv Ullmann's nipples, which, if he remembered correctly, and he did, were not as plain as plain can be. That night, after the film and the coffee and the talk about everything but the film, when they climbed into bed when he should have been his most attentive, he fell sound asleep and dreamed. And from that night his dreams began, habitually, to welcome other women. He couldn't remember dreaming about other women before, not habitually.

The marriage lasted only four more fretful years and then off she'd gone with the kids and her nipples and most of the best family photographs. She'd finished her stalled degree at John's expense, tit for tat, she'd said, at another university and began teaching computer science. She was a respected member of one of the hottest faculties in the country, or so their old friends told him, whenever they could work it in. And she'd married a moderately successful architect. They lived with the kids who were still at home in a house overlooking the Pacific, which they'd built on a great slab of smooth brown rock. John had been welcomed there often, for the sake of the children. He'd never once manoeuvred the preposterous slope of the driveway without feeling like an impotent uncle, but he'd endured, he'd wanted to hold his kids as they grew. And everyone understood. There were lots of books on this kind of stuff.

For a time, he'd attributed their marital disaster to the dull-witted Yank at the barbeque, but then he'd relented and acknowledged the debilitating habits, many of them his own, and the hard knots of temperament that appeared and reap-peared like rocks thrown up by a field. On really good days he was content simply that they'd made it as far as they had, and that the damage, if his accounting could be trusted, had been minimal. He'd never told her what he dreamed of, habitually, only that he dreamed. And she'd had the decency to keep the worst of her secrets to herself. He had watched her keeping them.

He'd sold the house; he had no interest whatsoever in screwing her around financially, although his lawyer indicated, with some enthusiasm, that it could be done. She'd worked as hard as he'd worked and what she had with the kids wasn't exactly tenure. And no one else really knew or cared how great the kids were turning out, no one else knew or cared that she'd laughed them all through more than one rough spot.

He'd found an apartment and was no sooner into it and lonely than they started to show up in his office, the women from his dreams, with their nipples. Not the exact women, but very close. In retrospect, those years, seven or eight of them, would run in his mind like a long raunchy film, one naked young body following another. Not that they weren't fine women, some of them. Occasionally, more than occasionally, he remembered their fineness.

Most of them were simply young. They didn't talk in sentences. They wouldn't eat anything, wouldn't cook or sit still to eat a decent dinner. They wore T-shirts and only T-shirts with their jeans. And they expected him to make love to them with a wisdom he couldn't count on all night long and half the next day. They were enthralled by nakedness and long stretches of time and their own capacity to enjoy skin and nerve endings and they lied to him about his virility, not huge lies, but lies just the same, and necessary.

They installed in him a status which was false, although flattering beyond anything he'd ever known. They looked up to him, literally, with sweet smooth cheeks.

He consoled himself with the conviction that he'd freed them all to go after what they wanted and most of them did. Some had returned to his office boasting degrees better than his own and two had come back to show off babes in arms and fuller hips and breasts relaxed into a new purpose. Given the chance, he would have carefully set the infants on the floor beside his filing cabinets to nap inside their downy sleepers while he jumped their still familiar mothers.

The victorious visits had more or less stopped when he found Marion. He was marching alone down the library steps one balmy Indian summer evening, gazing up through the trees, and he might actually have fallen over her if she hadn't spoken. "Careful," she'd said, and he'd excused himself, feeling clumsy, certainly potentially clumsy. She sat near the bottom of the long flight with eight or ten books piled beside her on the step, exposed by one of the high new lights installed for campus security. He noticed immediately that her cheeks were wet. She wasn't young. A young woman in tears on the library steps would not have slowed him down.

He assumed that a public display from a woman this age did not indicate anything personal, he guessed she was in some kind of physical discomfort, that she'd been hurt, and he was right. She said she was just back to work and was likely pushing it too hard but she was so damned tired of waiting to feel herself again. She said she supposed she should get the books back inside and then get home and watch David Letterman or something. He told her he didn't see that such drastic action was necessary, and he began to load her books, economics texts, two geography, one Welty and one Hardy, into his briefcase and then into his arms.

"Can you stand?" he asked. "My car is just over in the north lot. I'll bring it around and then I'll take you home." And he hauled her books across the cool grass to the north lot. It didn't occur to him until he was back and helping her into his car to ask her who she was. She said she was Marion Alderson; she taught economics, had done so for three years on this campus and for many other years on other campuses across the country. Maid Marion he'd called her and she'd raised her eyebrows, smiling only slightly. She said she was just getting over a little bit of surgery and that she lived in one of the high rises on the other side of the bridge. After he got her home, up the elevator and into her suite with her books settled on an elegant glass desk in her living room, he saw, when her back was turned, that she had a set of those perfect calves that actresses from the fifties used to have, with heavier thighs, he could read them under her dress as she walked. He accepted her graceful thanks and took his leave, feeling a little bit the hero, feeling decent and light on his feet.

He didn't phone her, didn't even think of phoning her until one cold morning two months later when he was marking a particularly fine paper on the Boer War. He found his directory and there she was, name, rank and telephone number. He told her he wanted to know only if she was feeling herself yet and she said yes she was and thanks again for the gallant assistance and when he didn't take the conversation to its natural close she asked if she could buy him lunch in the Talbot faculty dining room as a token of her gratitude. Sure she could, he said.

So they met, properly, surrounded by economics people he recognized but didn't know. And she was much better, much stronger. She wore an expensive shirtwaist, paisley, Carol had wanted such dresses when they couldn't afford them, and very fine leather shoes with narrow high heels. The shoes, he knew, were worn to show off the legs. Her hair looked especially clean and full, it was a dark grey blonde and it swayed around her head as she talked. Only her eyes, a guarded deep brown set off by rays of crow's feet, disappointed him. As he ate his grilled cheese he imagined her eyes unguarded and bright, throwing off a phrase or two from the accumulated vocabulary of experienced eyes.

Now that she was well, her voice was clipped and businesslike and funny. She was one of those women who wear no rings but talk without apology about their grown-up children. Her breasts seemed full and solid although he couldn't begin to find her nipples; they were lost beneath the swirling blue paisley. After two hours they counted between them, with some guilt, five students left waiting in the halls outside their offices.

He liked her, he decided he liked her tremendously and by the time the woman came to clear their plates he felt a potent urge to be in love again. As he walked back across the grass to his office he very deliberately resurrected everything he knew to be true and ridiculous and daunting about this urge. He lined it all up, chose what he wanted to believe, and dumped the rest into the bunkers long since dug at the back of his brain. He was going to get into her pants and he was going to fall in love, in whichever order was necessary. She could decide the order.

It didn't take him long to fall in love. She was available and game. They went to concerts in the city park put on by a youth orchestra and to a fall fair thirty miles out of the city and once to the horse races, where he lost forty dollars and she came away even, and smug. They talked about her ex-husband and about Carol over Caesar salad and beer and about books she'd had a chance to read that year and about recent economic theories he'd wanted to comprehend. And she said one evening, while putting down a twenty for her part of the diner, that she had no credit cards. She said she thought unnecessary debt was very unwise. That night he'd stood in his kitchen in his boxers and cut his Visa card into pieces with his nail scissors. The next day he transferred enough money out of his savings account to pay off every cent owned to everyone for everything.

They even had a short Sunday afternoon at her apartment with two of her children and one of his own, all gathered in the city for their own youthful, compelling reasons. The young visitors eyed each other tenuously as they threw back beer nuts and pretzels and they circled their parents warily, as had been predicted, but they did give brief, spontaneous lip service to companionship and fun, for anyone. The companionship line, full of good cheer, had come from his own long-legged son, gratis. "Just drink your beer," he'd told him.

He expected by this time, quite honourably he thought, to be in love. She was friendly almost beyond bearing, she touched his arm or his back whenever there was even the mildest excuse to do so. But she'd said no twice to his offer to tuck her up and she kissed him chastely.

Because he knew no other way he asked her flat out one night, over a late dinner after an economics lecture which he'd enjoyed and agreed with, why they weren't making love. "I want to bite those thighs," he said. He didn't broach her nipples; he wasn't entirely without discipline.

She plopped sour cream over her baked potato and loaded it with chives. "I'm forty-seven years old," she said. "I would bet you've never been with a forty-seven-year-old woman."

"No," he said, grinning.

"It's no joke," she said.

He knew what had to be done. He was sure he could match her. He listened to her go on about Dostoyevsky over dessert and as soon as they were into the car in the parking lot he pulled his shirt out of his pants and let his stomach hang out over his belt, although it wasn't as disgusting in the dark as he'd hoped. He took her hand and placed it on his soft, hairy pot.

"There," he said. "Isn't that nice?"

She took her hand away.

He hiked up his pant leg and pointed to a long lumpy vein just under the skin. He'd been watching its steady movement to the surface for years.

"Look at this," he said. "Like an old log bobbing up."

She watched his excitement calmly for a minute and then she lifted her bum off the seat and pulled her dress up to expose her thighs.

"Yes indeed," he said. "I'd recognize them anywhere." He started the car and got them on their way, sticking to the passing lane of the main thoroughfare from the city core out to the campus.

"There's more," she said.

He turned off onto a quiet side street, continuing home at a steady fifty kilometers an hour. She had unbuttoned her shirt-waist, this one a soft green print, and was pulling her arms out of it as he drove. He saw, glancing as often as he could in the intermittent light from the street, what she wanted him to see. Her lacy black bra was filled with something other than flesh, something similar in texture and shape to the kids' old bean bags. She reached around and unhooked her bra, letting it fall heavily into her lap. He was looking at a war zone.

He slowed and pulled the car over to the side of the road. As soon as his hands were free he turned and used them to cover the two nearly healed slices. His thumbs moved involuntarily, up and down, up and down, over the rough dark texture.

Her eyes were bright, finally, but not with the sulky passion he'd put there in his dreams. Her smile looked empty, and raw.

"They don't hurt much anymore," she said.

He leaned over and buried his face in her. The scars felt tough and final against his cheek, as if the cells had hardened and said, This is it, don't ever cut here again. He was astounded by their warmth, scars as warm as flesh can be.

"You might have told me," he said.

She put her hand into his thinning hair, lifted it between her fingers and let it fall back into itself, soft and orderly. She said, "I'm telling you now."

He could hear her heart as clearly as he'd heard his own when he'd been alone and listening for it. He took what he could into his mouth, the thick layers of tissue where the needle had gathered the skin, the sturdy ridges rising like a mountain chain where all other land had disappeared.

He knew escape was a possibility. There were ways, and he'd had some practice. He could be bravely direct or he could be subtle, clever, cowardly. It wouldn't matter much. She was braced for anything. He could feel her fingers drifting absently through what was left of his hair. She might have been on Mars.

"They're in my mind," he said. He rubbed his cheek against her. "I've got them." He bent down to her thigh, sank his teeth, gently. He took her firm and shapely flesh between his teeth. He could hear the sharp intake of her breath above him and then a sound that might have been laughter, if laughter is sometimes brutal.

ANGELA CARTER

BLACK VENUS

On March 13, 1856, Charles Baudelaire woke in the early hours of the morning from an extraordinary dream. Wandering through the streets of Paris, he had met a friend who had insisted that they drive together to a brothel where Jeanne Duval, the poet's Caribbean mistress, was working. Before entering, Baudelaire gave the madam (who in the dream was also Baudelaire's mother) a copy of his newly published translation of Poe's stories, which had become a volume of pornography. As Baudelaire entered the brothel, he found he was exposing himself, and reflected that it was indecent to appear like this; he was also barefoot, and had stepped into a puddle. Inside the brothel was a series of galleries where the prostitutes stood talking to their customers, a few of them young students. On the walls hung obscene pictures as in a museum. But not only pictures were shown in this brothel: there was also a live exhibit, a monster who had been born here and who had been placed on a pedestal, crouching in a fetal position. Just as Baudelaire had begun *to engage the monster in conversation, he woke up, exhausted, and immediately wrote to a friend describing the dream. It is the only dream Baudelaire recorded.*

If the dream is a depiction of the poet's obsessive soul, then Angela Carter's story is a portrait of Jeanne Duval, "the nursemaid" Baudelaire said, of his obsessions, his reluctant muse, the woman he called "Black Venus." "To constancy, to opium, to the night," he wrote to her, "I prefer the elixir of your mouth where love is on display." Their quarrels were legendary; the poems he wrote to her form the core of his most famous book, The Flowers of Evil, *which was available only in a bowdlerized version until 1917.*

S AD; SO SAD, those smoky-rose, smoky-mauve evenings of late Autumn, sad enough to pierce the heart. The sun departs the sky in winding sheets of gaudy cloud; anguish enters the city, a sense of the bitterest regret, a nostalgia for things we never knew, anguish of the turn of the year, the time of impotent yearning, the inconsolable season. In America, they call it "the Fall," bringing to mind the Fall of Man, as if the fatal drama of the primal fruit-theft must recur again and again, with cyclic regularity, at the same time of every year that schoolboys set out to rob orchards, invoking, in the most everyday image, any child, every child, who, offered the choice between virtue and knowledge, will always choose knowledge, always the hard way. Although she does not know the meaning of the word "regret" the woman sighs, without any precise reason.

Soft twists of mist invade the alleys, rise up from the slow river like exhalations of an exhausted spirit, seep in through the cracks in the window frames so that the contours of their high, lonely apartment waver and melt. On these evenings, you see everything as though your eyes are going to lapse to tears.

She sighs.

———————

The custard-apple of her stinking Eden she, this forlorn Eve, bit – and was all at once transported here, as in a dream; and yet she is a *tabula rasa*, still. She never experienced her experience *as* experience, life never added to the sum of her knowledge; rather, subtracted from it. If you start out with nothing, they'll take even that away from you, the Good Book says so.

Indeed, I think she never bothered to bite any apple at all. She wouldn't have known what knowledge was *for*, would she? She was in neither a state of innocence nor a state of grace. I will tell you what Jeanne was like.

She was like a piano in a country where everyone has had their hands cut off.

On these sad days, at those melancholy times, as the room sinks into dusk, he, instead of lighting the lamp, fixing drinks, making all cozy, will ramble on: "Baby, baby, let me take you back where you belong, back to your lovely, lazy island where the jewelled parrot rocks on the enamel tree and you can crunch sugar-cane between your strong, white teeth, like you did when you were little, baby. When we get there, among the lilting palm-trees, under the purple flowers, I'll love you to death. We'll go back and live together in a thatched house with a veranda over-grown with flowering vine and a little girl in a short white frock with a yellow satin bow in her kinky pigtail will wave a huge feather fan over us, stirring the languishing air as we sway in our hammock, this way and that way … the ship, the ship is waiting in the harbour, baby. My monkey, my pussy-cat, my pet … think how lovely it would be to live there …"

But, on these days, nipped by frost and sulking, no pet nor pussy she; she looks more like an old crow with rusty feathers in a miserable huddle by the smoky fire which she pokes with spiteful sticks. She coughs and grumbles, she is always chilly, there is always a draught gnawing the back of her neck or pinching her ankles.

Go, where? Not *there*! The glaring yellow shore and harsh blue sky daubed in crude, unblended colours squeezed directly from the tube, where the perspectives are abrupt as a child's drawing, your eyes hurt to look. Fly-blown towns. All there is to eat is green bananas and yams and a brochette of rubber goat to chew. She puts on a theatrical shudder, enough to shake the affronted cat off her lap. She hates the cat, anyway. She can't look at the cat without wanting to strangle it. She would like a drink. Rum will do. She twists a flute of discarded manuscript from the waste-paper basket into a spill for her small, foul, black cheroot.

Night comes in on feet of fur and marvellous clouds drift past the windows, those spectral clouds of the night sky as if they were living in the gondola of a balloon such as the one in which his friend Nadar made triumphant ascents.

At the inspiration of a gust of wind such as now rattles the tiles above us, this handsome apartment with its Persian rugs, its walnut table off which the Borgias served poisons, its carved armchairs from whose bulbous legs grin and grimace cinque-cento faces, the crust of fake Tintorettos on the walls (he's an indefatigable connoisseur, if, as yet, too young to have that sixth sense that tells you when you're being conned) – at the invitation of the mysterious currents of the heavens, this well-appointed cabin will loose its moorings in the street below and take off, depart, whisk across the dark vault of the night, tangling a stillborn, crescent moon in its ropes, nudging a star at lift-off, and will deposit us –

"*No!*" she said. "Not the bloody parrot forest! Don't take me on the slavers' route back to the West Indies, for godsake! And let the bloody cat out, before it craps on your precious Bokhara!"

They have this in common, neither has a native land, although he likes to pretend she has a fabulous home in the bosom of a blue ocean, he will force a home on her whether she's got one or not, he cannot believe she is as dispossessed as he is … Yet they are only at home together when contem-plating flight; they are both waiting for the wind to blow that will take them to a miraculous elsewhere, a happy land, far, far away, the land of delighted ease and pleasure.

After she's got a drink or two inside her, however, she stops coughing, grows a bit more friendly, will consent to unpin her hair and let him play with it, the way he likes to. And, if her native indolence does not prove too much for her – for she is capable of sprawling, as in a vegetable trance, for hours, for days, in the dim room by the smoky fire – nevertheless, she will sometimes lob the butt of her cheroot in the fire and be persuaded to take off her clothes and dance for Daddy who, she will grudgingly admit when pressed, is a good Daddy, buys her pretties, allocates her the occasional lump of hashish, keeps her off the street.

Nights of October, of frail, sickle moons, when the earth conceals the shining accomplice of assassins in its shadow, to make everything all the more mysterious – on such a night, you could say the moon was black.

This dance, which he wanted her to perform so much and had especially devised for her, consisted of a series of voluptuous poses one following another; private-room-in-a-bordello stuff but tasteful, he preferred her to undulate rhythmically rather than jump about and shake a leg. He liked her to put on all her bangles and beads when she did her dance, she dressed up in the set of clanking jewellery he'd given her, paste, nothing she could sell or she'd have sold it. Meanwhile, she hummed a Créole melody, she liked the ones with ribald words about what the shoemaker's wife did at Mardi Gras or the size of some fisherman's legendary tool but Daddy paid no attention to what song his siren sang, he fixed his quick, bright, dark eyes upon her decorated skin as if, sucker, authentically entranced.

"Sucker!" she said, almost tenderly, but he did not hear her.

She cast a long shadow in the firelight. She was a woman of immense height, the type of those beautiful giantesses who, a hundred years later, would grace the stages of the Crazy Horse or the Casino de Paris in sequin cache-sexe and tinsel pasties, divinely tall, the colour and texture of suede. Josephine Baker! But vivacity, exuberance were never Jeanne's qualities. A slumbrous resentment of anything you could not eat, drink or smoke, i.e. burn, was her salient characteristic. Consumption, combustion, these were her vocations.

She sulked sardonically through Daddy's sexy dance, watching, in a bored, fascinated way, the elaborate reflections of the many strings of glass beads he had given her tracking about above her on the ceiling. She looked like the source of light but this was an illusion; she only shone because the dying fire lit his presents to her. Although his regard made her luminous, his shadow made her blacker than she was, his shadow could eclipse her entirely. Whether she had a good heart or not underneath, is anybody's guess; she had been raised in the School of Hard Knocks and enough hard knocks can beat the heart out of anybody.

Though Jeanne was not prone to introspection, sometimes, as she wriggled around the dark, buoyant room that tugged at its moorings, longing to take off on an aerial quest for that Cythera beloved of poets, she wondered what the distinction was between dancing naked in front of *one* man who paid and dancing naked in front of a group of men who paid. She had the impression that, somewhere in the difference, lay morality. Tutors in the School of Hard Knocks, that is, other chorus girls in the cabaret, where, in her sixteenth summer, she had tunelessly croaked these same Créole ditties she now hummed, had told her there was all the difference in the world and, at sixteen, she could conceive of no higher ambition than to be kept; that is, kept off the streets. Prostitution was a question of number; of being paid by more than one person at a time. That was bad. She was not a bad girl. When she slept with anyone else but Daddy, she never let them pay. It was a matter of honour. It was a question of fidelity. (In these ethical surmises slumbered the birth of irony although her lover assumed she was promiscuous because she *was* promiscuous.)

Now, however, after a few crazy seasons in the clouds with him, she sometimes asked herself if she'd played her cards right. If she was going to have to dance naked to earn her keep, anyway, why shouldn't she dance naked for hard cash in hand and earn enough to keep herself? Eh? Eh?

But then, the very thought of organizing a new career made her yawn. Dragging herself around madams and music halls and so on; what an effort. And how much to ask? She had only the haziest notion of her own use value.

She danced naked. Her necklaces and earrings clinked. As always, when she finally got herself up off her ass and started dancing, she quite enjoyed it. She felt almost warm towards him; her good luck he was young and handsome. Her bad luck his finances were rocky, the opium, the scribbling; that he … but, at "that," she snapped her mind off.

Thinking resolutely of her good luck, she held out her hands to her lover, flashed her teeth at him – the molars might be black stumps, already, but the pointed canines still white as vampires' – and invited him to join in and dance with her. But he never would, never. Scared of muzzing his shirt or busting his collar or something, even if, when stoned, he would clap his hands to the rhythm. She liked it when he did that. She felt he was appreciating her. After a few drinks, she forgot the other thing altogether, although she guessed, of course. The girls told over the ghoulish litany of the symptoms together in the dressing-room in hushed, scared voices, peeking at the fortune-telling mirror and seeing, not their rosy faces, but their own rouged skulls.

When she was on her own, having a few drinks in front of
the fire, thinking about it, it made her break out in a horrible
hag's laughter, as if she were already the hag she would become
enjoying a grim joke at the expense of the pretty, secretly
festering thing she still was. At Walpurgisnacht, the young
witch boasted to the old witch: "Naked on a goat, I display my
fine young body." How the old witch laughed! "You'll rot!" I'll
rot, thought Jeanne, and laughed. This cackle of geriatric cynicism ill became such a creature made for pleasure as Jeanne,
but was pox not the emblematic fate of a creature made for
pleasure and the price you paid for the atrocious mixture of
corruption and innocence this child of the sun brought with
her from the Antilles?

For herself, she came clean, arrived in Paris with nothing
worse than scabies, malnutrition and ringworm about her
person. It was a bad joke, therefore, that, some centuries before
Jeanne's birth, the Aztec goddess, Nanahuatzin, had poured a
cornucopia of wheelchairs, dark glasses, crutches and mercury
pills on the ships of the conquistadores as they took their
spoiled booty from the New World to the Old; the raped
continent's revenge, perpetrating itself in the beds of Europe.
Jeanne innocently followed Nanahuatzin's trail across the
Atlantic but she brought no erotic vengeance – she'd picked up
the germ from the very first protector. The man she'd trusted to
take her away from all that, enough to make a horse laugh,
except that she was a fatalist, she was indifferent.

She bent over backwards until the huge fleece of a black
sheep, her unfastened hair, spilled onto the Bokhara. She was a
supple acrobat; she could make her back into a mahogany
rainbow. (Notice her big feet and huge, strong hands, capable

enough to have been a nurse's hands.) If he was a connoisseur of the beautiful, she was a connoisseur of the most exquisite humiliations but she had always been too poor to be able to afford the luxury of acknowledging a humiliation as such. You took what came. She arched her back so much a small boy could have run under her. Her reversed blood sang in her ears.

Upside down as she was, she could see, in the topmost right-hand window-pane he had left unfrosted, the sickle moon, precise as if pasted on the sky. This moon was the size of a broad nail-paring; you could see the vague outline of the rest of its surface, obscured by the shadow of the earth as if the earth were clenched between the moon's shining claw-tips, so you could say the moon held the world in its arms. An exceptionally brilliant star suspended from the nether prong on a taut, invisible leash.

The basalt cat, the pride of the home, its excretory stroll along the quay concluded, now whined for readmittance outside the door. The poet let Puss in. Puss leapt into his waiting arms and filled the apartment with a happy purr. The girl plotted to strangle the cat with her long, agile toes but, indulgent from the exercise of her sensuality, she soon laughed to see him loving up the cat with the same gestures, the same endearments, he used on her. She forgave the cat for its existence; they had a lot in common. She released the bow of her back with a twang and plumped on the rug, rubbing her stretched tendons.

He said she danced like a snake and she said, snakes can't dance: they've got no legs, and he said, but kindly, you're an idiot, Jeanne; but she knew he'd never so much as *seen* a snake, nobody who'd seen a snake move – that quick system of transverse strikes, lashing itself like a whip, leaving a rippling snake in the sand behind it, terribly fast – if he'd seen a snake move, he'd never have said a thing like that. She huffed off and contemplated her sweating breasts; she would have liked a bath, anyway, she was a little worried about a persistent vaginal discharge that smelled of mice, something new, something ominous, something horrid. But: no hot water, not at this hour.

"They'll bring up hot water if you pay."

His turn to sulk. He took to cleaning his nails again.

"You think I don't need to wash because I don't show the dirt."

But, even as she launched the first darts of a shrew's assault that she could have protracted for a tense, scratchy hour or more, had she been in the mood, she lost the taste for it. She was seized with sudden indifference. What does it matter? we're all going to die; we're as good as dead already. She drew her knees up to her chin and crouched in front of the fire, staring vacantly at the embers. Her face fixed in sullen resentment. The cat drew silently alongside, as if on purpose, adding a touch of satanic glamour, so you could imagine both were having silent conversations with the demons in the flames. As long as the cat left her alone, she let it alone. They were alone together. The quality of the separate self-absorptions of the cat and the woman was so private that the poet felt outmanoeuvred and withdrew to browse in his bookshelves, those rare, precious volumes, the jewelled missals, the incunabula, those books acquired from special shops that incurred damnation if you so much as opened the covers. He cherished his arduously aroused sexuality until she was prepared to acknowledge it again.

He thinks she is a vase of darkness; if he tips her up, black light will spill out. She is not Eve but, herself, the forbidden fruit, and he has eaten her!

Weird goddess, dusky as night,
reeking of musk smeared on tobacco,
a shaman conjured you, a Faust of the savannah,
black-thighed witch, midnight's child.

Indeed, the Faust who summoned her from the abyss of which her eyes retain the devastating memory must have exchanged her presence for his soul; black Helen's lips suck the marrow from the poet's spirit, although she wishes to do no such thing. Apart from her meals and a few drinks, she is without many conscious desires. If she were a Buddhist, she would be halfway on the road to sainthood because she wants so little, but, alas, she is still pricked by needs.

The cat yawned and stretched. Jeanne woke from her trance. Folding another spill out of a dismantled sonnet to ignite a fresh cheroot, her bib of cut glass a-jingle and a-jangle, she turned to the poet to ask, in her inimitable half-raucous, half-caressing voice, voice of a crow reared on honey, with its dawdling accent of the Antilles, for a little money.

Nobody seems to know in what year Jeanne Duval was born, although the year in which she met Charles Baudelaire (1842) is precisely logged and the biographies of his other mistresses, Aglaé-Josephine Sabatier and Marie Daubrun, are well documented. Besides Duval, she also used the names Prosper and Lemer, as if her name was of no consequence. Where she came from is a problem; books suggest Mauritius, in the Indian Ocean, or Santo Domingo, in the Caribbean, take your pick of two different sides of the world. (Her *pays d'origine* of less importance than it would have been had she been a wine.) Mauritius looks like a shot in the dark based on the fact that Baudelaire spent some time on that island during his abortive trip to India in 1841. Santo Domingo, Columbus' Hispaniola, now the Dominican Republic, a troubled history, borders upon Haiti. Here Toussaint L'Ouverture led a successful slave revolt against French plantation owners at the time of the French Revolution.

Although slavery had been abolished without debate throughout the French possessions by the National Assembly in 1794, it was reimposed in Martinique and Guadeloupe – though not in Haiti – by Napoleon. These slaves were not finally emancipated until 1848. However, African mistresses of French residents were often manumitted, together with their children, and intermarriage was by no means a rare occurrence. A middle-class Créole population grew up; to this class belonged the Josephine who became Empress of the French on her marriage to the same Napoleon.

It is unlikely that Jeanne Duval belonged to this class if, in fact, she came from Martinique, which, since she seems to have been Francophone, remains a possibility.

He made a note in "Mon Coeur Mis à Nu": "Of the People's hatred of Beauty. Examples: Jeanne and Mme Muller." (Who was Mme Muller?)

Kids in the street chucked stones at her, she so tall and witchy and, when she was pissed, teetering along with the vulnerable, self-conscious dignity of the drunk which always invites mockery, and, always, she held her bewildered head with its enormous, unravelling cape of hair as proudly as if she were carrying upon it an enormous pot full of all the waters of Lethe. Maybe he found her crying because the kids in the street were chucking stones at her, calling her a "black bitch" or worse and spattering the beautiful white flounces of her crinoline with handfuls of tossed mud they scooped from the gutters where they thought she belonged because she was a whore who had the nerve to sashay to the corner shop for cheroots or *ordinaire* or rum with her nose stuck up in the air as if she were the Empress of all the Africas.

But she was the deposed Empress, royalty in exile, for, of the entire and heterogeneous wealth of all those countries, had she not been dispossessed?

Robbed of the bronze gateways of Benin; of the iron breasts of the Amazons of the court of the King of Dahomey; of the esoteric wisdom of the great university of Timbuktu; of the urbanity of glamorous desert cities before whose walls the horsemen wheel, welcoming the night on trumpets twice the length of their own bodies. The Abyssinia of black saints and holy lions was not even so much as a legend to her. Of those savannahs where men wrestle with leopards she knew not one jot. The splendid continent to which her skin allied her had been excised from her memory. She had been deprived of history, she was the pure child of the colony. The colony – white, imperious – had fathered her. Her mother went off with the sailors and her granny looked after her in one room with a rag-covered bed.

Her granny said to Jeanne: "I was born in the ship where

my mother died and was thrown into the sea. Sharks ate her. Another woman of some other nation who had just still-born suckled me. I don't know anything about my father nor where I was conceived nor on what coast nor in what circumstances. My foster-mother soon died of fever in the plantation. I was weaned. I grew up."

Nevertheless, Jeanne retained a negative inheritance; if you tried to get her to do anything she didn't want to, if you tried to erode that little steely nugget of her free will, which expressed itself as lethargy, you could see how she had worn away the patience of the missionaries and so come to inherit, not even self-pity, only the twenty-nine legally permitted strokes of the whip.

———

Her granny spoke Créole, patois, knew no other language, spoke it badly and taught it badly to Jeanne, who did her best to convert it into good French when she came to Paris and started mixing with swells but made a hash of it, her heart wasn't in it, no wonder. It was as though her tongue had been cut out and another one sewn in that did not fit well. Therefore you could say, not so much that Jeanne did not understand the lapidary, troubled serenity of her lover's poetry but, that it was a perpetual affront to her. He recited it to her by the hour and she ached, raged and chafed under it because his eloquence denied her language. It made her dumb, a dumbness all the more profound because it manifested itself in a harsh clatter of ungrammatical recriminations and demands which were not directed at her lover so much – she was quite fond of him – as at her own condition, great gawk of an ignorant black girl, good for nothing: correction, good for only one thing, even if the spirochetes were already burrowing away diligently at her spinal marrow while she bore up the superb weight of oblivion on her Amazonian head.

The greatest poet of alienation stumbled upon the perfect stranger; theirs was a match made in heaven. In his heart, he must have known this.

———

The goddess of his heart, the ideal of the poet, lay resplendently on the bed in a room morosely papered red and black; he liked to have her make a spectacle of herself, to provide a sumptuous feast for his bright eyes that were always bigger than his belly.

Venus lies on the bed, waiting for a wind to rise: the sooty albatross hankers for the storm. Whirlwind!

———

She was acquainted with the albatross. A scallop-shell carried her stark naked across the Atlantic; she clutched an enormous handful of dreadlocks to her pubic mound. Albatrosses hitched glides on the gales the wee black cherubs blew for her.

The Albatross can fly around the world in eight days, if only it sticks to the stormy places. The sailors call the huge birds ugly names, goonies, mollyhawks, because of their foolish clumsiness on the ground but wind, wind is their element; they have absolute mastery of it.

Down there, far down, where the buttocks of the world

slim down again, if you go far south enough you reach again the realm of perpetual cold that begins and ends our experience on this earth, those ranges of ice mountains where the bull-roaring winds bay and bellow and no people are, only the stately penguin in his frock coat not unlike yours, Daddy, the estimable but, unlike you, uxorious penguin who balances the precious egg on his feet while his dear wife goes out and has as good a time as the Antarctic may afford.

If Daddy were like a penguin, how much more happy we should be; there isn't room for two albatrosses in *this* house.

Wind is the element of the albatross just as domesticity is that of the penguin. In the "Roaring Forties" and "Furious Fifties," where the high winds blow ceaselessly from west to east between the remotest tips of the inhabited continents and the blue nightmare of the uninhabitable ice, these great birds glide in delighted glee, south, far south, so far south it inverts the notional south of the poet's parrot-forest and glittering beach; down here, down south, only the phlegmatic monochrome, flightless birds form the audience for the wonderful *aerielistes* who live in the heart of the storm – like the bourgeoisie, Daddy, sitting good and quiet with their eggs on their feet watching artistes such as we dare death upon the high trapeze.

––––––

The woman and her lover wait for the rising of the wind upon which they will leave the gloomy apartment. They believe they can ascend and soar upon it. This wind will be like that from a new planet.

The young man inhales the aroma of the coconut oil which

she rubs into her hair to make it shine. His agonized romanticism transforms this homely odour of the Caribbean kitchen into the perfume of the air of those tropical islands he can sometimes persuade himself are the happy lands for which he longs. His lively imagination performs an alchemical alteration on the healthy tang of her sweat, freshly awakened by dancing. He thinks her sweat smells of cinnamon because she has spices in her pores. He thinks she is made of a different kind of flesh than his.

It is essential to their connection that, if she should put on the private garments of nudity, its non-sartorial regalia of jewellery and rouge, then he himself must retain the public nineteenth-century masculine impedimenta of frock coat (exquisitely cut); white shirt (pure silk, London tailored); oxblood cravat; and impeccable trousers. There's more to "Le Déjeuner sur l'Herbe" than meets the eye. (Manet, another friend of his.) Man does and is dressed to do so; his skin is his own business. He is artful, the creation of culture. Woman is; and is, therefore, fully dressed in no clothes at all, her skin is common property, she is a being at one with nature in a fleshly simplicity that, he insists, is the most abominable of artifices.

Once, before she became a kept woman, he and a group of Bohemians contrived to kidnap her from her customers at the cabaret, spirited her, at first protesting, then laughing, off with them, and they'd wandered along the streets in the small hours, looking for a place to take their prize for another drink and she urinated in the street, right there, didn't announce it; nor go off into an alley to do it on her own; she did not even leave go his arm but straddled the gutter, legs apart, and pissed as if it was the most natural thing in the world. Oh, the unexpected Chinese bells of that liquid cascade!

(At which point, his Lazarus arose and knocked unbidden on the coffin-lid of the poet's trousers.)

Jeanne hitched up her skirts with her free hand as she stepped across the pool she'd made, so that he saw where she had splashed her white stockings at the ankle. It seemed to his terrified, exacerbated sensibility that the liquid was a kind of bodily acid that burned away the knitted cotton, dissolved her petticoat, her stays, her chemise, the dress she wore, her jacket, so that now she walked beside him like an ambulant fetish, savage, obscene, terrifying.

He himself always wore gloves of pale pink kid that fitted as tenderly close as the rubber gloves that gynecologists will wear. Watching him play with her hair, she tranquilly recollected a red-haired friend in the cabaret who had served a brief appren-ticeship in a brothel but retired from the profession after she discovered a significant proportion of her customers wanted nothing more of her than permission to ejaculate into her mag-nificent Titian mane. (How the girls giggled over that.) The red-haired girl thought that, on the whole, this messy business was less distasteful and more hygienic than regular intercourse but it meant that she had to wash her hair so often that her crowning, indeed – she was a squint-eyed little thing – unique glory was stripped of its essential, natural oils. Seller and com-modity in one, a whore is her own investment in the world and so she must take care of herself; the squinting red-head decided she dare not risk squandering her capital so recklessly but Jeanne never had this temperament of the tradesperson, she did not feel she was her own property and so she gave herself away to everybody except the poet, for whom she had too much respect to offer such an ambivalent gift for nothing.

"Get it up for me," said the poet.

"Albatrosses are famous for the courtship antics they carry on throughout the breeding season. These involve grotesque, awkward dancing, accompanied by bowing, scraping, snapping of bills, and prolonged nasal groans."

Birds of the World, Oliver L. Austin Jnr.

They are not great nest builders. A slight depression in the ground will do. Or, they might hollow out a little mound of mud. They will make only the most squalid concessions to the earth. He envisaged their bed, the albatross's nest, as just such a fleeting kind of residence in which Destiny, the greatest madam of all, had closeted these two strange birds together. In this transitory exile, anything is possible.

"Jeanne, get it up for me."

Nothing is simple for this fellow! He makes a performance worthy of the Comédie Française out of a fuck, bringing him off is a five act drama with farcical interludes and other passages that could make you cry and, afterwards, cry he does, he is ashamed, he talks about his mother, but Jeanne can't remember her mother and her granny swapped her with a ship's mate for a couple of bottles, a bargain with which her granny said she was well satisfied because Jeanne was already getting into trouble and growing out of her clothes and ate so much.

While they had been untangling together the history of transgression, the fire went out; also, the small, white, shining, winter moon in the top left-hand corner of the top left-hand pane of the few sheets of clear glass in the window had, accompanied by its satellite star, completed the final section of its low arc over the black sky. While Jeanne stoically laboured over her lover's pleasure, as if he were her vineyard, she laying up treasure in heaven from her thankless toil, moon and star arrived together at the lower right-hand window pane.

If you could see her, if it were not so dark, she would look like the victim of a robbery; her bereft eyes are like abysses but she will hold him to her bosom and comfort him for betraying to her in his self-disgust those trace elements of common humanity he has left inside her body, for which he blames her bitterly, for which he will glorify her, awarding her the eternity promised by the poet.

The moon and star vanish.

———————

Nadar says he saw her a year or so after, deaf, dumb and paralyzed, Baudelaire died. The poet, finally, so far estranged from himself that, in the last months before the disease triumphed over him, when he was shown his reflection in a mirror, he bowed politely, as to a stranger. He told his mother to make sure that Jeanne was looked after but his mother didn't give her anything. Nadar says he saw Jeanne hobbling on crutches along the pavement to the dram-shop; her teeth were gone, she had a mammy-rag tied around her head but you could still see that her wonderful hair had fallen out. Her face would terrify the little children. He did not stop to speak to her.

———————

The ship embarked for Martinique.

You can buy teeth, you know; you can buy hair. They make the best wigs from the shorn locks of novices in convents.

The man who called himself her brother, perhaps they *did* have the same mother, why not? She hadn't the faintest idea what had happened to her mother and this hypothetical, high-yellow, demi-sibling popped up in the nick of time to take over her disordered finances with the skill of a born entrepreneur – he might have been Mephistopheles, for all she cared. Her brother. They'd salted away what the poet managed to smuggle to her, all the time he was dying, when his mother wasn't looking. Fifty francs for Jeanne, here; thirty francs for Jeanne, there. It all added up.

She was surprised to find out how much she was worth.

Add to this the sale of a manuscript or two, the ones she hadn't used to light her cheroots with. Some books, especially the ones with the flowery dedications. Sale of cuff-links and drawerful upon drawerful of pink kid gloves, hardly used. Her brother knew where to get rid of them. Later, any memorabilia of the poet, even his clumsy drawings, would fetch a surprising sum. They left a portfolio with an enterprising agent.

In a new dress of black tussore, her somewhat ravaged but carefully repaired face partially concealed by a flattering veil, she chugged away from Europe on a steamer bound for the Caribbean like a respectable widow and she was not yet fifty, after all. She might have been the Créole wife of a minor civil servant setting off home after his death. Her brother went first, to look out the property they were going to buy.

Her voyage was interrupted by no albatrosses. She never thought of the slavers' route, unless it was to compare her grandmother's crossing with her own, comfortable one. You could say that Jeanne had found herself; she had come down to earth, and, with the aid of her ivory cane, she walked perfectly well upon it. The sea air did her good. She decided to give up rum, except for a single tot last thing at night, after the accounts were completed.

See her, now, in her declining years, every morning in decent black, leaning a little on her stick but stately as only one who has snatched herself from the lion's mouth can be. She leaves the charming house, with its vine-covered verandah; "Good morning, Mme Duval!" sings out the obsequious gardener. How sweet it sounds. She is taking last night's takings to the bank. "Thank you so much, Mme Duval." As soon as she had got her first taste of it, she became a glutton for deference.

Until at last, in extreme old age, she succumbs to the ache in her bones and a cortège of grieving girls takes her to the churchyard, she will continue to dispense, to the most privileged of the colonial administration, at a not excessive price, the veritable, the authentic, the true Baudelairean syphilis.

JOHN CHEEVER

THE WORLD OF APPLES

Whether the writer has or has not a moral responsibility, is a question that has probably been debated since the days when paleolithic bards improvised dubious hymns in praise of tentative hunters. For Plato, the writer was responsible for communicating the truth, and he consequently banned poets, those composers of fantasies, from his Republic. *In our time, writers have argued that their responsibility is to their contemporaries or to a political ideal or to nothing but their writing. In the end, the readers decide. Writers who have believed themselves responsible for social change — Jonathan Swift, for instance — are remembered as authors of children's stories — such as his work,* Gulliver's Travels. *And others who have repeatedly denied any responsibility to society — William Golding comes to mind — become known for their social acumen — as in the classic,* Lord of the Flies.*

But as all writers (and some readers) discover, words themselves are tendentious. There are passages of seemingly stern prose that suddenly seem to strip the reader naked and fill the page with sensuousness and longing, and other, amorous texts where every image is buttoned up to the neck and every adjective carefully censored. The Countess of Noailles refused to allow her teenage daughters to read St Augustine's Confessions *because she felt (quite rightly) that the saint's autobiographical prose was so redolent with carnal desire that the girls' concentration in their studies might be adversely affected. In John Cheever's story "The World of Apples," the words the writer does not want to write have an urgency which he cannot understand, an erotic appeal which becomes stronger and coarser as his fear of them becomes greater, until the final transformation into a perfect text.*

ASA BASCOMB, the old laureate, wandered around his work house or study – he had never been able to settle on a name for a house where one wrote poetry – swatting hornets with a copy of *La Stampa* and wondering why he had never been given the Nobel Prize. He had received nearly every other sign of renown. In a trunk in the corner there were medals, citations, wreaths, sheaves, ribbons, and badges. The stove that heated his study had been given to him by the Oslo P.E.N. Club, his desk was a gift from the Kiev Writers' Union, and the study itself had been built by an international association of his admirers. The presidents of both Italy and the United States had wired their congratulations on the day he was presented with the key to the place. Why no Nobel Prize? Swat, swat. The study was a barny, raftered building with a large northern window that looked off to the Abruzzi. He would sooner have had a much smaller place with smaller windows but he had not been consulted. There seemed to be some clash between the altitude of the mountains and the disciplines of verse. At the time of which I'm writing he was eighty-two years old and lived in a villa below the hill town of Monte Carbone, south of Rome.

He had strong, thick white hair that hung in a lock over his forehead. Two or more cowlicks at the crown were usually disorderly and erect. He wet them down with soap for formal receptions, but they were never supine for more than an hour or two and were usually up in the air again by the time champagne was poured. It was very much a part of the impression he left. As one remembers a man for a long nose, a smile, birthmark, or scar, one remembered Bascomb for his unruly cowlicks. He was known vaguely as the Cézanne of poets. There was some linear preciseness to his work that might be thought to resemble Cézanne but the vision that underlies Cézanne's paintings was not his. This mistaken comparison might have arisen because the title of his most popular work was *The World of Apples* – poetry in which his admirers found the pungency, diversity, colour, and nostalgia of the apples of the northern New England he had not seen for forty years.

Why had he – provincial and famous for his simplicity – chosen to leave Vermont for Italy? Had it been the choice of his beloved Amelia, dead these ten years? She had made many of their decisions. Was he, the son of a farmer, so naïve that he thought living abroad might bring some colour to his stern beginnings? Or had it been simply a practical matter, an evasion of the publicity that would, in his own country, have been an annoyance? Admirers found him in Monte Carbone, they came almost daily, but they came in modest numbers. He was photographed once or twice a year for *Match* or *Epoca* – usually on his birthday – but he was in general able to lead a quieter life than would have been possible in the United States. Walking down Fifth Avenue on his last visit home he had been stopped by strangers and asked to autograph scraps of paper. On the streets of Rome no one knew or cared who he was and this was as he wanted it.

Monte Carbone was a Saracen town, built on the summit of a loaf-shaped butte of sullen granite. At the top of the town were three pure and voluminous springs whose water fell in pools or conduits down the sides of the mountain. His villa was below the town and he had in his garden many fountains, fed by the springs on the summit. The noise of falling water was loud and unmusical – a clapping or clattering sound. The water was stinging cold, even in midsummer, and he kept his gin, wine, and vermouth in a pool on the terrace. He worked in his study in the mornings, took a siesta after lunch, and then climbed the stairs to the village.

The tufa and pepperoni and the bitter colours of the lichen that takes root in the walls and roofs are no part of the consciousness of an American, even if he has lived for years, as Bascomb had, surrounded by this bitterness. The climb up the stairs winded him. He stopped again and again to catch his breath. Everyone spoke to him. *Salve, maestro, salve!* When he saw the bricked-up transept of the twelfth-century church he always mumbled the date to himself as if he were explaining

the beauties of the place to some companion. The beauties of
the place were various and gloomy. He would always be a
stranger there, but his strangeness seemed to him to be some
metaphor involving time as if, climbing the strange stairs past
the strange walls, he climbed through hours, months, years,
and decades. In the piazza he had a glass of wine and got his
mail. On any day he received more mail than the entire population of the village. There were letters from admirers, proposi-
tions to lecture, read, or simply show his face, and he seemed to
be on the invitation list of every honorary society in the
Western world excepting, of course, that society formed by the
past winners of the Nobel Prize. His mail was kept in a sack,
and if it was too heavy for him to carry, Antonio, the *postina's*
son, would walk back with him to the villa. He worked over his
mail until five or six. Two or three times a week some pilgrims
would find their way to the villa and if he liked their looks he
would give them a drink while he autographed their copy of
The World of Apples. They almost never brought his other
books, although he had published a dozen. Two or three
evenings a week he played backgammon with Carbone, the
local padrone. They both thought that the other cheated and
neither of them would leave the board during a game, even if
their bladders were killing them. He slept soundly.

Of the four poets with whom Bascomb was customarily
grouped one had shot himself, one had drowned himself, one
had hanged himself, and the fourth had died of delirium
tremens. Bascomb had known them all, loved most of them,
and had nursed two of them when they were ill, but the broad
implication that he had, by choosing to write poetry, chosen to
destroy himself was something he rebelled against vigorously.

He knew the temptations of suicide as he knew the temptations of every other form of sinfulness and he carefully kept out
of the villa all firearms, suitable lengths of rope, poisons, and
sleeping pills. He had seen in Z – the closest of the four – some
inalienable link between his prodigious imagination and his
prodigious gifts for self-destruction, but Bascomb in his stubborn, countrified way was determined to break or ignore this
link – to overthrow Marsyas and Orpheus. Poetry was a lasting
glory and he was determined that the final act of a poet's life
should not – as had been the case with Z – be played out in a
dirty room with twenty-three empty gin bottles. Since he
could not deny the connection between brilliance and tragedy
he seemed determined to bludgeon it.

Bascomb believed, as Cocteau once said, that the writing of
poetry was the exploitation of a substratum of memory that was
imperfectly understood. His work seemed to be an act of recollection. He did not, as he worked, charge his memory with any
practical tasks but it was definitely his memory that was called
into play – his memory of sensation, landscapes, faces, and the
immense vocabulary of his own language. He could spend a
month or longer on a short poem but discipline and industry
were not the words to describe his work. He did not seem to
choose his words at all but to recall them from the billions of
sounds that he had heard since he first understood speech.
Depending on his memory, then, as he did, to give his life use-
fulness he sometimes wondered if his memory were not failing.
Talking with friends and admirers he took great pains not to
repeat himself. Waking at two or three in the morning to hear
the unmusical clatter of his fountains he would grill himself for
an hour on names and dates. Who was Lord Cardigan's adver-

sary at Balaklava? It took a minute for the name of Lord Lucan
to struggle up through the murk but it finally appeared. He
conjugated the remote past of the verb *esse*, counted to fifty in
Russian, recited poems by Donne, Eliot, Thomas, and
Wordsworth, described the events of the Risorgimento beginning with the riots in Milan in 1812 up through the coronation
of Vittorio Emanuele, listed the ages of pre-history, the number
of kilometres in a mile, the planets of the solar system, and the
speed of light. There was a definite retard in the responsiveness
of his memory but he remained adequate, he thought. The only
impairment was anxiety. He had seen time destroy so much that
he wondered if an old man's memory could have more strength
and longevity than an oak; but the pin oak he had planted on
the terrace thirty years ago was dying and he could still remember in detail the cut and colour of the dress his beloved Amelia
had been wearing when they first met. He taxed his memory to
find its way through cities. He imagined walking from the railroad station in Indianapolis to the memorial fountain, from the
Hotel Europe in Leningrad to the Winter Palace, from the
Eden-Roma up through Trastevere to San Pietro in Montori.
Frail, doubting his faculties, it was the solitariness of this inqui-
sition that made it a struggle.

   His memory seemed to wake him one night or morning,
asking him to produce the first name of Lord Byron. He could
not. He decided to disassociate himself momentarily from his
memory and surprise it in possession of Lord Byron's name but
when he returned, warily, to this receptacle it was still empty.
Sidney? Percy? James? He got out of bed – it was cold – put on
some shoes and an overcoat and climbed up the stairs through
the garden to his study. He seized a copy of *Manfred* but the

author was listed simply as Lord Byron. The same was true of *Childe Harold.* He finally discovered, in the encyclopedia, that his lordship was named George. He granted himself a partial excuse for this lapse of memory and returned to his warm bed. Like most old men he had begun a furtive glossary of food that seemed to put lead in his pencil. Fresh trout. Black olives. Young lamb roasted with thyme. Wild mushrooms, bear, venison, and rabbit. On the other side of the ledger were all frozen foods, cultivated greens, overcooked pasta, and canned soups.

In the spring, a Scandinavian admirer wrote, asking if he might have the honour of taking Bascomb for a day's trip among the hill towns. Bascomb, who had no car of his own at the time, was delighted to accept. The Scandinavian was a pleasant young man and they set off happily for Monte Felici. In the fourteenth and fifteenth centuries the springs that supplied the town with water had gone dry and the population had moved halfway down the mountain. All that remained of the abandoned town on the summit were two churches or cathedrals of uncommon splendour. Bascomb loved these. They stood in fields of flowering weeds, their wall paintings still brilliant, their facades decorated with griffins, swans, and lions with the faces and parts of men and women, skewered dragons, winged serpents, and other marvels of metamorphoses. These vast and fanciful houses of God reminded Bascomb of the boundlessness of the human imagination and he felt lighthearted and enthusiastic. From Monte Felici they went on to San Giorgio, where there were some painted tombs and a little Roman theatre. They stopped in a grove below the town to have a picnic. Bascomb went into the woods to relieve himself and stumbled on a couple who were making love. They had not bothered to undress and the only flesh visible was the stranger's hairy backside. *Tanti, scusi,* mumbled Bascomb and he retreated to another part of the forest but when he rejoined the Scandinavian he was uneasy. The struggling couple seemed to have dimmed his memories of the cathedrals. When he returned to his villa some nuns from a Roman convent were waiting for him to autograph their copies of *The World of Apples.* He did this and asked his housekeeper, Maria, to give them some wine. They paid him the usual compliments – he had created a universe that seemed to welcome man; he had divined the voice of moral beauty in a rain wind – but all that he could think of was the stranger's back. It seemed to have more zeal and meaning than his celebrated search for truth. It seemed to dominate all that he had seen that day – the castles, clouds, cathedrals, mountains, and fields of flowers. When the nuns left he looked up to the mountains to raise his spirits but the mountains looked then like the breasts of women. His mind had become unclean. He seemed to step aside from its recalcitrance and watch the course it took. In the distance he heard a train whistle and what would his wayward mind make of this? The excitements of travel, the *prix fixe* in the dining car, the sort of wine they served on trains? It all seemed inno-cent enough until he caught his mind sneaking away from the dining car to the venereal stalls of the Wagon-Lit and thence into gross obscenity. He thought he knew what he needed and he spoke to Maria after dinner. She was always happy to accommodate him, although he always insisted that she take a bath. This, with the dishes, involved some delays but when she left him he definitely felt better but he definitely was not cured.

In the night his dreams were obscene and he woke several

times trying to shake off his venereal pall or torpor. Things were no better in the light of morning. Obscenity – gross obscenity – seemed to be the only factor in life that possessed colour and cheer. After breakfast he climbed up to his study and sat at his desk. The welcoming universe, the rain wind that sounded through the world of apples had vanished. Filth was his destiny, his best self, and he began with relish a long ballad called The Fart That Saved Athens. He finished the ballad that morning and burned it in the stove that had been given to him by the Oslo P.E.N. The ballad was, or had been until he burned it, an exhaustive and revolting exercise in scatology, and going down the stairs to his terrace he felt genuinely remorseful. He spent the afternoon writing a disgusting confession called The Favourite of Tiberio. Two admirers – a young married couple – came at five to praise him. They had met on a train, each of them carrying a copy of his *Apples*. They had fallen in love along the lines of the pure and ardent love he described. Thinking of his day's work, Bascomb hung his head.

On the next day he wrote The Confessions of a Public School Headmaster. He burned the manuscript at noon. As he came sadly down the stairs onto his terrace he found there fourteen students from the University of Rome who, as soon as he appeared, began to chant "The Orchards of Heaven" – the opening sonnet in *The World of Apples*. He shivered. His eyes filled with tears. He asked Maria to bring them some wine while he autographed their copies. They then lined up to shake his impure hand and returned to a bus in the field that had brought them out from Rome. He glanced at the mountains that had no cheering power – looked up at the meaningless blue sky. Where was the strength of decency? Had it any reality at all? Was the gross bestiality that obsessed him a sovereign truth? The most harrowing aspect of obscenity, he was to discover before the end of the week, was its boorishness. While he tackled his indecent projects with ardour he finished them with boredom and shame. The pornographer's course seems inflexible and he found himself repeating that tedious body of work that is circulated by the immature and the obsessed. He wrote The Confessions of a Lady's Maid, The Baseball Player's Honeymoon, and A Night in the Park. At the end of ten days he was at the bottom of the pornographer's barrel; he was writing dirty limericks. He wrote sixty of these and burned them. The next morning he took a bus to Rome.

He checked in at the Minerva, where he always stayed, and telephoned a long list of friends, but he knew that to arrive unannounced in a large city is to be friendless, and no one was home. He wandered around the streets and, stepping into a public toilet, found himself face to face with a male whore, displaying his wares. He stared at the man with the naïveté or the retard of someone very old. The man's face was idiotic – doped, drugged, and ugly – and yet, standing in his unsavoury orisons, he seemed to old Bascomb angelic, armed with a flaming sword that might conquer banality and smash the glass of custom. He hurried away. It was getting dark and that hellish eruption of traffic noise that rings off the walls of Rome at dusk was rising to its climax. He wandered into an art gallery on the Via Sistina where the painter or photographer – he was both – seemed to be suffering from the same infection as Bascomb, only in a more acute form. Back in the streets he wondered if there was a universality to this venereal dusk that had settled over his spirit. Had the world, as well as he, lost its way? He passed a concert hall where a program of songs was advertised and thinking that music might cleanse the thoughts of his heart he bought a ticket and went in. The concert was poorly attended. When the accompanist appeared, only a third of the seats were taken. Then the soprano came on, a splendid ash blonde in a crimson dress, and while she sang *Die Liebhaber der Brücken* old Bascomb began the disgusting and unfortunate habit of imagining that he was disrobing her. Hooks and eyes? he wondered. A zipper? While she sang *Die Feldspar* and went on to *Le Temps des lilas et le temps des roses ne reviendra plus* he settled for a zipper and imagined unfastening her dress at the back and lifting it gently off her shoulders. He got her slip over her head while she sang *L'Amore Nascondere* and undid the hooks and eyes of her brassiere during *Les Rêves de Pierrot*. His reverie was suspended when she stepped into the wings to gargle but as soon as she returned to the piano he got to work on her garter belt and all that it contained. When she took her bow at the intermission he applauded uproariously but not for her knowledge of music or the gifts of her voice. Then shame, limpid and pitiless as any passion, seemed to encompass him and he left the concert hall for the Minerva but his seizure was not over. He sat at his desk in the hotel and wrote a sonnet to the legendary Pope Joan. Technically it was an improvement over the limericks he had been writing but there was no moral improvement. In the morning he took the bus back to Monte Carbone and received some grateful admirers on his terrace. The next day he climbed to his study, wrote a few limericks, and then took some Petronius and Juvenal from the shelves to see what had been accomplished before him in this field of endeavour.

Here were candid and innocent accounts of sexual merriment. There was nowhere that sense of wickedness he experi-

enced when he burned his work in the stove each afternoon.
Was it simply that his world was that much older, its social
responsibilities that much more gruelling, and that lewdness
was the only answer to an increase of anxiety? What was it that
he had lost? It seemed then to be a sense of pride, an aureole of
lightness and valour, a kind of crown. He seemed to hold the
crown up to scrutiny and what did he find? Was it merely some
ancient fear of Daddy's razor strap and Mummy's scowl, some
childish subservience to the bullying world? He well knew his
instincts to be rowdy, abundant, and indiscreet and had he
allowed the world and all its tongues to impose upon him some
structure of transparent values for the convenience of a conser-
vative economy, an established church, and a bellicose army and
navy? He seemed to hold the crown, hold it up into the light, it
seemed made of light and what it seemed to mean was the genuine and tonic taste of exaltation and grief. The limericks he had
just completed were innocent, factual, and merry. They were
also obscene, but when had the facts of life become obscene and
what were the realities of this virtue he so painfully stripped
from himself each morning? They seemed to be the realities of
anxiety and love: Amelia standing in the diagonal beam of light,
the stormy night his son was born, the day his daughter married. One could disparage them as homely but they were the
best he knew of life – anxiety and love – and worlds away from
the limerick on his desk that began: "There was a young consul
named Caesar / Who had an enormous fissure." He burned his
limerick in the stove and went down the stairs.

The next day was the worst. He simply wrote F—k again
and again covering six or seven sheets of paper. He put this into
the stove at noon. At lunch Maria burned her finger, swore

lengthily, and then said: "I should visit the sacred angel of Monte Giordano." "What is the sacred angel?" he asked. "The angel can cleanse the thoughts of a man's heart," said Maria. "He is in the old church at Monte Giordano. He is made of olivewood from the Mount of Olives, and was carved by one of the saints himself. If you make a pilgrimage he will cleanse your thoughts." All Bascomb knew of pilgrimages was that you walked and for some reason carried a seashell. When Maria went up to take a siesta he looked among Amelia's relics and found a seashell. The angel would expect a present, he guessed, and from the box in his study he chose the gold medal the Soviet government had given him on Lermontov's Jubilee. He did not wake Maria or leave her a note. This seemed to be a conspicuous piece of senility. He had never before been, as the old often are, mischievously elusive, and he should have told Maria where he was going but he didn't. He started down through the vineyards to the main road at the bottom of the valley.

As he approached the river a little Fiat drew off the main road and parked among some trees. A man, his wife, and three carefully dressed daughters got out of the car and Bascomb stopped to watch them when he saw that the man carried a shotgun. What was he going to do? Commit murder? Suicide? Was Bascomb about to see some human sacrifice? He sat down, concealed by the deep grass, and watched. The mother and the three girls were very excited. The father seemed to be enjoying complete sovereignty. They spoke a dialect and Bascomb understood almost nothing they said. The man took the shotgun from its case and put a single shell in the chamber. Then he arranged his wife and three daughters in a line and put their hands over their ears. They were squealing. When this was all arranged he stood with his back to them, aimed his gun at the sky, and fired. The three children applauded and exclaimed over the loudness of the noise and the bravery of their dear father. The father returned the gun to its case, they all got back into the Fiat and drove, Bascomb supposed, back to their apartment in Rome.

Bascomb stretched out in the grass and fell asleep. He dreamed that he was back in his own country. What he saw was an old Ford truck with four flat tires, standing in a field of buttercups. A child wearing a paper crown and a bath towel for a mantle hurried around the corner of a white house. An old man took a bone from a paper bag and handed it to a stray dog. Autumn leaves smouldered in a bathtub with lion's feet. Thunder woke him, distant, shaped, he thought, like a gourd. He got down to the main road, where he was joined by a dog. The dog was trembling and he wondered if it was sick, rabid, dangerous, and then he saw that the dog was afraid of thunder. Each peal put the beast into a paroxysm of trembling and Bascomb stroked his head. He had never known an animal to be afraid of nature. Then the wind picked up the branches of the trees and he lifted his old nose to smell the rain, minutes before it fell. It was the smell of damp country churches, the spare rooms of old houses, earth closets, bathing suits put out to dry – so keen an odour of joy that he sniffed noisily. He did not, in spite of these transports, lose sight of his practical need for shelter. Beside the road was a little hut for bus travellers and he and the frightened dog stepped into this. The walls were covered with that sort of uncleanliness from which he hoped to flee and he stepped out again. Up the road was a farmhouse – one of those schizophrenic improvisations one sees so often in Italy. It seemed to have been bombed, spatch-cocked, and put together not at random but as a deliberate assault on logic. On one side there was a wooden lean-to where an old man sat. Bascomb asked him for the kindness of his shelter and the old man invited him in.

The old man seemed to be about Bascomb's age but he seemed to Bascomb enviably untroubled. His smile was gentle and his face was clear. He had obviously never been harried by the wish to write a dirty limerick. He would never be forced to make a pilgrimage with a seashell in his pocket. He held a book in his lap – a stamp album – and the lean-to was filled with potted plants. He did not ask his soul to clap hands and sing, and yet he seemed to have reached an organic peace of mind that Bascomb coveted. Should Bascomb have collected stamps and potted plants? Anyhow it was too late. Then the rain came, thunder shook the earth, the dog whined and trembled, and Bascomb caressed him. The storm passed in a few minutes and Bascomb thanked his host and started up the road.

He had a nice stride for someone so old and he walked, like all the rest of us, in some memory of prowess – love or football, Amelia, or a good dropkick – but after a mile or two he realized that he would not reach Monte Giordano until long after dark and when a car stopped and offered him a ride to the village he accepted it, hoping that this would not put a crimp in his cure. It was still light when he reached Monte Giordano. The village was about the same size as his own, with the same tufa walls and bitter lichen. The old church stood in the centre of the square but the door was locked. He asked for the priest and found him in a vineyard, burning prunings. He explained that he wanted to make an offering to the sainted angel and showed the priest his golden medal. The priest wanted to know if it was true gold and Bascomb then regretted his choice. Why hadn't he chosen the medal given him by the French government or the medal from Oxford? The Russians had not hallmarked the gold and he had no way of proving its worth. Then the priest noticed that the citation was written in the Russian alphabet. Not only was it false gold; it was Communist gold and not a fitting present for the sacred angel. At that moment the clouds parted and a single ray of light came into the vineyard, lighting the medal. It was a sign. The priest drew a cross in the air and they started back to the church.

It was an old, small, poor country church. The angel was in a chapel on the left, which the priest lighted. The image, buried in jewellery, stood in an iron cage with a padlocked door. The priest opened this and Bascomb placed his Lermontov medal at the angel's feet. Then he got to his knees and said loudly: "God bless Walt Whitman. God bless Hart Crane. God bless Dylan Thomas. God bless William Faulkner, Scott Fitzgerald, and especially Ernest Hemingway." The priest locked up the sacred relic and they left the church together. There was a cafe on the square where he got some supper and rented a bed. This was a strange engine of brass with brass angels at the four corners, but they seemed to possess some brassy blessedness since he dreamed of peace and woke in the middle of the night finding in himself that radiance he had known when he was younger. Something seemed to shine in his mind and limbs and lights and vitals and he fell asleep again and slept until morning.

On the next day, walking down from Monte Giordano to the main road, he heard the trumpeting of a waterfall. He went into the woods to find this. It was a natural fall, a shelf of rock and a curtain of green water, and it reminded him of a fall at the edge of the farm in Vermont where he had been raised. He had gone there one Sunday afternoon when he was a boy and sat on a hill above the pool. While he was there he saw an old man, with hair as thick and white as his was now, come through the woods. He had watched the old man unlace his shoes and undress himself with the haste of a lover. First he had wet his hands and arms and shoulders and then he had stepped into the torrent, bellowing with joy. He had then dried himself with his underpants, dressed, and gone back into the woods and it was not until he disappeared that Bascomb had realized that the old man was his father.

Now he did what his father had done – unlaced his shoes, tore at the buttons of his shirt, and knowing that a mossy stone or the force of the water could be the end of him he stepped naked into the torrent, bellowing like his father. He could stand the cold for only a minute but when he stepped away from the water he seemed at last to be himself. He went on down to the main road, where he was picked up by some mounted police, since Maria had sounded the alarm and the whole province was looking for the maestro. His return to Monte Carbone was triumphant and in the morning he began a long poem on the inalienable dignity of light and air that, while it would not get him the Nobel Prize, would grace the last months of his life.

COLETTE

ONE EVENING

In 1893, when she was only twenty years old, Colette married the celebrated journalist and man-about-town Henry Gauthier-Villars, who signed his books as "Willy" and was openly unfaithful to her. Willy was in the habit of having books written by others and then publishing them under his own name, and suggested to his wife that she try her hand at this ghost-writing. Colette produced a memoir of her school years but Willy thought it uninteresting and locked it away in a drawer. A couple of years later, he came across it again and changed his opinion drastically. He asked Colette to add "a few spicy details" and published the memoir, signed with his own name, under the title Claudine at School. *The book was a huge success, and Colette produced (always for Willy) several sequels. Only in 1904 did Colette add her name to that of her husband, when* Animal Dialogues *was published. Four years later, Colette divorced him and went on to become one of the most successful and illuminating chroniclers of women's lives.*

Colette explored the intricacies of different erotic relationships with meticulous craft and elegance. She wrote about teenage love, love between women, love of an older woman and a younger man, love in married couples, and even about the absence of love. Without ever being graphic she succeeded in being explicit, a feature that earned her the condemnation of the Catholic Church and the inclusion of her work in the Index of Forbidden Books. *In spite of this injunction, when she died, in 1954, hers was the first state funeral ever accorded to a woman in France.*

———

THE MOMENT the gate closed behind us and we saw the lantern in the gardener's hand dancing in front of us, under a covering of clipped yews where the heavy downpour filtered through only in scattered drops, we felt that shelter was very near and agreed laughingly that the car trouble which had just left us stranded in the countryside clearly belonged in the category of "happy accidents."

It just so happened that Monsieur B., a country councillor and the owner of the château, who welcomed these two rain-soaked and unexpected women out on the terrace, knew my husband slightly, and his wife – a former student at the Schola Cantorum – remembered having met me at a Sunday concert.

Around the first wood fire of the season, there rose a talkative gaiety. My friend Valentine and I felt it only right to accept a potluck of cold meat washed down with champagne; our hosts had only just finished their dinner.

An old plum brandy and some still-steaming coffee made us feel almost intimate. The electric light, rare for the region, the smell of mild tobacco, fruits, the blazing, resinous wood – I savoured these familiar delights like gifts from a newfound isle.

Monsieur B., square-shouldered, with just a hint of grey and the handsome, white-toothed smile of a man from the south, took my friend Valentine aside, and I chatted with Madame B. less than I observed her.

Blond, slim, and dressed as if for an elegant dinner and not for receiving stranded motorists, she surprised me with eyes so light that the least reflection robbed them of their pale blue. They became mauve like her dress, green like the silk of her chair, or disturbed, in the lamplight, by a fleeting red glimmer like the blue eyes of a Siamese cat.

I wondered if the entire face did not owe its vacant look, its empty amiability, its sometimes somnambulistic smile to these overlight eyes. A somnambulist, in any case, singularly attentive to everything that might please us and shorten the two or three hours it would take our chauffeur, with the help of Monsieur B.'s mechanic, to repair the car.

"We have a room you're welcome to use," Madame B. said to me. "Why not spend the night here?"

And her eyes, as though untenanted, expressed only an unlimited and almost unthinking solitude.

"It's not so bad here, really," she continued. "Look at my husband, he's getting on quite well with your friend!"

She laughed, while her wide-open, deserted eyes seemed not to hear what she said. Twice she made me repeat some phrase or other, starting slightly each time. Morphine? Opium? An addict would never have those rosy gums, that relaxed brow, that soft, warm hand, or that youthful flesh, firm and rounded beneath the low-cut dress.

Was I dealing with a silent conjugal victim? No. A tyrant, even a Machiavellian one, does not say "Simone" so tenderly, never bestows upon his slave so flattering a look …

"Why, yes, Madame, they do exist," Monsieur B. was saying to my friend Valentine. "There are couples who live in the country eight months out of the year, are never out of each other's sight, and don't complain about their fate! They do exist, don't they, Simone?"

"Yes, thank God!" replied Simone.

But in her eyes, just barely blue, there was nothing, nothing but a tiny yellow cinder, very far away – the lamp's reflection in a potbellied samovar. Then she stood up and poured us cups of steaming hot tea flavoured with rum "for the dark road." It was ten o'clock. A young man came in, bareheaded, and before being introduced gave some opened letters to Monsieur B., who asked my friend to excuse him as he leafed quickly through his mail.

"He's my husband's secretary," Madame B. explained to me as she cut a lemon into thin slices.

I responded by saying exactly what I was thinking: "He's very good-looking."

"Do you think so?"

She raised her eyebrows like a woman surprised, saying, "I've never thought about it." However, what was striking about this svelte young man was his air of stubborn, completely unself-conscious persistence, a habit of lowering his eyelids which, when he raised them, made his brusque, wild, quickly masked glance all the more arresting, and more disdainful than shy. He accepted a cup of tea and sat in front of the fire, next to Madame B., thus occupying the other place on one of those horrid, handy, S-shaped settees which the style of the 1880s named love seats.

Suddenly everyone fell silent for a moment and I was afraid our amiable hosts had tired of us. In order to break the silence I said softly, "How cozy! I'm going to remember this charming house I will have been in without ever knowing what it looks like set in the countryside ... This fire will warm us again, won't it, Valentine, if we close our eyes in the wind, a while from now."

"It will be your own fault," Madame B. cried out. "If it were me, I wouldn't need any sympathy. I love driving at night, with the rain streaking the air in front of the headlights and the drops of rain on my cheeks like tears. Oh, I love all that!"

I looked at her with surprise. She glowed all over with a delicious, human flame, which shyness had perhaps stifled for the first few hours. She no longer held herself back and the most attractive self-confidence showed her to be gay, sensible, well informed about local politics and her husband's ambitions, which she scoffed at by imitating him, the way little girls do when playacting. There was no lamp on the mantel, and only the crackling hearth, far from the central light, coloured or left in shadow this young woman whose sudden animation made me think of the gaiety of canaries, awakened in their cage at the hour when the lamps are lit. The dark back of Monsieur B.'s secretary was angled against the S-shaped armrest which separated him from Madame B. While she was talking to her husband and my friend from a slight distance, turned toward them, I rose in order to set down my empty cup and I saw that the young man's concealed hand held Madame B.'s bare arm in a steady and perfectly motionless grip above the elbow. Neither one of them moved, the young man's visible hand held a cigarette he was not smoking, and Madame B.'s free arm waved a small fan. She was speaking happily, attentive to everyone, her eyes limpid, in a voice interrupted now and then by her quickened breathing, like the urge to laugh, and I could see the veins in one of her hands begin to swell, so amorous and strong had the hidden embrace become.

Like someone who feels another's glance weighing down on him, Monsieur B.'s secretary suddenly rose, bowed to everyone, and left.

"Isn't that our motor I hear?" I asked Madame B. a moment later. She did not answer. She was staring into the fire, inclining her head toward a sound beyond her hearing, and slightly slumped over, looked like a woman who had just taken a bad fall. I repeated my question; she gave a start.

"Yes, yes, I believe so …" she said hastily. She blinked her eyes and gave me a smile of frozen grace, her eyes overtaken by a cold emptiness.

"What a shame!"

We left, carrying with us autumn roses and black dahlias. Monsieur B. walked alongside the car, which started slowly, as far as the first turn in the drive. Madame B. stood on the lighted terrace, smiling at us from a face abandoned by the momentary certainty of being alive; one of her hands, rising up beneath a transparent scarf, clasped her bare arm above the elbow.

Translated by
Matthew Ward

JULIO CORTÁZAR

FIRST CHAPTER

In the early sixties, the Argentinian writer Julio Cortázar, who had been living in Paris since 1954, undertook the writing of a huge novel which would allow the reader unprecedented freedom since the chapters would be written in such a way that they could be followed in any order one wished. The plot, therefore, would depend on chance and the reader's whim, a privilege or burden now advocated by postmodernism. Cortázar set the novel in Paris and London, but the characters belong to the Buenos Aires Cortázar had long left behind. Hopscotch *was published in 1967 and soon became recognized as one of the most inventive novels of our time. Several years later, the Canadian playwright John Krizanc wrote* Tamara *along similar principles, allowing the members of the audience to follow any character they chose throughout a mansion that was also the stage.*

Cortázar began Hopscotch *by writing a chapter in which the main character, obsessed with the body of a woman, effects on her a curious erotic ritual. Later, as the novel progressed, Cortázar realized that this first chapter was superfluous and abandoned it. Years afterwards, however, he re-read it, liked it, and decided to publish it in a Cuban magazine, as an independent short story. As the characters now had their own life in a separate book, he took their names out of the text and left blanks in their place since "one cannot give a character a name that is not his." Anonymously (as suits the nature of erotic literature) the characters conduct their intimate performance at which the reader is a bewildered voyeur.*

———————

        started because after gulping down the last of the coffee, he signalled but   stared at him blankly and went to get the paper to read the obituary column as is only proper after coffee.   waited for a moment and then said he would make some more coffee because he still felt like drinking real coffee and not the whitish juice   made with the excuse that there was no ground coffee left in the blue tin. To this   answered with an equally whitish look, and, when   made the sign again, her eyes allowed themselves to be lowered and began to search (in a morning paper) for Juan Roberto Figueredo, r.i.p., passed away peacefully on 13 January 195–, with the blessing of the Church and the benefit of last rites. His wife, et cetera. Isaac Feinsilber, r.i.p., et cetera. Rosa Sánchez de Morando, r.i.p. No one she knew, not today, not even one name that sounded like someone she knew and would allow the doubt and the genealogy.   came back with the coffee pot and started by spooning a good amount of sugar into   's cup who wasn't looking, deep in the paper, reading about Remigio Díaz, r.i.p. He then poured the coffee up to the rim of her cup, and filled his own, while with the free hand he took out a packet of cigarettes and put it to his mouth as if he were about to bite it, but it was only dexterously to extract a cigarette without touching the others with his lips.

"I'm very sleepy," said   after ten minutes.

"With the kind of news you read," said   who had been waiting for those words and was beginning to get seriously worried.

          yawned delicately.

"Take advantage now that the bed isn't made," said   . "You'll save yourself work afterwards."   looked at him as if she hoped he would do his signalling again, but   had begun to whistle with his eyes glued to the ceiling, and more precisely on a cobweb. Then   thought   was miffed because she had not answered his signalling with the expected answer (passing her hand over her left ear as a sign of tenderness and compliance) and went off to take her nap, leaving the table with the remains of a splendid casserole.

          waited three minutes, took off his pyjama top and entered the bedroom.   was fast asleep, on her back. As it was hot, she had taken the blanket off as well as the top sheet; it was exactly what   wanted, and also the fact that   should have nothing on except the nightdress in which she had got up that morning. The blue dressing-gown was lying at the foot of the bed, covering her feet, and hooked it on his slipper and kicked it into a corner. He missed his shot and the dressing-gown almost flew out of the window, which would have been a nuisance.

Out of the left pocket of his trousers   took a tube of Secotine glue and a ball of black thread. The thread was shiny and rather thick, almost like wrapping-string. Carefully,   put his hand inside the right pocket of his trousers and took out a razor blade wrapped up in a piece of toilet paper. The toilet paper was torn and one could see the blade's edge. Sitting on the bed,   began to work while loudly whistling a bit from an opera. He was certain she would not wake up, because large quantities of coffee always made her sleep profoundly, and also he would have been very surprised if she did wake up, considering the penumbrate of oxtaline he had slipped in with the sugar. On the contrary,   's sleep was quite extraordinary; she huffed to take the air in, so that every five seconds her upper lip would blow up like the frill of a curtain, while the air blew underneath it in a noisy puff.   used this as a pacemaker to carry on whistling the opera while cutting the black thread, after calculating approximately how much he needed.

A tube of Secotine glue is opened by taking out the round-headed pin that serves both to cover and uncover it, a detail that gives one an idea of the maker's ability. Once the pin is out, it is more than likely that a drop will appear on the tip of the tube, a drop of a rather revolting substance, with its already famous smell and certified mucilaginous properties. Very carefully, and while he embroidered variations on *Bella figlia dell'amore*,   wet the tip of the black thread with Secotine and, leaning over   , pressed the wet tip in the middle of her forehead, leaving his finger in place long enough for the thread to stick to the forehead without sticking to his finger, that is to say, about four seconds more or less. He then climbed on a chair (after placing the tube, the pin and the ball of thread on the chest-of-drawers) and stuck the other end of the thread to one of the cut-glass prisms of the chandelier that hung over the bed and that   had refused to throw out of the window in spite of his (now past and not repeated) pleading.

  Satisfied that the thread remained sufficiently tense, because he loathed sagginess in any human creation,
placed himself on the left side of the bed armed with the razor blade, and cut with a single stroke   's nightdress begin-ning with the armpit. Then he cut the turn of the sleeve, and did the same on the other side. The sleeves fell like snakeskins, but   proceeded with a certain solemnity when he came to lifting the front of the nightdress, leaving   stark naked. There was nothing on   's body that could be unknown to him, but the sudden contemplation of her body always dazzled him, although the Great Custom always managed to stale the effect.   's navel, more than any-thing else, made him giddy at first glance; it had something of confectionery, of failed transplant, or a pillbox thrown into a drum. Every time he saw it from above,   felt the urgent desire to fill his mouth with saliva, very white and very sweet, and delicately spit on the navel, filling it to the rim with warm birthday lace. He had done so many times, but now was not the right moment, so he turned to look for the ball of thread and began cutting threads of different lengths, first measuring out certain distances. The first piece of thread (because the one leading from the forehead to the chandelier was like a previous pledge that could not be taken into account) he stuck on the

big toe of   's left foot; this piece went from the toe to the
bathroom doorknob. The second piece of thread he stuck to
the second toe and also to the doorknob; the third to the third
toe and also to the doorknob; the fourth, to the fourth toe and
to a carving in the shape of the horn of plenty on the oak chest-
of-drawers, split in three parts; the fifth thread was drawn from
the little toe to another cut-glass prism of the chandelier. All
this on the left side of the bed.

  Satisfied,   stuck another piece of thread to   's
left knee and fixed it to the top of the window frame that looked
out onto the hotel courtyard. At precisely that moment an enormous bluebottle fly flew in through the open window and
began to buzz over   's body. Without paying any attention to it,   stuck another thread to   's groin, at the
top of her left thigh, and also to the upper rim of the window
frame. He thought for a moment before making up his mind,
and then took the tube of Secotine and squeezed it
against   's navel till it was full. He immediately stuck six
threads there and fixed them onto five cut-glass prisms hanging
from the chandelier, and onto the window frame. This did not
seem enough, so he stuck eight more pieces of thread to the
navel, which he stuck to seven more prisms and to the window
frame. Stepping back two feet (he was somewhat cornered
between the bed, the window and the pieces of thread that led
from   to the window frame),   gave the finished
work an appreciative look and found it satisfactory. He took out
another cigarette and lit it with the butt that was already burning his lips. Suddenly he cut another half-dozen more pieces of
thread, and stuck one to   's left nipple, another among
the hairs of the left armpit, another to the earlobe, another to

the left corner of the mouth, another to the left nostril and another to the corner of the left eye. The first three he stuck to the cut-glass prisms of the chandelier, and the others to the window frame, with a great deal of difficulty because he hardly had any room to move. After doing this, he stuck pieces of thread to each and every finger of the left hand, to the elbow and to the shoulder on that same side. Then he put the lid back on the Secotine with the pin provided for that purpose, wrapped the razor blade in the piece of toilet paper he had carefully kept in the hip pocket of his trousers, and tucked away both things and the ball of thread in the hip pocket of his trousers, and tucked away both things and the ball of thread in the left pocket of the above-mentioned article of clothing. Bending over very carefully so as not to touch the threads which looked amazingly tense, he crept under the bed until he came out on the other side, completely covered in fluff and dust. He shook himself against the window that opened onto the street, took out once again his working utensils, and cut a number of pieces of thread that he stuck successively to different parts of the right side of   's body, in general keeping a symmetry with the left side but allowing himself certain variations; for instance, the piece of thread corresponding to the right earlobe was drawn between the earlobe and the bathroom doorknob; the thread leaving the corner of the right eye was stuck to the window frame opening onto the street. Finally (even though he was under no obligation to finish that task in a hurry),   cut a fair number of pieces of thread, put a good quantity of Secotine on them, and plunged into   a   vehement   improvisation,   spreading   them among   's hair and eyebrows, and sticking most of them to the cut-glass prisms of the chandelier, and yet keeping some for the window frame opening onto the street, the bathroom doorknob and the carved horn of plenty.

Sliding under the bed, after putting away the tube, the razor blade and the ball of thread in his trousers,   dragged himself along till he came out at the foot of the bed, and kept sliding till he came to the bathroom door. Very slowly, so as not to touch any of the threads that led to the doorknob, he stood up and admired his work. Through the windows came a yellowish, rather dirty light, like the reflection of the peeling wall opposite that still held onto the remains of a painting depicting a baby sucking on something with a delighted look on his face; but the paint had come off in strips, and instead of a mouth the baby had a kind of purplish sore that seemed a poor recommendation for the nutritive product praised below in rather stuttering letters. The street was immensely narrow and the windows on one side were no more than five feet away from the other side. At that time not one window was open, except   's, but   would probably not be there at that time, or would be napping. The fly began to bother   intensely, and he would have liked to shoo it out of the window, but in order to do this he would have had to step forward to the foot of the bed and wave his hand next to the chandelier, which would have been impossible due to the large quantity of threads stretched in that direction.

"It's hot," thought   , wiping his forehead with the back of his hand. "It's really terribly hot."

On the one hand he would have liked to close the blinds, but quite apart from the fact that it was difficult to wind one's way through the threads, he would not have had enough light to see with the perfect clarity he needed   's body.

's nakedness seemed cut out against the background, not so much because she lay on her back on the bed, but because the black threads seemed to converge from everywhere and fall upon her. Had they not been that tense, the overall effect would have been completely bungled, and   congratulated himself on his dexterity, even though his naturally demanding spirit led him to notice that the thread that led from the window frame to the corner of the right eye was slightly slack. For a moment he thought that   had moved, altering the general balance of tensions, but it was enough for him to eye the total array of threads to dismiss that possibility. Furthermore, the amount of sleeping powder he had put into   's coffee would not have allowed even to blink.   thought of sliding down to the slackest thread and tightening it, but he would probably have spoiled some of the threads that met with this one on the window frame. He concluded that all in all the work was fine, and that he could allow himself a rest and another cigarette.

Eight minutes later he threw the butt out of the window into the street, and took off his clothes without moving from where he was. His tall, thin body seemed to have come out of an engraving (a frequent opinion of   's). Even though   could not see him, he gave the convened signal, and waited for an answer for about thirty seconds. Then he began to draw nearer the bed, avoiding little by little, with infinite care, the threads that led to the bathroom doorknob. To do this he bent down and then stood up every time it was necessary, until he was standing exactly at the foot of the bed, closing a triangle formed by   's two feet and his own body. He waited a while, until   opened her eyes and stared at him.

As soon as he was sure that she could see him (because sometimes the state of unconsciousness lasted a few minutes after
waking up) he lifted a finger and pointed to one of the
threads.   's eyes began to wander up and down the
threads, beginning by the ones that sprang from her eyebrows
and the corners of her eyes, and following the entire length of
her body. They rose to the cut-glass prisms of the chandelier
and back to their starting-point; they left again, travelling to
the window that looked onto the courtyard, and then returned
to fix themselves to a knee or a nipple; they followed the black
track to the window that opened onto the street, and returned
to the groin or to the toes.   was waiting with his arms
crossed, identical to a   painting of the blue period.

When   finished reconnoitring the threads, something like a sigh lifted her chest and projected her lips forwards.
Cautiously she moved her right arm, but she stopped when she
heard the cut-glass prisms of the chandelier tinkle. The bluebottle fly flew heavily, slid among the threads, swirled around
          's stomach and was about to land on her mount of
          , but then it ascended to the ceiling and stuck to one of
the mouldings.   and   followed its flight with exasperated attention; they did not look at each other until they
were sure that the fly had settled down on the ceiling with
every intention of staying there.

Putting one knee down on the edge of the bed,   bent
his head and began leaning forwards towards   , who
stared at him, motionless. The other knee appeared on the edge
of the bed, while the torso advanced horizontally and one of the
hands tried to grip the mattress, exactly in between   's
legs. The pieces of thread surrounded him, but his movements

were so precise that he did not so much as touch one when he lifted a knee and put it on the mattress; then the second knee together with the other hand, and remained on bent knees, completely arched between 's legs, breathing heavily because the manoeuvre had been slow and difficult, and his calves hurt him, still perched as he was on the edge of the bed.

Lifting his head, looked at . Both were sweating, but while the sweat wrapped in a fine mesh of transparent droplets, had both her face and shoulders sodden, even though her breasts and stomach were dry.

"One makes the signal, but the other plays with the clouds," said.

"Clouds are also an answer," said.

"A borrowed phrase."

"Exactly what you deserve."

waited.

"You did it, at last," said . "You've been preparing me for months for this. First with your obsession with teaching me to recite filth, to dance like a Tibetan woman, to eat like an Eskimo, to make love like a dog. Then you forced me to cut my nails, you threw me into the street that day when it was hailing, you locked me in a wooden box with an infrared lamp, you bought me a stamp album. All that was nothing."

"You know how much I love you," said in a voice so low that opened her eyes as if in surprise. "My love is held tight in this fist, crumpled and broken till it becomes a screeching ball, a portable star that I can take out of my pocket and put next to your body, to burn it, to tattoo it. Every time I signal you, you don't answer, and the star fries my legs, runs over my ribs like a storm in the Sargasso Sea, that inexistence where the Kraken floats, where the jellyfish couple in thousands, slowly turning in the night, in a bath of phosphorus and plankton."

"And is all that my fault?"

"You'll move the threads," said   . "When you move your mouth, two of the threads change position."

"So what, the threads?" said   .

"What do you mean, so what the threads?" said   . "It took me half an hour's work, I'm covered in dust and fluff. You never sweep under the bed. Even worse, you sweep the room and then hide the rubbish under the bed. I've just found out. My love is also like that, bits and pieces that come together and join and merge and stick onto one another. But I sweat, which rubbish doesn't."

"It seems as if I've slept for a hundred years," said   . "How long did I sleep,   ?"

"A hundred years," said   .

"That's a lot, a hundred years."

"For the one who stays awake."

"You must have been terribly bored."

"Exactly," said   . "When you fall asleep you take the world away with you, and I am left in sort of nothing crossed by lines of perspective. After a while it becomes boring."

"That's why you play like this," said   , staring at the threads.

"This is not playing. To be naked looking at one another."

"I swear," said   . "I think I didn't see the signal."

"Of course you saw it."

"Had I seen it I would have answered it. I'd rather be awake, with you."

"Explanations never suckled bees," said   .

"Maybe I saw it and didn't answer it, but that was because of the heat and because after all I'd have had to do the dishes before coming to bed."

"First the dishes," said   . "An excellent motto. At the bottom of how many knifings lies this excuse that no judge would accept. You'd lick the dirty dishes rather than lick my chest like an industrious little snail. Leaving a track in the shape of a four or an eight. Or better still, a seven, a number drunk in sacredness. But no, first we'll lick the dishes, as Queen Victoria would say. First we'll lick the dishes."

"But they're so filthy,   ," said   . "It's been fifteen days since we've washed anything in the kitchen. You noticed we had our lunch on dirty dishes, we can't go on like this."

"You're disturbing the threads," said   .

"And if now you'd signal to me, if even now you'd …"

A whistle was heard, in the shape of an S. It came in through the window that opened onto the street.

"It's   ," said   . "Calling me."

"Put something on before leaning out," said   . "You always forget you're naked."

"I'm always naked. You are the one who forgets that."

"Fine," said   . "But at least put the pyjama pants on. And till when do I have to stay like this?"

"I don't know," said   . "First I've got to see what   wants."

"To ask for something, I'm sure. A cigarette or matches, something like that."

"He's an addict."

"But you protect him."

"Well, if you're going to protect normal people …"

"True," said   . "After all,   is a good guy. Listen how he whistles. It's unbelievable how he can whistle. My mouth would fall to bits if I tried."

"   is an alchemist," said   . "He changes the air into a strip of mercury. Shit, he's fucked up."

"Why don't you look out and see what he wants? I'm not too comfortable here with these threads."

          stood for a moment silently studying   's words.

"I know," he said. "What you want is that I let you go so that you can wash those dirty dishes."

"I swear I don't. I'll stay here with you. If you give me the signal, I swear I'll …"

"Bitch, bitch, you bitch," said   . "If I give you the signal, eh? Now you come making up to me with the signal. Why should I care about the signal, if I had you any way I wanted while you slept? Even now all I have to do is slide down some twenty inches, making my way like a seagull through that wonderful black web, those ropes on the mast of a galley, and enter you in one single thrust so that you scream out, because you always scream out when I take you by surprise. And you're longing for it, I've been smelling you for the past five minutes and I know you're longing for it, I could enter you like a hand into a used glove, you have the perfect level of humidity advised by the specialists in copulatory matters, you hot sea-slug."

"Did you really do it while I slept?" said   .

"I did it in the most perfect way, but you would never understand," said   , looking at the threads in profound admiration. "Beyond the signal, beyond your dirty kitchen, and above all beyond your animal desire. Keep quiet, you're moving the threads."

"Please," said   . "Go and see what   wants, and then close the blinds and come to me. I swear I won't move, but hurry up."

        once again studied   's words in silence.

"Maybe," he said. "You don't move. Do you want me to dry you a bit with a towel? You're sweating like a stoat."

"Stoats don't sweat," said   .

"They sweat gallons," said   .

They always talked about stoats when they were making up.

"Now the problem is to see how I can get out of here," said   . "There are so many pieces of string that I could bump into one, and when you go backwards you don't have the same clairvoyance as when you go forwards. It's incredible how man was born for going forwards. From behind we're nothing. Like driving in reverse, even the cockiest will run over a post box at the first change of gears. Guide me. First I'll take this leg out and put this knee on the edge of the bed."

"A little further to the right," said   .

"I think I'm touching a thread with my foot," said   , looking behind him and correcting his movement.

"You hardly grazed it. Now put the other knee there, but slowly. You look beautiful, all in a sweat. And the light from the window seems to bathe you in green. You look like something rotten, I swear. I never saw you look so lovely."

"Stop flattering me and guide me instead," said   , furious. "You think I should put my foot down on the floor or should I slide down? I'll scrape my shins if I do that, this bed has a very sharp edge."

"First put the right foot down," said   . "The thing is
that I can't see the floor; how can I guide you if I can't even
move?"

"There," said   . "Now I'll bend down slowly and go
back inch by inch, like in   's novels."

"Don't name that bird of ill omen," said   .

Crawling like an everglades alligator,   passed little by
little under the threads that led to the window frame. He did
not look up at   again, concentrating on the study of the
chest-of-drawer's horn of plenty, and the problem of over-
coming the threads that went from the horn of plenty to one of
the toes, and to   's hair and eyebrows. Like that he
passed under the greater part of the threads, but the last one he
jumped. Only then, with his hand on the doorknob, he looked
back at   who seemed asleep. He realized that instead of
going to the window he was standing next to the door, and that
from there it was easy to reach the head of the bed without
disturbing the pieces of thread. Approaching her on tiptoes, he
began to blow on her hair. The threads wavered, and the cut-
glass prisms tinkled.

"Come here," said   in a very low voice.

"Oh no," said   , walking away. "I signalled you and
you didn't answer."

"Come, come here immediately."

          looked towards the door.   was breathing with
difficulty, as if the black threads were sucking her blood. The
crystal-clear note of one last cut-glass prism was heard, and then
the silence of the afternoon nap. From the house opposite came
a terrible whistle, and from below it was answered by something
very similar to someone breaking wind.

"They've sent him a splendid fart," said   . "He really deserves it."

"Please come here," she begged. "   . It's painful to wait for you like this, I feel I'm going to die. Who'll cook your steak tonight?"

          opened his arms, took a deep breath, and jumped onto the bed, sweeping the threads with a fabulous swing. The racket made by the cut-glass prisms coincided with the crash of his feet touching the floor on the other side of the bed and with   's yell, clutching her stomach with both hands.

          was still screaming in pain when   fell on her, squashing her, weighing her down, biting her and fucking her. "My belly-button hurts terribly,"   managed to say, but   could not hear her, completely on the far side of words. The air smelt more and more of Secotine, and the bluebottle fly circled around the shaken chandelier. Bits of black thread twisted like insect legs all over the place, falling from the edge of the bed, crossing over each other and tearing with tiny snaps.

          had bits of thread in his mouth, under his nose, another coiled around his neck, and   was moving her hands almost unconsciously, mingling caresses with desperate waves to rid herself of the threads that sprang from her every-where. And all this seemed to last forever, and the horn of plenty was lying on the floor broken in three pieces, one bigger and the other two almost the same, as divine proportion requires.

Translated by
Alberto Manguel

ANDRE DUBUS

THE LOVER

Married love is supposed to deaden passion. Because in time the immediate force of an attachment becomes less surprising, we find fault in the system and not in the sentiment itself. So strong is our impulse to blame marriage, that the image of matrimony as a suburb of hell has become a cliché. The English poet Louis MacNeice wrote:

So they were married, to be the more together
And found that they were never again so much
   together
Divided by the morning tea,
By the evening paper,
By children and tradesmen's bills.

Rainer Maria Rilke seems closer to the truth. "A good marriage," he suggested, "is that in which each appoints the other the guardian of his solitude." Andre Dubus's characters never seem to reach these mutual agreements. Their marriages are largely places of despair, and it is in the world outside the home where they seek challenges and find their expectations raised. Dubus describes them after they have left their marriage, as they enter a new situation, exploring how they act, what impulses drive them, how they fall in and out of love, what they find sensual and erotic, observing them without comment or judgement. This detached tone is Dubus's trademark. Once, in an interview, he quoted his favorite short-story writer, Anton Chekhov, who was told by a reader that the story "Thieves" was immoral because it didn't explain that horse-stealing was an immoral activity. "Everybody knows it's immoral to steal horses," Chekhov answered. "I wanted you to know what it feels like to be a man who steals horses."

L EE TRAMBATH was a fifty-five-year-old restaurant manager, with three ex-wives and five children. He was a slender, dark-haired man with a trimmed beard that was mostly grey, and he lived and worked in a small Massachusetts town, near the sea. The children were from his first two marriages, three daughters and two sons, grown now and spread up and down the Eastern seaboard from Charleston to Portland, all in places he liked to visit. None of them were married; they all had lovers. Lee was on good terms with the two mothers of his children; time had healed him, had allowed him to forget whatever he and the women had done to each other, or removed the precision of pain from his memory; and sometimes, sitting alone in his apartment or strolling on the boardwalk along the river flowing a mile or so to the ocean, he wished as a boy does: that in some way his first marriage had never ended, yet that his second had occurred, so the daughter and son from that one would be on the earth; and that he and the two women and five children were one family. This frequent wish was never erotic: his images were of him and the two women and five children in living rooms, dining rooms, on lawns. It was the third wife, and the women in their forties whom he dated after his divorce from her, who made him refer to his last marriage as absolutely his last.

His third wife was nearly forty when they married. She had two daughters who were aging her with their listless work in high school, slovenly lives at home, strong-willed disobedience, and unsavoury boyfriends whose tight clothing seemed only a cover to get from their cars to the house and, with the girls, back to their cars. Lee did what he could, with tender hesitance; the girls' father had moved to Houston when they were six and eight, and sent them cheques on birthdays and at Christmas. Lee silently predicted pregnancies, abortions, and a few years of too much drinking and cocaine. Then after college, which even they would be able to attend and muddle through, they would work at jobs to pay for clothes, cars, and apartments; and, like most people, they would settle softly into mundane lives. For Lee, the household was often frenzied and barely tolerable, with three females crying at once, but he was forty-nine, he had spent most of his adult life with families, and he could bear it.

His wife did not hold up as well, and told him to get a

vasectomy. He did not want to. Gently and reasonably he said he would not mind being sterile if it simply happened to him, if nature retired him from the ranks of fertility; but he did not want it done to him by a doctor; and, more importantly, he did not want to choose to have it done, but this was a hair he could not split for her. She was not gentle, and if her argument was reasonable, her scorn for his feelings, her crying and cursing him for not loving her, made reason hard to discern. She would not make love with him until he gave in; and he did, because he understood her fears more than he understood his resistance, and he wanted to keep peace, so when he consented he began to see her demand as a request that could not be made calmly. Who could turn away from a drowning woman because her plea for help came not as a whisper but a scream? Undressing for surgery, he felt he was giving up his life as he had known it; and afterward, when he brought his sperm to be tested, he hoped the surgeon had failed; or, rather, that his sperm remained, undaunted by scalpel, or his wife, or himself. His wife was relieved, and soon he was, too, and peace returned, or they returned to it.

When it did not last, when its not lasting slowly burned to ashes all kindness and respect in the marriage, when the marriage ended and Lee Trambath was in a bachelor apartment again, and seeing his two stepdaughters there and in restaurants, and dating again, he thought of his vasectomy as a concealed deformity, something he was hiding from women. No one he dated wanted more children, but still he always felt he was dissembling, until he told them, and one and all looked into his eyes as though he had spread yellow roses between them on the bar, the dinner table, or the bed.

He had married his first two wives when they were in their twenties, and he was the first husband of both; and always, however small, the shadows of sadness and failure were cast upon him: all his love and serious intent had increased the population of divorcées by two. His union with his third wife was his first with a divorcée; and her ex-husband, or what he had done to her, or what she believed he had done to her with no provocation at all, was a fulcrum in her marriage to Lee: he could trace the extremities of her anger and sorrow to that man he had never known. Now, dating, he collided with the presence of a man, or men, he only knew because a woman was pouting or crying or yelling or throwing a kitchen utensil at him, once a potholder, once a breadboard. The pain and bitterness, fear and distrust, of these women seemed all to be caused by one of his gender, not only husbands and lovers, but fathers and stepfathers as well. Confronted by these lives in which not one woman, including the woman herself, had ever been anything but kind, generous, and consoling, he began not only to believe it but to feel responsible for it, and he tried to atone. No one he dated ever accused him of being harsh, cruel, inattentive. They praised his patient listening, his lack of fear and cynicism in the face of love. They never accused him of anything; still, they made him feel like a drugged coral snake, sleeping and beautiful, which they took the risk of wearing around their throats while the clock ticked and the effect of the drug subsided: with the first slow movement of his flesh, they would grab him and hold him on the table and, with an oyster fork, pierce his brain.

He began to wonder what he had done to his wives. The first had never remarried, had kept his last name, and for the past seventeen years had lived on Cape Cod with one man. The second had married again, and the third was dating. What cracks had he left in their hearts? Did they love less now and settle for less in return, as they held on to parts of themselves they did not want to give and lose again? Or – and he wished this – did they love more fully because they had survived pain, so no longer feared it? This could not be true of his third wife: she would need a strong, gentle, and older man, someone like a father without the curse of incest. But perhaps the first two wives were free of him, were saved. Lee was so afraid of what he might have done to his daughters, even his stepdaughters whose lives he had entered when they were already in motion at a high and directionless speed, that he wondered about them as he did about the time and manner of his death: seldom, and with either terrible images or a silent blankness in his mind, like a window covered with shining white paint. With the women he loved after his last marriage, he started smoking again, and drinking more.

There were three of these women, separated by short intervals of pain, remorse, and despair. When he and the last one had their final quarrel – she threw the breadboard – he was nearly fifty-five, and he gave up on love, save the memory of it. Always his aim had been marriage. He had never entered what he considered to be an affair, something whose end was an understood condition of its beginning. But he had loved and wanted for the rest of his life women who took him in their arms, and even their hearts, but did not plan to keep him. He had known that about them, they had told him no lies about what they wanted, and he had persisted, keeping his faith: if he could not change their hearts, then love itself would.

As a young man, in his first marriage, he had done some erotic dabbling: one-night stands whose causes, he now knew, were alcohol, night, and vanity. This had only scratched his marriage: a little blood showed, nothing more; for his wife had also fallen from grace, and in the same way. Theirs was a confessional marriage, and the purging of one and forgiving by the other deepened their love. The marriage ended much later, when their sexual mischief was far behind them, and Lee would never understand all of its ending any more than he could explain why, on their first date in college, there was already enough love between them to engender the years it would take to have three children and let their love die. He learned how quickly love died when you weren't looking; if you weren't looking.

At the restaurant he managed, a flaxen-haired young waitress flirted with him as a matter of course. This was Doreen Brodie. She was tall, and her limbs looked stronger than his. Some nights he had an after-hours drink with her, sitting at the bar, and her blue eyes and thin red lips aroused his passion and, more tempting, swelled his loneliness till it nearly brimmed over, nearly moved his arms to hold her. He did not touch her. She was younger than his children; he was old, a marital leftover wearing a jacket and tie.

He had come to believe that only young women still trusted love, believed in it. He knew this could not be true, that it was the inductive reasoning of his bad luck, that he simply had not met resilient older women because they lived someplace else, or lived here in this little town but somehow had not crossed his path. Yet even if he met such a woman, wasn't he the common denominator in three divorces? Perhaps he was a sleeping snake.

He slipped into masturbation and nearly always, afterward, felt he was too old for this, too, and what he wiped from his hand onto the sheet was his dignity. But sometimes on long afternoons when he could think of nothing but Doreen Brodie, of phoning her and asking her for a date, of having dinner with her, of making love with her, and so falling in love with her, he resorted to the dry and heartless caress of his hand; then, his member spent and limp as his soul, he focused clearly on his life again, and he did not call Doreen.

He had married friends and went to their homes for dinner, or joined them at bars, but mostly he was alone in his apartment. So working nights, which had been an intrusion on his marriages and an interference with his dating, became a blessing. He started reading history or philosophy during the day, going for long walks, and keeping a journal in spiral notebooks. He wrote every morning before breakfast: reflections on what he read, on people at the restaurant, sketches of the town and river and sky as he saw them on his walks. He wrote slowly, used a large dictionary, and took pleasure in precise nouns, verbs, and adjectives. He liked working with colours. He wrote nothing painful or erotic; he did not want his children to feel pity or shame when they went through his effects after his death. For a summer and fall, a winter and part of a spring, Lee Trambath lived like this, till an April morning when he woke to the sound and smell of rain.

As he dressed he remembered that yesterday he had meant to buy coffee but, drawn by sunshine and a salty breeze from the sea, he had walked along the river, instead of to the store. He wanted to write about rain, try to put its smell and sound on paper. But he had no coffee, and he put on his raincoat and a felt hat and went downstairs and outside. At once his face and throat and hands were pleasantly wet. Across the street was the grey river. He watched rain falling on it, and cars moving slowly, their headlights glowing. Then he walked to the end of the block and turned left, onto the main street. He smelled rain and the sea. The grocery store was in the next block but his stride was slowing as he approached a newsstand with a kitchen for breakfast and lunch. In front of it, he stopped. Until nearly a year ago he had come here for breakfast, read newspapers, bought paperback books. Some time after he ducked the breadboard and backed out of her kitchen, backed out of her dining and living rooms and front door, he had begun his rituals of abstinence: his journal; his breakfast at home; his study of America, hoping to find in that huge canvas perhaps one brushstroke to illuminate the mystery of his life; his walks whose purpose was for at least one hour of light to see where he lived, smell it, touch it, listen to its sounds. Standing in the cool rain he lost his eagerness to write about it, but he kept its thrill. The rain on his race was like joyful tears, given him by the clouds; he could not recall when he had last wept. Now a new excitement welled in him: that of a holiday, and he moved to the door and swung it open and went inside, looking first to his left at the counter for tobacco and boxed candy at that wall, and beyond it the shelves of magazines and racks of books, then he looked to this right at tables for two and four where people were eating, and a long counter facing a mirror. Seated at the counter were a policeman, a young couple looking at each other as they talked, a grey-haired man alone, and Doreen Brodie reading a newspaper. To her right were three empty stools. He walked between tables and sat beside her. He had never seen her in daylight, had never seen her anywhere save at the restaurant. She looked at the mirror opposite the counter, saw him there, smiled at his reflection, then turned the smile to him and said: "Well. What brings you out in the rain?"

He took off his hat and placed it on the counter and was about to say he was going to buy coffee, but he looked at Doreen's blue eyes and said: "I woke to the sound of rain. It was the first thing I smelled." From behind her a waitress approached and he signalled with thumb and forefinger as if gripping a cup. "Some was splashing through the screen, onto the windowsill. I didn't close the window. I wanted to write about rain, but I was out of coffee." He was unbuttoning his coat, removing his arms from its sleeves. "I've been writing things. I wanted to write its smell and sound. Its feel in April." He let his coat fall to the back of his stool. The waitress brought his coffee, and he stopped talking to pay. She was a young brunette wearing glasses, probably a year out of high school and waiting, happily enough, it seemed, for something to happen. He looked at Doreen's eyes: "It would be a separate section; the rain. Coming right after something I wrote yesterday about William James. He said that fear doesn't cause running away. Running away causes fear. So if you hold your ground you'll be brave. And that sadness doesn't cause crying. Crying makes us sad. So we should act the way we want to feel. And he said if that doesn't work, nothing else will anyway." Then he blushed. "He was a philosopher. I've been reading all kinds of things."

"Does it work?"

"What?"

"Acting the way you want to feel."

"Sometimes." He looked away from her, stirred sugar and cream into his cup. Still he felt her eyes.

"What is it you want to feel?"

Beneath his heart, wings fluttered. He looked at her eyes and the wings paused like a hawk's, and glided.

"You," he said, and they rushed in his breast, and someplace beneath them he felt the cool plume of a lie. "I want to feel you."

The lie spread upward but light was in her eyes, and she was standing, was saying softly: "Let's go."

He stood and put on his coat and hat; she had a black umbrella; she left her newspaper on the counter and he followed her out the door. She opened the umbrella, held it between them, and he stepped under it. His arm touched hers; perhaps it was the first time he had ever touched her. He went with her up the street, away from the river; at the corner she stopped and faced traffic, and watched the red light. He looked at her profile. Suddenly he felt the solidity of the earth beneath his feet. Were gravity and grave rooted in the same word? In that moment, looking at her left eye and its long upturning lashes, her nose and lips, and the curve of her chin, he could have told her they must not do this, he was a waste of her time, her fertility. Then she turned to him, and her eyes amazed him; he was either lost or found, he could not know which, and he surrendered.

The traffic light changed and they crossed the street and she led him down a brick alley between brick shops, then across a courtyard. His life was repeating itself, yet it felt not repetitious but splendid, and filled with grace. He lowered his eyes to rain moving on darkened bricks. God in heaven, he thought, if there is one, bless us. As a boy he was an Episcopalian. Then, with his first wife, he became his flesh and what it earned. Only his love for his children felt more spiritual than carnal. Holding one in his arms, he felt connected with something ancient, even immortal. In the arms of his passionate wife he felt a communion he believed was the supreme earthly joy. It had ended and he had found it again with other wives and other women, and always its ending had flung him into a dark pit of finitude, whose walls seeped despair as palpable as the rain he walked in now, after too many years.

Doreen's kiss dispelled those years. She gave it to him just across the threshold of her apartment, and he marvelled at the resilience of nature. So many kisses in his lifetime, yet here he was, as though kissed for the first time on a front porch in summer in Dayton, Ohio. O plenitude, O spring rain, and new love. He did not see the apartment; it was objects and shadows they moved through. Her unmade bed was box springs and a mattress on the floor, and quickly they were in it, his hat and clothes on the carpet with hers. He did not want it to end: he made love to her with his lips, his hands, his tongue. The muscles of her arms and stomach and legs were hard, her touch and voice soft; he spoke her name, he called her sweet, he called her my lovely, he perspired, and once from his stomach came a liquid moan of hunger. Finally she rolled away from him, toward the bedside table, and opened a drawer; he heard a tearing sound, and she sat up holding a golden condom.

"I have a vasectomy."

"What a guy. I've got an IUD."

"I've mostly been married."

"You never know." He watched her hands as she placed the

condom and unrolled it. Then she kneeled above him, guided him in, and said: "I had given up on you."

"So had I."

Here it was again, the hot love of a woman, and he closed his eyes and saw the ocean at night, and squid mating on its gentle swell, a documentary he watched on television one afternoon last winter; sharks swam up and ate swaths of squid, but the others kept on, just kept on. Fucking and eating, he thought. They were why he left home, to marry and work, and here he was, over thirty years later, with a woman nearly as young as his first wife when passion drove them out of their parents' homes and into the world, into a small apartment that was first an enclosure for their bed and second for a kitchen to prepare food in and a table to eat it on, and third for plumbing so they could bathe, and flush body waste. All vitality radiated from the bed, enough of it to give him the drive and direction to earn money and father children; he fell in love with them, a love that was as much a component of his flesh as the flow of his blood; and in fact it could only end with that flow's ending. Now another flow was about to leave his body: the pleasure started in the muscles of his legs where masturbation never reached, and he saw the mockery of himself and his hand, and to rid his mind of this comparison he said her name. He said it again and again, naming her flesh and his delight but the truth was as loud as their quick breath. His passion spurted from him, was gone, a bit of sterile liquid in a condom, a tiny bit if it were blood. It was enough to stain a sheet, make a child. His children would smile if they knew of this, if he told them he had waked to rain but had no coffee, so – There was nothing to smile about here. He opened his eyes. Doreen's were closed.

Soon he would soften inside her, and she was racing against the ebbing of his blood. He watched her face. Long ago he had learned that in lovemaking the one giving pleasure felt the greater intimacy; beyond a certain pitch of passion, the one receiving was isolated by muscles and nerves. He could have been watching her suffer pain; he could have been watching her die. She cried out. Then she was still, her eyes open, her breath deep and slowing. Before moving away, she reached between them and pinched the condom's opening. She took it with her, hanging from her fingers as she stood and smiled at him, and left the room.

He closed his eyes and listened to rain on the window. It saddened him now, all that rain and grey. He heard her footsteps in the hall, then soft on the carpet, and her lighter twice, and blown smoke; she sat on the bed and he spread his fingers for the cigarette, then she lay beside him and placed a cool glass ashtray on his stomach. He opened his eyes and looked at hers and said: "What more could I ask?"

"You could have asked sooner."

"I was trying to do something. Learn something. Do you know I could *own* a restaurant by now, if I wanted to? I never wanted to. I have money. I'm not just solvent; I have *money*. When I die my children will be able to make down payments on houses. Big payments. I have five children. All grown, and none of them married. Nobody's in a hurry anymore. To marry."

"Nobody has to be."

"Exactly. And that's all I ever was. What are people now? Their jobs? I started behind the bar and in kitchens. Now I read all this stuff. History. Philosophy. Looking for myself, where I fit in. I must be part of it, right? I'm here. So I must be. You know where I fit? I earn and invest and spend money. You know why? Because I fell in love. When I was very young. If I hadn't I might have joined the French Foreign Legion. Then I'd know, wouldn't I? What my part was. My part was this —" He gestured with a hand toward his penis; then he touched his heart. "And this. If you look at the country today, you see families torn apart. Kids with blood splashed on them. It all started with families. Like this, you and me, naked. People made love, settled land, built towns. Now the beginning is dying and we're left with the end. I'm part of that, too. Three divorces. So that's where I fit. At the beginning and the end. It was always love for me, love of a woman. I look back and I think love needs tenacity. Maybe that's what I didn't have. And where is love in all this? It's not here. You don't love me." Her eyes were gentle as she shook her head. "Probably I could love you. But what for? Reverse my vasectomy and start over? Own a restaurant? Somewhere I missed something. Something my cock can't feel. Even my heart can't feel. Something that keeps you from fucking while sharks are eating your neighbours; while one is coming for you. I broke the hearts of three wives. It's not what I set out to do. We were in bed, and there were all those fins. I ripped childhood from five children. It'll always be with them, that pain. Like joints that hurt when it rains. There's more to it, but I can't find it. It's not walking with a cane and giving cigar rings to grandchildren. You know anyone in AA?"

She nodded. Her eyes were damp, and he knew from them what his own face showed.

"You know that look they have when it's really behind them? When they've been dry for years? Like there's a part of them that nothing in the world can touch. Not pain. Not grief. Not even love. But where do I go for that? What street is it on? Where's the door?" He held the ashtray and sat up. "Where?" Looking at Doreen, he felt tears in his throat then his eyes and on his face. "I want that door," he said, then he could not speak. His stomach tightened, his body jerked forward, and his head bowed as he wept. She took the ashtray and cigarette from him and tightly held him with one arm, and with a hand she petted his cheek, pressing it against hers; she gently rocked him.

"You poor man," she said.

He knew what she felt, at the core of her tender voice and touch. He had held in his arms suffering women and children, knew that all anyone could do was hold and touch and speak, watch and listen, and wish the pain would end. Gratefully he leaned against her, moving with the push and pull of her arm. He could see nothing beyond this sorrow, could not imagine what he might say or do when it left him in Doreen's embrace.

MARY GAITSKILL

A ROMANTIC WEEKEND

Locked up in the prisons of the Bastille and Vincennes, and later in the lunatic asylum of Charenton, the Marquis de Sade was punished both for his politics and his imagination. Ironically, the French Revolution which proclaimed equality, liberty and the brotherhood of men would not free him. The horrors Sade depicted in his so-called "philosophical novels" carried to the extreme fantasies common in every culture, from the ancient Greeks who told with admiration of the flaying alive of Marsyas, to the Christians who worshipped the image of their God nailed bleeding to a cross.

The infliction of pain has long been associated with ecstasy; Sade argued that this was a natural association, since Nature itself was cruel, and that it was our unnatural hypocrisy that condemned it. A century later, the aristocratic Leopold Sacher-Masoch gave, in The Venus in Furs, *an account not of the pain-inflicter but of the pain-seeker who longs for a beautiful and domineering woman who will punish him.*

In our time, the terms derived from the companionable names of these two outcasts have become trivial: we speak of the sadism of certain politicians who torture us with their speeches; we call ourselves masochists for agreeing to read the novels of Joyce Carol Oates. The erotic fantasies which these two terms might conjure up require, on the part of the fantasizers, concerted efforts to escape this triteness, to return to our dark depths. As Mary Gaitskill shows, two people who together agree on exploring this dangerous territory must work very hard, or they will fail miserably. Bad Behaviour, Gaitskill's collection of stories which included "A Romantic Weekend," is prefaced by a quotation from W. H. Auden:*

All the conventions conspire
To make this fort assume
The furniture of home;
Lest we should see where we are,
Lost in a haunted wood,
Children afraid of the night
Who have never been happy or good.

SHE WAS MEETING a man she had recently and abruptly fallen in love with. She was in a state of ghastly anxiety. He was married, for one thing, to a Korean woman whom he described as the embodiment of all that was feminine and elegant. Not only that, but a psychic had told her that a relationship with him could cripple her emotionally for the rest of her life. On top of this, she was tormented by the feeling that she looked inadequate. Perhaps her body tilted too far forward as she walked, perhaps her jacket made her torso look bulky in contrast to her calves and ankles, which were probably skinny. She felt like an object unravelling in every direction. In anticipation of their meeting, she had not been able to sleep the night before; she had therefore eaten some amphetamines and these had heightened her feeling of disintegration.

When she arrived at the corner he wasn't there. She stood against a building, trying to arrange her body in the least repulsive configuration possible. Her discomfort mounted. She crossed the street and stood on the other corner. It seemed as though everyone who walked by was eating. A large, distracted businessman went by holding a half-eaten hot dog. Two girls passed, sharing cashews from a white bag. The eating added to her sense that the world was disorderly and unbeautiful. She became acutely aware of the garbage on the street. The wind stirred it; a candy wrapper waved forlornly from its trapped position in the mesh of a jammed public wastebasket. This was all wrong, all horrible. Her meeting with him should be perfect and scrap-free. She couldn't bear the thought of flapping trash. Why wasn't he there to meet her? Minutes passed. Her shoulders drew together.

She stepped into a flower store. The store was clean and white, except for a few smudges on the linoleum floor. Homosexuals with low voices stood behind the counter. Arranged stalks bearing absurd blossoms protruded from sedate round vases and bristled in the aisles. She had a paroxysm of fantasy. He held her, helpless and swooning, in his arms. They were supported by a soft ball of puffy blue stuff. Thornless roses surrounded their heads. His gaze penetrated her so thoroughly, it was as though he had thrust his hand into her chest and begun feeling her ribs one by one. This was all right with her. "I have never met anyone I felt this way about," he said. "I love you." He made her do things she'd never done before, and then they went for a walk and looked at the new tulips that were bound to have grown up somewhere. None of this felt stupid or corny, but she knew that it was. Miserably, she tried to gain a sense of proportion. She stared at the flowers. They were an agony of bright, organized beauty. She couldn't help it. She wanted to give him flowers. She wanted to be with him in a room full of flowers. She visualized herself standing in front of him, bearing a handful of blameless flowers trapped in the ugly pastel paper the florist would staple around them. The vision was brutally embarrassing, too much so to stay in her mind for more than seconds.

She stepped out of the flower store. He was not there. Her anxiety approached despair. They were supposed to spend the weekend together.

He stood in a cheap pizza stand across the street, eating a greasy slice and watching her as she stood on the corner. Her anxiety was visible to him. It was at once disconcerting and weirdly attractive. Her appearance otherwise was not pleasing. He couldn't quite put his finger on why this was. Perhaps it was the suggestion of meekness in her dress, of a desire to be inconspicuous, or worse, of plain thoughtlessness about how clothes looked on her.

He had met her at a party during the previous week. She immediately reminded him of a girl he had known years before, Sharon, a painfully serious girl with a pale, gentle face whom he had tormented off and on for two years before leaving for his wife. Although it had gratified him enormously to leave her, he had missed hurting her for years, and had been half-consciously looking for another woman with a similarly fatal combination of pride, weakness and a foolish lust for something resembling passion. On meeting Beth, he was astonished at how much she looked, talked and moved like his former victim. She was delicately morbid in all her gestures, sensitive, arrogant, vulnerable to flattery. She veered between extravagant outbursts of opinion and sudden, uncertain halts, during which she seemed to look to him for approval. She was in love with the idea of intelligence, and she overestimated her own. Her sense of the world, though she presented it aggressively, could be, he sensed, snatched out from under her with little or no trouble. She said, "I hope you are a savage."

He went home with her that night. He lay with her on her sagging, lumpy single mattress, tipping his head to blow smoke into the room. She butted her forehead against his chest. The mattress squeaked with every movement. He told her about Sharon. "I had a relationship like that when I was in college," she said. "Somebody opened me up in a way that I had no control over. He hurt me. He changed me completely. Now I can't have sex normally."

The room was pathetically decorated with postcards, pictures of huge-eyed Japanese cartoon characters, and tiny, maddening toys that she had obviously gone out of her way to find, displayed in a tightly arranged tumble on her dresser. A frail model airplane dangled from the light above her dresser. Next to it was a pasted-up cartoon of a pink-haired girl cringing open-mouthed before a spike-haired boy-villain in shorts and glasses. Her short skirt was blown up by the force of his threatening expression, and her panties showed. What kind of person would put crap like this up on her wall?

"I'm afraid of you," she murmured.

"Why?"

"Because I just am."

"Don't worry. I won't give you any more pain than you can handle."

She curled against him and squeezed her feet together like a stretching cat. Her socks were thick and ugly, and her feet were large for her size. Details like this could repel him, but he felt tenderly toward the long, grubby, squeezed-together feet. He said, "I want a slave."

She said, "I don't know. We'll see."

He asked her to spend the weekend with him three days later.

It had seemed like a good idea at the time, but now he felt an irritating combination of guilt and anxiety. He thought of his wife, making breakfast with her delicate, methodical movements, or in the bathroom, painstakingly applying kohl under her huge eyes, flicking away the excess with pretty, birdlike finger gestures, her thin elbows raised, her eyes blank with concentration. He thought of Beth, naked and bound, blindfolded and spread-eagled on the floor of her cluttered apartment. Her cartoon characters grinned as he beat her with a whip. Welts rose on her breasts, thighs, stomach and arms. She screamed and twisted, wrenching her neck from side to side.

She was going to be scarred for life. He had another picture of her sitting across from him at a restaurant, very erect, one arm on the table, her face serious and intent. Her large glasses drew her face down, made it look sombre and elegant. She was smoking a cigarette with slow, mournful intakes of breath. These images lay on top of one another, forming a hideously confusing grid. How was he going to sort them out? He managed to separate the picture of his wife and the original picture of blindfolded Beth and hold them apart. He imagined himself travelling happily between the two. Perhaps, as time went on, he could bring Beth home and have his wife beat her too. She would do the dishes and serve them dinner. The grid closed up again and his stomach went into a moil. The thing was complicated and potentially exhausting. He looked at the anxious girl on the corner. She had said that she wanted to be hurt, but he suspected that she didn't understand what that meant.

He should probably just stay in the pizza place and watch her until she went away. It might be entertaining to see how long she waited. He felt a certain pity for her. He also felt, from his glassed-in vantage point, as though he were torturing an insect. He gloated as he ate his pizza.

At the height of her anxiety she saw him through the glass wall of the pizza stand. She immediately noticed his gloating countenance. She recognized the coldly scornful element in his watching and waiting as opposed to greeting her. She suffered, but only for an instant; she was then smitten by love. She smiled and crossed the street with a senseless confidence in the power of her smile.

"I was about to come over," he said. "I had to eat first. I was starving." He folded the last of his pizza in half and stuck it in his mouth.

She noticed a piece of bright orange pizza stuck between his teeth, and it endeared him to her.

They left the pizza stand. He walked with wide steps, and his heavy black overcoat swung rakishly, she thought, above his boots. He was a slight, slender boy with a pale, narrow face and blond hair that wisped across one brow. In the big coat he looked like the young pet of a budding secret police force. She thought he was beautiful.

He hailed a cab and directed the driver to the airport. He looked at her sitting beside him. "This is going to be a disaster," he said. "I'll probably wind up leaving you there and coming back alone."

"I hope not," she said. "I don't have any money. If you left me there, I wouldn't be able to get back by myself."

"That's too bad. Because I might." He watched her face for a reaction. It showed discomfort and excitement and something that he could only qualify as foolishness, as if she had just dropped a tray full of glasses in public. "Don't worry, I wouldn't do that," he said. "But I like the idea that I could."

"So do I." She was terribly distressed. She wanted to throw her arms around him.

He thought: There is something wrong. Her passivity was pleasing, as was her silence and her willingness to place herself in his hands. But he sensed another element present in her that he could not define and did not like. Her tightly folded hands were nervous and repulsive. Her public posture was brittle, not pliant. There was a rigidity that if cracked would yield nothing. He was disconcerted to realize that he didn't know if he could crack it anyway. He began to feel uncomfortable. Perhaps the weekend would be a disaster.

———————

The arrived at the airport an hour early. They went to a bar and drank. The bar was an open-ended cube with a red neon sign that said "Cocktails." There was no sense of shelter in it. The furniture was spindly and exposed, and there were no doors to protect you from the sight of dazed, unattractive passengers wandering through the airport with their luggage. She ordered a Bloody Mary.

"I can't believe you ordered that," he said.

"Why not?"

"Because I want a bloody Beth." He gave her a look that made her think of a neurotic dog with its tongue hanging out, waiting to bite someone.

"Oh," she said.

He offered her a cigarette.

"I don't smoke," she said. "I told you twice."

"Well, you should start."

They sat quietly and drank for several minutes.

"Do you like to look at people?" she asked.

She was struggling to talk to him. He saw that her face had become very tense. He could've increased her discomfort, but for the moment he had lost the energy to do so. "Yes," he said. "I do."

They spent some moments regarding the people around them. They were short on material. There were only a few customers in the bar; most of them were men in suits who sat there

seemingly enmeshed in a web of habit and accumulated rancour that they called their personalities, so utterly unaware of
their entanglement that they clearly considered themselves men
of the world, even though they had long ago stopped noticing
it. Then a couple walked through the door, carrying luggage.
The woman's bright skirt flashed with each step. The man
walked ahead of her. He walked too fast for her to keep up. She
looked harried. Her eyes were wide and dark and clotted with
makeup; there was a mole on her chin. He paused, as though
considering whether he would stop for a drink. He decided not
to and strode again. Her earrings jiggled as she followed. They
left a faint trail of sex and disappointment behind them.

Beth watched the woman's hips move under her skirt.
"There was something unpleasant about them," she said.

"Yes, there was."

It cheered her to find this point of contact. "I'm sorry I'm
not more talkative," she said.

"That's all right." His narrow eyes became feral once again.
"Women should be quiet." It suddenly struck her that it would
seem completely natural if he lunged forward and bit her face.

"I agree," she said sharply. "There aren't many men around
worth talking to."

He was nonplussed by her peevish tone. Perhaps, he
thought, he'd imagined it.

He hadn't.

———————

They had more drinks on the plane. They were served a hunk
of white-frosted raisin pastry in a red paper bag. He wasn't

hungry, but the vulgar cake appealed to him so he stuck it in his baggage.

They had a brief discussion about shoes, from the point of view of expense and aesthetics. They talked about intelligence and art. There were large gaps of silence that were disheartening to both of them. She began talking about old people, and how nice they could be. He had a picture of her kneeling on the floor in black stockings and handcuffs. This picture became blurred, static-ridden, and then obscured by their conversation. He felt a ghastly sense of longing. He called back the picture, which no longer gave him any pleasure. He superimposed it upon a picture of himself standing in a nightclub the week before, holding a drink and talking to a rather combative girl who wanted his number.

"Some old people are beautiful in an unearthly way," she continued. "I saw this old lady in the drugstore the other day who must've been in her nineties. She was so fragile and pretty, she was like a little elf."

He looked at her and said, "Are you going to start being fun to be around or are you going to be a big drag?"

She didn't answer right away. She didn't see how this followed her comment about the old lady. "I don't know."

"I don't think you're very sexual," he said. "You're not the way I thought you were when I first met you."

She was so hurt by this that she had difficulty answering. Finally, she said, "I can be very sexual or very unsexual depending on who I'm with and in what situation. It has to be the right kind of thing. I'm sort of a cerebral person. I think I respond to things in a cerebral way, mostly."

"That's what I mean."

She was struck dumb with frustration. She had obviously

disappointed him in some fundamental way, which she felt was completely due to misunderstanding. If only she could think of the correct thing to say, she was sure she could clear it up. The blue puffball thing unfurled itself before her with sickening power. It was the same image of him holding her and gazing into her eyes with bone-dislodging intent, thinly veiling the many shattering events that she anticipated between them. The prospect made her disoriented with pleasure. The only problem was, this image seemed to have no connection with what was happening now. She tried to think back to the time they had spent in her apartment, when he had held her and said, "You're cute." What had happened between then and now to so disappoint him?

She hadn't yet noticed how much he had disappointed her.

He couldn't tell if he was disappointing her or not. She completely mystified him, especially after her abrupt speech on cerebralism. It was now impossible to even have a clear picture of what he wanted to do to this unglamorous creature, who looked as though she bit her nails and read books at night. Dim, half-formed pictures of his wife, Sharon, Beth and a sixteen-year-old Chinese hooker he'd seen a month before crawled aimlessly over each other. He sat and brooded in a bad-natured and slightly drunken way.

She sat next to him, diminished and fretful, with idiot radio songs about sex in her head.

———

They were staying in his grandmother's deserted apartment in Washington, D.C. The complex was a series of building blocks seemingly arranged at random, stuck together and painted the least attractive colours available. It was surrounded by bright green grass and a circular driveway, and placed on a quiet highway that led into the city. There was a drive-in bank and an insurance office next to it. It was enveloped in the steady, continuous noise of cars driving by at roughly the same speed.

"This is a horrible building," she said as they travelled up in the elevator.

The door slid open and they walked down a hall carpeted with dense brown nylon. The grandmother's apartment opened before them. Beth found the refrigerator and opened it. There was a crumpled package of French bread, a jar of hot peppers, several lumps covered with aluminum foil, two bottles of wine and a six-pack. "Is your grandmother an alcoholic?" she asked.

"I don't know." He dropped his heavy leather bag and her white canvas one in the living room, took off his coat and threw it on the bags. She watched him standing there, pale and gaunt in a black leather shirt tied at his waist with a leather belt. That image of him would stay with her for years for no good reason and with no emotional significance. He dropped into a chair, his thin arms flopping lightly on its arms. He nodded at the tray of whiskey, Scotch and liqueurs on the coffee table before him. "Why don't you make yourself a drink?"

She dropped to her knees beside the table and nervously played with the bottles. He was watching her quietly, his expression hooded. She plucked a bottle of thick chocolate liqueur from the cluster, poured herself a glass and sat in the chair across from his with both hands around it. She could no longer ignore the character of the apartment. It was brutally

ridiculous, almost sadistic in its absurdity. The couch and
chairs were covered with a floral print. A thin maize carpet
zipped across the floor. There were throw rugs. There were artificial flowers. There was an abundance of small tables and
shelves housing a legion of figures; grinning glass maidens in
sumptuous gowns bore baskets of glass roses, ceramic birds
warbled from the ceramic stumps they clung to, glass horses
galloped across teakwood pastures. A ceramic weather poodle
and his diamond-eyed kitty-cat companions silently watched
the silent scene in the room.

"Are you all right?" he asked.

"I hate this apartment. It's really awful."

"What were you expecting? Jesus Christ. It's a lot like yours,
you know."

"Yes. That's true, I have to admit." She drank her liqueur.

"Do you think you could improve your attitude about this
whole thing? You might try being a little more positive."

Coming from him, this question was preposterous. He
must be so pathologically insecure that his perception of his
own behaviour was thoroughly distorted. He saw rejection
everywhere, she decided; she must reassure him. "But I do feel
positive about being here," she said. She paused, searching for
the best way to express the extremity of her positive feelings.
She invisibly implored him to see and mount their blue puffball bed. "It would be impossible for you to disappoint me.
The whole idea of you makes me happy. Anything you do will
be all right."

Her generosity unnerved him. He wondered if she realized
what she was saying. "Does anybody know you're here?" he
asked. "Did you tell anyone where you were going?"

"No." She had in fact told several people.

"That wasn't very smart."

"Why not?"

"You don't know me at all. Anything could happen to you."

She put her glass on the coffee table, crossed the floor and dropped to her knees between his legs. She threw her arms around his thighs. She nuzzled his groin with her nose. He tightened. She unzipped his pants. "Stop," he said. "Wait." She took his shoulders – she had a surprisingly strong grip – and pulled him to the carpet. His hovering brood of images and plans was suddenly upended, as though it had been sitting on a table that a rampaging crazy person had flipped over. He felt assaulted and invaded. This was not what he had in mind, but to refuse would make him seem somehow less virile than she. Queasily, he stripped off her clothes and put their bodies in a viable position. He fastened his teeth on her breast and bit her. She made a surprised noise and her body stiffened. He bit her again, harder. She screamed. He wanted to draw blood. Her screams were short and stifled. He could tell that she was trying to like being bitten, but that she did not. He gnawed her breast. She screamed sharply. They screwed. They broke apart and regarded each other warily. She put her hand on his tentatively. He realized what had been disturbing him about her. With other women he had been with in similar situations, he had experienced a relaxing sense of emptiness within them that had made it easy for him to get inside them and, once there, smear himself all over their innermost territory until it was no longer theirs but his. His wife did not have this empty quality, yet the gracious way in which she emptied herself for him made her submission, as far as it went, all the more poignant.

This exasperating girl, on the other hand, contained a tangible somethingness that she not only refused to expunge, but that seemed to wilfully expand itself so that he banged into it with every attempt to invade her. He didn't mind the somethingness; he rather liked it, in fact, and had looked forward to seeing it demolished. But she refused to let him do it. Why had she told him she was a masochist? He looked at her body. Her limbs were muscular and alert. He considered taking her by the neck and bashing her head against the floor.

He stood abruptly. "I want to get something to eat. I'm starving."

She put her hand on his ankle. Her desire to abase herself had been completely frustrated. She had pulled him to the rug certain that if only they could fuck, he would enter her with overwhelming force and take complete control of her. Instead she had barely felt him, and what she had felt was remote and cold. Somewhere on her exterior he'd been doing some biting thing that meant nothing to her and was quite unpleasant. Despairing, she held his ankle tighter and put her forehead on the carpet. At least she could stay at his feet, worshipping. He twisted free and walked away. "Come on," he said.

The car was in the parking lot. It was because of the car that this weekend had come about. It was his wife's car, an expensive thing that her ex-husband had given her. It had been in Washington for over a year; he was here to retrieve it and drive it back to New York.

Beth was appalled by the car. It was a loud yellow monster

with a narrow, vicious shape and absurd doors that snapped up from the roof and out like wings. In another setting it might have seemed glamorous, but here, behind this equally monstrous building, in her unsatisfactory clothing, the idea of sitting in it with him struck her as comparable to putting on a clown nose and wearing it to dinner.

They drove down a suburban highway lined with small businesses, malls and restaurants. It was twilight; several neon signs blinked consolingly.

"Do you think you could make some effort to change your mood?"

"I'm not in a bad mood," she said wearily. "I just feel blank."

Not blank enough, he thought.

He pulled into a Roy Rogers fast food cafeteria. She thought: He is not even going to take me to a nice place. She was insulted. It seemed as though he was insulting her on purpose. The idea was incredible to her.

She walked through the line with him, but did not take any of the shiny dishes of food displayed on the fluorescent-lit aluminum shelves. He felt a pang of worry. He was no longer angry, and her drawn white face disturbed him.

"Why aren't you eating?"

"I'm not hungry."

They sat down. He picked at his food, eyeing her with veiled alarm. It occurred to her that it might embarrass him to eat in front of her while she ate nothing. She asked if she could have some of his salad. He eagerly passed her the entire bowl of pale leaves strewn with orange dressing. "Have it all."

He huddled his shoulders orphanlike as he ate; his blond

hair stood tangled like pensive weeds. "I don't know why you're not eating," he said fretfully. "You're going to be hungry later on."

Her predisposition to adore him was provoked. She smiled.

"Why are you staring at me like that?" he asked.

"I'm just enjoying the way you look. You're very airy."

Again, his eyes showed alarm.

"Sometimes when I look at you, I feel like I'm seeing a tank of small, quick fish, the bright darting kind that go every which way."

He paused, stunned and dangle-forked over his pinched, curled-up steak. "I'm beginning to think you're out of your fucking mind."

Her happy expression collapsed.

"Why can't you talk to me in a half-normal fucking way?" he continued. "Like the way we talked on the plane. I liked that. That was a conversation." In fact, he hadn't liked the conversation on the plane either, but compared to this one, it seemed quite all right.

———

When they got back to the apartment, they sat on the floor and drank more alcohol. "I want you to drink a lot," he said. "I want to make you do things you don't want to do."

"But I won't do anything I don't want to do. You have to make me want it."

He lay on his back in silent frustration.

"What are your parents like?" she asked.

"What?"

"Your parents. What are they like?"

"I don't know. I don't have that much to do with them. My mother is nice. My father's a prick. That's what they're like." He put his hand over his face; a square-shaped album-style view of his family presented itself. They were all at the breakfast table, talking and reaching for things. His mother moved in the background, a slim, worried shadow in her pink robe. His sister sat next to him, tall, blond and arrogant, talking and flicking at toast crumbs in the corners of her mouth. His father sat at the head of the table, his big arms spread over everything, leaning over his plate as if he had to defend it, gnawing his breakfast. He felt unhappy and then angry. He thought of a little Italian girl he had met in a go-go bar a while back, and comforted himself with the memory of her slim haunches and pretty high-heeled feet on either side of his head as she squatted over him.

"It seems that way with my parents when you first look at them. But in fact my mother is much more aggressive and, I would say, more cruel than my father, even though she's more passive and soft on the surface."

She began a lengthy and, in his view, incredible and unnecessary history of her family life, including descriptions of her brother and sister. Her entire family seemed to have a collectively disturbed personality characterized by long brooding silences, unpleasing compulsive sloppiness (unflushed toilets, used Kleenex abandoned everywhere, dirty underwear on the floor) and outbursts of irrational, violent anger. It was horrible. He wanted to go home.

He poked himself up on his elbows. "Are you a liar?" he asked. "Do you lie often?"

She stopped in midsentence and looked at him. She seemed to consider the question earnestly. "No," she said. "Not really. I mean, I can lie, but I usually don't about important things. Why do you ask?"

"Why did you tell me you were a masochist?"

"What makes you think I'm not?"

"You don't act like one."

"Well, I don't know how you can say that. You hardly know me. We've hardly done anything yet."

"What do you want to do?"

"I can't just come out and tell you. It would ruin it."

He picked up his cigarette lighter and flicked it, picked up her shirt and stuck the lighter underneath. She didn't move fast enough. She screamed and leapt to her feet.

"Don't do that! That's awful!"

He rolled over on his stomach. "See. I told you. You're not a masochist."

"Shit! That wasn't erotic in the least. I don't come when I stub my toe either."

In the ensuing silence it occurred to her that she was angry, and had been for some time.

"I'm tired," she said. "I want to go to bed." She walked out of the room.

He sat up. "Well, we're making decisions, aren't we?"

She re-entered the room. "Where are we supposed to sleep, anyway?"

He showed her the guest room and the fold-out couch. She immediately began dismantling the couch with stiff, angry movements. Her body seemed full of unnatural energy and purpose. She had, he decided, ruined the weekend, not only for him but for herself. Her wilful, masculine, stupid some-thingness had obstructed their mutual pleasure and satisfaction. The only course of action left was hostility. He opened his grandmother's writing desk and took out a piece of paper and a Magic Marker. He wrote the word "stupid" in thick black letters. He held it first near her chest, like a placard, and then above her crotch. She ignored him.

"Where are the sheets?" she asked.

"How'd you get so tough all of a sudden?" He threw the paper on the desk and took a sheet from a dresser drawer.

"We'll need a blanket too, if we open the window. And I want to open the window."

He regarded her sarcastically. "You're just keeping yourself from getting what you want by acting like this."

"You obviously don't know what I want."

They got undressed. He contemptuously took in the muscular, energetic look of her body. She looked more like a boy than a girl, in spite of her pronounced hips and round breasts. Her short, spiky red hair was more than enough to render her masculine. Even the dark bruise he had inflicted on her breast and the slight burn from his lighter failed to lend her a more feminine quality.

She opened the window. They got under the blanket on the fold-out couch and lay there, not touching, as though they really were about to sleep. Of course, neither one of them could.

"Why is this happening?" she asked.

"You tell me."

"I don't know. I really don't know." Her voice was small and pathetic.

"Part of it is that you don't talk when you should, and then you talk too much when you shouldn't be saying anything at all."

In confusion, she reviewed the various moments they had spent together, trying to classify them in terms of whether or not it had been appropriate to speak, and to rate her performance accordingly. Her confusion increased. Tears floated on her eyes. She curled her body against his.

"You're hurting my feelings," she said, "but I don't think you're doing it on purpose."

He was briefly touched. "Accidental pain," he said musingly. He took her head in both hands and pushed it between his legs. She opened her mouth compliantly. He had hurt her after all, he reflected. She was confused and exhausted, and at this instant, anyway, she was doing what he wanted her to do. Still, it wasn't enough. He released her and she moved upward to lie on top of him, resting her head on his shoulder. She spoke dreamily. "I would do anything with you."

"You would not. You would be disgusted."

"Disgusted by what?"

"You would be disgusted if I even told you."

She rolled away from him. "It's probably nothing."

"Have you ever been pissed on?"

He gloated as he felt her body tighten.

"No."

"Well, that's what I want to do to you."

"On your grandmother's rug?"

"I want you to drink it. If any got on the rug, you'd clean it up."

"Oh."

"I knew you'd be shocked."

"I'm not. I just never wanted to do it."

"So? That isn't any good to me."

In fact, she was shocked. Then she was humiliated, and not in the way she had planned. Her seductive puffball cloud deflated with a flaccid hiss, leaving two drunken, bad-tempered, incompetent, malodorous people blinking and uncomfortable on its remains. She stared at the ugly roses with their heads collapsed in a dead wilt and slowly saw what a jerk she'd been. Then she got mad.

"Do you like people to piss on you?" she asked.

"Yeah. Last month I met this great girl at Billy's Topless. She pissed in my face for only twenty bucks."

His voice was high-pitched and stupidly aggressive, like some weird kid who would walk up to you on the street and offer to take care of your sexual needs. How, she thought miserably, could she have mistaken this hostile moron for the dark, brooding hero who would crush her like an insect and then talk about life and art?

"There's a lot of other things I'd like to do too," he said with odd self-righteousness. "But I don't think you could handle it."

"It's not a question of handling it." She said these last two words very sarcastically. "So far everything you've said to me has been incredibly banal. You haven't presented anything in a way that's even remotely attractive." She sounded like a prim, prematurely adult child complaining to her teacher about someone putting a worm down her back.

He felt like an idiot. How had he gotten stuck with this prissy, reed-voiced thing with a huge forehead who poked and picked over everything that came out of his mouth? He longed for a dim-eyed little slut with a big, bright mouth and black vinyl underwear. What had he had in mind when he brought this girl here, anyway? Her serious, desperate face, panicked and tear-stained. Her ridiculous air of sacrifice and abandonment as he spread-eagled and bound her. White skin that marked easily. Frightened eyes. An exposed personality that could be yanked from her and held out of reach like...oh, he could see it only in scraps; his imagination fumbled and lost its grip. He looked at her hatefully self-possessed, compact little form. He pushed her roughly. "Oh, I'd do anything with you," he mimicked. "You would not."

She rolled away on her side, her body curled tightly. He felt her trembling. She sniffed.

"Don't tell me I've broken your heart."

She continued crying.

"This isn't bothering me at all," he said. "In fact, I'm rather enjoying it."

The trembling stopped. She sniffed once, turned on her back and looked at him with puzzled eyes. She blinked. He suddenly felt tired. I shouldn't be doing this, he thought. She is actually a nice person. For a moment he had an impulse to embrace her. He had a stronger impulse to beat her. He looked around the room until he saw a light wood stick that his grandmother had for some reason left standing in the corner. He pointed at it.

"Get me that stick. I want to beat you with it."

"I don't want to."

"Get it. I want to humiliate you even more."

She shook her head, her eyes wide with alarm. She held the blanket up to her chin.

"Come on," he coaxed. "Let me beat you. I'd be much nicer after I beat you."

"I don't think you're capable of being as nice as you'd have to be to interest me at this point."

"All right. I'll get it myself." He got the stick and snatched the blanket from her body.

She sat, her legs curled in a kneeling position. "Don't," she said. "I'm scared."

"You should be scared," he said. "I'm going to torture you." He brandished the stick, which actually felt as though it would break on the second or third blow. They froze in their positions, staring at each other.

She was the first to drop her eyes. She regarded the torn-off blanket meditatively. "You have really disappointed me," she said. "This whole thing has been a complete waste of time."

He sat on the bed, stick in lap. "You don't care about my feelings."

"I think I want to sleep in the next room."

They couldn't sleep separately any better than they could sleep together. She lay curled up on the couch pondering what seemed to be the ugly nature of her life. He lay wound in a blanket, blinking in the dark, as a dislocated, manic and unpleasing review of his sexual experiences stumbled through his memory in a queasy scramble.

In the morning they agreed that they would return to Manhattan immediately. Despite their mutual ill humour, they fornicated again, mostly because they could more easily ignore each other while doing so.

They packed quickly and silently.

"It's going to be a long drive back," he said. "Try not to make me feel like too much of a prick, okay?"

"I don't care what you feel like."

———————

He would have liked to dump her at the side of the road somewhere, but he wasn't indifferent enough to societal rules to do that. Besides, he felt vaguely sorry that he had made her cry, and while this made him view her grudgingly, he felt obliged not to worsen the situation. Ideally she would disappear, taking her stupid canvas bag with her. In reality, she sat beside him in the car with more solidity and presence than she had displayed since they met on the corner in Manhattan. She seemed fully prepared to sit in silence for the entire six-hour drive. He turned on the radio.

"Would you mind turning that down a little?"

"Anything for you."

She rolled her eyes.

Without much hope, he employed a tactic he used to pacify his wife when they argued. He would give her a choice and let her make it. "Would you like something to eat?" he asked. "You must be starving."

She was. They spent almost an hour driving up and down the available streets trying to find a restaurant she wanted to be in. She finally chose a small, clean egg-and-toast place. Her humour visibly improved as they sat before their breakfast. "I like eggs," she said. "They are so comforting."

He began to talk to her out of sheer curiosity. They talked about music, college, people they knew in common and drugs they used to take as teenagers. She said that when she had taken LSD, she had often lost her sense of identity so completely that she didn't recognize herself in the mirror. This pathetic statement brought back her attractiveness in a terrific rush. She noted the quick dark gleam in his eyes.

"You should've let me beat you," he said. "I wouldn't have hurt you too much."

"That's not the point. The moment was wrong. It wouldn't have meant anything."

"It would've meant something to me." He paused. "But you probably would've spoiled it. You would've started screaming right away and made me stop."

The construction workers at the next table stared at them quizzically. She smiled pleasantly at them and returned her gaze to him. "You don't know that."

He was so relieved at the ease between them that he put his arm around her as they left the restaurant. She stretched up and kissed his neck.

"We just had the wrong idea about each other," she said. "It's nobody's fault that we're incompatible."

"Well, soon we'll be in Manhattan, and it'll be all over. You'll never have to see me again." He hoped she would dispute this, but she didn't.

They continued to talk in the car, about the nature of time, their parents and the injustice of racism.

She was too exhausted to extract much from the pedestrian conversation, but the sound of his voice, the position of his body and his sudden receptivity were intoxicating. Time took on a grainy, dreamy aspect that made impossible conversations and unlikely gestures feasible, like a space capsule that enables its inhabitants to happily walk up the wall. The peculiar little car became a warm, humming cocoon, like a miniature house she had, as a little girl, assembled out of odds and ends for invented characters. She felt as if she were a very young child, when every notion that appeared in her head was new and naked of association and thus needed to be expressed carefully so it didn't become malformed. She wanted to set every one of them before him in a row, as she had once presented crayon drawings to her father in a neat many-coloured sequence. Then he would shift his posture slightly or make a gesture that suddenly made him seem so helpless and frail that she longed to protect him and cosset him away, like a delicate pet in a matchbox filled with cotton. She rested her head on his shoulder and lovingly regarded the legs that bent at the knee and tapered to the booted feet resting on the brakes or the accelerator. This was as good as her original fantasy, possibly even better.

"Can I abuse you some more now?" he asked sweetly. "In the car?"

"What do you want to do?"

"Gag you? That's all, I'd just like to gag you."

"But I want to talk to you."

He sighed. "You're really not a masochist, you know."

She shrugged. "Maybe not. It always seemed like I was."

"You might have fantasies, but I don't think you have any concept of a real slave mentality. You have too much ego to be part of another person."

"I don't know, I've never had the chance to try it. I've never met anyone I wanted to do that with."

"If you were a slave, you wouldn't make the choice."

"All right, I'm not a slave. With me it's more a matter of love." She was just barely aware that she was pitching her voice higher and softer than it was naturally, so that she sounded like a cartoon girl. "It's like the highest form of love."

He thought this was really cute. Sure it was nauseating, but it was feminine in a radio-song kind of way.

"You don't seem interested in love. It's not about that for you."

"That's not true. That's not true at all. Why do you think I was so rough back there? Deep down, I'm afraid I'll fall in love with you, that I'll need to be with you and fuck you ... forever." He was enjoying himself now. He was beginning to see her as a locked garden that he could sneak into and sit in for days, tearing the heads off the flowers.

On one hand, she was beside herself with bliss. On the other, she was scrutinizing him carefully from behind an opaque facade as he entered her pasteboard scene of flora and fauna. Could he function as a character in this landscape? She imagined sitting across from him in a Japanese restaurant, talking about anything. He would look intently into her eyes....

He saw her apartment and then his. He saw them existing a nice distance apart, each of them blocked off by cleanly cut boundaries. Her apartment bloomed with scenes that spiralled toward him in colourful circular motions and then froze suddenly and clearly in place. She was crawling blindfolded across the floor. She was bound and naked in an S&M bar. She was sitting next to him in a taxi, her skirt pulled up, his fingers in her vagina.

... and then they would go back to her apartment. He would beat her and fuck her mouth.

Then he would go home to his wife, and she would make dinner for him. It was so well balanced, the mere contemplation of it gave him pleasure.

The next day he would send her flowers.

He let go of the wheel with one hand and patted her head. She gripped his shirt frantically.

He thought: This could work out fine.

HELEN GARNER

CIVILIZATION AND
ITS DISCONTENTS

*The Argentinian writer Eduardo Quiroga imagined the
following story: Don Quixote, fully aware that every knight
must have a lady, fixes his love on a peasant woman,
Aldonza Lorenzo, and renames her Dulcinea del Toboso.
After many misfortunes and countless battles, Don Quixote
is carried wounded to his bed and asks that Dulcinea be
brought to his side, that he may look upon her once before
dying. She appears and he sees her, for the first time, as she
really is: dishevelled, grubby, red-faced, wringing her large
brutish hands and wiping her nose on her sleeve.
"Dulcinea," says the dying knight, "evil wizards and nefar-
ious sorcerers have clouded my mind and make me see you
now, in my final hour, as a hideous hag. No matter. Ages
from this day, readers will look back on our lives and then it
will be true that I was a gallant knight and you a graceful
lady, and that we — not those two tawdry creatures we now*

are, but those we know ourselves to be – loved each other."

In a brilliant short essay on eroticism, the Polish critic Jan Kott remarked that when we make love, it is in fact four people who go to bed together: the pair of lovers and the pair of lovers those lovers have invented, "two bodies and two partners of imagination and desire, created mutually by each other." We are ourselves, but we are also that extraordinary monster made up of bits of someone else's longing, memories, dreams, fears, needs, experiences and hopes. We are the ill-trained, badly rehearsed actor in a play which our lover writes, directs, attends and reviews. Not all of us – witness the protagonists of Helen Garner's story, for instance – survive these gruelling performances.

P HILIP CAME. I went to his hotel: I couldn't get there fast enough. He stepped up to me when I came through the door, and took hold of me.

"Hullo," he said, "my dear."

People here don't talk like that. My hair was still damp.

"Did you drive?" he said.

"No. I came on the bus."

"The *bus?*"

"There's never anywhere to park in the city."

"You've had your hair cut. You look like a boy."

"I know. I do it on purpose. I dress like a boy and I have my hair cut like a boy. I want to *be* a boy. So I can have a homosexual affair with *you*."

He laughed. "Good girl!" he said. At these words I was so flooded with well-being that I could hardly get my breath. "If you were a boy some of the time and a girl the rest," he said, "I'd be luckier. Because I could have both."

"No," I said. "I'd be luckier. Because I could *be* both."

I scrambled out of my clothes.

"You're so thin," he said.

"I don't eat. I'm sick."

"Sick? Are you?" He put his two hands on my shoulders and looked into my eyes like a doctor.

"Sick with love."

"Your eyes are healthy. Lustrous. Are mine?"

His room was on the top floor. Opposite, past some roofs and a deep street, was the old-fashioned tower of the building in which a dentist I used to go to had his rooms. That dentist was so gentle with the drill that I never needed an injection. I used to breathe slowly, as I had been taught at yoga: the pain was brief. I didn't flinch. But he made his pile and moved to Queensland.

The building had a flagpole. Philip and I stood at the window with no clothes on and looked out. The tinted glass made the cloud masses more detailed, richer, more spectacular than they were.

"Look at those," I said. "Real boilers. Coming in from somewhere."

"Just passing through," said Philip. He was looking at the building with the tower. "I love the Australian flag," he said. "Every time I see it I get a shiver."

"I'm like that about the map." Once I worked in a convent school in East London. I used to go to the library at lunchtime, when the nuns were locked away in their dining room being read to, and take down the atlas and gaze at the page with Australia on it: I loved its upper points, its vast inlets, its fat sides, the might of it, the mass from whose south-eastern corner my small life had sprung. I used to crouch between the stacks and rest the heavy book on the edge of the shelf: I could hardly support its weight. I looked at the map and my eyes filled with tears.

"Did I tell you she's talking about coming back to me?" said Philip.

"Do you want her to?"

"Of course I do."

"We'll have to start behaving like adults," he said. "Any idea how it's done?"

"Well," I said, "it must be a matter of transformation. We have to turn what's happening now into something else."

"You sound experienced."

"I am."

"What can we turn it into?"

"Brother and sister? A lifelong friendship."

"Oh," he said. "I don't know anything about that. Can't people just go on having a secret affair?"

"I don't like lying."

"You don't have to. I'm the liar."

"What makes you so sure she won't find out? People always know. She'll take one look at you and know. That's what wives are for."

"We'll see."

"How can you stand it?" I said. "It's dishonourable. How can you lie to someone and still love her?"

"Forced to. Forced by love to be a hypocrite."

I thought for a second he was joking.

"We could drop it now," I said.

"What are you *saying?*"

"I don't mean it."

Not yet. The sheets in those hotels are silky, but crisp. How do they get them like that? A lot of starch, and ironing, things no housewife in her right mind could be bothered doing. The bed was wide enough for another two people to have lain in it, and still none of us would have had to touch sides. I don't usually go to bed in the daylight. And as if the daylight were not enough, the room was full of lamps. I started to switch them off, one after another, and thinking of the phrase "full of lamps" I remembered something my husband said to me, long after we split up, about a Shakespearean medley he had seen performed by doddering remnants of a famous British company that was touring Australia. "The stage," he said, "was covered in *thrones*," and his knees bent with laughter. He was the only man I have ever known who would rejoice with you over the petty triumphs of the day. I got under the sheet. I couldn't help laughing to myself, but it was too complicated to explain why.

Philip had a way of holding me, when we lay down: he made small rocking movements, so small that I sometimes wondered if I were imagining them, if the comfort of being held were translating itself into an imaginary cradling.

"I never told anyone I love them, before," said Philip.

"Don't be silly," I said.

"You don't know anything about me."

"At your age?" I said. "A married man? You've never loved anyone before?"

"I've never *said* it before."

"No wonder she went away," I said. "Men are really done over, aren't they. At an early age."

"Why do you want to fuck like a boy, then?"

"Just for play."

"Is it allowed?" he said.

"Who by?" I said. I was trying to be smart; but seriously, who says we can't? Isn't that why women and men make love? To bend the bars a little, just for a little; to let the bars dissolve? Philip pinched me. He took hold of the points of my breasts, between forefingers and thumbs. I could see his teeth. He pinched hard. It hurt. I liked it. And he bit me. He *bit* me. When I got home I looked in the mirror and my shoulders and arms were covered in small round bruises.

———

I went to his house, in the town where he lived. I told him I would be passing through on my way south, and he invited me, and I went, though I had plenty of friends I could have stayed with in that city.

There was a scandal in the papers as I passed through the airport that evening, about a woman who had made a contract to have a baby for a childless couple. The baby was born, she changed her mind, she would not give it up. Everyone was talking about her story.

I felt terrible at his house, for all I loved him, with his wife's forgotten dressing gown hanging behind the door like a witness. I couldn't fall asleep properly. I "lay broad waking" all night long, and the house was pierced by noises, as if its walls were too flimsy to protect it from the street: a woman's shoes striking the pavement, a gate clicking, a key sliding into a lock, stairs breathing in and out. It never gets truly dark in cities. Once I rolled over and looked at him. His face was sleeping, serene, smiling on the pillow next to mine like a cherub on a cloud.

He woke with a bright face. "I feel unblemished," he said, "when I've been with you." This is why I love him, of course: because he talked like that, using words and phrases that most people wouldn't think of saying. "When I'm with you," he'd say, "I feel happy and free."

He made the breakfast and we read the papers in the garden.

"She should've stuck to her word," he said.

"Poor thing," I said. "How can anyone give a baby away?"

"But she promised. What about the couple? They must be dying to have a kid."

"Are you?"

"Yes," he said, and looked at me with the defiant expression of someone expecting to be crossed. "Yes, I am."

The coffee was very strong. It was bad for me in the mornings. It made my heart beat too fast.

"I think in an ideal world everyone would have children," I said. "That's how people learn to love. Kids suck love out of your bones."

"I suppose you think that only mothers know how to love."

"No. I don't think that."

"Still," he said. "she signed a contract. She *signed*. She made a promise."

"Philip," I said, "have you ever smelled a baby's head?"

The phone started to ring inside the house, in the room I didn't go into because of the big painting of her that was hanging over the stereo. Thinking that he loved me, though I understood and believed I had accepted the futurelessness of it, I amused myself by secretly calling it The Room in Which the First Wife Raved, or Bluebeard's Bloody Chamber: it repelled me with an invisible force, though I stood at times outside its open door and saw its pleasantness, its calm, its white walls and wooden floor on which lay a bent pattern of sunlight like a child's drawing of a window.

He ran inside to answer the phone. He was away for quite a while. I thought about practising: how it is possible to learn with one person how to love, and then to apply the lesson learnt to somebody else: someone teaches you to sing, and then you wait for a part in the right opera. It was warm in the garden. I dozed in my chair. I had a small dream, one of those shockingly vivid dreams that occur when one sleeps at an unaccustomed time of day, or when one ought to be doing something other than sleeping. I dreamed that I was squatting naked with my vagina close to the ground, in the posture we are told primitive women adopt for childbearing ("They just squat down in the fields, drop the baby, and go on working"). But someone was operating on me, using sharp medical instruments on my cunt. Bloody flesh was issuing from it in clumps and clots. I could watch it, and see it, as if it were somebody else's cunt, while at the same time experiencing it being done to me. It was not painful. It didn't hurt at all.

I woke up as he came down the steps smiling. He crouched down in front of me, between my knees, and spoke right into my face.

"You want me to behave like a married man, and have kids, don't you?"

"*Want* you to?"

"I mean you think I should. You think everyone should, you said."

"Sure – if that's what you want. Why?"

"Well, on the phone just now I went a bit further towards it."

"You mean you *lined* it *up*?"

"Not exactly – but that's the direction I'm going in."

I looked down at him. His forearms were resting across my knees and he was crouching lightly on the balls of his feet. He was smiling at me, smiling right into my eyes. He was waiting for me to say, *Good boy!*

"Say something reassuring," he said. "Say something close, before I go."

I took a breath, but already he was not listening. He was ready to work. Philip loved his work. He took on more than he could comfortably handle. Every morning he came home with his pockets sprouting contracts. He never wasted anything: I'd hear him whistling in the car, a tiny phrase, a little run of notes climbing and falling as we drove across the bridges, and then next morning from the room with the synthesizer in it would issue the same phrase but bigger, fuller, linked with other ideas, becoming a song: and a couple of months after that I'd hear it through the open doors of every cafe, record shop and idling car in town. "Know what I used to dream?" he said to me once.

"I used to dream that when I pulled up at the lights I'd look into the cars on either side of me and in front and behind, and everyone would be singing along with the radio, and they'd all be singing the same song. Even if the windows were wound up we'd read each other's lips, and everyone would laugh, and wave."

I made my own long distance call. "I'll be home tonight, Matty," I said.

His voice was full of sleep. "They rang up from the shop," he said. "I told them you were sick. Have you seen that man yet?"

"Yes. I'm on my way. Get rid of the pizza boxes."

"I need money, Mum."

"When I get there."

Philip took me to the airport. I was afraid someone would see us, someone he knew. For me it didn't matter. Nothing was secret, I had no-one to hide anything from, and I would have been proud to be seen with him. But for him I was worried. I worried enough for both of us. I kept my head down. He laughed. He would not let me go. He tried to make me lift my chin; he gave it soft butts with his forehead. My cheeks were red.

"I'm always getting on planes with tears in my eyes," I said.

"They'll be getting to know you," he said. "Are you too shy to kiss me properly?"

I bolted past the check-in desk. I looked back and he was watching me, still laughing, standing by himself on the shining floor.

On the plane I was careful with myself. I concentrated on the ingenuity of the food tray, its ability to remain undisturbed by the alterations in position of the seatback to which it was attached. I called for a Scotch and drank it. My mistake was to look inside a book of poems, the only reading matter I had on me. They were poems so charged with sex and death and longing that it was indecent to read them in public: I was afraid that their power might leak out and scandalize the onlookers. Even as I slammed the book shut I saw "*I want to know, once more,/how it feels/to be peeled and eaten whole, time after time.*" I kept the book turned away from two men who were sitting between me and the window. They were drinking German beer and talking in a European language of which I did not recognize a single word. One of them turned his head and caught my eye. I expected him to look away hastily, for I felt myself to be ugly and stiff with sadness; but his face opened into a dazzling smile.

My son was waiting for the plane. He had come out on the airport bus. He saw how pleased I was, and looked down with an embarrassed smile, but he permitted me to hug him, and patted my shoulder with little rapid pats.

"Your face is different," he said. "All sort of emotional."

"Why do you always pat me when you hug me?" I said.

"Pro'ly 'cause you're nearly always in a state," he said.

He asked me to wait while he had a quick go on the machines. His fingers swarmed on the buttons. *Death By Acne* was the title of a thriller he had invented to make me laugh: but his face in concentration lost its awkwardness and became beautiful. I leaned on the wall of the terminal and watched the people passing.

A tall young man came by. He was carrying a tiny baby in a sling against his chest. The mother walked behind, smooth-faced and long-haired, holding by the hand a fat-nappied toddler. But the man was the one in love with the baby. He walked slowly, with his arms curved round its small bulk. His head was bowed so he could gaze into its face. His whole being was adoring it.

I watched the young family go by in its peaceful procession, each one moving quietly and contentedly in place, and I heard the high-pitched death wails of the space creatures my son was murdering with his fast and delicate tapping of buttons, and suddenly I remembered walking across the street the day after I brought him home from hospital. The birth was long and I lost my rhythm and made too much noise and they drugged me, and when it was over I felt that now I knew what the prayer-book meant when it said *the pains of death gat hold upon me*. But crossing the road that day, still sore from knives and needles, I saw a pregnant woman lumbering towards me, a woman in the final stages of waiting, putting one heavy foot in front of the other. Her face as she passed me was as calm and as full as an animal's: "a face that had not yet received the fist." And I envied her. I was stabbed, pierced with envy, with longing for what was about to happen to her, for what she was ignorantly about to enter. I could have cried out, Oh, let me do it again! Give me another chance! Let me meet the mighty forces again and struggle with them! Let me be rocked again, let me lie helpless in that huge cradle of pain!

"Another twenty cents down the drain," said my son. We set out together towards the automatic doors. He was carrying my bag. I wanted to say to him, to someone, "Listen. Listen. I am *hopelessly in love*." But I hung on. I knew I had brought it on myself, and I hung on until the spasm passed. And then I began to recreate from memory the contents of the fridge.

ALLAN GURGANUS

ADULT ART

"All my stories," says Allan Gurganus, "are about a kind of struggle against a puritan ethic." Largely, this puritan ethic is concerned with compartments, with deciding what is "family viewing" and what should be "rated X," what is art and what is pornography, what can be pulled off the shelves by anyone, and what must be hidden away in brown paper bags. Certain words, certain images – the puritans tell us – fit strictly into one category or another.

Not even the most clinical depictions of the human body are beyond this fanatical labelling. Dozens of precious medieval medical treatises were thrown into the fire by a volunteer librarian early this century at the municipal library of Sémur-en-Auxois because they showed gynecological images which the rigorous librarian found arousing. And in recent years, the fact that a Vanity Fair *cover featuring a nude Demi Moore caused a huge controversy because she was also pregnant – thereby embodying both*

family values and X-rated iconography – suggests that the
puritan ethic has lost little of its zeal.

Since something innocent, a pregnant woman, for
instance, can be branded pornographic, then pornography
– "adult art" – can stand for something innocent, can
become, as in Gurganus's ironic story, an allegory for the
pain of amorous desire. "There are as many kinds of pain as
fiction," Gurganus writes, "and because I find being in
trouble comic, my ambition has been to write the funniest
things possible about the worst things that can happen to
you as a human being."

I'VE GOT AN EXTRA TENDERNESS. It's not legal.

I see a twelve-year-old boy steal a white Mercedes off the
street. I'm sitting at my official desk – Superintendent of
Schools – it's noon on a weekday and I watch this kid wiggle a
coat hanger through one front window. Then he slips into the
sedan, straight-wires its ignition, squalls off. Afterward, I can't
help wondering why I didn't phone the police. Or shout for
our truant officer just down the hall.

Next, a fifty-nine Dodge, black, mint condition, tries to
parallel park in the Mercedes' spot (I'm not getting too much
paperwork done today). The driver is one of the worst drivers
I've ever seen under the age of eighty. Three pedestrians take

turns waving him in, guiding him back out. I step to my window and hear one person yell, "No, left, sharp *left*. Clown." Disgusted, a last helper leaves.

When the driver stands and stretches, he hasn't really parked his car, just stopped it. I've noticed him around town. About twenty-five, he's handsome, but in the most awkward possible way. His clothes match the old Dodge. His belt's pulled up too high. White socks are a mistake. I watch him comb his hair, getting presentable for downtown. He whips out a handkerchief and stoops to buff his shoes. Many coins and pens spill from a shirt pocket.

While he gathers these, a second boy (maybe a brother of the Mercedes thief?) rushes to the Dodge's front, starts gouging something serious across its hood. I knock on my second-story window – nobody hears. The owner rises from shoe-polishing, sees what's happening, shouts. The vandal bolts. But instead of chasing him, the driver touches bad scratches, he stands – patting them. I notice that the guy is talking to himself. He wets one index fingertip, tries rubbing away scrawled letters. Sunlight catches spit. From my second-floor view, I can read the word. It's an obscenity.

I turn away, lean back against a half-hot radiator. I admire the portrait of my wife, my twin sons in Little League uniforms. On a far wall, the art reproductions I change every month or so. (I was an art history major, believe it or not.) I want to rush downstairs, comfort the owner of the car, say, maybe, "Darn kids, nowadays." I don't dare.

They could arrest me for everything I like about myself.

At five sharp, gathering up valise and papers, I look like a regular citizen. Time to leave the office. Who should pass? The owner of the hurt Dodge. His being in the Municipal Building shocked me, as if I'd watched him on TV earlier. In my doorway, I hesitated. He didn't notice me. He tripped over a new two-inch ledge in the middle of the hall. Recovering, he looked around, hoping nobody had seen. Then, content he was alone, clutching a loaded shirt pocket, the guy bent, touched the spot where the ledge had been. There was no ledge. Under long fingers, just smoothness, linoleum. He rose. I stood close enough to see, in his pocket, a plastic caddy you keep pens in. It was white, a gift from WOOTEN'S SMALL ENGINES, NEW AND LIKE-NEW. Four old fountain pens were lined there, name-brand articles. Puzzled at why he'd stumbled, the boy now scratched the back of his head, made a face. "Gee, *that's* funny!" An antiquated cartoon drawing would have shown a decent cheerful hick doing and saying exactly that. I was charmed.

——————

I've got this added tenderness. I never talk about it. It only sneaks up on me every two or three years. It sounds strange but feels so natural. I know it'll get me into big trouble. I feel it for a certain kind of other man, see. For any guy who's even clumsier than me, than "I."

You have a different kind of tenderness for everybody you know. There's one sort for grandparents, say. But if you waltz into a singles' bar and use that type of affection, you'll be considered pretty strange. When my sons hit pop flies, I get a strong wash of feeling – and yet, if I turned the same sweetness on my Board of Education, I'd soon find myself both fired and committed.

Then he saw me.

He smiled in a shy cramped way. Caught, he pointed to the spot that'd given him recent trouble, he said of himself, "Tripped." You know what I said? When I noticed – right then, this late – how kind-looking he was, I said, "Happens all the time. Me too." I pointed to my chest, another dated funnypaper gesture. "No reason." I shrugged. "You just *do*, you know. Most people, I guess."

Well, he liked that. He smiled. It gave me time to check out his starched shirt (white, buttoned to the collar, no tie). I studied his old-timey overly wide belt, its thunderbird-design brass buckle. He wore black pants, plain as a waiter's, brown wingtips with a serious shine. He took in my business suit, my early signs of greying temples. Then he decided, guileless, that he needed some quick maintenance. As I watched, he flashed out a green comb and restyled his hair, three backward swipes, one per side, one on top. Done. The dark waves seemed either damp or oiled, suspended from a part that looked incredibly white, as if my secretary had just painted it there with her typing correction fluid.

This boy had shipshape features – a Navy recruiting poster, forty years past due. Some grandmother's favourite. Comb replaced, grinning, he lingered, pleased I'd acted nice about his ungainly little hop. "What say to a drink?" I asked. He smiled, nodded, followed me out. – How simple, at times, life can be.

───────────

I'm remembering: During football practice in junior high gym-class, I heard a kid's arm break. He was this big blond guy, nice but out of it. He whimpered toward the bleachers and perched there, grinning, sweating. Our coach, twenty-one years old, heard the fracture too. He looked around: somebody should walk the hurt boy to our principal's office. Coach spied me, frowning, concerned. Coach decided that the game could do without me. I'd treat Angier right. (Angier was the kid – holding his arm, shivering.)

"Help him." Coach touched my shoulder. "Let him lean against you."

Angier nearly fainted halfway back to school. "Whoo …" He had to slump down onto someone's lawn, still grinning apologies. "It's okay," I said. "Take your time." I finally got him there. The principal's secretary complained – Coach should've brought Angier in himself. "These *young* teachers." She shook her head, phoning the rescue squad. It all seemed routine for her. I led Angier to a dark waiting room stacked with textbooks and charts about the human body. He sat. I stood before him holding his good hand. "You'll be fine. You'll see." His hair was slicked back, as after a swim. He was always slow in class – his father sold fancy blenders in supermarkets. Angier dressed neatly. Today he looked so white his every eyelash stood out separate. We could hear the siren. Glad, he squeezed my hand. Then Angier swooned back against the bench, panting, he said something hoarse. "What?" I leaned closer. "Thank you," he grinned, moaning. Next he craned up, kissed me square, wet, on the mouth. Then Angier fainted, fell sideways.

Five days later, he was back at school sporting a cast that everybody popular got to sign. He nodded my way. He never asked me to scribble my name on his plaster. He seemed to have forgotten what happened. I remember.

———

As we left the office building, the Dodge owner explained he'd been delivering insurance papers that needed signing – flood coverage on his mother's country property. "You can never be too safe. That's Mother's motto." I asked if they lived in town; I was only trying to get him talking, relaxed. If I knew his family, I might have to change my plans.

"Mom died," he said, looking down. "A year come March. She left me everything. Sure burned my sisters up, I can tell you. But they're both in Florida. Where were *they* when she was so sick? She appreciated it. She said she'd remember me. And Mom did, too." Then he got quiet, maybe regretting how much he'd told.

We walked two blocks. Some people spoke to me, they gave my companion a mild look as if thinking, What does Dave want with *him*?

———

He chose the bar. It was called The Arms, but whatever word had been arched between the "The" and the "Arms" – six Old

English golden letters – had been stolen; you could see where glue had held them to the bricks. He introduced himself by his first name: Barker. Palms flat on the bar, he ordered beers without asking. Then he turned to me, embarrassed. "Mind reader," I assured him, smiling and – for a second – cupped my hand over the bristled back of his, but quick. He didn't seem to notice or much mind.

My chair faced the street. His aimed my way, toward the bar's murky back. Bathrooms were marked kings and queens. Some boy played a noisy video game that sounded like a jungle bird in electronic trouble.

Barker's head and shoulders were framed by a window. June baked each surface on the main street. Everything out there (passersby included) looked planned, shiny and kind of ceramic. I couldn't see Barker's face that clearly. Sun turned his ears a healthy wax red. Sun enjoyed his cheekbones, found highlights waiting in the wavy old-fashioned hair I decided he must oil. Barker himself wasn't so beautiful – a knotty wiry kid – only his pale face was. It seemed an inheritance he hadn't noticed yet.

Barker sitting still was a Barker almost suave. He wasn't spilling anything (our beer hadn't been brought yet). The kid's face looked, back-lit, negotiable as gems. Everything he said to me was heartfelt. Talking about his mom put him in a memory-lane kind of mood. "Yeah," he said. "When *I* was a kid..." and he told me about a ditch that he and his sisters would wade in, building dams and making camps. Playing doctor. Then the city landfill chose the site. No more ditch. Watching it bulldozed, the kids had cried, holding on to one another.

Our barman brought us a huge pitcher. I just sipped; Barker knocked four mugs back fast. Foam made half a white moustache over his sweet slack mouth; I didn't mention it. He said he was twenty-nine but still felt about twelve, except for winters. He said after his mother's death, he'd joined the Air Force but got booted out.

"What for?"

"Lack of dignity." He downed a fifth mug.

"You mean … 'lack of discipline'?"

He nodded. "What'd I say?" – I told him.

"'Dignity,' 'discipline,'" he shrugged to show they meant the same thing. The sadder he seemed the better I liked it, the nicer Barker looked.

Women passing on the street (he couldn't see them) wore sundresses. How pretty their pastel straps, the freckled shoulders; some walked beside their teenaged sons; they looked good too. I saw folks I knew. Nobody'd think to check for me in here.

Only human, under the table, my knee touched Barker's, lingered a second, shifted. He didn't flinch. He hadn't asked about my job or home life. I got the subject around to things erotic. With a guy as forthright as Barker, you didn't need posthypnotic suggestion to manage it. He'd told me where he lived. I asked wasn't that out by Adult Art Film and Book. "You go in there much?"

He gave me a mock-innocent look, touched a fingertip to his sternum, mouthed Who, me? Then he scanned around to make sure nobody'd hear. "I guess it's me that keeps old Adult Art open. Don't tell, but I can't help it, I just love that stuff. – You too?"

I nodded.

"What kind?"

I appeared bashful, one knuckle rerouting sweat beads on my beer mug. "I like all types, I guess. You know, boy/girl, girl/girl, boy/boy, girl/dog, dog/dog." Barker laughed, shaking his fine head side to side. "Dog/dog," he repeated. "That's a good one. *Dog*/dog!"

He was not the most brilliantly intelligent person I'd ever met. I loved him for it.

——————

We went in my car. I didn't care to chance his driving. Halfway to Adult Art, sirens and red lights swarmed behind my station wagon. This is it, I thought. Then the white Mercedes (already mud-splattered, a fender dented, doing a hundred and ten in a thirty-five zone) screeched past. Both city patrol cars gave chase, having an excellent time.

We parked around behind; there were twelve or fourteen vehicles jammed back of Adult Art's single dumpster; seven phone-repair trucks had lined up like a fleet. Adult's front asphalt lot, plainly visible from US 301 Business, provided room for forty cars but sat empty. This is a small town, Falls. Everybody sees everything, almost. So, when you *do* get away with something, you know it; it just means more. Some people will tell you Sin is old hat. Not for me. If, once it starts, it's not going to be naughty, then it's not worth wasting a whole afternoon to set up. Sin is bad. Sex is good. Sex is too good not to have a whole lot of bad in it. I say, Let's keep it a little smutty, you know?

Barker called the clerk by name. Barker charged two films –
slightly discounted because they'd been used in the booths –
those and about thirty bucks in magazines. No money changed
hands; he had an account. The section marked LITERATURE
milled with phone linemen wearing their elaborate suspension
belts. One man, his pelvis ajangle with wrenches and hooks,
held up a picture book, called to friends, "Catch *her*, guys. She
has got to be your foxiest fox so far." Under his heavy silver
gear, I couldn't but notice on this hearty husband and father,
jammed up against workpants, the same old famous worldwide
pet and problem poking.

———

I drove Barker to his place; he invited me in for a viewing. I'd
hoped he would. "World premiere," he smiled, eyes alive as
they hadn't been before. "First show on Lake Drive anyways."

The neighbourhood, like Barker's looks, had been the rage
forty years ago. I figured he must rent rooms in this big
mullioned place, but he owned it. The foyer clock showed I
might not make it home in time for supper. Lately I'd overused
the excuse of working late; even as Superintendent of Schools
there're limits on how much extra time you can devote to your
job.

I didn't want to miff a terrific wife.

I figured I'd have a good hour and a half; a lot can happen in
an hour and a half. We were now safe inside a private place.

The house had been furnished expensively but some years
back. Mission stuff. The Oriental rugs were coated with dust
or fur; thick hair hid half their patterns. By accident, I kicked a

chewed rubber mouse. The cat toy jingled under a couch, scaring me.

In Barker's kitchen, a crockpot bubbled. Juice hissed out under a Pyrex lid that didn't quite fit. The room smelled of decent beef stew. His counter was layered with fast-food takeout cartons. From among this litter, in a clay pot, one beautiful amaryllis lily – orange, its mouth wider than the throat of a trombone, startled me. It reminded you of something from science fiction, straining like one serious muscle toward daylight.

In the dark adjacent room, Barker kept humming, knocking things over. I heard the clank of movie reels. "Didn't expect company, Dave," he called. "Just clear off a chair and make yourself at home. Momma was a cleaner-upper. Me...less. I don't *see* the junk till I get somebody to...till somebody drops over, you know?"

I grunted agreement, strolled into his pantry. Here were cans so old you could smell them for the labels. Here was a 1950s tin of vichyssoise I wouldn't have eaten at gunpoint. I slipped along the hall, wandered upstairs. An archive of *National Geographics* rose in yellow columns to the ceiling. "Dave?" he was hollering. "Just settle in or whatever. It'll only take a sec. See, they cut the leaders off both our movies. I'll just do a little splice. – I'm fast, though."

"Great."

On the far wall of one large room (windows smothered by outside ivy) a calendar from 1959, compliments of a now-

defunct savings and loan. Nearby, two Kotex cartons filled
with excelsior and stuffed, I saw on closer inspection, with
valuable brown and white Wedgwood place settings for forty
maybe. He really should sell them – I was already mothering
Barker. I'd tell him which local dealer would give top dollar.

In one corner, a hooked rug showed a Scottie terrier
chasing one red ball downhill. I stepped on it, three hundred
moths sputtered up, I backed off, arms flailing before me.
Leaning in the doorway, waiting to be called downstairs for
movietime, still wearing my business clothes, I suddenly felt a
bit uneasy, worried by a famous thought: What are you *doing*
here, Dave?

Well, Barker brought me home with him, is what. And, as
far back as my memory made it, I'd only wanted just such guys
to ask me over. Only they held my interest, my full sympathy.

The kid with the terrible slouch but (for me) an excellent
smile, the kid who kept pencils in a plastic see-through satchel
that clamped into his looseleaf notebook. The boy whose mom
– even when the guy'd turned fourteen – *made* him use his
second-grade Roy Rogers/Dale Evans lunchbox showing them
astride their horses, Trigger and Buttermilk. He was the kid
other kids didn't bother mocking because – through twelve
years of schooling side by side – they'd never noticed him.

Of course I could tell, there were other boys, like me,
studying the other boys. But they all looked toward the pink
and blond Stephens and Andrews: big-jawed athletic office
holders, guys with shoulders like baby couches, kids whose legs
looked turned on lathes, solid newels – calves that summer
sports stained mahogany brown, hair coiling over them,
bleached by overly chlorinated pools and an admiring sun:

yellow-white-gold. But while others' eyes stayed locked on them, I was off admiring finer qualities of some clubfooted Wendell, a kindly bespectacled Theodore. I longed to stoop and tie their dragging shoestrings, one unfastened so long that the plastic tips had worn to frayed cotton tufts. Math geniuses who forgot to zip up: I wanted to give them dating hints. I'd help them find the right barber. I dreamed of assisting their undressing – me, bathing them with stern brotherly care, me, putting them to bed (poor guys hadn't yet guessed that my interest went past buddyhood). While they slept (I didn't want to cost them any shut-eye), I'd just reach under their covers (always blue) and find that though the world considered these fellows minor minor, they oftentimes proved more major than the muscled boys who frolicked, unashamed, well-known, pink-and-white in gym showers.

What was I *do*ing here? Well, my major was art history. I was busy being a collector, is what. And not just someone who can spot (in a museum with a guide to lead him) any old famous masterpiece. No, I was a detective off in the odd corner of a side street thrift shop. I was uncovering (on sale for the price of the frame!) a little etching by Wyndham Lewis – futuristic dwarves, or a golden cow by Cuyp, one of Vuillard's shuttered parlours painted on a shirt cardboard.

Maybe this very collector's zeal had drawn me to Carol, had led me to fatherhood, to the underrated joys of community. See, I wanted everything – even to be legit. Nothing was so obvious or subtle that I wouldn't try it once. I prided myself on knowing what I liked, and going shamelessly after it. Everybody notices grace. But appreciating perfect clumsiness, that requires the real skill.

"Won't be long now!" I heard Barker call.

"All *right*," I hollered, exactly as my sons would.

———————

I eased into a messy office upstairs and, among framed documents and pictures, recognized Barker's grandfather. He looked just like Barker but fattened up and given lessons. During the Fifties, the granddad served as mayor of our nearby capital city. Back then, such collar-ad looks were still admired, voted into office.

A framed news photo showed the mayor, hair oiled, presenting horse-topped trophies to young girls in jodhpurs. They blinked up at him, four fans, giggling. Over the wide loud tie, his grin showed an actor's worked-at innocence. He'd been a decent mayor – fair to all, paving streets in the black district, making parks of vacant lots. Good till he got nabbed with his hand in the till. Like Barker's, this was a face almost too pure to trust. When you observed the eyes of young Barker downstairs – it was like looking at a *National Geographic* close-up of some exotic Asian deer – you could admire the image forever, it wouldn't notice or resist your admiration. It had the static beauty of an angel. Designed. That unaffected and willing to serve. His character was like an angel's own – the perfect go-fer.

I heard Barker humming Broadway ballads, knocking around ice trays. I opened every door on this hall. Why not? The worse the housekeeping got, the better I liked it. The tenderer I felt about the guy downstairs. One room had seven floor lamps in it, two standing, five resting on their sides, one plugged in. Shades were snare-drum shaped, the delicate linings frayed and split like fabric from old negligées.

I closed all doors. I heard him mixing drinks. I felt that buzz and ringing you learn to recognize as the sweet warning sign of a sure thing. Still, I have been wrong.

I checked my watch. "Ready," he called, "when you are." I passed the bathroom. I bet Barker hadn't done a load of laundry since last March or April. A thigh-high pile made a moat around the tub. I lifted some boxer shorts. (Boxers show low self-esteem, bodywise; my kind of guy always wears them and assumes that every other man on earth wears boxers, too.) These particular shorts were pin-striped and had little red New York Yankee logos rashed everywhere. They surely needed some serious bleaching.

There he stood, grinning. He'd been busy stirring instant iced tea, two tall glasses with maps of Ohio stencilled on them. I didn't ask, Why Ohio? Barker seemed pleased, quicker moving, the host. He'd rolled up his sleeves, the skin as fine as sanded ashwood. The icebox freezer was a white glacier dangling roots like a molar's. From one tiny hole in it, Barker fished a gin bottle; he held the opened pint to one tea glass and smiled. "Suit you?"

"Gin and iced tea? Sure." Seducers/seducees must remain flexible.

"Say when, pal." I said so. Barker appeared full of antsy mischief.

For him, I saw, this was still his mother's house. With her

dead, he could do as he liked; having an illicit guest here
pleased him. Barker cultivated the place's warehouse look. He
let cat hair coat his mom's prized rugs; it felt daring to leave the
stag-movie projector and screen set up in the den full-time, just
to shock his Florida sisters.

I couldn't help myself. "Hey, buddy, where *is* this cat?" I
nodded toward the hallway's grey fluff balls.

"Hunh? Oh. There's six. Two mother ones and four kid
ones. All super-shy but each one's really different. Good
company."

He carried our tea glasses on a deco chrome tray; the film-
viewing room was just ten feet from the kitchen. Dark in here.
Ivy vines eclipsed the sunset; leaf green made our couch feel
underwater. I slumped deep into its dated scalloped cushions.

Sipping, we leaned back. It seemed that we were waiting
for a signal: Start. I didn't want to watch a movie. But, also, I
did. I longed to hear this nice fellow tell me something, a
story, anything, but I worried: talking could spoil whatever
else might happen. I only half knew what I hoped for. I felt
scared Barker might not understand my particular kind of
tenderness. Still, I was readier and readier to find out, to risk
making a total fool of myself. Everything worthwhile requires
that, right?

I needed to say something next.

"So," is what I said. "Tell me. So, tell me something …
about yourself. Something I should know, Barker." And I
added that, Oh, I really appreciated his hospitality. It was
nothing, he shrugged then pressed back. He made a throaty
sound like a story starting. "Well. Something plain, Dave? Or
something…kind of spicy?"

"Both," I said. Education does pay off. I know to at least ask for everything.

———

"Okay." His voice dipped half an octave. The idea of telling had relaxed Barker. I could see it. Listening to him relax relaxed me.

———

– "See, they sent my granddad to jail. *For* something. I won't say what. He did do it, still, we couldn't picture prison – for him. My mom and sisters were so ashamed that, at first, they wouldn't drive out to see him. I wanted to. Nobody'd take me. I called up Prison to ask about visiting hours. I made myself sound real deep, like a man, so they'd tell me. I was eleven. So when the prison guy gave me the times, he goes, 'Well, thank you for calling, ma'am.' I had to laugh.

They'd put him in that state pen out on the highway, the work farm. It's halfway to Tarboro and I rode my bike clear out there. It was busy, a Saturday. I had to keep to the edge of the Interstate. Teenagers in two convertibles threw beer cans at me. Finally when I got to the prison, men said I couldn't come in, being a minor and all. Maybe they smelled the beer those hoods'd chucked at my back.

I wondered what my granddad would do in the same spot (he'd been pretty well known around here), and so I started mentioning my rights, *loud.* The men said 'okay okay' and told me to pipe down. They let me in. He sat behind heavy-gauge chicken wire. He looked good, about the same. All the uniforms were grey but his was pressed and perfect on him – like he'd got to pick the colour of everybody else's outfit. You couldn't even hold hands with him. Was like going to the zoo except it was your granddaddy. Right off, he thanks me for coming and he tells me where the key is hid. Key to a shack he owned at the back side of the fairgrounds. You know, out by the pine trees where kids go park at night and do you-know-what?

He owned this cottage, but, seeing as how he couldn't use it – for six to ten – he wanted me to hang out there. Granddad said I should use it whenever I needed to hide or slack off or anything. He said I could keep pets or have a club, whatever I liked.

He said there was one couch in it, plus a butane stove but no electric lights. The key stayed under three bricks in the weeds. He said, 'A boy needs a place to go.' I said, 'Thanks,' – Then he asked about Mom and the others. I lied: how they were busy baking stuff to bring him, how they'd be out soon, a carful of pies. He made a face and asked which of my sisters had driven me here.

I said, 'Biked it.' Well, he stared at me. 'Not nine miles and on a Saturday. No. I've earned this, but you shouldn't have to.' He started crying then. It was hard, with the wire between us. Then, you might not believe this, Dave, but a black guard comes over and says, 'No crying.' I didn't know they could do that – boss you like that – but in jail I guess they can do anything they please. Thing is, Granddad stopped. He told me, 'I'll make this up to you, Barker. Some of them say you're not exactly college material, Bark, but we know better. You're the best damn one. But, listen, hey, you walk that bike home, you hear me? Concentrate on what I'm saying. It'll be dark by the time you get back to town but it's worth it. Walk, hear me?' I said I would. I left and went outside. My bike was missing. I figured that some convict's kid had taken it. A poor kid deserved it more than me. Mom would buy me another one. I walked."

Barker sat still for a minute and a half. "What else?" I asked. "You sure?" He turned my way. I nodded. He took a breath.

"Well, I hung out in my new cabin a lot. It was just two blocks from the busiest service station in town but it seemed way off by itself. Nobody used the fairgrounds except during October and the County Fair. You could smell pine straw. At night, cars parked for three and four hours. Up one pine tree, a bra was tied – real old and grey now – a joke to everybody but maybe the girl that'd lost it. Out there, pine straw was all litterbugged with used rubbers. I thought they were some kind of white snail or clam or something. I knew they were yucky, I just didn't know *how* they were yucky.

I'd go into my house and I'd feel grown. I bought me some birds at the old mall with my own money. Two finches. I'd always wanted some Oriental type of birds. I got our dead parakeet's cage, a white one, and I put them in there. They couldn't sing, they just looked good. One was red and the other one was yellow, or one was yellow and one was red, I forget. I bought these seed balls and one pink plastic bird type of toy they could peck at. After school, I'd go sit on my man-sized sofa, with my birdcage nearby, finches all nervous, hopping, constant, me reading my comics – I'd never felt so good, Dave. I knew why my granddad liked it there – no phones, nobody asking him for favours. He'd take long naps on the couch. He'd make himself a cup of tea. He probably paced around the three empty rooms – not empty really: full of cobwebs and these coils of wire.

I called my finches Huey and Dewey. I loved my Donald Duck comics. I kept all my funny-books in alphabetical order in the closet across from my brown sofa. Well, I had everything I needed, a couch, comics, cups of hot tea. I hated tea but I made about five cups a day because Granddad had bought so many bags in advance and I did like holding a hot mug while I read. So one day I'm sitting there curled up with a new comic – comics are never as good the second time, you know everything that's next – so I'm sitting there happy and I hear my back door slam wide open. Grownups.

Pronto, I duck into my comics closet, yank the door shut except for just one crack. First I hoped it'd be Granddad and his bust-out gang from the state pen. I didn't believe it, just hoped, you know.

In walks this young service-station guy from our busy Sunoco place, corner of Sycamore and Bolton. I heard him say, 'Oh yeah, I use this place sometimes. Owner's away a while.' The mechanic wore a khaki uniform that zipped up its front. 'Look, birds,' a woman's voice. He stared around. 'I guess somebody else is onto Robby's hideaway. Don't sweat it.' He heaved right down onto my couch, onto my new comic, his legs apart. He stared – mean-looking – at somebody else in the room with us. Robby had a reputation. He was about twenty-two, twice my age then – he seemed pretty old. Girls from my class used to hang around the Coke machine at Sunoco just so they could watch him, arm-deep up under motors. He'd scratch himself a lot. He had a *real* reputation. Robby was a redhead, almost a blond. His cloth outfit had so much oil soaked in, it looked to be leather. All day he'd been in sunshine or up underneath leaky cars and his big round arms were brown and greasy like...cooked food. Well, he kicked off his left loafer. It hit my door and about gave me a heart attack. It did. Then – he was flashing somebody a double-dare kind of look. Robby yanked down his suit's big zipper maybe four inches, showing more tanned chest. The zipper made a chewing sound.

I sat on the floor in the dark. My head tipped back against a hundred comics. I was gulping, all eyes, arms wrapped around my knees like going off the high-dive in a cannonball.

When the woman sat beside him, I couldn't believe this. You could of knocked me over with one of Huey or Dewey's feathers. See, she was my best friend's momma. I decided, No, must be her identical twin sister (a bad one) visiting from out of town. This lady led Methodist Youth Choir. Don't laugh but she'd been my Cub Scout den mother. She was about ten years older than Robby, plump and prettyish but real real scared-looking.

He says, 'So, you kind of interested, hunh? You sure been giving old Rob some right serious looks for about a year now, ain't it? I was wondering how many lube jobs one Buick could take, lady.'

She studies her handbag, says, 'Don't call me Lady. My name's Anne. Anne with an E.' She added this like to make fun of herself for being here. I wanted to help her. She kept extra still, knees together, holding on to her purse for dear life, not daring to look around. I heard my birds fluttering, worried. I thought: If Robby opens this door, I am dead.

'Anne with a E, huh? An-nie? Like Li'l Orphan. Well, Sandy's here, Annie. Sandy's been wanting to get you off by yourself. You ready for your big red dog Sandy?'

'I didn't think you'd talk like that,' she said.

I wanted to bust out of my comics closet and save her. One time on a Cub Scout field trip to New York City, the other boys laughed because I thought the Empire State Building was called something else. I said I couldn't wait to see the Entire State Building. Well, they sure ragged me. I tried to make them see how it *was* big and all. I tried to make them see the logic. She said she understood how I'd got that. She said it was right 'original.' We took the elevator. I tried to make up for it by eating nine hot dogs on a dare. Then I looked off the edge. That didn't help. I got super-sick, Dave. The other mothers said I'd brought it on myself. But she was so nice, she said that being sick was nobody's fault. Mrs. ... the lady, she wet her blue hankie at a water fountain and held it to my head and told me not to look. She got me a postcard so, when I got down to the ground, I could study what I'd almost seen. Now, with her in trouble in my own shack, I felt like I should rescue her. She was saying, 'I don't know what I expected you to talk like, Robby. But not like this, not cheap, please.'

Then he grinned, he howled like a dog. She laughed anyway. Huey and Dewey went wild in their cage. Robby held both his hands limp in front of him and panted like a regular hound. Then he asked her to help him with his zipper. She wouldn't. Well then, Robby got mad, said, 'It's my lunch hour. You ain't a customer *here*, lady. It's your husband's silver-grey Electra parked out back. You brought me here. – You've got yourself into this. You been giving me the look for about a year. I been a gentleman so far. Nobody's forcing you. It ain't a accident you're here with me. – But, hey, you can leave. Get out. Go on.'

She sighed but stayed put, sitting there like in a waiting room. Not looking, kneecaps locked together, handbag propped on her knees. Her fingers clutched that bag like her whole life was in it. 'Give me that.' He snatched the purse, and swatting her hands away, opened it. He prodded around, pulled out a tube of lipstick, said, 'Annie, sit still.' She did. She seemed as upset as she was interested. I told myself, She *could* leave. I stayed in the dark. So much was happening in a half-inch stripe of sunshine. The lady didn't move. Robby put red on her mouth – past her mouth, too much of it. She said, 'Please, Robby.' '"Sandy,"' he told her. 'You Annie, me Sandy Dog. Annie Girl, Sandy Boy. Sandy show Annie.' He made low growling sounds. 'Please,' she tried but her mouth was stretched from how he kept painting it. 'I'm not sure,' the lady said. 'I wanted to know you better, yes. But now I don't feel...sure.' 'You will, Annie Mae. Open your Little Orphan shirt.' She didn't understand him. '"Blouse" then, fancy pants, open your "Blouse," lady.' She did it but so slow. 'Well,' she said. 'I don't know about you, Robby. I really don't.' But she took her shirt off anyhow.

˙ My den mother was shivering in a bra, arms crossed over

her. First his black hands pushed each arm down, studying her. Then Robby pulled at his zipper so his whole chest showed. He put the lipstick in her hand and showed her how to draw circles on the tops of his – you know, on his nipples. Then he took the tube and made X's over the dots she'd drawn. They both looked down at his chest. I didn't understand. It seemed like a kind of target practice. Next he snapped her bra up over her collarbones and he lipsticked hers. Next he threw the tube across the room against my door – but, since his shoe hit, this didn't surprise me so much. Robby howled like a real dog. My poor finches were just chirping and flying against their cage, excited by animal noises. She was shaking her head. 'You'd think a person such as myself … I'm having serious second … I'm having serious second thoughts here, Robert, convinced … that … that we …'

Then Robby got up and stood in front of her, back to me. His hairdo was long on top, the way boys wore theirs then. He lashed it side to side, kept his hands, knuckles down, on his hips. Mrs....the lady must have been helping him with the zipper. I heard it slide. I only guessed what they were starting to do. I'd been told about all this. But, too, I'd been told, say about the Eiffel Tower (we called it the Eye-ful). I no more expected to have this happening on my brown couch than I thought the Eye-ful would come in and then the Entire State Building would come in and they'd hop on to one another and start...rubbing … girders, or something.

I wondered how Bobby had forced the lady to. I felt I should holler, 'Methodist Youth Choir!' I'd remind her who she really was around town. But I knew it'd be way worse for her – getting caught. I had never given this adult stuff much thought before. I sure did now. Since, I haven't thought about too much else for long. Robby made worse doggy yips. He was a genius at acting like a dog. I watched him get down on all fours in front of the lady – he snouted clear up under her skirt, his whole noggin under cloth. Robby made rooting and barking noises – pig, then dog, then dog and pig mixed. It was funny but too scary to laugh at.

He asked her to call him Big Sandy. She did. 'Big Sandy,' she said. Robby explained he had something to tell his Orphan gal but only in dog talk. 'What?' she asked. He said it, part-talking part-gargling, his mouth all up under her white legs. She hooked one thigh over his shoulder. One of her shoes fell off. The other – when her toes curled up, then let loose – would snap, snap, snap.

I watched her eyes roll back then focus. She seemed to squint clear into my hiding place. She acted drowsy then completely scared awake – like at a horror movie in the worst part – then she'd doze off, then go dead, perk up overly alive, then half dead, then eyes all out like being electrocuted. It was something. She was leader of the whole Methodist Youth Choir. Her voice got bossy and husky, a leader's voice. She went, 'This is wrong, Robby. You're so low, Robert. You are a sick dog, we'll get in deep trouble, Momma's Sandy. Hungry Sandy, thirsty Sandy. Oh – not that, not there. Oh Jesus Sandy God. You won't tell. How *can* we. I've never. What are we *do*ing in this shack? Whose shack? We're just too...It's not me here. I'm not *like* this.'

He tore off her panties and threw them at the birdcage. (Later I found silky britches on top of the cage, Huey and Dewey going ga-ga, thinking it was a pink cloud from heaven.)

I watched grownups do everything fast then easy, back to front, speeding up. They slowed down and seemed to be feeling sorry, but I figured this was just to make it all last longer. I never heard such human noises. Not out of people free from jail or the state nuthouse. I mean, I'd heard boys make car sounds, 'Uh-dunn. Uh-dunn.' But this was like Noah's ark or every zoo and out of two white people's mouths. Both mouths were lipsticked ear to ear. They didn't look nasty but pink as babies. It was wrestling. They never got all the way undressed – I saw things hooking them. Was like watching grownups playing, making stuff up the way kids'll say, 'You be this and I'll be that.' They seemed friskier and younger, nicer. I didn't know how to join in. If I'd opened my door and smiled, they would have perished and *then* broke my neck. I didn't join in but I sure was dying to.

By the end, her pale Sunday suit had black grease hand-prints on the bottom and up around her neck and shoulders. Wet places stained both people where babies get stained. They'd turned halfway back into babies. They fell against each other, huffing like they'd forgot how grown-ups sit up straight. I mashed one hand over my mouth to keep from crying or panting, laughing out loud. The more they acted like slobbery babies, the older I felt, watching.

First she sobbed. He laughed, and then she laughed at how she'd cried. She said, 'What's come over me, Sandy?'

'Sandy has.' He stroked her neck. 'And Annie's all over Sandy dog.' He showed her. He blew across her forehead, cooling her off.

She made him promise not to tell. He said he wouldn't snitch if she'd meet him and his best buddy someplace else.

'Oh no. No way.' She pulled on her blouse and buttoned it. 'That wasn't part of our agreement, Robert.'

'"Agreement"?' I liked that. My lawyers didn't exactly talk to your lawyers about no agreement. Show me your contract, Annie with a E.' Then he dives off the couch and is up under her skirt again. You could see that he liked it even better than the service station. She laughed, she pressed cloth down over his whole working head. Her legs went straight. She could hear him snuffling down up under there. Then Robby hollered, he yodelled right up into Mrs. ... up into the lady.

They sort of made up.

After adults finally limped from sight and even after car doors slammed, I waited – sure they'd come back. I finally sneaked over and picked the pants off my birds' roof. What a mess my couch was! I sat right down on such wet spots as they'd each left. The room smelled like nothing I'd ever smelled before. Too, it smelled like everything I'd ever smelled before but all in one room. Birds still went crazy from the zoo sounds and such tussling. In my own quiet way, Dave, I was going pretty crazy too.

After that I saw Robby at the station, him winking at everything that moved, making wet sly clicking sounds with his mouth. Whenever I bent over to put air into my new bike's tires, I'd look anywhere except Robby. But he noticed how nervous I acted and he got to teasing me. He'd sneak up behind and put the toe of his loafer against the seat of my jeans. Lord, I jumped. He liked that. He was some tease, that Robby, flashing his hair around like Lash LaRue. He'd crouch over my Schwinn. The air nozzle in my hand would sound like it was eating the tire. Robby'd say, real low and slimy, 'How you like your air, regular or hi-test, slick?' He'd made certain remarks, 'Cat got your tongue, Too-Pretty-By-Half?' He didn't know what I'd seen but he could smell me remembering. – I dreaded him. Of course, Dave, Sunoco was not the only station in town. I worried Robby might force me into my house and down onto the couch. – I thought, 'But he couldn't do anything to *me*. I'm only eleven. Plus, I'm a boy.' But next, I made pictures in my head, and I knew better. There were ways, I bet …

I stayed clear of the cabin. I didn't know why. I'd been stuck not nine feet from everything they did. I was scared of getting trapped again. I wanted to just live in that closet, drink tea, eat M & M's, praying they'd come back. – Was about six days later I remembered: my birds were alone in the shack. They needed water and feeding every other day. I'd let them down. I worried about finches, out there by their lonesomes. But pretty soon it'd been over a week, ten days, twelve. The longer you stay away from certain things, the harder it is, breaking through to do them right. I told myself, 'Huey and Dewey are total goners now.' I kept clear of finding them, stiff – feet up on the bottom of the cage. I had dreams.

I saw my den mother uptown running a church bake sale to help hungry Koreans. She was ordering everybody around like she usually did, charming enough to get away with it. I thought I'd feel super-ashamed to ever see her again. Instead I rushed right up. I chatted too much, too loud. I wanted to show that I forgave her. Of course, she didn't know I'd seen her do all such stuff with greasy Robby. She just kept looking at me, part-gloating part-fretting. She handed me a raisin cupcake, free. We gave each other a long look. We partly smiled.

After two and a half weeks, I knew my finches were way past dead. I didn't understand why I'd done it. I'd been too lazy or spooked to bike out and do my duty. *I* belonged in prison – Finch Murderer. Finally I pedalled my bike in that direction. One day, you have to. The shack looked smaller, the paint peeled worse. I found the key under three bricks, unlocked, held my breath. I didn't hear one sound from the front room, no hop, no cheep. Their cage hung from a hook on the wall and, to see into it, I had to stand up on my couch. Millet seed ground between my bare feet and the cushions. Birds had pecked clear through the back of their plastic food dish. It'd been shoved from the inside out, it'd skidded to a far corner of the room. My finches had slipped out their dish's slot. Birds were gone – flown up a chimney or through one pane of busted window glass. Maybe they'd waited a week. When I didn't show up and treat them right, birds broke out. They were now in pinewoods nearby. I wondered if they'd known all along that they could leave, if they'd only stayed because I fed them and was okay company.

I pictured Huey and Dewey in high pines, blinking. I worried what dull local sparrows would do to such bright birds, hotshots from the Mall pet store. Still, I decided that being free sure beat my finches' chances of hanging around here, starving.

Talk about relief. I started coughing from it, I don't know why. Then I sat down on the couch and cried. I felt something slippery underneath me. I wore my khaki shorts, nothing else, it was late August. I stood and studied what'd been written on couch cushions in lipstick, all caked. Words were hard to read on nappy brown cloth. You could barely make out 'I will do what Robby wants. What Sandy needs worst. So help me Dog.'

I thought of her. I wanted to fight for her but I knew that, strong as the lady was, she did pretty much what she liked. She wouldn't be needing me. I sat again. I pulled my shorts down. Then I felt cool stripes get printed over my brown legs and white butt. Lipstick, parts of red words stuck onto my skin – 'wi' from 'will,' the whole word 'help.' I stretched out full length. My birds didn't hop from perch to perch or nibble at their birdie top. Just me now. My place felt still as any church. Something had changed. I touched myself, and – for the first time, with my bottom all sweetened by lipstick – I got real results.

Was right after this, I traded in my model cars, swapped every single comic for one magazine. It showed two sailors and twin sisters in a hotel, doing stuff. During the five last pictures, a dark bellboy joined in. Was then that my collection really started. The End, I guess. The rest is just being an adult."

———

Barker sat quiet. I finally asked what'd happened to his grandfather. How about Robby and the den mother?

"In jail. My granddad died. Of a broken heart, Mom said. Robby moved. He never was one to stay any place too long. One day he didn't show up at Sunoco and that was it. Mrs....the lady, she's still right here in Falls, still a real leader. Not two days back, I ran into her at the Mall, collecting canned goods to end World Hunger. We had a nice chat. Her son's a lawyer in Marietta, Georgia now. She looks about the same, really – I love the way she looks, always have. Now when we talk, I can tell she's partly being nice to me because I never left town or went to college and she secretly thinks I'm not too swift. But since I kept *her* secret, I feel like we're even. I just smile back. I figure, whatever makes people kind to you is fine. She can see there's something extra going on but she can't name it. It just makes her grin and want to give me little things. It's one of ten trillion ways you can love somebody. We do, love each other. I'm sure. – Nobody ever knew about Robby. She got away with it. More power to her. Still leads the Youth Choir. Last year they won the Southeast Chorus prize, young people's division. They give concerts all over. Her husband loves her. She said winning the prize was the most fulfilling moment of her life. I wondered. I guess everybody does some one wild thing now and then. They should. It's what you'll have to coast on when you're old. You know?" I nodded. He sat here, still.

"Probably not much of a story." Barker shrugged. "But, back then it was sure something, to see all that right off the bat, your first time out. I remember being so shocked to know that – men want to. *And* women. I'd figured that only one person at a time would need it, and they'd have to knock down the other person and force them to, every time. But when I saw that, no, everybody wants to do it, and how there are no rules in it – I couldn't look straight at a grown-up for days. I'd see that my mom's slacks had zippers in them, I'd nearabout die. I walked around town, hands stuffed deep in my pockets. My head was hanging and I acted like I was in mourning for something. But, hey, I was really just waking up. – What got me onto all *that*? You about ready for a movie, Dave? Boy, I haven't talked so much in months. It's what you get for asking, I guess." He laughed.

I thanked Barker for his story. I told him it made sense to me.

"Well, thanks for saying so anyhow."

————

He started fidgeting with the projector. I watched. I knew him better now. I felt so much for him. I wanted to save him. I couldn't breathe correctly.

"Here goes." He toasted his newest film then snapped on the large and somehow sinister antique machine.

The movie showed a girl at home reading an illustrated manual, hand in dress, getting herself animated. She made a phone call; you saw the actor answering and, even in a silent film, even given this flimsy premise, you had to find his acting absolutely awful. Barker informed me it was a Swedish movie; they usually started with the girl phoning. "Sometimes it's one guy she calls, sometimes about six. But always the telephones. I don't know why. It's like they just got phones over there and are still proud of them or something." I laughed. What a nice funny thing to say. By now, even the gin and iced tea (with lemon and sugar) tasted like a great idea.

He sat upright beside me. The projector made its placid motorboat racket. Our couch seemed a kind of quilted raft. Movie light was mostly pink; ivy filtered sun to a thin green. Across Barker's neutral white shirt, these tints carried on a silent contest. One room away, the crockpot leaked a bit, hissing. Hallway smelled of stew meat, the need for maid service, back issues, laundry in arrears, one young man's agreeable curried musk. From a corner of my vision, I felt somewhat observed. Cats' eyes. To heck with caution. Let them look!

Barker kept elbows propped on knees, tensed, staring up at the screen, jaw gone slack. In profile against windows' leaf-spotted light, he appeared honest, boyish, wide open. He unbuttoned his top collar button.

I heard cars pass, my fellow Rotarians, algebra teachers from my school system. Nobody would understand us being here, beginning to maybe do a thing like this. Even if I went public, dedicated an entire Board of Education meeting to the topic, after three hours of intelligent confession, with charts and flannel boards and slide projections, I knew that when lights snapped back on I'd look around from face to face, I'd see they still sat wondering your most basic question:

Why, Dave, why?

I no longer noticed what was happening on screen. Barker's face, lit by rosy movie light, kept changing. It moved me so. One minute: drowsy courtesy, next a sharp manly smile. I set my glass down on a Florida-shaped coaster. Now, slow, I reached toward the back of his neck – extra-nervous, sure – but that's part of it, you know? My arm wobbled, fear of being really belted, blackmailed, worse. I chose to touch his dark hair, cool as metal.

"Come *on*," he huffed forward, clear of my hand. He kept gazing at the film, not me. Barker grumbled, "The guy she phoned, he hasn't even got to her *house* yet, man."

I saw he had a system. I figured I could wait to understand it.

———————

I felt he was my decent kid brother. Our folks had died; I would help him even more now. We'd rent industrial-strength vacuum cleaners. We'd purge this mansion of dinge, yank down tattered maroon draperies, let daylight in. I pictured us, stripped to the waists, painting every upstairs room off-white, our shoulders flecked with droplets, the hair on our chests flecked with droplets.

I'd drive Barker and his Wedgwood to a place where I'm known, Old Mall Antiques. I bet we'd get fifteen to nineteen hundred bucks. Barker would act amazed. In front of the dealer, he'd say, "For *that* junk?" and, laughing, I'd have to shush him. With my encouragement, he'd spend some of the bonus on clothes. We'd donate three generations of *National Geographics* to a nearby orphanage, if there are any orphanages anymore and nearby. I'd scour Barker's kitchen, defrost the fridge. Slowly, he would find new shape and meaning in his days. He'd commence reading again – nonporn, recent worthy hardbacks. We'd discuss these.

He'd turn up at Little League games, sitting off to one side. Sensing my gratitude at having him high in the bleachers, he'd understand we couldn't speak. But whenever one of my sons did something at bat or out in centre field (a pop-up, a body block of a line drive), I would feel Barker nodding approval as he perched there alone; I'd turn just long enough to see a young bachelor mumbling to himself, shaking his head Yes, glad for my boys.

After office hours, once a week, I'd drive over, knock, then walk right in, calling, "Barker? Me."

No answer. Maybe he's napping in a big simple upstairs room, one startling with fresh paint. Six cats stand guard around his bed, two old Persians and their offspring, less Persian, thinner, spottier. Four of them pad over and rub against my pant cuffs; by now they know me.

I settle on the edge of a single bed, I look down at him. Barker's dark hair has fallen against the pillow like an open wing. Bare-chested, the texture of his poreless skin looks finer than the sheets. Under a blue blanket, he sleeps, exhausted from all the cleaning, from renewing his library card, from the fatigue of clothes shopping. I look hard at him; I hear rush-hour traffic crest then pass its peak. Light in here gets ruddier.

A vein in his neck beats like a clock, only liquid.

– I'm balanced at the pillow end of someone's bed. I'm watching somebody decent sleep. – If the law considers this so wicked – then why does it feel like my only innocent activity? Barker wakes. The sun is setting. His face does five things at once: sees somebody here, gets scared, recognizes me, grins a good blurry grin, says just, "You."

———

(They don't want a person to be tender. They could lock me up for everything I love about myself, for everything I love.)

———

Here on the couch, Barker shifted, "Look *now*, Dave. Uh oh, she hears him knocking. See her hop right up? Okay, walking to the door. It's him, all right. He's dressed for winter. That's because they're in Sweden, right, Dave?"

I agreed, with feeling. Then I noted Barker taking the pen caddy from his pocket, placing it on the table before him.

Next, with an ancient kind of patience, Barker's torso twisted inches toward me; he lifted my hand, pulled my whole arm up and around and held it by the wrist, hovering in air before his front side as if waiting for some cue. Then Barker, clutching the tender back part of my hand, sighed, "Um-kay. *Now* they're really starting to." And he lowered my whole willing palm – down, down onto it.

I touched something fully familiar to me, yet wholly new.

––––––

He bucked with that first famous jolt of human contact after too long, too long alone without. His spine slackened but the head shivered to one side, righted itself, eager to keep the film in sight. I heard six cats go racing down long hallways, then come thumping back, relaxed enough to play with me, a stranger, in their house. Praise.

Barker's voice, all gulpy: "I think … this movie's going to be a real good one, Dave. Right up there on my Ten Favourites list. And, you know?…" He *almost* ceased looking at the screen, he *nearly* turned his eyes my way instead. And the compliment stirred me. "You know? You're a regular fellow, Dave. I feel like I can trust you. You seem like … one real nice guy."

Through my breathing, I could hear him, breathing, losing breath, breathing, losing breath.

"Thank you, Barker. Coming from you, that means a lot."

––––––

Every true pleasure is a secret.

STEVEN HEIGHTON

TO EVERYTHING A SEASON

Old age, we are told, is the season of experience, not of passion. Traditional imagery opposes the spring of youth to the winter of senility and associates the colours of grass and budding leaves with young love and those of ice and snow with sages and crones. An old person in love is a foolish thing. Even a great wise man, such as Merlin the Magician, is duped by the young enchantress Vivien and sealed up for all eternity in a giant oak tree. And someone as ancient as the centuries-old boatman, Charon, destined to row souls from this life to the next, is as susceptible as an adolescent to the traps of Eros, so that the poet Walter Savage Landor has to ask the crowd of the ghosts to protect Charon from the sight of a beautiful, dead woman:

Stand close around, ye Stygian set,
With Dirce in one boat convey'd,
Or Charon, seeing, may forget
That he is old, and she a shade.

For Steven Heighton, our wonder at love flourishing again in old age is increased by the realization that love can nevertheless come to an end. In the present, if it is to be reborn it must overcome the weaknesses of the body and the unpleasantness of decay. Compared to the fiery first encounters, the last lovemaking takes place (to use the geographical imagery of Heighton's story) in a familiar, much studied landscape, weathered by experience and yet still astonishing.

———

A time to embrace, and a time to refrain from embracing
ECCLESIASTES

I   Winter Earth

How does it happen for the last time? The lovemaking. Two bodies joining once, twice, a thousand times, then never again. How?

———

Over the city a vault of winter clouds as grey and cold as limestone. Like the walls of the old house, the walls of the garden, where the raised beds of frozen earth pushed through snow like islands in an ice-bound lake.

Through a circle he had cleared in the frost of his study window Alden looked out across the garden and over ranks of snowy roofs to the lake, where the ferry was crossing to Wolfe Island. At this distance it seemed to glide above the ice and only the mist rising around it from a slim, tenuous lead of open water proved otherwise. The newspaper open on his desk advised commuters that tonight the channel would freeze hard in the few hours the ferry docked; from tomorrow till the lake warmed in early March, the much longer, winter route would be used.

Perfect. Yes! And those scales – the ones in D minor? You won't forget? So – next week at the same time?

Holly dismissing her last student downstairs, playing her own voice with virtuoso skill – touching all the lively, pert, high trilling notes.

Alden? Alden? Her own voice again, weary and dissonant, turned back to the cracked muffled chords of old age by the departure of outsiders, the front door's slam.

Alden got up from his hard chair and stood facing his great-great-grandfather Caleb MacLeod, the "rebel and exile," who glowered out of his framed old charcoal sketch as if from a prison casement. Chastened, Alden pocketed his glasses, crossed the small dim study and pulled open the door. The glassed-in parchment map on the back rattled softly as the door swung to. Alden's study was papered in maps, framed and unframed, contour, weather and relief maps, ancient, old, or recent, the former tools and current mementoes of thirty-six years in the Geography Department at the college. Alden had been – and in retirement remained – an authority on historical cartography, especially as it applied to the mapping of south-eastern Ontario and the Thousand Islands. The *Garden of the*

Spirits, the Iroquois had called it, *Garden of the Gods*, before
they and their names were written over or erased.

After Holly's Sunday afternoon lessons a blessed silence
settled over the house. After eighteen years with his own children at home and with students at school, then fifteen more
among the swelling undergraduate hordes, Alden had been
ready for retirement, for the cozy undemanding silence and
setness of the old limestone house, for a study untrespassed by
students who sprang lately from a world for which he had no
maps, and which continued to spawn junior colleagues of an
increasingly remote and radical stripe. *Post-colonial revisionings
of the mapping process. Marxist demography. The cartographer as
rapist.* Before his departure, Alden had made a few listless bids
at befriending and understanding his new colleagues, but they
had not really wanted that any more than he had. He did have
a few friends – one left in the department, the other retired –
and they still met sometimes for a drink or two, at the faculty
club, Friday afternoons.

He had always been more comfortable with maps than
people anyway.

Alden?

He started downstairs. Holly had taken on the piano
students soon after Caleb and Annie had left home, within a
year, one after another, the house suddenly silent after all that
time. She had said the students were to give her something to
do besides the garden and her winter reading – and he had seen
her point. It was good for her to get out of the house and to
meet new people. But in the last few years her back problems
had worsened, and her students had begun to come to her.
And, inescapably, to him.

He could hardly object, out loud, to such a necessity.

She was waiting for him at the dining room table, a dull grey cardigan over the ochre paisleyed dress she had worn for her lessons. He sat down across from her. Her three students, who came one after another for an hour each, had made distressing inroads on the plate of biscuits she had set out earlier in the day – but a few of his favourites remained. He heard the kettle steaming in the kitchen. Snow fell behind her, beyond the picture window giving onto the garden, and it seemed to fall around and onto her head, whitening her hair, which had been white now for a decade and grew whiter each year so her shrinking face seemed each year redder against the white, her blue eyes refined to an eerie brilliance.

"Really, Alden, there's no need for you to hide away in your study whenever they come."

He selected a small piece of her shortbread.

"Or to look at me like that."

"I was watching the snow. Behind you."

She half-turned in her chair and winced, her rouged mouth pinched and puckering. Alden started to his feet, and then, seeing she was all right, settled back down.

She said, "I would have thought it was too cold to snow."

"Well, the paper predicts the ferry channel will freeze tonight and they'll have to change to the winter route tomorrow. So tonight would be better for the island."

"Yes ..."

"Is your back too painful? We don't have to go."

"Alden, *please* ..." The faint, exasperated quaver that betrays deep weariness. A yellowing key, accidentally touched, on a worn old piano.

"I only meant – "

"No, I want to, we go every New Year and we'll go tonight. I want to."

"I realize the food isn't as good as it used to be."

She smiled. "That's us. We don't taste things the same way." She started to get up for the kettle but he waved her off with a quick, teacherly sweep of the hand. He rose and strode briskly past her as if entering a crowded classroom.

"To hear you talk," he chided from the kitchen, quickly finishing his shortbread, "you'd think we were in our eighties."

He poured a stream of boiling water into the white stoneware pot she had already sprinkled with leaves. He checked his watch. Beyond the kitchen window snow sifted into the garden, filling the furrows between the raised beds; tucked invisibly under the sill, the stiff frozen stalks and clenched, faded flowers of the snapdragons would be sinking under the snow.

Alden brought in the teapot and cups and saucers on an heirloom tray. As he served her, Holly frowned and fidgeted with the brooch pinned over her thin breast, the grey cardigan that grew looser by the week. How much longer, he wondered, would she be able to go on teaching? He did wish she could still go out to do it.

They drank tea in silence. The room went darker, the clear corners growing dusty with shadow and the dust seeming to creep outward and suffuse the whole room. Above the piano there was a small Krieghoff that had been in Alden's family for years, and by the time he had finished his third cup of tea the voyageurs heaving their sledge through snowdrifts, pipes pluckily chomped in their mouths, were almost imperceptible.

He squinted again at his watch.

"Shall we get ready?"

She swallowed the last of her tea, as if bracing for an ordeal.

"You really don't want to go," he told her, sensing her fatigue and how it mirrored his own and accusing her of both. But her back, he thought, her spine – the bones there dissolving. A woman who had loved more than anything else *to go out,* for dinner, for walks, for drinks and dancing when a sitter was found and it was Friday night or even on weeknights when the children were older and Alden willing to go along. To the theatre, then, or a pub by the harbour – or, more recently, on her own, to the warm houses of students where she would be offered such delicacies, such delicacies, Alden, you can't imagine! Things we never ate when we were young. *Sushi, samosas,* blue corn chips with homemade *salsa,* pickled ginger! How our old city has changed!

Each New Year as they got ready for the drive to the ferry and the island for their annual celebration she would grow spry, sprightly as Caleb and Annie years before at Christmas: the drive down Princess Street crowded with students under the green and spruce-blue lights and then aboard the ferry, pulling out, the half-hour passage with the boat grinding through the ice-clogged channel or taking the longer route past Fort Henry and the lights of Marysville to the winter dock, then a short drive to the old limestone inn, the Sir John A., and the table they reserved each year by the window with the lights of the city reflected in long tapering rays over the ice….

He helped her upstairs and in their bedroom turned on the dim lamp on the oak table between the beds. Her idea, these matching single beds; not long after his retirement she had pointed them out in a catalogue and said that with her pain and her waking at night for pills it might be better for him, he might rest a bit better. "Well," he'd said after a time – a short time during which his mind flashed over a broad, sombre spectrum of feelings – "I suppose it's a good idea. It would be better for you, I suppose, your back."

And he'd added, "Besides, we never really make love anymore."

"We never much did," she'd snapped. And after all there had been a time when only he was indifferent – once the children were born, and his academic standing and responsibilities increased, when sex had seemed, as often as not, just too much fuss. He wondered sometimes if he'd left his most passionate efforts in the lecture hall – or perhaps at his desk? He could not be sure. He couldn't say. He could only wonder how a man put in thirty-five years at "an esteemed institution of higher learning," reading and thinking and teaching, and forty-one years in the institution of marriage, perfectly faithful (in marked contrast to his colleagues, or most of them); how it happened he raised two good children and cared for his wife in health and now in sickness and did everything one is supposed to do only to end up so baffled, bled dry, alone in a study scanning the legends of priceless old parchment maps for a clue to where he was and what had happened. *One of the country's foremost authorities on. The author of respected volumes concerning.* Lies, on one level. *A stranger to his most basic desires.*

He eased shut the bathroom door and shaved for the second time that day. The light above the mirror granted, as usual, no quarter at all: his dull eyes trapped in a cobweb of wrinkles: deep shadow in the wattled folds of his neck. But a full head of silver hair, swept off the forehead and back from the sides, still handsome....

When he stepped into the bedroom the lamp was off, the room almost dark. Holly sat on the side of her quilt, knees in the furrow between the beds – her knees bare. She was naked. They always undressed separately these days, not exactly hiding from each other but with a kind of coy, Victorian stealth, discreet contortions and turnings-away, Holly stiffer, more clumsy all the time, Alden more precise and methodical.

It had been a while since he'd seen her naked. Thinner now. Sitting on her bedside in the near-dark.

"Alden...?"

Faint stirrings, a quickening in the belly, not the rushing spring-melt of early youth but an echo of that, muted as so many things now seemed, as if age were gradually cooling, burying him in drifts of softly falling – what? Not only snow. Cheques and bills? A storm, maybe, of calendar leaves blown from the old black-and-white films of his youth. Blurring his eyes, frosting his brows and hair. His ears filling up. His senses shrouded, deadened – yet alive.

He undressed. Snow slipped past the darkening window and for a moment a gust rattled the pane and snow whirled and flocked against it.

"Of course I want to go," she said softly as he eased down beside her. "I still look forward to it. Every year. Here, kiss me."

Her face looked different, smoothed out by the near-dark; in bright light her papery skin seemed almost translucent, as if she were melting from outside as well as from within, but this dimness filled out and deepened her face so she seemed now more solid, substantial, less likely to fold up and crumple if he held her....

And as they lay back together on her bed and began again,

with great patience, for the first time in a year and the second in three years and for the last time, a thought drifted through Alden's mind and he wondered if it mattered and thought it must but then he lost it, he let it go and only recalled later, when they arrived an hour late at the Sir John A., that he'd been worried about missing the next ferry. Their pale bodies stirring like snow outside the window, blending, settling through grey air then churned to life by occasional gusts and floating down again to sift white over the frozen earth like seed. But cold. And as Alden made slow and difficult, blissful love to Holly he wondered why they had never much done it and why they did not do it more often now in spite of everything, to let it heal and bind them, and he vowed he would not let the intensity and purity of this moment melt away, he would keep it alive inside him, he would make this happen more often, again. But afterward as they lay on her bed he felt the warmth and rapture beginning to fade and bleed away: stored heat drawn from the body of the earth as summer ends, and autumn, and ice embalms the dead stalks of flowers and glazes over the lake – an old woman's eyes dulled, glassed-over with time.

So they came home later that night from the island to their separate beds, and went on as before, and Alden failed to keep his vow. And kept on asking himself how, and why. How was it that the love and gravity stored in the lodestones of the body – the organs and the brain – were strong enough one day to draw two people together but the next day not quite strong enough? Or the next, or the next. A threshold crossed. The body's brief half-life ending.

He holds her arm tightly as they come downstairs, he in a wool suit, dark grey, she in a pleated maroon skirt and jacket.

Telling her he wants to clear snow from the steps he carefully bundles up and hurries out around the house for a shovel. The air is clear and cold. Orion's belt hangs over the chimney like three sparks, and in the back garden light from the picture window maps a gold square on the beds of soil. Huddled by the limestone in deep shadow under the kitchen are the stalks and wizened heads of the snapdragons; each year he records the date they last until and this year has been the latest ever. A few hardy survivors, closest to the wall, were still waving gamely from the snows a month before.

A faint high trilling of music. Through the dining room window Alden sees Holly at the piano, hunched painfully over the keyboard, her face flushed and her lips, half-open, budding into a smile. He can't quite make out the piece she is playing but he stands a long time, leaning on his shovel in that parcel of light, and watches.

II   To the Sea in Spring

That spring I was twenty years old and I was going out to the coast – the ocean. West.

Jess and I had been working since March in a small hotel in Banff where we'd wound up after leaving Toronto. I first met her there in a Queen Street place called the Cutting Edge where I knew the bass guitarist in a local band – the Cargo Cult. Back then I was serious about guitar and this friend kept promising me a place in the band but nothing ever seemed to come up. "Caleb," he kept at me, "it won't be long," but in those days I didn't know how to wait. Night and day I was busking Yonge Street to keep afloat and sharing a small attic off College with another guitarist – Kathy. We weren't getting along too well. I couldn't really cover my share of the rent and I was thinking I'd maybe go home and finish school – which in hindsight didn't look too bad – but I kept thinking of Kerouac and Ginsberg and of Neil Young heading west in his beat-up old hearse, and wondering what they would have done.

My dog-eared secondhand Scriptures (*On the Road, Dharma Bums, Desolation Angels*) made it pretty clear: the safe smooth expressway back to school and a white-collar noose was mortal sin and I would lose my soul. Go West, young man. "Man, you gotta *Go*."

Jess herself had left art college a few years before. She was twenty-three. She was waiting tables at the Edge but wanted to leave since she'd just broken up with the sax player for the Cult and he was giving her a hard time. He was also a friend of a friend, bitter about Jess and by all accounts a mean drunk so there was nothing left when we hit it off but to skip town. We caught the eighty-nine-buck cross-country Greyhound and rolled out across what Kerouac (that exile *Canadien*) might have called *the big gone breathtaking vastness of Canada* sharing smokes and necking in the cramped seats and trying without much luck to go further as the lights of the prairie farms and wheat-towns washed past behind our reflections like phosphorescence on the sea around a ferry. When the sun came up on the snowy outskirts of Swift Current and sloped in the windows it made her long ringlets of ginger hair glint and ripened her face and hands to a freckled grain-gold. Jeans and snug sweater dazzling blue, wide eyes as green as – what? I settled for the Strait of Juan de Fuca – another name from my father's maps. I'd never been there. But I'd be there soon. Jess doing quick sketches of me or gesture drawings of the other passengers while I cheerfully played requests, rock, folk, or country, my pliant voice always the voice of the song's famous singer.

I was happy. I was who I wanted to be. Not the feeble *myself* I'd been tied to at home and still cousined to two-and-a-half hours west in Toronto but something better, infinitely, a character I'd come to love, to chase, somebody with a myth and a story. And the myth and the story gave me a future. I still hadn't read *Big Sur*.

We got off in Banff, for Jess, for the mountains. She'd seen them with her folks when she was a child and the minute we cleared Calgary and they soared up out of the snowed-in plains and foothills she said we had to stop there, and we did.

So I got a job in the great northwoods/Working as a cook for a spell.... Well, really a cook's helper. Who helped by washing dishes, pots – a dirty job, but I could take it for a while. Jess got another waitress position and we shacked up in a small lopsided room in the old staff barracks behind the hotel. The place smelled of sawdust and mildew, stale beer. Browsing elk and blasé "garbage-bears" peeped in the windows of the staff lounge like boorish, unshaven tourists, drawn I guess by the sounds of our jamming. One night the bellman with the off-key twelve-string brought in a Yukon mickey and the jam session kept going till way past dawn and when I wrote home I made sure my folks knew all about it. I told my father how much his maps and atlases had made me want to light out and see the world.

Jess and I walked hand-in-hand in the snow with our necks

sore as Michelangelo in the Sistine Chapel from looking up at the Rockies. That was how she liked to put it. She kept a little sketchbook in her jacket pocket with a small box of charcoal and in the barracks after work she could sit for hours by the window, drawing. How? I could never sit that still – not even for Kerouac's *Lonesome Traveller*, my latest Book. Hearing sounds of guitar or voices or bottles clinking up the hall or in the lounge I'd be pulled out of the room irresistibly, a passenger sucked from a damaged jet. Between my impatience and the way she'd always put her pencil down soon after starting to draw me, smile, say, *Caleb, let's get undressed,* she never did quite finish a portrait, though more and more that's what she wanted to do – sit in the room drawing or reading or cleaning up and saying we should look around town for new jobs, a nicer place. And still I kept telling myself she really loved our nights off, singing and drinking, dancing, then at midnight under a sea of stars stumbling out for coffee and rushing back to the lounge and jamming again till dawn. But now I see. Like when you read some complex, eerie book and wake up a few nights later in a sweat because out of the blue some small, subtle detail makes terrible sense? That's how it is with me now. I'll remember something she said in passing, some subtle gesture, and I get to know better what she was, what she wanted. I haven't seen her in a dozen years but each year that goes by I get to know her more. Too late. Guess I've finally fallen in love.

I can see it now – what she liked best was what we did only on the nights we were tired, or I was – a possibility *On the Road* hadn't really prepared me for. We'd lie in bed after making love and read together, taking turns reading aloud, the wings of an open book balanced on our chests. In March we'd read parts of

The Horse's Mouth (I'd chosen it for her and she'd liked it, though the artist Gulley sometimes riled her) and now in April it was *On the Road*. In hindsight I see she never liked the book at all and only put up with it for my sake. As she had to – as she put up with me. For a while.

Then one night in bed she turned to me, propping her head on one hand – long ginger curls spooling over her cheeks, breasts flopping together – to ask if I didn't think those guys were sometimes a bit, you know, a bit *immature*. They were in their thirties, after all.

I sat up in bed, cradling in my right hand The Book.

"Now Caleb, don't get angry, all I mean is … I mean do you really want to be driving around the country wrecking cars when you're middle-aged? Drinking till you pass out? Like a schoolkid. Looking for Mom."

I informed her The Beats were just more alive than most people. Burning with life, with a hunger for life. Wanting to swallow it whole. *Living*.

"Sure. And treating women as if they're just a bunch of – just – "

"What?"

She brushed a curl off her breast and looked down, smiling slightly, shaking her head.

"Look," I told her, "Jess, I'm not *making* you read anything. I can get along just fine reading this on my own."

She sighed. "I know it."

"What's that supposed to mean?"

She just smiled again, said she'd had enough of books for now, and asked me to turn out the light. She took my *On the Road* and set it on the floor and pulled me down to her.

In late April I was promoted to the position of third cook, which meant I got to ladle soup and slap eggs onto plates as well as help with the dishes. Jess and I saw each other on the job all the time, me passing her breakfasts over the steam table while the Swiss-German chefs made bad jokes in broken English about me slipping the pretty painter the bacon. I just shook my head and smiled. Jess never seemed to hear, so I didn't think it mattered. I ignored them when they ribbed me about Chantal, too, since she was from a small town in the Gaspé and barely knew a word of English. It was strange – we'd barely exchanged a word since meeting and it wasn't till the chefs started smirking and teasing me about her that I realized they'd long seen what I was just starting to feel.

In early May Jess told me she'd tracked down a nice apartment in town that was free from the first of June, and I said I guessed that sounded all right, but when were we going on to the coast? She suggested a week's holiday after we moved in to the new place – the overnight bus to Vancouver and maybe a couple days on the island, Long Beach. I told her that sounded fine to me too, but I warned her once we got out to the sea we might never want to come back.

"I think *I* will," she said, setting aside *Mad Shadows* and turning in bed to face me. I put down my own book; it was one of our quiet nights but we weren't reading together much anymore. "In fact I'm sure I'll want to come back. I've never been any place like this before. It's the light, I think – so much clearer than back east."

"Really," I said. "You think so?"

"Caleb you *know* I do. You told me it was growing on you, too."

I was hungover and tired. I was now struggling through the terminal stages of Kerouac's Canon and the later books painted a pretty bleak picture of life for a Lonesome Traveller, getting old. All I really wanted then was to make love – to forget – and go to sleep. So I told her she was right, the light here *was* really special, it was growing on me too, it must be perfect for her drawing and painting and all.

She kissed me and I reached for the bare bulb above our heads.

The light really was something through May and Jess spent all her free time outside painting the landscape as it thawed, and, especially when I was least in the mood, talking about June and our new place. It had been a rough month in some ways and I wanted to avoid more arguing, so I just nodded and told myself – and her – how tired I was of the barracks crowd anyway. Meantime my body, without my knowledge, went on mapping out its own plans.

It was a few days before the end of May when Jess tried again to draw me. She sat me at the foot of the bed so her drawing would take in most of our little room and even the window where evening sunlight flooded in with the year's first mellow wind. Her hair riffled over her forehead as she studied me, her face still, eyes now and then dipping to the page.

Like all the other times I'd posed for her I found myself torn between vanity and impatience. The scratch of her charcoal mixed rhythmically into the undertow of sounds from the lounge up the hall: jamming guitars, singing, voices always swelling into laughter and then subsiding in a slow tidal rhythm, waves breaking on a shore. A shore where new friends sit by a bonfire and sing, smoke hash and pass around bottles of wine? Or was it the Big Sur coast, where Kerouac's dream of a highway endlessly running finally slowed and skidded over the cliffs…? I was almost finished *Big Sur* and strangely enough that elegy to the Beat years, along with my own growing fatigue, just made me more restless and anxious to prove it didn't all have to end in nausea: Kerouac kneeling like Narcissus in the shallows and puking, weeping into his own wavery image; me going back east hat in hand to my father and maybe ending up an accountant or a teacher and recluse like him….

Whatever feelings had surfaced in my eyes, Jessie seemed to find them riveting. Frightening. I'd never seen her stare so intensely, her own eyes so transfixing and transfixed that she hardly ever seemed to look down at the page. As usual I was anxious to see the drawing in process, to see what was there so far. Then another wave of laughter from the lounge. I found my fingers tapping on my knee, as if in time to a music I couldn't hear…. *I don't know, Caleb…. Those guys are in their thirties after all…. Do you want to be driving around the country wrecking cars when you're an old man…?*

"Caleb?" She was frowning at me, setting down her charcoal. "Caleb, what is it? What's wrong? You look …"

"What?"

"I can't finish with your look changing that way."

"I'm tired," I lied, "that's all. I need a walk. Think I'll go up the hall, see what's happening, maybe have a drink."

She turned over her pad and came to me.

"You don't need another drink, Caleb – that's why you're so tired to begin with." Her mouth tightened. "Unless maybe you've just been working a bit too hard on your French."

I glared at her. She looked away.

"You don't *need* another drink, Caleb, it's the last thing –"

"A change of scene, that's what I really need. A real change. They're going to fire me soon anyhow."

A sharp rapping at some door a few rooms down, then footsteps rushing up the hall.

She was shaking her head, eyes downcast, smiling tightly. "Caleb…?"

I watched her blackened fingers form fists. I looked up at her. She seemed to force the words out, an actress delivering a line she didn't believe in:

"Caleb, I swear, you touch her and I'll get my palette knife and …"

"And *what?*" I grabbed her wrist, as if she held the knife already. "I know you wouldn't."

She shook her wrist free and gripped my hand and held it till it hurt. "No," she said softly. "Of course not. Of *course* not. But isn't that what I'm supposed to say? Something like that? Anyway you half-deserve it, you know, you and your stupid – stupid Dharma Bums and their – goddamn empty – "

She was pushing me back onto the bed and kissing me sharply, clawing at my shirt. I found myself kissing and biting her lips and roughly undressing her as we fell back into the blankets. She made a quick swiping motion with her arm. There was a faint smack as my books slid off the bed to the floor. All the angry blood seemed to be draining down out of my face into my body and suddenly I was hard and wanting her as badly as I ever had, or maybe ever could – as if I really did love her and we were back in Toronto on our first night together.

Looking back now I try to remember just how it was that

last time, but who can ever remember how it felt, how it feels to make love? Details, that's all. As if Nature's worked things out so we have to fuck again and again to remember and that need to remember keeps us doing it, keeps us feeling unhappy – restless. Just details. Feeling my jeans slide around my ankles, the breeze on my thighs. Warm melon-musk of her breasts in my face, my mouth. Her tongue seeming to paint its way down and down my belly to my cock then rushing up again to my nipples and throat then a force like my own anger seeming to fuel her hips so she rammed herself onto me with a cry and bit her own lower lip, hard, her body so brine-wet we slid smack together and I bit her neck and shoulders scratching as we fucked and the welts and bruises she left me were still there two nights later when I got to Vancouver and the sea.

Lights of the north shore and the mountains above, lights strung up like Orion over the freighters in English Bay and the sweep and spread of it all tugs your eye and heart way out after the close stony walls of the Rockies. The sea. For the first time ever. And every time after is a first time.

Because afterwards I left Jess calmly sleeping and found a party up the hall, but I couldn't leave her words behind. The anger ebbed back, blood rising back out of my heart and body into my face – ashamed. Drinking made it worse. *Cale*, my friends said, *you're so quiet tonight*, and Chantal slipped her arm round me and asked if I was okay.

No. I thought of rushing back to the room and waking Jess and telling her she was wrong and bound for a life of clock-punching dullness and domestic mediocrity – but I just kept drinking and sometime before dawn I tumbled into bed with Chantal.

Late next morning I collected my things off the floor of a room I now thought of as Jess's. She was at work. My *On the Road* lay atop a neat pile of my stuff she'd stacked in the corner by the door. The cover was partly torn, as if she'd started to shred it with the palette knife that lay on the floor nearby – then stopped. For a moment I thought of taking the knife and thrusting it through last night's portrait – very dark and blurred, the borders of the head rough and broken as a shore-line – then I grabbed a pencil instead and scrawled in the margin a brief, bitter goodbye.

I stood and stared down at it for a minute or two, then hurried out.

My pack with guitar strapped on the top felt so fine, so light on my shoulders as I hiked to the station. Chantal was already there. Such black, black hair, her eyes pale blue; *like the waters off Vancouver Island.* I scrawled a postcard to my folks and we boarded the Vancouver bus and pulled away twelve hours over the mountains and through the interior to the sea – Golden, Revelstoke, Salmon Arm, Kamloops, Boston Bar and Hope, the marvellous names from my father's maps scrolling through my mind with the warm foreign word Chantal kissed into my ear when we first sensed, on the soft humid wind gusting up the Fraser Valley an hour from the coast, *la mer.* Our lips and tongues sweetly sore from hours of necking but no need now for speech and so few words we knew in common anyway and it seemed perfect like that and I was sure that was the secret, Chantal and I had dropped anchor off an island of calm: shared language led to strife and pain and ice-cold familiarity (my folks!) and paradise was a lover who could never perjure herself or you with a spoken word. The secret. We'd be together a long time.

Bullshit.

In the cramped, rumbling washroom just before we got in, I stared at my face in the mirror – dimly lit and warped, uneven, as in a mountain pool. Had Jess really seen through me? I leaned closer to the smeared glass and a reek of piss and disinfectant washed up from below. Peering into my eyes I wondered – I wonder – what Chantal saw there. Herself? The bus swerved and braked for something on the road and I pitched off-balance, felt my face crack into the glass and for a moment I was stunned. Numb, breathless. Awash in a dim reflection. Drowned.

III   Summer Fires

How does it happen for the last time? The lovemaking. Two bodies joining once, twice, a thousand times, then never again. How?

———————

In the early summer of 1839 Alden's great-great-grandfather Caleb MacLeod found his way back to Brockville, his wife Charlotte and their three small children. He arrived long after midnight. He was filthy and sunburnt, his stern, bulging blue eyes had sunk back in his skull, and the fierce determined jut of the chin so striking in his portrait was hidden under a matted bush of beard. His prematurely thin red hair had thinned still further and his fiery brows had thickened in the seven months since his capture and five weeks since his escape. Alden pictured him standing in the doorway before his wife, a storybook giant grown thin as the cut-out silhouette figurines his children would have eyed in vain through shop windows last Christmas, soon after his capture. So changed now, face flickering in the weak glow of the candle Charlotte has brought to the door....

The story of Caleb's famous insurgency, flight and exile had been heirloomed along through the generations as far as Alden, then his children, Annie and Caleb, the known facts hammered down during its passage to the gritty essentials – as a fugitive will gradually jettison all but the most basic possessions, yet build around him a portable mansion of memories as shelter for the long, fetal nights cringing under scrub-pines and in caves and deserted cabins. Likewise Caleb's story had grown in spirit as it shrivelled in fact, so by the time it was entrusted to Alden his ancestor loomed as a mythic, romantic giant who both inspired and intimidated his heirs. Alden could trace his fascination with the rugged and fickle geography of the region to the story of Caleb's escape from Fort Henry in mid-May 1839 – a few days before he was to be shipped out for Quebec, Portsmouth, and Van Diemen's Land – and his five-week wilderness journey north to the edge of the Shield country, then furtively east and south again to Brockville. Alden felt sure, too, that the unruly wanderlust of his son Caleb's youth (Banff, Vancouver, Australia) had sprung also from Caleb senior – from his example as much as his genes. Alden, after all, had never much liked to travel or even leave his solid house, let alone his study. But who could tell? Perhaps his ancestor had been the same. After all, young Caleb's footloose enthusiasms had cooled and he now lived a steady productive life as a prison literacy and music teacher, married, in Winnipeg.

So perhaps Caleb senior, a blacksmith by trade, had loved the warm confines of his shop? Alden pictured him on a winter's day flushed with the crackling heat of the forge, his great red eyebrows singed and curling, the firelight mirrored above his temples on the bald scalp. He whistles quietly, mumbles to himself and grins. He savours the warm private manual work – the mundane spectacle of golden sparks cascading from the hammered anvil, its rhythmic clanging as intimate as his own pulse, his muscles rippling smoothly under the warm wool shirt and leather apron…. Alden did not believe, as some of his old academic friends believed about the radical new scholars in the department, that inside every rebel there skulks a sullen child anxious to seize the attention of the world, or, failing that, to destroy it. He believed he'd seen through a few bandwagon radicals but he had also met some young people – and older ones – who seemed driven by solid and reasoned convictions to challenge the status quo. Sometimes Alden saw their point, and for a while he'd done some teaching in the prisons, but he loved too much the stillness and setness of his maps and study ever to throw himself wholly into the fray. But his great-great-grandfather had done that – thrown himself in. Surely, though, the injustices of his age had been harsher, more sharply defined? Sometimes Alden was not so sure. But Caleb, a mild giant of a man who loved the confines of his workshop and the hearthlike heat of the forge – who loved his hearth, his wife Charlotte and three small children – Caleb had made up *his* mind and beat his dead father's ploughshare into a sword.

The story first joins him in the fall of 1837 when he is thirty-six years old and established as one of four blacksmiths in the town of Brockville. He is a hardworking pious man who reads to his wife and children from the Bible each night before supper. His blood, steeped in the sober egalitarianism of his Scots forbears, has warmed at the despotic pranks and machinations of the ruling Family Compact, steamed at their summer decrees, and comes to a rolling boil in the fall of '37 after a run of incendiary sermons by local politicoes and the visiting radical William Lyon Mackenzie.

In November Caleb closes shop and canters toward York, or Toronto, with twelve other Brockville men. A few of them are armed with muskets; Caleb carries a kind of lance he has improvised by lashing a long, home-beaten blade onto a staff. In York, family tradition casts our hero willy-nilly in a starring role on a decidedly ill-starred stage: during the rebels' pell-mell flight from Montgomery's Tavern the gallant blacksmith holds off a body of militiamen with his shining lance and thus helps scores of comrades evade capture, even death.

Here the family storysmiths beat a hurried retreat and Caleb is seen back in his workshop, with markedly less work to lay on the anvil because customers have switched to other shops during his three-week absence, and the Tories among them, hearing rumours of his treason, have sworn never to come back.

Nothing is told here of Charlotte, but surely her feelings can be guessed. For three weeks no income, and now an income greatly reduced. Three weeks alone with the children at night wondering if her husband has been shot, imprisoned, hanged. Rising at dawn and stirring the coals, feeling their faint, lukewarm breath waft up to her face, blinking down at their dim, infernal glow. *Van Diemen's Land.*

Unrest smoulders again through the hot summer of '38 and
the autumn winds, like a bellows by the forge at dawn, fan it to
high flame. More fighting in Lower Canada. A hundred
soldiers and *patriotes* dead in the snow near Beauharnois. So
the rumour runs. And in November a force of Canadian
patriots and sympathetic Yankees is ferried across the St.
Lawrence below Brockville, hoping to seize Ft. Wellington.
Caleb and his comrades, undaunted by last autumn's debacle,
are there to join them. The whole force falls back on an old
windmill above the river and is soon besieged by British
soldiers and Canadian militia. Four days inside the yard-thick
limestone walls while fire rages and fades in the buildings
round the mill – then bursts through the oak floor of the mill
inside. The crackle of musket fire echoing madly, the bark of
British cannons, the thud as the balls pound the limestone and
soundwaves smash through to pummel the ribs like the butt of
a rifle.

Flame-red jackets moving over the brown grasses of the
field. Like a brush-fire. Closing in.

Caleb is captured, trussed and carted with over a hundred
others to Fort Henry in Kingston where a young lawyer named
Sir John A. Macdonald defends their leader, but to no avail.
The leader is to be hanged, along with ten others. And along
with fifty-nine others Caleb is sentenced to transportation – to
Van Diemen's Land, in May.

In March when the worst of the winter is past, Charlotte
and the children accomplish the rough two-day journey from
Brockville to Kingston to say farewell. The children weep and
shiver in the damp grey corridors of Fort Henry, Dickensian
waifs clinging to the full skirts of their pallid, frightened

mother. A rushed visit. Kisses for the children who hardly recognize their father, his face, his clothing, his smell. A few moments in private for Caleb and Charlotte – Charlotte torn by fear and regret and anger and desire and who knows what else? Her desire, such as it is, damped by dreary circumstance. Her fear by now familiar, hidden, like her feelings of regret.

And anger? But there is so little time. And so much anger. *Your smithy is lost and your children halfway orphaned and I –* But the guards have come. An iron door clangs shut.

In mid-May, a few days before he is to be shipped out for Quebec, Portsmouth, and Australia, Caleb escapes a work detail outside the fort walls. With the hammer that he wields to crush rock, his expert hands (so the story goes) neatly smash the shackles, and he is spotted (too late) in full stride over the newly green fields, his prison trousers flapping round bloodied ankles as he lopes downhill for the river. A single erratic musket blast. A blast of Cockney cursing as the second guard's gun misfires. Already the balding red-bearded giant is at the river's edge, and gone.

It has been a warm spring and had it been otherwise Caleb could hardly have survived his first night: shivering, wet, in the soft needled shelter of a small pine, after running north along the Cataraqui and braving its unusually mild waters at a ford. In the morning he cuts inland and thrashes north through the wilderness above Kingston. Near Westport, it is said, he finds in a deserted shack some old moth-ravaged woollens and a bit of dried food. He stays for several days to recoup his strength, then moves on. North. Through the forest a stone's throw east of the Perth Road so that he hears and sometimes catches a glimpse of traffic on the road, a troop of red-coated cavalry cantering south – on the lookout for someone? – or farmers and settlers bound north from Kingston on one-horse carts laden with topsoil and seed potatoes and sacks of grain. Caleb, a beanstalk of a giant not born for stealth, sidling through the undergrowth and darting barefoot for silence onto the King's road behind a clattering cart. Grabbing whatever he can. A few seed potatoes. A turnip. Sometimes only seed.

For a few days he camps on Foley Mountain, above the hamlet of Westport, where the farmlands end and the Shield rears up. At night he slinks down the pine-covered mountain-side to the sleeping hamlet and scavenges what he can. There is little enough – a meat-pie on a sill, a small bag of flour in a shed behind the baker's. Two more days on the mountain resting, eating cold flour mush till his stomach rebels, regretting his forge and hearth but not daring to light a fire....

He sets out for home. Stronger now and more acquainted with stealth, he escapes even the mythmakers who lose him in dense forest east of Westport and only catch him in passing glances through the woods or darting at nightfall with his giant strides over the new-seeded fields north of Brockville. He surprises them, and Charlotte, sometime after midnight on mid-summer's eve 1839 when he appears, a bearded, sun-burned ghost, in the doorway of his home.

The mythmakers usher him to the table where his devoted Charlotte serves him his first substantial meal in weeks, and they grant him a brief last look at his sleeping children before he and his wife retire for the night and he sleeps in a good bed for the first time in months – and the last time in his life. With a modesty and discretion suited to the authors of stories that may be told to children, the mythmakers do not shadow the reunited pair over the threshold of their room, or even grant us a keyhole peep, but in his later years, especially after he and Holly had moved to separate rooms, Alden often wondered what his forbear's last night had been like, Charlotte desperately afraid. And angry. But by all accounts Caleb was a fiery impetuous giant of a man and Alden felt sure, in his study under that smouldering charcoal gaze, that he would have squeezed his wife in a last mighty bearhug.

It is a sultry windless night so that even with the window above the bed propped open the flame of the candle on the bedside table does not stir. Caleb peels off his matted clothing and washes quickly at the basin, sighing richly but with now-instinctive softness as the water streams over his body and face. Charlotte sits on the side of the bed in her summer nightgown, bare feet on the floor. She stares into the flame of the candle then looks down at her lap, the patient hands folded together – a little too tightly. Caleb in his old nightshirt on the bed beside her. Mumbled words. Where will he go in the morning? Away. Again? He must go away again.

No. *No.* But she admits that, yes, men have come to the house many times, men with firearms and pointed questions. Her hands clench tighter, the knuckles blanched and angry – then she turns on Caleb with a sudden embrace. He responds with his usual clumsy ardour and the candle flame wavers in the breeze of their coupling. How thin he is under his shirt! She kisses his balding scalp, his massive brow and eyes and beard. Their hands and fingers clawing and flickering like flames, impatient, as if fearing interruption – as if after long absence every half-forgotten half-embellished part must be re-explored and so relearned, reclaimed. *Stay*, she says, *for the sake of your children, hide here until they forget,* and he clenches her tighter till she can hardly breathe, or move, or say another word. This man she has cursed every day of his absence and craved, Alden thinks, every night.

As usual it is over too soon. Sadness, deeper than usual, and the old, embering coals of shame.

Van Diemen's Land.

They are sweating with the heat, as if the single candle is a hearth, a forge. They have never before made love in the light. Charlotte blows out the candle and Caleb, within seconds, is snoring heavily so she must lean across his long enfeebled frame and yank down the sash. She lies back, turning from him, the ache inside her unfilled. Anger flaring up to fill it. For with morning he will leave and start fading from his family's eyes to something as dim as the light this glowing wick still casts: a character in a story read once as a child, his name forgotten with the story's name, nothing left but an aura, a tone of voice, a few flickering details.

The story has it that he did not leave, he was taken. At first light a platoon of redcoated soldiers hammered on the door and Caleb was seized by four strong men as he leapt in his nightshirt from the bedroom window. And here the forgers of the story follow him for the last time as he is marched in irons down the cobbled streets of Brockville to the river and up the gangplank of a sloop bound for Quebec, then Portsmouth, then Australia. They lose him as the ship leans out and ferries him away with the current and a clean summer wind.

Who can add further chapters? His own son, thought Alden, the son he named Caleb, who has seen Botany Bay and Tasmania.

The story ends that Charlotte conceived her third daughter that night – Alden's great-grandmother Sarah. Sarah in her cradle by the hearth in late March, cooing, her cries a dim high echo of her father's deep bass. Reading from Scripture, at table, in a much brighter season: *After the fire a still small voice.*

IV   *The Fall Wind*

A Chinook wind blew in over the passes and the clean powder snow falling since Remembrance Day turned soft and wet and began to vanish. The streets of Banff, full of skiers and sight-seers up for the day from Calgary, ran with meltwater smelling of spring, while the sun in the clear sky was summer-hot. Jessie and Stratis stood at the plate-glass window of their busy cafe gazing up over the bright crowded streets and dripping roofs of the facing shops to the peak of Mount Rundle, where snow was being churned and spun by the mild winds like spume off the tip of a wave. And Rundle did look like a wave, a huge tidal wave of blue-grey water frozen solid in the second before breaking. So Jessie thought. She was a painter, part-time – a too-small part of the time – and she'd told Stratis how the mountain looked to her but he always said he just couldn't see it, a mountain was a mountain, wasn't it?

She turned to him. The sunlight through the plate-glass window did him good, brushed his greyed face with colour. For two weeks he'd been in a state of unexpected remission and ten days back he'd come home from the hospital in Calgary. The doctors, Stratis warned her, were not optimistic. She knew that. She knew not to expect miracles. But on a day like today anything seemed possible, even likely, with Rundle holding its precarious poise against the blue sky, the sunlight, the Chinook breathing sweetly through the open door of the shop, winter deferred for a few more days, the shop full of cheerful customers and the new help, Glen, working out just fine – much better than the last student she'd hired in June when Stratis first went into hospital.

"Jess?"

Glen needed help at the till. Jessie spun round and in a few strides crossed the tiny Olympos Cafe. She and Stratis had long fought over the decor – he wanted posters and framed, doctored tourist photos of Greece, she planned to cover the walls with the sketches and paintings of Bow Valley artists – but from the start of his illness she had acquiesced, so in his absence the cafe had come to look exactly as he had always hoped. A few of her paintings he could live with, he said, gladly he could, but all that other stuff? There were enough mountains out the window, who wanted airbrushed Alps when you had the real thing a few steps out the door? So while a few of her watercolour landscapes still hung behind the till, it had been months since she'd hung any new work by friends. A yellowing map of Greece instead, the Acropolis from at least five angles and through lenses aimed with wildly differing degrees of skill, Mt Olympos viewed from the sea, sunny beaches with fresh-painted fishing boats drawn up, the Aegean in implausible postcard blue and the matching forgery of Grecian skies.

A tightness now in her throat and belly as she passed them, these aquamarine clichés, these touched-up dreams that would soon remind her of a fresh and unretouched sorrow. But no. Stratis looked so well these days; he was cheered by the cafe's increasing success, and the weather, and most of all by being back in Banff with his children. And Jessie. He had smiled weakly then laughed out loud and hugged her on seeing how she had put up all those extra images of Greece.

"But soon my dear you will take them down."

He said it softly, without malice.

Jessie had met him eight years before in Calgary, where, at twenty-six, she was trying to finish a Fine Arts degree part-time while waitressing wherever she could. Stratis managed the dining room where she worked weekends. He was the owner's son and he'd surprised her, over time, by erasing her stereotyped image of the Classical Greek Boss. "My father, mind you, is the real thing," he would laugh, his long black feminine lashes meeting. "Me, I hate it here."

Stratis had no particular interest in art and that suited Jessie just fine, she'd had enough of dating art students. Stratis's consuming interest, she learned, was family – not the one he had, mind you, but the one he hoped to have. He wanted a small business of his own somewhere a long way from his father's city and he wanted his own big family as well. So his lean olive features lit up and furrowed in a broad smile whenever a family with small children came into his father's place – partly, Jessie teased, because he didn't have to serve them.

"Strange," he opened up to her one night after work, over his beer and cigarettes, "we were never happy as children. I think sometimes I want to do right what my father didn't."

Stratis was ready to settle down, it was clear, and Jessie had long been ready. So after getting her degree she moved with him to Banff, which she loved and he didn't think was really far enough from Calgary but did offer good prospects for the future. They both got work in another restaurant through one of Stratis's seemingly countless uncles. They lived frugally and began to save. They were made floor-managers, Jessie days and Stratis nights, and the money was better. After a year they got married and a year later had their first child – a girl, Calla. Then twins, Larissa and Paul. They made an offer on a closing crafts-shop and did it over as a cafe.

With each passing year Jessie smuggled a few more of her friends' paintings into the cafe and deported a few more of her husband's Grecian atrocities. Stratis fought a stubborn rear-guard action and sometimes resorted to guerilla tactics, one night replacing three watery Alpscapes with chromatically similar Greek scenes, then pleading, "Jessie, *pethi*, we're a Greek-style cafe, think of the customers!" And she had to nod. But this was no more than a minor check. Eventually, she was sure, the Olympos Cafe would be a kind of local art gallery....

The impending realization of her dream could do little now but depress her – as if the dream itself were partly to blame for what had happened? Stratis looked so thin here, silhouetted in the window with the mountain above him; snow churning steadily off the crest.

She showed Glen how to unjam the drawer of the till and, when she looked up, saw Stratis weaving his way back through the tables. He riffled the hair of a small blond girl who grinned up at him, her chin, lips and teeth flecked with nuts and sticky bits of *filo*. For a moment he seemed to flush, to glow with that contact, but as he neared the till his face faded again from rich colour to shades of chalk and charcoal, black-and-white. The furrows in his cheeks and round his eyes sank deeper. Deeper still as he tried to smile.

"It's such a nice day, Jessie. Too busy to leave Glen here alone. Let's close at four and go for supper with the kids."

———

After the children were in bed Jessie asked Glen to come down from his upstairs apartment so she and Stratis could go out for a while. The Chinook wind was still blowing and the streets still ran with meltwater and the Bow River, sluggish and half-frozen just a day before, was flowing quickly in the dark. But the air did seem colder and Jessie wondered if it was more than just the absence of the sun. A change in the weather? They walked arm-in-arm along the river, slowly. The path was deserted. Then, straight ahead, a black, massive shape bulked out of the river onto the banks: a huge elk, his hide and antlers dripping, glistening in the faint lamplight, his body like a great barrel rocking back and forth as he shook off the cold water of his crossing.

Jessie and Stratis stood very still. The elk ignored them, his heavy snout upraised and snuffling the wind. After a few moments he ambled, with solemn dignity, into the pines.

They lagged back up Wolf Street toward the cafe. Stratis said he wanted to check the place seeing as they'd closed early – and since Stratis was the kind of man who would stop the car halfway to Calgary and turn around and drive back to Banff just to check if he'd turned off the coffee machine, Jessie was not surprised. She was not even exasperated, as she had been in the past by his worrying, his occasional laziness in the shop, his stubborn matter-of-factness (*a mountain is a mountain!*) – and his refusal to quit smoking till it was too late. How strange, how very wasteful such exasperation now seemed! Even about the smoking, perhaps....

Rundle brooded above them again, a tidal wave in silhouette. Jessie would never tire of its power, its tension, the sense of massive implacable movement, stopped. Yet always in motion; never complete. It was a masterpiece of tension and whoever could reflect it perfectly in paint – and not just its essence but its *shape*, which could never be improved on – would have a masterpiece on her hands. She had sketched and painted it many times, in charcoal, *conté*, watercolour and oils, in as many versions as there were tourist views of the Acropolis. By the path near the bridge over the Bow River where she and Caleb had come walking years before, she would set up her easel in the warm sun. Mondays, for a few stolen hours. So that when she came home, Stratis – making the *baklava* that had added, with the children, twenty pounds to her frame – smiled at her freckles and said it looked like someone had sprinkled her face with nutmeg.

And she would laugh. But the mountain escaped her.

They came back to the modest clapboard two-storey on Marten Street and thanked Glen. Jessie noticed how uneasy the boy looked on seeing Stratis' face, and when she and Stratis were alone and she got a good look at him under the hall-light, she realized he did look worse. And she sensed he knew it.

He told her he felt fine.

In bed, the mountain and its halo of blue air were still above them – a kind of abstract Greek Orthodox icon, framed above their heads, in watercolour. Jessie's. She frowned up at it as she got under the down quilt beside her husband, who was almost asleep now but seemed to stir himself, to rub his long-lashed eyes like a child resisting sleep. And with those white pyjamas he had started wearing in the hospital after years of sleeping nude, he looked even more like a child. So small and shrunken, even now, after a week of eating well.

His body giving off the faint sour odour they had both noticed in June. For the last week it had been gone and his body had seemed, to Jessie, fresh and pure as a wind off the snowfields.

"I smell again, Jess. I stink."

A kiss of denial. "*Hush.*"

He puts his arms round her and pulls her naked body onto him. His clasp is so gentle, she thinks; and then she thinks, weak.

She helps him undress. Gently she holds him and rubs her body over his. He is so weak, not like two nights ago when he seemed almost as before, laughing, reminding her of when sex was something lively, raunchy, a terrific joke with endless variations and the same gut-wrenching punchline that seemed new every time.... A warm fragrant gust of Chinook rattles the blinds and passes over them and perhaps it stirs him, wakes him a little, breathes strength back into his lungs for his cock hardens in her hand and quickly she guides him inside her and moves over him, and over him. They go on for a long time in near-silence, Stratis with his eyes closed and a look on his face so peaceful, the long lashes twinned, parted lips like a sleeping child's. She with her mouth open near to his. Exhaling deep as if to revive him. Now his eyes open, widen and he clutches her buttocks with hands so gentle she could weep, she arches harder and rubs against him and pulls back and feels a kind of fear as if the smooth motion of her cunt soon to clasp and suck the crisis from deep inside him with his seed will weaken him too much, bleed the life from his core. He is coming, groaning weakly and she lets herself go, she pushes, and as the storm breaks under her womb and pumps long sweet warming gusts to the tips of her arching toes and clinched fingers a breeze blows through the room and just to feel it caress her bare skin as she comes is too much, the sweetness is too much, the pain, goddamn it, the sorrow. A second climax wells from her belly but this time it is all pain, an orgasm of pain that racks her whole body dredging up all the things she has kept down as she sobs and collapses on top of this man, this good man, this fucking heartless bastard who is going to leave her.

So soon. So soon his cock softens, wilts and slips out of her. She can't stop crying, her head pressed into the bony crook between his neck and shoulder. The sour reek of his poor body.

"It's all right, Jessie. Please. It's all right."

It's not goddamn it and you know it's not. It's not. You're going to leave me. What the fuck am I going to do?

At four she wakes and his side of the bed is empty. For a moment she lies propped on an elbow staring at the imprint his body has etched into the sheet. That sour smell again, stronger.

She stumbles into the hall. A white form glides toward her out of the dark. "*Stratis…?*"

"The children," he whispers, short of breath. "Just checking. You know how I am. To close their windows."

She guides him back into the bedroom, so cold now, icy, the weather has turned and by dawn the unmelted snow in the yard will have a crust a child can walk on without sinking. Ice knitting up in the melt-pools and forming along the banks of the Bow. Cold air bleeding in through the walls and settling into the drawer by the window where she keeps all her portraits.

She tucks Stratis in and closes the window for winter.

"In the morning," she says lightly, trying to sound casual, in control, "darling? In the morning we should probably go see the doctors. In Calgary."

His mouth is open as if to form a response, but he says nothing. Asleep, so soon. She lies beside him and studies the familiar yet subtly changed contours of his face, thinking of the weeks to come, and Rundle: the blue sky above it and the Chinook blowing snow like foam off the grey rock crest of a shape she'll always be painting. Down the sloping backside of the frozen wave to a small graveyard of crooked limestone slabs. She has painted there, too, but she won't be able to do that again.

She leans over and sets her palm, like a mirror, an inch above the open mouth and feels the warm soft breath of her husband moistening her skin.

Coda

Alden and Holly stand in the blunt bow of the ferry crossing to the island and peer into a slim channel clogged with broken ice – ice that buckles and cracks and gets sucked under by the ferry as it grinds along. A cold wind burns their cheeks and stings their squinted eyes and they huddle together for warmth. Everyone else is in the heated cabin or in cars with engines running but Holly has insisted they leave their car and stand in the bow, as they used to do years back, to feel the wind. And it is bracing, it does slap them awake: Alden feels his chest fill with a kind of boyish joy and expectation so that even squinting down stiffly at his watch he seems a young explorer – a mapmaker – poring over a compass as his ship nears new land. Wind and black water in the channel and the snowy hill where the old prison looms and the lights of the town like flickering amber spots in a damped, cooling fire.

"What were you playing on the piano," he says, then has to shout over the roaring, "*what were you playing when I went out to clear the ice?*"

The trickling of the notes, so faint, but two or three in sequence clear enough to rouse the ghost of some forgotten passage.

"*Holly?*"

She kisses him, smiles, excited by the wind, her back forgotten, the fire-warmed inn and the dinner to come. The way she smiled at the keyboard, caught in the window while the snapdragons disappeared below…. Laughing, she says she's forgotten. Think of that! She recalls sitting down and playing the piano, but forgets now what she played.

AMELIA
HOUSE

CONSPIRACY

One of the immediate aims of censorship is to limit experi-
ence. Whether in books and art or in readers and viewers, it
constructs exclusive compartments that take the place of
definitions. A censored novel becomes defined by a single
characteristic – its erotic scenes, its political passages; a
person censored becomes recognizable through one feature
alone – a poem, a film, a professed religion, the colour of the
skin. The policy of apartheid in South Africa, which began
in 1913 with the Natives Land Act separating European
from non-European residents, established categories so strict
that the Nobel Prize-winning writer Nadine Gordimer
declared that an artist who was not censored under such a
regime would be forced to question the validity of his or her
work.

In such circumstances, every aspect of life is contami-
nated and every act becomes political, including the erotic
act. Private desire and individual choices – choosing a
partner, finding someone mysteriously attractive, falling in

love with a face or a voice or a pair of hands – become huge symbols of acceptance or rebellion far beyond the limits of the bedroom. In the following story, Amelia House, who left South Africa in 1963 to settle first in England and then in the United States, transforms one such small moment into a public act of treason in which intimacy is subversive and coming together, a conspiracy.

Pretoria: Immorality Act: 1957 Session of Parliament increased the maximum penalty for illicit carnal intercourse between whites and non-whites to seven years imprisonment. It also became an offence to conspire to commit an act.

Amy stared at the window high in the wall. The row of windows met the ground level of the basement room. Through the ivy she watched the feet of passing students. A starling pecked at the window. The University of Cape Town nestled against the slope of the mountain at Rondebosch. The marble pillars of Jameson Hall shone out over the ivy covered walls. Amy liked to stop at the entrance of Jameson Hall where she could look back and take a full view of the campus. All those steps leading up from the road – she always meant to count and never did: the student residences (for Whites Only); the playing fields (for Whites Only); and then she let her gaze go out to the horizon across the Cape Flats. This panorama she enjoyed again and again. Amy usually enjoyed working in the archives, but today she felt trapped inside the mountain.

As she sat trying to imagine from the books what the Cape looked like when Simon van der Stel was Governor, the view from the top of the steps kept obtruding. She could sit in this room undisturbed because not many students came to this section.

"How much would I have to pay to know those deep and profound thoughts?" Saimon broke into Amy's reverie.

"You shouldn't creep up on me like that. Me heart can't stand it."

"Admit it's my presence that sends your heart pounding. This six-foot Adonis makes his little five-foot and-a-dot mere mortal woman tremble."

"The conceit of the cave man – not god. How did you know I was here?"

"Don't I always know where to find you? I changed into a butterfly and peeped in at each window. You waved to me when I fluttered by five minutes ago."

"A butterfly? Why not just send your spirit to inhabit Prof. Grayson's poodle? It gets all over campus."

"I know you like butterflies better. You'll try to catch me and stroke my wings. You stroking my body – what a thought!"

Saimon held Amy's hands and kissed her forehead, her eyelids, each cheek and then took her in his arms as she turned up her mouth to respond to his kiss.

"Enough. I might just forget how immoral we are and let you kiss me the rest of the morning." Amy broke away hurriedly. Looked up at the windows. Only the passing feet; no eyes peering in. Even the starling had flown away.

"I managed to get two tickets for the Roman Catholic Students' Annual Ball. So here, Miss Baptist, is yours, and this one is for Mr Jew. I bet we'll be the most devout Catholics present. I've also thought of a plan for us to meet on my parents' boat."

"Kristina and John are going to the dance. I can arrange for John to take me and you can escort Kristina. Nothing more respectable – a coloured couple and a white couple – no immorality there."

"You've become quite a schemer too. Want to see more of me, hey? Not content with kisses in the archives and pecks behind the book stacks? I'll have to watch it. I think my downfall is being plotted."

"I don't have to take risks for you, Saimon Zolkov. There are any number of safe dates I can have."

"Only joking, my little black bird."

"An English literature major resorts to clichés. Even your Romantic poets could give you a better image. Black bird. Be careful where you call me that name. I've already been told not to allow myself to be insulted. You never forget my colour."

"Why so touchy today? You know it was your raven black curls that first caught my eye. Shall I say, my little raven black bird?"

"I wish I was thousands of miles from this place. I want to laugh and run across a sunny beach with you. Not sneak around. A peck on the cheek behind the Social Science book stack. A quick squeeze near Humanities. I could write a paper on a catalogue of our courtship."

"It's hard for me too. We're not ashamed. But we have to

behave as if we are. Please, Amy, don't get bitter. Soon our exams will be over. Graduation will be over and we'll have a honeymoon on the Costa Brava." Amy was almost smiling. "We can't feel the warm sands of *these* beaches between our toes," Saimon pulled Amy close to him. "But I promise you, my little Amy, we'll run across the beaches of Spain."

"And no looking around for policemen to spring out like cockroaches from any crack."

"Mr. and Mrs. Zolkov in sunny Spain."

"I didn't even want to think about that. I'm glad your mother approved of me and will let you go to England. But then there's still your father."

"Amy, with him it's not colour. It's religion. You know that. He probably has a good Jewish girl in mind for me."

"I accept that. My mother is anxious to see me leave here. I don't suppose she'll ever sleep easy until I'm safely out of Cape Town."

"I forgot to ask. How did your passport interview go?"

"If Prof. Inskip were handing out acting awards, I could've won it for the acting I did at that interview. I was ever so humble and my mother did herself proud too. She went on about how she kept money from my late father's insurance to send me on this trip and what a good girl I was and how I deserved a nice holiday and I would be back to teach our coloured children. Our schools need good children and teachers. She went on and on. There the old man was, with his broken-down typewriter trying to fill in responses to his set questions: 'What do you know about Communism? Do you belong to any banned organization? Why are you going? How long will you stay? How much money have you got?'"

"You're not serious, are you? All those questions just to get a passport?"

Amy sat still a second or two. It struck her that Saimon really knew very little of the life of coloureds. Very little of her life.

"An interview at the main police station, Caledon Square, no less. You ought to have seen the poor old *Boer* trying to type with two fingers. I could hardly keep a straight face."

"A no-laugh pantomime, hey?"

"I wanted to laugh, but couldn't risk one slip. I was desperate for that passport and had to give all the correct responses. There was me, a History major, saying 'Communism? I have no time to read rubbish!' with raised eyebrows and a suitably disgusted expression."

"Why didn't you give him a lecture on the ideological differences between Marx and Lenin?"

"He probably hadn't ever heard of those two gentlemen. I played it straight. I had a good rehearsal. John went for his interview last week. He briefed me. I passed, I guess, because the *Boer* said he would see that I get the passport as soon as I have my return ticket. My mother went to buy it today. I sail on the Windsor Castle seven days after Graduation."

"I don't suppose you realize that I first declared my love to you one year ago today."

"Declared your love, no less. I'll excuse you that quaint expression considering you are busy with a paper on the Romantic Poets. Yes. I do remember being caught on the top gallery behind the History books. I also remember you stared at me a whole year during English II classes."

"But you stared back, you bold hussy."

"You found a timid little black bird behind the bold hussy."

"Not timid. Bold and ready to hold on to the worm she caught."

"I didn't see the worm putting up any fight. He was only too willing to be carried off to be devoured."

"I do believe there is something metaphysical about that image, or is it a metaphor?"

"A final year English student, doubting his images and metaphors?"

"Gosh. It's time for our lecture. We'll have a lecture on Revenge Tragedy if our dear Prof. remembers his topic."

"You go first. I'll follow later. I can't face any suspicious looks from our librarian."

"Will you be back here this afternoon?"

"No. I'll see you tomorrow in my History tutor's office. She'll give me a key. I don't want us to meet here anymore. I feel we're being watched. Kristina says to watch out for Mr. Alex."

"Mr. Alex?"

"You know him. The coloured man who sits at the back of the class."

"Oh yes, that old man. What about him?"

"Don't you wonder why he's taken six years for a three-year course?"

"I know he's been around a long time, but judging by the questions he asks, I didn't wonder why he took two years for each course."

"That's all part of his act. Do you know what his major is? He's a government agent. Kristina told me. She should know. You know who her father is, don't you?"

"Yes. Chief of Police. But I also think you mustn't imagine surveillance. He's probably here to report on the political opinions of the students."

"No, Saimon. I'm not going to take a chance on that. Even if it's not Mr. Alex watching us, I feel somebody is."

"Okay. We'll be careful."

"Remember my History tutor's office tomorrow."

"See you then. Don't forget the big ball. Save a few dances for me. The last dance. I'll catch Kristina later. See her after class. Kolbe House at eight. Don't fly away."

"Stomp on any cockroaches you see."

John and Amy joined the other students gathered around the two fountains in the centre of the ballroom. Every year the engineering students rigged up a unique way of serving the wine. The previous year a big steam engine puffed away burning brandy. After the remarks about the waste, the planning committee promised to make every drop available for drinking. This year they had constructed two fountains – one spouting red wine and the other white wine. Mugs hung around the base of each fountain. Although John and Amy were as intrigued as the other students by the beautiful fountains, they were both more interested in trying to locate Saimon and Kristina.

Amy wore a long yellow organza sheath dress. Huge butterfly sleeves were an eye-catching feature. She had tied her waist-length black curls together at the nape of her neck with a big yellow bow. She wore no make-up and no jewellery. She was aware that she was getting second glances from many of the men.

"Ladies and Gentlemen, dinner is served. Stand not on the order of your seating, but be seated or words to that effect. As a Law student I'm allowed to misquote Shakespeare," boomed out Bertram Davidson, the President of the Roman Catholic Students' Union.

Katrina and Saimon sat at the other end of the table from John and Amy. Neither couple paid much attention to the speeches and food. They waited for the dancing to begin.

"As President of the Union, I wish to welcome all members and friends. Tonight we say farewell to Father McInnis who helped to keep Kolbe House truly Catholic and not just Roman Catholic. This is the only place at the University of Cape Town where everybody, regardless of colour and creed can mix freely. As we are here for festivities, I don't intend making a political speech, but I would like everybody to be reminded of the great-ness of Kolbe House. As a non-white on this campus, I know what it feels like to pay recreation fees for tennis courts and swimming pools I'm not allowed to use. Not to be welcomed at the Freshmen's Ball because my colour denies me the right to a ticket. So I wish to propose a toast to Kolbe House, Father McInnis, and all true Catholics among us."

"Hear, hear. Long live Kolbe."

"I wish to thank all our friends for their continued support. Now to the dancing."

John and Amy hurried to the ballroom and swung into a quick-step. Although they had to continue to be absorbed in each other, both looked around for Saimon and Kristina. Although Kolbe House boasted its liberal attitudes, all the mixed couples knew they had to tread softly. Spies and cock-roaches hide in cracks.

"Good evening, Kristina, Saimon. Glad you could make it. Hope you enjoy yourselves. As a Roman Catholic member with a Baptist partner, I would like to welcome my Jewish friend with his Dutch Reformed partner. As our President said – a truly Catholic gathering. Could I have the next dance with your lovely partner?"

"Only if I'm allowed a dance with your lovely partner."

Amy floated in Saimon's arms totally oblivious to anybody or anything around her. To be held by him for such a long time sent a chill of fear and excitement through her.

"What's that shiver for? Not scared again? You look so beau-tiful, I can't bear to see you hanging on John's arm. That was the longest dinner I've ever had to sit through. I don't know what I ate."

"John is jealous of Katrina on your arm and so am I and I daresay Katrina doesn't like me with John – but we have to fool the cockroaches."

"Kolbe House will be seeing a lot of us. I've agreed to join a symposium on Comparative Religions next week. They might convert me yet."

"I'm glad you'll be there. I offered to help Francis with the catering. See you there."

"John invited Katrina and me to join the two of you on a tour of the grounds in half-an-hour. It's the best time to go into the woods to see Father McGeown's ghost."

Amy became vaguely aware of other couples dancing around her. Some of them she had suspected of going together. She felt safer, knowing there were others like her and Saimon, but she could never shake off the deep fear of knowing what the penalty was if she and Saimon were ever caught.

Saimon returned a dazed Amy to John.

"Saimon, Katrina has agreed to view the ghost. We'll meet you on the back verandah. Meanwhile the key word is, circulate. Nobody sticks to his partner so move around. Don't forget to stomp the cockroaches!"

The game had to be played convincingly. Each one had to appear to be completely unattached and ready to play the field. Katrina and Amy did not see John and Saimon during the next hour. They were constantly claimed for one dance after the other.

"Time for a breath of fresh air, Amy," John announced when he returned. "The ghost will be walking soon. Not scared I hope?"

Saimon watched John and Amy leave the ballroom hand in hand. He caught the pained expression on Katrina's face.

"We can go out the front door and walk around the side of the house. There seem to be many interesting nooks to explore," said Saimon as he led Katrina outside.

Chinese lanterns swung in the breeze on the front verandah. Bright coloured lights glowed in the two big oak trees at the gate. Katrina and Saimon were anxious to get out of the light to the dark side of the house.

"A bit spooky this old house. I won't venture upstairs," remarked Katrina.

"Won't venture upstairs. A little spooky. But willing to see Father McGeown's ghost walking in the woods?"

"I'm not afraid when I'm with John."

"Thanks, kind lady. I thought all women felt protected in my presence."

"Be serious. You know what I mean. In case I forget – thanks for escorting me here. It means so much to get to be alone with John."

"No thanks necessary, Katrina. That score is even. You and John – Amy and me."

Saimon and Katrina wondered who was left in the ballroom since they seemed to stumble over one couple after another, until their eyes got used to the dark. The back of the house was not lit at all.

"Thought you'd eloped with my girl. Amy is no company out here under the stars when all she talks about is Saimon, her man," John teased. "We four have to go into the woods together and then we can pair off. Saimon, you'll have to watch for a light in that top window. It's Father McInnis' signal for every-body to return to the ballroom. I'll escort Amy back in, okay?"

"Thanks, John. Long live Kolbe. Come, my little black bird, off to the woods to build a nest."

"Stomp the cockroaches," John and Saimon chorused as they parted company ... seven years imprisonment...offence to conspire to commit an act ...

    conspire to ...

        conspire to ...

            offence ...

––––––––

Amy approached the gate at the Table Bay Yacht Basin with outward defiance. She gave an extra tug at the turban she had tied around her head to hide her long curls. She hoped her old, lace-up brown brogues looked shabby enough. She made certain that her floral overall was longer than her coat. Although she never smoked, this afternoon she dangled a cigarette from the corner of her disguise, but she could not relax until she was past the guard and on the yacht.

"Where do you think you're going? No hawkers allowed here. What're you selling? I have to inspect that basket," the guard growled at Amy.

"No, Baas, I'm not selling nothing. Young Master Zolkov's having a party tonight on the boat. I have to clean up the rooms and prepare the table."

"They usually send their houseboy. And they always let me know who's coming."

"The boy is busy at the house. The old Master and Madam is having a dinner. I work by the family next door. I said I would help Young Master Zolkov. Which boat is it?"

"The white and blue one second on the left. I'll have to ask Mr. Zolkov not to forget to let me know who's coming to the party. Security is my job."

"Yes, Baas. You do you job good."

Amy lifted her basket and tried to seem not too eager to get to the boat. As she reached the gangway, she noticed Saimon sunbathing on deck. She hoped he would not laugh at her disguise.

"Master Saimon. Security wants to know about your guests tonight," she shouted. She made certain the guard heard.

"Go tell him I'll be down later with the list. He was at lunch when I came through," Saimon shouted back, hardly looking at Amy.

She did not really want to face the guard again but she had to obey her "Master Saimon."

When Amy returned, Saimon had gone below. As she descended the stairs into the galley, Saimon doubled up with laughter.

"I'll close my eyes and open my arms. I think I could kiss you if I keep my eyes closed."

"No, Master Saimon, no kisses. I have to go up and clean the deck. I don't want the Security to worry. No, no, Master Saimon, don't forget about the Immorality Act. If the police catch you kissing a coloured girl who will be arrested?" Amy acted the shocked servant pushing off her boss's advances. "Patience, Saimon. I have to clean the decks first. The guard might come around to see what's happening. I'll have to keep on my beautiful outfit."

Amy collected the bucket of water and brooms and clattered up the stairs. She set to work with loud mumblings about having to waste her time cleaning when all those wild young people would only be messing everything with wine tonight.

Saimon returned from his talk with the Security Officer and started up the engine.

"Hey, Master Saimon, I'm not working on no moving boat. I don't swim. Where're you going?" Amy tried to sound indignant.

"I'm taking it around to False Bay to meet the Shapiros. You can work on the way."

"Master Saimon, your mother said nothing about no trip. I'll work inside while we go. No big wave is gonna knock me off the top. I'm going to ask for danger money." Amy shouted as she hurried below. She collapsed on the nearest bunk, grateful that she need no longer play a role.

"Shouldn't you be navigating this vessel, Master Saimon? We can't risk running aground."

"Don't worry. Zolly is at the helm. He was in the shower when you arrived so you didn't notice. Now don't get upset. Zolly has known about us even before I was brave enough to approach you. He has a girl-friend of colour too (as our Prime Minister says). Zolly knows how we feel."

Amy stiffened for a moment but then relaxed as Saimon pulled off the turban.

"Let's get the real Amy out from under all this. Everything off – including that hideous lipstick."

Saimon took off Amy's overall, while she untied her shoes. Both shivered with excitement. Amy wore a bikini under her overall. As soon as Saimon got the overall off, he started kissing her all over.

"I still have to remove my hideous lipstick, remember?"

"To hang with the lipstick. We've waited too long to be together like this. We've waited. A whole year sneaking kisses behind book stacks and accidental hand brushing. This is our day."

"Slowly. Have you forgotten the Roman Catholic Students' Ball? What happened under the willow between a certain Jew and a Baptist?"

"We're alone here and nothing to stop us."

"Police patrol in boats too. I can't help feeling a little afraid."

"Zolly will signal long before any Coast Guard can come near."

Saimon had removed the top of her bikini. Amy instinctively pulled her long, black curls over her breasts. Even if she was in love with Saimon and knew she wanted him to touch her, all the guilt of her strict Baptist upbringing caused her to stiffen in his embrace.

"I'm sorry, Saimon. I'm just too scared. No. I can't think straight: guilt, fear, love. I want you. But I'm scared to go all the way. Let's just stop right now. I'm bound to mess things up. Saimon, please don't be angry. We can wait another three months. London doesn't seem so far off. Graduation – London – us together without fear. Right now I'm scared stiff and that's not how I want the first time to be. Please under-stand."

"Speech over? We've had all the academic discussions about your virginity. I respect your views. So relax, little Amy. I'll know when to stop. Just let's enjoy what we can of each other."

Amy relaxed as best she could with half an ear open for a Coast Guard whistle.

"Time to stop, Saimon. Have you forgotten the Shapiros don't know about us? Can't take any chances. I'd better get into my work clothes and finish the cleaning."

"Okay. You get the food and table organized. I'll check everything above."

"Yes, Sir. Right, young Master Saimon."

———

Maximum penalty for illicit carnal intercourse between whites and non-whites increased to seven years' imprisonment ... also an offence to conspire ...

———

"A gathering of the penguins," Amy bounced into Miriam's room. There were eight others in the room, all trying to freshen up their make-up and comb their hair. All wore white dresses and black graduation gowns.

"What a day! I thought the graduation ceremony would never end. Especially as I was almost last. Miriam and Saimon Zolkov bringing up the rear."

"Although Amy Abrahams went up first, I just wanted it to be all over. I only waited to see you and Saimon," Amy remarked.

"I looked at that piece of neatly rolled-up paper and couldn't believe that that was what the three years of slogging was all about."

"The great anti-climax is what graduation is all about," remarked another girl.

"Maybe we will all feel less cynical tomorrow."

"Tomorrow, tomorrow. I wonder how I will feel after tonight," Amy thought out aloud.

"Cheer up, Amy. What about three weeks from tomorrow?" Miriam tried to be cheerful. "By the way, Linda, what did Prof. Smit find to talk about at dinner? You hung on his every word," Miriam added trying to distract attention from Amy and her problems.

"He invited me to see his etchings."

"That old line!" chorused all the girls.

"Miriam, why has Saimon decided to fly to London this evening instead of Sunday?"

"Yes. Isn't that a sudden change?"

"Nothing sudden or sinister. The 10:30 tonight makes it more convenient for my uncle to meet him tomorrow evening instead of Monday. We'd better join the rest of the party now," Miriam replied.

"I'll be out in a moment. I need to repair my slip strap. Do you have a little pin for me, Miriam?" asked Amy.

"Be right with you. I'll take everybody else in first to meet Mummy and Daddy."

Amy sat down at the dressing table recalling the day's events. Graduation, lunch with the English Faculty, tea with the German Faculty, dinner with the History Faculty and now Saimon's farewell. Such a short one.

"Now let's fix that non-existent broken slip strap. Since I'm soon to be your big sister, you might as well use my shoulder to cry on," Miriam spoke as she came into the room.

"Do you think that we're panicking for nothing. Saimon and I haven't been alone at any time for the past two weeks. Do you think the police are still suspicious? Must he leave tonight? Can't the 10:30 go without him? Will he be waiting for me in London?"

"Amy, you know you can't take any chances. You'll only be separated for three weeks. We have our spies too. We've been assured that the police are on to your involvement with Saimon."

"I'm sure Kristina told her father when John broke off with her. She's so bitter against coloureds now. The Chief of Police's daughter crazy about coloureds!"

"No. It's not Kristina. She's also meeting John overseas. The break-off was a front."

"So who could have spied on us? Oh, yes I know. It's that old man, Mr. Alex. He told me he was a Government Investigation Officer. 'A fancy name for a spy,' I said. I'm sure I made him angry. You know the one that has been at 'varsity goodness knows how long and nobody can figure out what his major is. How long does it take for a major in spying to graduate?"

"Amy there's no use upsetting yourself like this. You are wasting precious time. Let's join the party. Saimon leaves here for the airport in two hours. Don't you want to be near him?"

"I'm sorry, Miriam. Parting is such sweet sorrow and yet I can't say goodbye till it be morrow. We won't even be alone before he leaves."

"Cheer up. Good news. Join the party, then we can slip away down to the end of the garden to Isaac's studio. I'll show you his latest canvas until Saimon can get away."

"You mean Isaac has decided to accept me into this family?"

"Everybody is batting for you. Saimon wants to tell Daddy tonight, but I think he shouldn't. Mummy also wants him to wait until after the wedding. Daddy will accept the deed done."

"I'm ready to join the mob." Amy bit back some tears. She hurried over to the bar. A drink would be something to hang onto. Only when she reached the bar, did she notice Saimon there. A slight panic made her pull up short. Above all, she must avoid obvious contact with him. There could be a spy at the party. Now she was face to face with him, she had to behave as casually as possible.

"Glad to see you here. I didn't know whose party you were going to first. Did you hear I'm leaving for London this evening?"

"Miriam told me. She told me to come here first. I've three

other parties tonight. Mine is tomorrow. We'll have a week of parties if I survive tonight."

"You can drink my health at some of those parties. I'll be busy with interviews. I hope I get into Cambridge."

"I thought you were going to get a job on your uncle's newspaper."

"No. He wants me to study at a British University for at least a year first."

Amy had heard this all before, but she and Saimon had got used to this special casual public conversation.

"I have to go now. I see Miriam signalling to me. She's going to show me Isaac's new painting. I'm so excited. If you have to go before I get back in, I wish you all the best. Good luck in England. I'll be in England in three weeks' time. Might bump into you at Speakers' Corner or the Tower of London. One never knows," Amy threw over her shoulder as she hurried to join Miriam.

Amy did not really see any of the pictures. It seemed like hours before Saimon came.

"No, Miriam. No need for all the lights. Light the lamp," Saimon suggested.

"I'll light some candles instead."

As soon as one candle was lit, Miriam switched off the lights and hurried back to the house.

"My little Amy Abrahams. Three weeks hence, little Amy Zolkov." Saimon held her close. "Shaking all over as usual. Still. Quiet, little black bird."

"I'm trying not to cry. Tonight one-and-a-half hours and then nothing. Nothing for three weeks. Saimon, you're sure you'll be waiting for me?"

"Don't doubt me now, Amy. Our love is the only thing that has meaning in this crazy country. My eyes can tell colours apart, but not my heart."

"I wish I could fly away tonight too. I'm so very, very scared."

"Come here. Sit on the floor. Can't cast shadows on the windows then."

"You're still scared too, aren't you, Saimon? Just hold tight. I don't want you to let go of me."

Amy responded to Saimon's kisses as she had never done before. For the first time she wanted to give herself to him completely. She took off her graduation gown and spread it on the floor.

"Tonight I can't believe in my Baptist doctrine. I might never see you again. I can't help feeling as if you're going off to war. You might be killed on duty. Separation. Death. It's the same."

"I'll be waiting. I'll be at Southampton when the Windsor Castle docks. My wife."

Saimon blew out the candles then returned to their place on the floor.

"Come here, my wife."

"Yes. Your wife. I'll be that tonight. I'm not scared anymore. We can stay in this studio for an hour at the most and you're not going to forget this hour ever."

"Promises. Promises."

Amy stopped any further remarks from him by kissing him. She wrapped her tongue around his. Tickled his palate. Ran her tongue along his gums. Gently sucked his tongue into her mouth.

"I'm not dreaming still, am I? My little Amy, you do surprise me."

"I'd better stop, if you object."

"More. More..."

"Well, I must live up to the idea of being a hot, black woman. Isn't that why you fell for me? For the promises?" Amy tried to be flippant.

"Amy, my Amy, I love you. We don't have time for analysis now. Don't ever forget I love you – not because of colour. I love you – you the person – my little black bird."

"Deep down I know that. Sometimes I just can't think it's all true. I believe in my love for you. Yes. I do believe in your love."

Saimon ran his fingers over her face and down her arms. Clasped her hands between his and kissed each cheek. Soon Amy had discarded her white dress and Saimon was in his underwear. Amy felt free, but still afraid to enjoy her freedom. "I'm frightened. Will it hurt? I want you. I'm not cheap. I love you. Love you … love you. Don't hurt me."

"You know I'll be gentle." Saimon suddenly became very quiet as he tried to make certain he had not heard some movement outside.

"Somebody's outside, isn't there?" Amy could hardly get the words out.

"No. It's just the dog. Relax, Amy, relax."

Amy lay still for a few moments to reassure herself that there was nobody out there.

"You have to relax, little bird. There will be some pain when I go in, but not much if you relax."

"Pain. A sweet pain. I want to be your wife tonight. You believe me, don't you?" Amy tried to reassure herself. She had been running her tongue over his body but stopped suddenly. "I don't know now though. Perhaps we should wait another three weeks," Amy mused for a second or two. "No. No. It's right for it to be now. You love me? Don't you? Saimon?"

Saimon sat up because he thought he had heard some steps on the gravel. He crawled over to the window, tried to peer outside. He could see the party guests in the house and on the porch dancing, eating and laughing.

"Nobody anywhere near here. Miriam will see to that. I see her on the porch."

Saimon and Amy settled back on their spot. Amy felt the need to keep talking. "Wait until you're married. The man will lose respect for you." She pictured her mother giving her that oft-repeated advice. "If he loves you, he'll wait. You have to be extra certain, remember he might be playing a trick on a coloured girl. They use you, but they marry their own kind." Amy recalled her mother's very earliest remarks. Does he really love me? She lay with her legs tight together, but as he rolled onto her, he pushed them apart without resistance from her. She was not going to allow herself to be haunted. Saimon was in no hurry. He wanted Amy to be at ease. The music from the party drifted down to them. They were far from the crowd. They had time just to explore each other.

Saimon was ready. He thrust, deep. Beautiful pain. Amy yelled. Flashlights. Flashlights through the window. The door kicked open. Lights … more lights. Saimon and Amy lay in the middle of a sea of brilliant lights. Their world caving in around them. Two very tiny people viewed by giants in boots. Lights. Policemen everywhere like cockroaches. Even more lights. More cockroaches.

Saimon could hear his mother and Miriam screaming down the path. The music from the party drifted on. Saimon tried to wrap Amy in the cloak as he grabbed his clothes.

———

The shiny 10:30 South African Airways bird left for London on time. One passenger did not make it.

ISABEL
HUGGAN

SAWDUST

Eros is often depicted as a pudgy, rosy-cheeked, winged, and mischievous baby boy who shoots his arrows through St Valentine cards. Perhaps in the belief that Eros is essentially as innocent as a child, we have wishfully imagined that the messy clumsiness of first love might be otherwise; that if a young couple were isolated from the perversions of society and returned to pristine Arcadia, they would find, all by themselves, a primordial erotic innocence. In 1747, the French playwright Marivaux wrote a comedy, La Dispute, *in which a young boy and a young girl are placed on a desert island by curious adults wishing to observe their discovery of the true nature of love. In 1908, the English novelist Henry Stacpoole retold a version of the story in* The Blue Lagoon, *which Hollywood twice made into a film. The possibility of the innocent pleasures of love is still, apparently, an appealing notion.*

For Isabel Huggan, who so carefully followed the erotic awakening of a young girl in The Elizabeth Stories, *our adult fear overrides any appeal this notion might have. Paradoxically, even though we like to think of Eros as young, we are seldom inclined to allow the young to explore Eros. As a child, I was given the infamous nineteenth-century German children's book called* Struwwelpeter. *Each double page contained a rhymed story with a moral lesson: the little girl who was burnt to death because she played with matches, the little boy who became a skeleton because he wouldn't eat his soup. Most terrifying of all, to me, was the story of the child who, in spite of his mother's prohibition, persisted in the erotic pleasure of sucking his thumbs. One day, as he was busy enjoying himself, a diabolical tailor with huge scissors appeared suddenly and, as a punishment, snipped off his thumbs. I still remember the drops of blood dripping from the cuts, and how this image pursued me through countless terrible dreams.*

———————

I'VE HAD WARM, tingling feelings between my legs for as long as I can remember. One of my earliest, most vivid memories is being made to stand penitent at my grandmother's knee, made to tell her what awful indignities I had performed upon the teddy she'd given me only months before for my third birthday. It was Easter, and her front parlour was cold with damp April chill. There was a pot of lilies on a lace-covered window and I could smell their perfume as I waited for her wrath.

"You rub it? Where?" She glared down at me, having been coached in the questions to this catechism by my parents. "We've simply got to get her to stop," they must have said. "Maybe if *you* shame her."

"There, Nana," I remember saying, and pointed quickly to my plump little crotch, hidden away beneath layers of cotton and velvet. Hoping that, somehow, she would smile. Maybe she did this secret thing, too, and would say, "Oh, how nice. I'm sure teddy doesn't mind." But no such luck. There were white-faced intakes of breath, there were slappings and scoldings and tears, and the forbidding of any candy eggs, before or after supper.

The withholding of candy was old hat to my grandmother. She would always proffer her tray of Black Magic with the reminder, as my hand hovered by the liquid cherry, "You may have any but the soft centres. Your Nana loves the soft centres." And my resigned teeth would fasten on some terrible toffee she'd offer me, or clamp down on a chewy nougat for what seemed hours. I still hate hard centres, and find them, with their dreadful inedible interiors concealed beneath sweet chocolate, a shock and a cheat.

Teddy was confiscated as punishment and replaced in my private activities by other furry dolls. I knew now it was a bad thing I did, yet oddly enough my name for the rubbing and ensuing sensation was a particularly open and public one. I called it "greeting," and I have no idea what series of connective leaps my mind must have made to arrive at that. But greeting it was, and I would greet myself before sleep, my loneliness temporarily allayed.

By the time I turned five, greeting was no longer a solitary pursuit but involved either the observation or participation of Joyce and Sharon and Dennis and Dieter and Rudy. In those months before kindergarten, we'd be put in our yards to play during the mornings, and eventually there'd be a gathering in one spot or another and then a trek to the large vacant lot that backed onto my side of Brubacher Street. Along one edge of the field stood a row of poplars whose heavy low branches afforded easy access to more lofty places from which scouts could look out for mothers. Beside the trees lay the collapsed remains of a wooden bread waggon, abandoned by old man Kenny once he got rid of his horse and bought himself a real delivery truck. The waggon was dark brown with BREAD painted in gold on each side and with gilt scrolling around the edges. A square box of a waggon, not unlike a loaf itself. Inside there were three rows of shelves on either side of the door where the hot loaves would sit on their trip from bakery to table. There was just enough room on a shelf for one child to lie down, and so there we'd lie, stacked like loaves, greeting ourselves and giggling.

It was dark in the waggon except for the shaft of light cut by the door, and there was a heavy yeasty smell that must have engrained itself in the wood over the years. It was a comforting smell, not unlike the smell of life itself, sweat and skin and breathing.

There was a security and safety in that companionable place, as if by playing like this together we achieved mass absolution for our sins. God only knows who first suggested the activity or how we all came to trust each other. I can't remember. But it was Rudy and I who first took off our clothes and felt each other's bodies with exploring fingers. Once, at the end of the summer before we went off to school for the first time, I took off my cotton sundress and he his shorts and shirt, and we lay together on one of the shelves, first squeezed side by side and then with him on top of me. I can feel the heat inside the waggon, and the weight of his body on mine, and how we just lay very still.

Our mothers must have assumed that we played "store" or "house" inside the bread waggon, and so could not understand our dismay the following spring when the trees were chopped down and the waggon removed and the field cleared to make way for the new Pentecostal church. They were upset themselves, but about the noise and dirt of construction, and about the threat to the neighbourhood's tone. Except for the Roman Catholic Falconers on the corner, everyone on Brubacher Street was United Church or Lutheran, and the prospect of fundamentalist fervour on their doorstep made them nervous. My father, who had been chief among those trying to block the land sale by tightening the zoning laws, ranted for weeks. "Just one hallelujah," he'd say. "Just one hallelujah comes floating out one window and I go to council. Disturbing the peace."

What most infuriated my father was that he had been powerless to stop the deal in the first place, because there had been no need for the Pentecostals to go through his bank or any bank – they had paid Mr. Myers, who owned the land, cash. "Cash, Mavis," he'd say to my mother at dinner during those trying days. "Where have those holyrollers got that kind of money from? Nobody has cash these days." I listened to these conversations intently, my mind a guilty welter of questions. What would happen to a church built on such a wicked spot?

My father was manager of the Imperial, which was the only bank in Garten if you didn't count the trust company or the farmers' co-op. And my father certainly didn't count them. He had a pride and dignity that came from his absolute assurance that his was the only game in town. In all but wet and snowy weather he walked to and from the bank each day, and I think his motivation rose not from love of exercise but of being viewed. He had the idea that people should respect him, and so strong was his notion that there came a kind of validity on the heels of his vanity. He dressed in navy and his heavy tubular body filled out his suits so exactly that there was never excess fabric to make a wrinkle or unwanted crease. Even in the way his brown hair was clipped close to his bullet-shaped head there was a precision that seemed evidence of his profession. His stance, his measured speech all said, "Yes, I am a man who deals with money. I cannot afford to make mistakes. Banking is not a career for the careless."

Rudy's father, on the other hand, didn't look like what he was at all. Butchers in nursery rhyme pictures are slightly porcine in build, with suety fingers and bright beefy cheeks. But Mr. Shantz was small and pale and dry, with a sharp, ferrety face. He wore a white apron with long string ties that wound around him twice and knotted at the front, and he seemed able to slice and saw through hunks of meat and bone without ever spattering himself for he was always clean, pristine. Only when I found a row of fresh aprons, hanging on nails just inside the back room, was the mystery of his marvellous neatness solved. The day of that discovery was to change his life, and mine, forever.

The church was built within a year of the land sale, and the field of tall grass was replaced by the plainest of low brick buildings. The bread waggon would probably have lain unused even if it had been there, for once we entered civilized society we became self-conscious beings. Now we learned to jeer and sneer at each other's sex and, by the end of Grade 1, joined the other children in the playground game of Girls After Boys, or Boys After Girls.

The game was simply a variety of tag, in which opposing teams took turns chasing each other, the object being to catch and drag prisoners to a base, the enormous sandbox in the middle of the yard. Years ago pines had been planted at each corner of the box, and now stood at least 30 feet high, shading the sand so that the centre was always cool and damp and dark. Prisoners were guarded there by the less swift members of the offensive side until the recess bell rang. Then there would be a counting and marking down of the number on the side of the box. Then, in the next recess, there'd be a switching of position, and the chasing and catching would have an extra zest springing from revenge. Day after week after month it went on, wavering only now and again for skipping and baseball or skating and snow-forts. It was a merciless game with only the most unpleasant sexual overtones – kisses were given as the gravest humiliation, and retaliation was inevitable. The kisser's face would be pushed down into the sandbox during the following recess.

Rudy and I played with as much vigour as any, and if we caught each other were as rough and mean as the rules demanded. Yet periodically we would play with each other after school, returning to our touching and feeling games of the bread waggon days. It was a secret thing now, to which we never invited the other children.

It was at his house we played this way because his mother was often down at the shop tending the cash register. She was just as small and dry and neat as her husband, as unlikely a butcher's wife as she was the mother of four boys. Rudy was the youngest, and shared a bedroom with his eldest brother who was seven years older and never home after school. The other brothers had a room down the hall where they built model train sets and made engine noises. They were a couple of grades ahead of us and treated us with disdain, knowing that there was nothing we could ever think of to do that would interest them.

What we thought of to do was to take off our clothes and stand before the enormous oval mirror on the dressing-table, and examine our nakedness together. My body was smooth and round, heavy and thickened from waist to knees like all the women in my father's family. But I had the creamy skin of my mother, and her heart-shaped face and surprising blue eyes. Mine were magnified by my glasses, which I had to keep on during this game or else our reflections blurred into unrecognizable beige.

Rudy was thin and dark with lovely moles dotting his skin all over. He had a long, thoughtful face and heavy straight hair that fell forward over his forehead. He would place his finger between the folds of my vulva and I would feel the bunchy, ruffled skin of his scrotum and we'd laugh when his penis would nod its approval. It was a strange, disembodied curiosity we felt, quite divorced from the clothed selves we ordinarily were. Sometimes we would return to the greeting of our early explorations, and sit, each on a separate bed, touching our own bodies until there were small explosions of pleasure leaping up from our hands.

Once Otto, the brother who shared the room, came home unexpectedly. We heard his entry, and his feet landing heavily on the stairs as he came up three steps at a time. Rudy always locked the door when we were there, and within seconds Otto was rattling the handle, saying, "Look, you little bugger, let me in!" Rushing, rushing, pulling on our clothes, all the while Rudy arguing back. "It's my room too, you know" and "I can lock the door if I want" and "just cause you're older doesn't mean I have to do what you say." Rudy holding the door handle until I had my ribbed stockings fastened in their garters, and had scattered a few comic books around to make it look as if we'd been reading. Feeling scared, and amazed at my own guile. Otto, when the door opened, looked suspiciously around and said, "What are you two little buggers up to?" but was too intent on his own business to care.

But that frightened us, and we stopped. And even in the closed world of Brubacher Street there began to be an unease between us. We were growing older and guilt, even shared guilt, made us awkward instead of intimate. Our childhood was passing, but all we knew was that there was no more safety, anywhere. In the game of Boys After Girls, Rudy would purposely bang my head on the wooden sides of the sandbox whenever he'd drag me in, prisoner. And when it was my turn, if I could grab him, which was rare because I was seldom fast enough, I would dig my fingernails into his arm, trying to bruise or mark him in some way. He had forsaken me and I would get him back if I could.

By the time we were ten, Rudy always played with boys after schools and we hardly ever walked home together. But in the spring we were both on the class spelling team, and often had to stay late for drills. On those days we'd go along together and sometimes stop by the meat store to get a few slices of summer sausage from Mr. Shantz to eat on the way home.

One afternoon in April, two or three weeks before the big spelling contest, we left the school together and Rudy said, "We have to go by downtown. I have to go to the shop." And I said, "But it's Wednesday, stupid," since Wednesday was half-day closing in Garten.

"I know, dummy," he said, "but my Dad is going to pay me 50¢ every week if I go in and do a cleaning. If you want to come, you can help."

"Do I get half then?" I asked, knowing I'd go whether or not he ever gave me a quarter. I had a deep sense of loyalty to Rudy, and a belief that our lives would be connected forever. Because we had begun our lives together, I thought we would probably marry when we grew up. We were perfectly matched, the same age and height, and were equally good in school, although sometimes he was a better speller. Just that afternoon he had spelled "interregnum" right after I missed it.

When we reached the store we ran down the side alley and around the back, and Rudy drew a key out of his shoe and unlocked the door. Something in that action made my heart race with excitement. He'd had that key in his shoe all day long and I hadn't even known. What else might he have hidden I couldn't see?

Inside, the smell of sawdust and blood filled our nostrils. I had never been in the back before and the odour was stronger there. Rudy showed me the cold locker where sides of beef and pork hung on large hooks, and a freezer where pale plucked chickens were mounded in rows. On the walls there were all kinds of calendars, pink girls in low dresses holding red roses, fluffy dogs on blue velvet cushions, autumn wildernesses and smiling babies. Wonderful photographs that kept me walking around the room looking at them all. And then I came to the six hooks by the door, and the clean white aprons hanging there. I turned to tell Rudy I'd always wondered how his father kept so spotless, but he had had enough of my wandering. "You do the shelves in the shop," he ordered, "and I'll do the floor."

I went out round the glass-faced counter to where cans of stew and jars of horseradish were arranged on side shelves along the walls. I dusted and stacked, and shone up the cash register. The room was a shady green colour because the front blinds were down and I felt the kind of calm you do in a summer forest. I could hear Rudy sweeping in the back, and it seemed such a cheerful sound. We were working together, just like his mother and father did.

He came into the shop then, cleaning the floor behind the counter, gathering up the old sawdust and sprinkling fragrant new shavings everywhere. All the enamel trays of shiny purple kidneys and liver, of fat-speckled chuck and repulsive sweet-breads, had been put away in the refrigerator at noon when Mr. Shantz closed up. All that was left in the display case was sausage. Rudy slid open the door and reached in for a large salami. With a daring I envied, he turned on the slicing machine and held the hard sausage up to the blade until there was a pile of mottled slices on the metal plate.

I came round to where he stood without invitation and he divided the pile so we each had a handful of the spicy meat. It was foreign and exciting, the kind of food I never had at home. For although my father's background was German, as it was for many of the people in town, my mother's was English, and she deplored garlic and anything the least bit European as being not quite clean. Still, she shopped at Shantz's store for her weekly roast and bacon, and simply avoided looking at any of the sausages. I, on the other hand, loved those meats with so many flavours you couldn't tell what it was you were tasting as it moved around in your mouth. I stood there chewing the salami, smiling as Rudy put the rest back in the display, fully and completely happy. He turned back toward me then, with an odd smile.

"Do you want to greet?" he said, and the colour rose in his face.

"I don't do that any more," I lied.

"I mean with each other," he said. "Here, on the floor, here. Nobody will ever know. C'mon, Elizabeth, let's." He reached out and touched my waist and such shudders ran through my legs I felt as if he had lifted me up. I didn't know what he meant to do, but the sudden old memory of his soft, hot body on top of mine in the yeasty dark made me want more than anything to capture again that closeness, that secret time.

"Okay," I said, and quickly went down on my knees behind the counter, waiting for what his next move would be.

"Take off your pants," he said, and he began pulling down his own trousers. From under my skirt I took off my pants and bunched them in my hand. "Now lie down," he said, and I lay back in the fresh sawdust, not minding at all that it would coat my clothes and hair. He lay down on me immediately, as if he were shy that I should see his partly naked body. I, who knew his shape and size as well as my own. And yet, it did seem different, not the same at all when he lay on me, and I felt the jutting of his penis against my bare skin. There was an urgency to his squirming on top of me that had never been part of the game before. I felt the first shreddings of female dread, the coming apart of the dream.

"Don't greet so hard," I whispered, and tried to push him away a little bit. All the warm feelings I'd been having had dissipated with the discomfort of being pressed down so heavily. But he wouldn't stop, he kept moving rhythmically on top of me, saying, "Shut up, Elizabeth, shut up."

And of course, no sooner had I begun to wish for some way to stop him than his father came through from the back room. In a suit, without his apron on, he looked even smaller and drier, and his face broke into a bright, angular rage at the sight of his son's naked buttocks. "What are you doing?" he asked, in a voice that was only a throaty gasp. Then, in a shout that sent Rudy reeling against the far wall, "Get up! Get off her! Get up!"

I stayed on the floor and pulled down my skirt, hoping that maybe he hadn't seen there were no pants beneath. I kept the bunched-up pants in my hand behind me. Mr. Shantz was looking at me with a wildness in his eyes like hatred, and I realized afterward how much he must have guessed at that moment what the sequence of events would be. But all I knew then was that I was as guilty as Rudy, and as frightened, but that somehow I was safer than he. I was safer because I was the girl, because he was the boy and had been on top.

Mr. Shantz moved with quick steps across the sawdust toward his shaking son, and raised his arm as he spoke. "Scum!" he rasped, and brought his hand down on the side of Rudy's head. "Scum, worse than scum!" and he hit him again and again. "Put your clothes on, you, you...." Words failed him, and he turned again to me. "You too, Elizabeth, get up, put those panties on."

Humiliation, anger that he had seen all, knew all, made me want to cry and cry. But at my first tremulous sob he reached out and wrenched my arm, pushing me toward the door. "You're okay," he said. "No crying. Get in the truck." I heard Rudy behind me, still pulling his trousers on. "You're going home now, both of you," said Mr. Shantz, and he sounded tired and sad instead of raging the way he had been.

We walked through the cool back room, past the butcher blocks and wrapping-table, slowly, all wishing we could go backwards in time. He must have been wishing, even more than we were, that he had never come back to the shop to see how Rudy was doing with his chores.

He drove us to Brubacher Street in the delivery truck, the three of us crowded together on the narrow bench seat. Afraid to speak or look at each other, Rudy and I stared straight ahead. My mind was busy with detail, wondering how I could possibly turn the events to my advantage once my parents were told. And I had no doubt that Mr. Shantz intended to tell.

But I knew in my heart that no matter what version my parents were given by anyone, it would all be my fault. My mother's view of the universe excluded chance and no matter what tragedy happened to whom, her final statement on the subject would be that they had brought it on themselves. I had an amazing capacity for sins that had the ability to bring on disaster – carelessness, showing off, selfishness, arrogance and what can only be described as innate badness. "Why are you such a bad girl?" my mother would cry. "What have I done to bring this on myself?"

But strangely, this time she had almost nothing to say. She stood at the door untying her flowered apron and folding it into a very small parcel as Mr. Shantz told her, in his harsh, dry voice, that he had found his son attempting to perform an indignity upon my body. He was sure he had prevented anything from actually happening, she was to understand, but nevertheless he thought it was his duty to tell her. Of course there must be no more contact between the children, and he and Mrs. Shantz would deal with Rudy in a severe fashion. Perhaps she and Mr. Kessler would also reprimand Elizabeth since, from what he had seen, she had not been unwilling. I was sent to my room as they finished their conversation in low tones, and told to wait until my father came home.

It was nearly five o'clock and as he always arrived promptly at twenty past, I knew there wasn't long. I was far too terrified now to cry, and stood instead at my dresser, arranging my dolls from many lands into neat rows. I heard the front door close; that was Mr. Shantz going. I wondered if he was going to hit Rudy some more. What frightened me then was what Rudy might say to defend himself. He might tell about all the other times, even the waggon times, and if he did, then there'd be no hope for me. I knew I would be locked in my room forever.

Then I heard the door open again and it was my father. I heard the rush of muttering voices as my mother met him and I heard his growing anger in the way he said "Disgusting!" three times as they were coming up the stairs. Her voice was a constant fret beneath his, supplying the details that brought on his vehemence. My father's skin, when he was really angry, always took on a bluish, nearly metallic cast, and when he entered my room I knew from the heavy, dull glow of his face I was in for a bad time. I began lying immediately, without really meaning to. I said that I had never wanted to lie down, that Rudy had made me, that he had taken off my panties and been very mean to me. I said I didn't understand what he wanted to do, and that no, of course we had never done anything like that before.

"But you must have done something to bring it on," my mother said, the planes of her face focused to an accusing point. "Good girls don't get themselves in situations like this."

"I didn't, I didn't, Mommy! Honestly, it wasn't me, it's not my fault." I cried and whimpered, and lied and lied.

My father seemed much more willing to believe me than my mother did, and he turned his outrage toward the Shantzes.

"And that bastard had the nerve to sit in my office this afternoon and ask for a loan. While his son was...My God! He thinks he'll expand and get into groceries, does he? Well, I'll teach him a lesson, the little weasel."

My mother suddenly shed her harping tone and took on the voice of reason. "Now really Frank, it's hardly Elvin Shantz's fault if his son...." I could feel her still blaming me, and I hated her with a furious hatred, even as I was constricting with fear that a chain of events had been begun that I would be helpless to ever unlink.

"Like father, like son," he said, with a kind of weightiness, secure in aphorism the way he was with interest rates and mortgages. "It must come from somewhere, Mavis."

"And where did your daughter get it then?" she asked, flushed and bitter and oddly aggressive.

"You heard what the child said, it had nothing to do with her. It's all the boy, he's a menace. They've done something wrong in his upbringing, the last child, who knows. I want that family out of town, I want them out." His body seemed to be ballooning, a navy serge sausage filling the doorway of my room. "Leave it to me, Mavis, you tend to Elizabeth here. Leave it to me."

I was taken to the bathroom and told to take a bath, while my mother sat on the toilet seat looking tired and hurt. "I just feel crushed, Elizabeth," she said. "I had really thought you were starting to be a good girl, and now this. Look at the shame you have brought on us, think what you have done." She raised her head and looked at me with the sorrow I knew so well, with eyes that had seen countless disappointments because of me. "Wash between your legs, Elizabeth," she said. "Get yourself clean. Oh, people will hear about this, I know they will. How will I be able to hold my head up in this town again?"

I was made to go to bed then, but was given a fresh flannelette nightgown to wear even though it was the middle of the week and we didn't ordinarily change except on Saturdays. I lay and watched the spring twilight flicker through the venetian blinds, sucking my thumb quietly, with my other hand tucked in my crotch, the way I liked best to go to sleep. I always remembered to remove both hands from their comfortable places just at the moment I felt the most sleepy so there would be no chance of my falling asleep and getting caught. I had never felt so lonely or so unable to soothe myself, and long after my parents had looked in and then gone to bed, I lay in the dark and heard Rudy's voice. "Shut up, Elizabeth, shut up."

In the days that followed I gathered from my parents' coded consultations that revenge was rearing its head and preparing to strike at the Shantzes. My father refused the loan. I heard him tell my mother that "I just said, 'Elvin, we've had a look at your assets and we don't think this is the time for you to expand. It's a tight money situation for everyone now, not only here at the Imperial, if you see what I mean, Elvin.' He saw what I meant, all right. He won't go anywhere else in town for the money."

I didn't really grasp the implications of that conversation until later. What I had to think about at the moment was how to endure the torment of each day at school. My mother had been right – somehow, everyone knew. I think what happened was that my parents spoke to the principal who told our teacher, Miss Cracken, that Rudy and I were no longer to sit near each other in class, and were not to be seen together at recess. Of course, human being that she was, Miss Cracken must have rushed to the staffroom with the news that the Shantz boy had done something indecent to the Kessler girl. And there were probably speculations about what exactly we had done, and some laughter, and in a matter of hours it had all filtered through the school.

By the end of the week there was a rhyme in the playground:

Rudy, Rudy, Rudy Shantz
He took off Elizabeth's pants.

And in Boys After Girls, both sides would shout, "Go after her, Rudy, let's see what you do to her!" Or they'd call to me, "C'mon, Elizabeth, lie down for Rudy!"

On the shed wall behind the school someone wrote in blue chalk "Rudy put it in Elizabeth" and beside the message made a crude drawing of massive, disembodied genitals. Many years later, travelling across North Africa, I came across these same gun-shapes and clam-shapes chalked on walls, but with exotic-looking Arabic inscriptions alongside. I viewed them with the same kind of horror I had back in Garten, unmoved by time or distance from that first awful recognition. But it wasn't like that, no, it couldn't be! The other children from our street must have remembered our shared investigations in the bread waggon, but mutual guilt kept them wisely silent. Or perhaps they really had forgotten, or didn't understand what was happening, as they later claimed.

I cried openly and deserved the taunts of "Sucky-baby" during their teasing. I think I hoped to bring on their pity and consequent kindness if I showed myself to be weak, a tactic it has taken me half a lifetime to learn doesn't pay off. Rudy, on the other hand, became ice itself, able to pass me by as if I were a ghost. I didn't exist for him; he abided by the rules to the letter, and preserved an adult kind of dignity while he did it. I think he probably hated me but there was no way of opening things up to see. I couldn't speak to him because of the rules, and also because I was so alarmed by his aloofness. Did he know how much I had lied? My parents must have repeated those denials to his parents, who would of course have accosted him with these fresh facts: "Elizabeth says you made her do it." What could I do?

Once I passed him a note on a very small piece of paper which I had folded and folded into a tiny ball. I slipped it into his fist as we came out of the classroom one morning on our way to assembly. On it I had written, "I'm sorry. I had to lie." But he took the paper and unfolded it, without reading it, and ripped it into tiny, tiny shreds. And didn't look at me. Wouldn't look at me. I would try to catch his eye in the class all day long but he would always turn away.

We were both taken off the spelling team, which lost quite badly in the school competition. My mother pointed out we had ruined things for the team, that the circles of consequence go out and out and out. Rudy was instructed to go to the butcher shop every day after school, alone. I was most often met by my mother, but occasionally walked home with Dieter and Joyce and Dennis and Celia who had all been told by their mothers not to speak to me. Or so they said.

I thought a lot about dying but no amount of concentration on the blackness in my head seemed to make it possible. Instead, that spring I discovered movie magazines, and in the pages of *Photoplay* and *Screen Lives* I lost myself. I fell in love with Jeff Chandler, whose craggy presence had already mesmerized me at Saturday matinees. I dreamed that he would find me walking alone on a long beach and ask me to come home with him and live with him forever and be a movie star. When I read a story that suggested he had a wife and two daughters, I extended the boundaries of my fantasy to include the family, and we all lived together in the forgiving California sunshine. My mother was appalled by my interest in film stars, and so I kept the magazines in my closet. At night, by flashlight, I would sit beneath my pleated skirts and navy jumpers, thrilling myself with the possibility of escape.

In June, the day after school ended, the Shantz family moved. My parents must have known where they were going but there was no way I could ask. In a peculiar, almost mystic way, Rudy was now a dead person, replaced by Jeff Chandler, whose rough, tender voice now haunted my waking and sleeping life. The family who moved into the Shantz house told my mother that it was spotless, amazing when you considered they'd had four boys living there. My mother implied that they may have been clean but not entirely wholesome and there the subject of the Shantzes was stopped. The butcher shop was taken over by the IGA up the street who eventually bought out three adjoining stores and made a real supermarket.

Several years later, I got up the courage to ask Dieter, who had been Rudy's best friend besides me, whether he knew where they had gone. He said he thought they'd gone to Winnipeg where Mrs. Shantz had some relatives, but he wasn't sure. Nobody had ever heard from Rudy again, he said, not even a postcard or a Christmas card. The kids who knew the older brothers were too far out of my reach and I could never ask any of them about the family's whereabouts.

And so my father was successful and in time the town closed over the space where the Shantzes had been, and they were forgotten. But not by me. I still find Rudy in my thoughts from time to time and wonder if I am ever in his. Once, passing through Winnipeg a few years ago, I found his name in the telephone book. I put a coin in the slot of the pay phone and said, "Hello, this is Elizabeth Kessler, is this the Rudolf Shantz who used to live in Garten?" But it wasn't, or if it was he lied, and said, "No, I'm sorry, you must have the wrong number."

NEIL JORDAN

SEDUCTION

An ex-convict, abandoned by his wife, forbidden to see his daughter, falls in love with a high-class prostitute whom he is employed to chauffeur; she becomes his unattainable ideal, perfect because he cannot ever have her. A young girl, warned by her grandmother to beware all men "whose eyebrows meet and who are hairy inside" comes across a series of seducers, all of whom reveal themselves to be wild wolfish beasts. An Irish revolutionary becomes enraptured with the beautiful girlfriend of the soldier whose death he has caused, only to discover that she is a man. Mona Lisa, The Company of Wolves, *and* The Crying Game *are three films in which Neil Jordan, the Irish writer and film-maker, attempts to capture the elusiveness and ambiguity of desire. This attraction to something that cannot be named is also the subject of his short story, "Seduction."*

The verb "to seduce" carries with it the curious notion of becoming attracted to someone or something that leads us astray. Religious poetry speaks of rapture as the moment in which the soul is seduced by God away from the banalities of our material body. Erotic literature shares this imagery, but instead of relinquishing solid flesh, erotic literature emphasizes it and finds its echoes in the world around us. In Jordan's story, the summer weather, the beach, and the sea anticipate the moment of erotic discovery in which the nameless attraction is allowed to come into being.

Y OU DON'T BELIEVE ME, do you," he said, "you don't believe anything, but I've seen her" – and he repeated it again, but I didn't have to listen this time, I could imagine it so vividly. The naked woman's clothes lying in a heap under the drop from the road where the beach was clumsy with rocks and pebbles, her fat body running on the sand at the edge of the water, the waves splashing round her thick ankles. The imagining was just like the whole summer, it throbbed with forbidden promise. I had been back in the town two days and each day we had hung around till twilight, when the hours seemed longest, when the day would extend its dying till it seemed ready to burst, the sky like a piece of stretched gauze over it, grey, melancholy, yet infinitely desirable and unknown. This year I was a little afraid of him, though he was still smaller than me. I envied and loved his pointed shoes that were turned up and scuffed white and his hair that curled and dripped with oil that did its best to contain it in a duck's tail. I loved his assurance, the nonchalant way he let the vinegar run from the chip bag onto the breast of his off-white shirt. But I kept all this quiet knowing there were things he envied about me too. I think each of us treasured this envy, longing to know how the other had changed but disdaining to ask. We loved to talk in monosyllables conscious of the other's envy, a hidden mutual delight underneath it like blood. Both of us stayed in the same guest-house as last year. My room faced the sea, his the grounds of the convent, the basketball pitch with the tennis-net running through it where the nuns swung rackets with brittle, girlish laughter. We sniffed the smell of apples that came over the town from the monastery orchard behind it and the smell of apples in late August meant something different to me this year, as did the twilight. Last year it would have meant an invitation to rob. I wondered did it mean the same to him. I concluded that it must, with his hair like that. But then he was tougher, more obscene.

"Look, she's coming out now." He nodded his head sideways towards the chip-shop and I stared in through the dripping steamed glass. It looked warm inside, warm and greasy. I saw the woman coming out of the tiny corridor in which the chips were fried, leaning against the steel counter. Some older boys waiting for orders threw jibes at her. She laughed briefly, then took out a cigarette, put it in her mouth and lit it. I knew that when the cigarette came out its tip would be covered in lipstick, the way it happens in films. When she took the coins from them two gold bangles slipped down onto her fat wrist. There was something mysterious, hard and tired about her, some secret behind those layers of make-up which those older boys shared. I watched them laughing and felt the hard excitement of the twilight, the apples. And I believed him then, though I knew how much he lied. I believed him because I wanted to believe it, to imagine it, the nakedness of this fat blonde woman who looked older than her twenty-five years, who sang every Saturday night at the dance in the local hotel.

"Leanche's her name. Leanche the lion."

"Lioness," I said, being the erudite one. He looked at me and spat.

"When'll you ever dry up." I spat too. "Here." He held out the chip bag.

I took one. It was like when I came to the guest-house and he had already been there a day. He stood in the driveway pulling leaves off the rhododendron bush as we took things off the rack of our Ford car. I looked over at him, the same as last year, but with a new sullenness in his face. I hoped my face was even more deadpan. He turned his face away when I looked but stayed still, pulling the oily leaves till the unpacking was finished. Then I went over to talk to him. He said that the town was a dump this year, that there was an Elvis playing in the local cinema. He said that Ford cars with high backs had gone out since the ark. I asked him had his people got a car yet and he said no. But somehow it seemed worse to have a car with a high back and rusted doors than no car at all. He said "Come on, we'll go to the town" and we both walked to the gate, to the road that ran from the pier towards the town where every house was painted white and yellow and in summer was a guest-house.

"Let's go inside" he said, just as it was getting dark and the last of the queue filed from the chipper. "We've no money" I said. "Anyway, I don't believe you." I hoped my fright didn't glare through. "It's true," he said. "The man in the cinema told me." "Did he see her?" I asked. "No, his brother did." There was disdain in the statement that I couldn't have countered.

We pushed open the glass door, he took out a comb as he was doing so and slicked it through his hair. I went over to the yellow jukebox and pushed idly at the buttons "Are ye puttin' money in it son." I heard. I turned and saw her looking at me, the ridiculously small curls of her hair tumbling round her large face. Her cheeks were red and her dress was low and her immense bosom showed white through it, matching the grease-stains on her apron. "No" I said and began to blush to the roots, "we just wanted to know …"

"Have you got the time," Jamie burst in. "Have you eyes in your head," she countered. She raised her arm and pointed to a clock in the wall above her. Twenty past ten.

We had walked past the harbour and the chip-shop and the Great Northern Hotel that were all the same as last year. The rich hotelier's son who had left the priesthood and had gone a little mad was on the beach again, turning himself to let his stomach get the sun now that his back was brown. Jamie told me about the two Belfast sisters who wore nylons and who were Protestants, how they sat in the cinema every night waiting for something. He asked me had I ever got anything off a girl that wore nylons. I asked him had he. He said nothing, but spat on the ground and stirred the spittle with the sole of his shoe. The difference in the town was bigger now, lurid, hemming us in. I borrowed his comb and slicked it through my hair but my hair refused to quiff, it fell back each time on my forehead, incorrigibly flat and sandy-coloured.

The woman in the chip-shop smiled and crooked her arm

on the counter, resting her chin on her fist. The folds of fat bulged round the golden bangles. "Anything else you'd like to know." I felt a sudden mad urge to surpass myself, to go one better than Jamie's duck-tailed hair. "Yeah," I began, "do you …" Then I stopped. She had seemed a little like an idiot to me but something more than idiocy stopped me. "Do I!" she said and turned her head towards me, looking at me straight in the eyes. And in the green irises underneath the clumsy mascara there was a mocking light that frightened me. I thought of the moon with a green mist around it like the Angel of Death in the Ten Commandments. I saw her cheeks and heard the wash of the sea and imagined her padding feet on the sand. And I shivered at the deeper, infinite idiocy there, the lurid idiocy that drew couples into long grass to engage in something I wasn't quite sure of. I blushed with shame, with longing to know it, but was saved by her banging hand on the silver counter. "If you don't want chips, hop it." "Don't worry," said Jamie, drawing the comb through his hair. "Don't worry," I said, listening to his hair click oilily, making for the glass door. "I still don't believe you," I said to him outside. "Do you want to wait up and see then." I didn't answer. Jamie drew a series of curves that formed a naked woman in the window-dew. We both watched them drip slowly into a mess of watery smudges.

We had gone to the cinema that first night, through the yellow-emulsioned doorway into the darkness of the long hall, its windows covered with sheets of brown paper. I smelt the smells of last year, the sweaty felt brass of the seats and the dust rising from the aisle to be changed into diamonds by the cone of light above. There was a scattering of older couples there, there was Elvis on the screen, on a beach in flowered bathing-trunks, but no Belfast sisters. "Where are they?" I asked him, with the ghost of a triumphant note in my voice. He saved himself by taking out a butt, lighting it and pulling harshly on it. We drank in Elvis silently. Later the cinema projectionist put his head between both our shoulders and said "Hey boys, you want to see the projection-room?" His breath smelt the same as last year, of cigarettes and peppermint. But this year we said no.

Later again I sat in my room and watched the strand, where two nuns were swinging tennis-rackets on a court they had scrawled on the sand. It was ten past nine and the twilight was well advanced, the balance between blue and grey almost perfect. I sat on my bed and pulled my knees to my chest, rocking softly, listening to the nuns' tinkling laughter, staring at the billows their habits made with each swing of their arms. Soon even the nuns left and the strand was empty but for the scrawled tennis-court and the marks of their high-heeled boots. But I watched on, hearing the waves break, letting the light die in the room around me, weeping for the innocence of last year.

We pressed ourselves against the wall below the road, trying to keep our feet from slipping off the large round pebbles. My father was calling my name from the drive of the guest-house. His voice seemed to echo right down the beach, seeming worried and sad. Soon even the echo died away and Jamie clambered up and peeped over the top and waved to me that no-one was there. Then we walked down the strand making a long trail of footsteps in the half-light. We settled ourselves behind an upturned boat and began to wait. We waited for hours, till Jamie's face became pinched and pale, till my teeth began to chatter. He stared at the sea and broke the teeth from his comb, one by one, scattering them at his feet. I spat in the sand and watched how my spittle rolled into tiny sandballs. The sea washed and sucked and washed and sucked but remained empty of fat women. Then Jamie began to talk, about kisses with the mouth open and closed, about the difference between the feel of a breast under and over a jumper, between nylons and short white socks. He talked for what seemed hours and after a while I stopped listening, I knew he was lying anyway. Then suddenly I noticed he had stopped talking. I didn't know how long he had stopped, but I knew it had been some time before I noticed it. I turned and saw he was hunched up, his face blank like a child's. All the teeth were broken from his comb, his hand was clutching it insensibly and he was crying softly. His hair was wild with curls, the oil was dripping onto his forehead, his lips were purple with the cold. I touched him on the elbow and when his quiet sobbing didn't stop I took off my coat and put it gingerly round his shoulders. He shivered and moved in close to me and his head touched my chest and lay there. I held him there while he slept, thinking how much smaller than me he was after all.

There was a thin rim of light round the edge of the sea when he woke. His face was pale, – though not as grey as that light, and his teeth had begun to chatter. "What happened?" he asked, shaking my coat off. "You were asleep," I said, "you missed it," and began a detailed account of how the woman had begun running from the pier right up past me to the end of the strand, how her breasts had bobbed as the water splashed round her thick ankles. "Liar" he said. "Yes" I said. Then I thought of home. "What are we going to do?" I asked him. He rubbed his eyes with his hand and drew wet smudges across each cheek. Then he got up and began to walk towards the sea. I followed him, knowing the sea would obliterate his tears and any I might have. When he came near the water he began to run, splashing the waves round him with his feet and I ran too, but with less abandon, and when he fell face down in the water I fell too. When I could see him through the salt water he was laughing madly in a crying sort of way, ducking his head in and out of the water the way swimmers do. I got to my feet and tried to pull him up but his clothes were clinging to every bone of his thin body. Then I felt myself slipping, being pulled from the legs and I fell in the water again and I felt his arms around my waist, tightening, the way boys wrestle, but more quietly then, and I felt his body not small any longer, pressing against mine. I heard him say "this is the way lovers do it" and felt his mouth on my neck but I didn't struggle, I knew that in the water he couldn't see my tears or see my smile.

YEHUDIT KATZIR

SCHLAFFSTUNDE

*In the sixteenth-century treasury of Chinese ghost stories
known as the* Tales of Night and Rain, *is told the story of
Wu-Ling who, at the age of six, had a dream. He saw, in
the branches of a peach tree, a pale woman of extraordinary
beauty beckoning him to join her. Frightened but curious,
he climbed the tree, and the lady – who was one of the
amorous vampires who haunt the temple of Kiang – kissed
him with a kiss that burned his lips. Wu-Ling awoke but,
for the rest of his life, he was never able to find any woman
in the least attractive because, whenever he met one, he
could not imagine her kiss to be as fiery as the kiss of the
peach-tree lady. Wu-Ling died an old man, ardent and
chaste.*

*Erotic memories sometimes become the vocabulary of
our erotic fantasies which, in turn, become our memories.
In this circle of desire and experience lie our pleasures and
our fears. Remembering a moment past we become the
participants of that moment and through the recollected*

images and words and sensations we grant ourselves the illusion that once again we can be happy. Yehudit Katzir's "Schlaffstunde" – the nap, literally, the "hour of sleep" – recollects a distant childhood transformed by the discovery of sex. Katzir's past erotic moments pinpoint her memory of Israel, of her family, of the collective Jewish history of pursuit, death or escape, and form on their own a private story, an intimate autobiography of the awakening of the senses.

―――――――

ONCE, when summer vacation stretched over the whole summer and tasted of sand and smelled of grapes and a redhead sun daubed freckles on your face and, after Sukkot, the wind whistled into a gang of clouds and we galloped home through the ravine in a thunderstorm and the rain stabbed your tongue with mint and pine and the neighbourhood dogs set up a racket, barking like uncles coughing at intermission in a winter concert, and suddenly spring attacked with cats shrieking and the lemon trees blossoming and again came a hamsin and the air stood still in the bus but we got up only for Mrs. Bella Blum from the Post Office, a dangerous-child-snatcher who comes to us in bed at night with the wild grey hair of a dangerous-child-snatcher and narrow glasses on the tip of the sharp-as-a-red-pencil nose of a dangerous-child-snatcher and who smiles with the cunning flattery of a dangerous-child-snatcher and pokes dry-ice fingers into our faces, and only if we'd give her all the triangular stamps could we somehow be saved or if we prayed to God, who disguised himself as a clown in the Hungarian circus and rocked, balancing himself on the tightrope under the blue canvas of the tent, in high-heeled shoes and wide red-and-white checked pants and then disguised himself as an elephant, turned his wrinkled behind to us and went off to eat supper.

Once, when the world was all golden through the sparkling Carrera vase in the living room on the credenza, which maybe vanished with all the other furniture as soon as we left the room and we peeked through the keyhole to see if it was still there but maybe it saw us peeking and rushed back and a horrible gang of thieves was hiding out in the garage under the supermarket and only Emil and you could solve the mystery because obviously you were going to be an important detective they'd write books about and I'd be your assistant and we experimented with invisible ink made of onion skins and we heated the note in the candle so the writing would emerge and then we trained ourselves to swallow it so it wouldn't fall into enemy hands and we did other training exercises, in self-defense and in not-revealing-secrets even if they torture you and tie you to a bed and put burning matches under your toenails, and we mixed up poison from dirt and leaves and crushed shells and we kept it in yogurt jars and we drew a skull and crossbones on them and hid them with all our other treasures.

When the summer vacation stretched over the whole summer and the world was all gold and everything was possible and everything was about to happen, and Uncle Alfred was still alive and came for afternoon tea and Grandfather and Grandmother

went to rest between two and four and left us endless time, we
snuck up the creaky wooden steps behind the house to our little
room in the attic which was headquarters and we stood at the
window where you could view the whole sea beyond the cemetery and you touched my face with your fingertips and said you
loved me.

Now we're gathered here, like sad family members at a
departure in an airport, around the departures-board at the
entrance, where somebody's written in white chalk, two zero
zero, Aaron Green, funeral, and I look at the woman sitting on
the stone bench next to you, a round straw hat shading her eyes
and ripening her mouth to a grape and the sun polishes two
knives of light along her tanned shins and then I go up to the
two of you, take off my sunglasses and say quietly, Hello, and
you stand up hastily, Meet each other, this is my wife. My
cousin. I discern the sparkle of the ring and the white teeth
among the shadows and touch her soft hand with long long fingers and say again, Hello. And the undertakers, busy at work
like angels in their white shirtsleeves, bearded faces, sweaty, carrying on a stretcher the shrivelled body under the dark dusty
cloth, the head almost touching the fat black behind of the
gravedigger, the legs dangling in front of the open fly of the second one, and a frosty wind blowing inside me, as then, and I
seek the memory in your eyes but you lower them to her, take
hold of her arm and help her up and my spy's eyes freeze on her
rounded belly in the flowered dress and see inside her all your
children you buried behind the house, in the grove, in the summer vacation between seventh and eighth grade, when on the
first morning, as every year, Grandfather came to pick me up
from home in his old black car, with Misha, the office chauffeur,

who dressed himself up in my honour in a white visor cap and a
huge smile with a gold tooth. Misha put my red suitcase in the
trunk and opened the back door for me with a bow and a wink
and we went to pick you up from the railroad station near the
port. On the way, I stuck my head between him and Grandfather and asked him to tell me again how he played for the king
of Yugoslavia and Misha sighed and said, That was a long time
ago, but I remember it as if it was yesterday. I was a child then,
maybe nine, maybe ten, and I played the trumpet better than
anybody in the whole school and one day they brought me a
blue suit with gold buttons and a tie and stockings up to my
knees and a cap with a visor and said, Get dressed, and they put
me next to a flag and said, Play, and I played so beautiful and
strong and King Pavel came in and the flag rose to the top of the
pole and the trumpet sparkled like that in the sun and so did the
gold buttons, who would have believed a little Jewish boy like
that playing trumpet for the king and he came to me and
stroked my head and asked, What's your name, and I told him,
Misha, and Mama was standing there and crying so they had to
hold her up and Papa said to her, Now I'm happy we have him,
because at first he didn't want me at all, they went to Austria just
for a vacation and when they came back Mama said, I'm pregnant, and Papa told her, Five is enough, get an abortion, but
Mama was very stubborn, like Albert Einstein's mother, his
father didn't want him either, and then he was terrible in school
and the teachers called the father and the father said to him,
Albert, you're seventeen years old now, not a child, what will
become of you, but when he was twenty-six he met Lenin and
Churchill and showed them the theory of relativity and there
were a lot of discussions, and he became famous all over the

world, so when I hear about abortions I say, Who knows what can come out of that child, why kill a human being. Misha sighed again and lit a cigarette. In the distance you could already see the big clock over the railroad station. At five to nine we arrived. Grandfather and I went down to the platform and Misha waited in the car. Two porters in grey caps were leaning on their rusty carts, looked at one another from time to time with half-closed eyes and smoked stinky cigarettes from yellow packs with a picture of black horses. I was so excited I had to pee and I hopped around from one foot to the other. At nine o'clock on the dot we heard a long happy whistle of the locomotive pulling five rumbling cars. The porters woke up, stomped on their cigarettes with huge shoes and started running back and forth along the platform shouting, Suitcases, suitcases. Terrified, I looked for your face among the hundreds of faces, crushed and scared, against the glass of the windows. Then the doors opened with a hiss and you came down, the very first one, wearing the short jeans all the kids had and a green shirt with emblems on the pockets that only a few had and a checked detective hat they had brought you from England and no other kid had, and you stood there like that next to your father's black suitcase, and looked around with eyes scrunched up like two green slits under your dishevelled fair curls, and once again I felt the pain between my throat and my stomach that clutched my breath every time I saw you and even when I thought about you, and I shouted, Here Uli, here Uli, and I ran to you, and then you saw me and smiled and we embraced, and Grandfather came too, and tapped you on the shoulder and said, How you've grown Saul, and he didn't take your suitcase because you were already thirteen and a half and stronger then he, and you

put it in the trunk, next to my red one. And Misha took us to
Grandfather's office on Herzl Street, whose walls were covered
with big shiny pictures with lots of blue, pictures of beautiful
places in Israel, the Kinneret and the Dead Sea and Rosh Ha-
Nikra and Elat, where there were rest homes, and the government paid him to send Holocaust survivors there, and I always
imagined how they arrived there by train, wearing funny coats
and hats with sad yellow faces underneath them as in the pictures they showed us in school on the day commemorating the
Holocaust-and-Heroism, and they line up there in a long row
with all their suitcases tied with rope, and everybody enters in a
line and takes off his coat and hat and gets bright-coloured
clothes and an orange pointy cap, and they sit in chaise longues
in the sun and swim in the sea and eat a lot and convalesce and
after a week grow fat and tanned and smiling like the people in
the advertisements and then they're sent home because new survivors came on the train and are already waiting in line. Until
once, on Saturday, we went with Grandfather and Grandmother and Misha to visit one of those rest homes, called Rosh
Ha-Nikra Recreation Village, and there was no line of survivors
at the entrance, and there was no way to know who was a Holocaust survivor and who was just a normal person because they
all had fat, droopy pot-bellies and nobody looked especially
sad, they were all swimming in the pool and gobbling sandwiches and guzzling juice and talking loud and playing bingo.
So we made up a system to check who was a real survivor, but I
didn't have the courage, I just watched from a distance as you
passed among the chaise longues on the lawn next to the pool
and whispered into everybody's ear, Hitler, and I saw that most
of the people didn't do anything, just opened their eyes wide in

a strange kind of look, as if they were waking up from some dream and hadn't had time yet to remember where they were and they closed their eyes right away and went on sleeping and only one man, big and fat with a lot of black hair on his chest and on his back like a huge gorilla, got up and chased you all over the lawn huffing and puffing, his eyes red and huge, and finally he caught you and slapped you and shook your shoulders hard and barked, *Paskutstve holerye, paskutstve holerye*, and you came back to me with red ears, and you didn't cry and you said it didn't really hurt, but from then on, every time they mentioned Hitler, in school or on television, I would think of the gorilla from the rest home instead of the real Hitler with the little moustache and dangling forelock.

In the afternoon we went down, as always on the first day of vacation, to eat in the Balfour Cellar, and the tall thin waiter, who looked like a professor, and Grandfather told us that many years ago he really had been a professor in Berlin, wearing glasses in a silver frame and a beard the same colour and a black bowtie, gave a little bow because he knew us, and especially Grandfather, who was a regular customer, and pulled out the chairs for us to sit down, and quickly put menus in front of us and said, What will you have, Herr Green, even though Grandfather always ordered the same thing, roast with puree of potatoes and sauerkraut, and a bunch of purple grapes for dessert, and the regular customers around the tables knew us and smiled and waved at us with white napkins, and as I ate I watched the two plywood cooks hung on the wall in their high chef-hats and long aprons and black moustaches curving upward like two more smiles on their mouths, and they looked back at me leaning on half a wooden barrel sticking out of the wall and full, I was sure, of very very good sauerkraut. And once you told me that the restaurant had a secret cellar right underneath us and that was why it was called the Balfour Cellar, and in the cellar there were lots more barrels like those and all of them were full of sauerkraut that could last a long time in case of another Holocaust, and then the limping newspaper-seller came in wearing a dirty grey undershirt soaked with sweat and yelled, Paper get your paper, until the whole restaurant was filled with his sour breath, and Grandfather beckoned to him, and he came to our table and gave him the paper with a black hand, and Grandfather paid him twenty cents even though right next door to the restaurant there was a clean kiosk that had papers and soda and ice-cream-on-a-stick. Then we went back home on the steep road that went by the gold dome and you could see the whole bay from there, and on the way we fooled around on the back seat and played pinch-me-punch-me and boxed and yelled and called each other names, and Grandfather suddenly turned around and said quietly and earnestly, Don't fight, children, human beings have to love and pity one another, for in the end we all die. And we didn't understand what he meant but we stopped, and Misha winked at us in the mirror, and told about Louis Armstrong, who was the greatest trumpet player and had the deepest lungs, and when Betty Grable who had the prettiest legs in Hollywood got cancer he came with his whole orchestra to play for her on the hospital lawn under her window. Then we got to the house, and Grandmother opened the door, her tight hairdo rolled in a braid around her scalp, and pecked each of us on the cheek and said, Now Schlaffstunde, which always sounded to me like the name of a cake like Schwartzwalder Kirschtorte or

Sachertorte or Apfelstrudel, which she would bake because
they reminded her of her home overseas, and the steamy
fragrant cafe when outside it was cold and snowing, but Dr.
Schmidt didn't allow her to eat them because she had high
blood sugar which is very dangerous for the heart. So she only
served it to us and Uncle Alfred and Grandfather, who always
said politely, No thank you, and refused to taste a single bit
even though he was very healthy. But sometimes, when he
went to walk Uncle Alfred to the gate, Grandmother would cut
herself a small slice and eat it with quick bites, bent over her
plate, and Grandfather would come back, stand in the door
and observe her back with a tender look, and wait until she was
finished, and only then would he come into the living room
and sit down with the newspaper, pretending he hadn't seen.
They went to their room, and we went out to the grove behind
the house and stretched a strong rope between two pine trees
and tried to balance on it like that clown we once saw when we
were little and Grandfather took us to the Hungarian circus in
Paris Square, where there were purebred horses and panthers
with yellow eyes and trained elephants and a beautiful acrobat
with long blond hair and the face of an angel who danced on
the tightrope with a golden parasol in her hand, and we
decided we'd run away and join that circus after we were
trained, but now we only managed to creep along on the rope,
and you explained to me that it's important to know in case
you have to cross over water. Then we climbed up to our espi-
onage headquarters under the roof, which sometimes was
Anne Frank's hiding-place, where we'd huddle together trembling under the table and munch on potato peels and call each
other Anne and Peter and hear the voices of German soldiers

outside and drop onto the green velvet sofa which Grandmother brought with her when she came to Israel in the ship,
and when one of the two wooden headrests collapsed they
bought a new sofa for the living room and brought this one
here, because it's a shame to throw out a good piece of furniture, and suddenly you said in a pensive voice, Interesting what
you feel after you die, and I said, After you die you don't feel
anything, and we tried to close our eyes tight and block our
ears and hold our breath to feel dead, but it didn't work because
even with our eyes closed we could see colours and you said,
Maybe by the time we get old they'll invent some medicine
against death, and I said, Maybe you'll be a scientist and invent
it yourself and you'll be famous like Albert Einstein. Then we
played writing words with our finger on each other's back and
whispering them. First we wrote the names of flowers,
narcissus and anemone and cyclamen, and names of animals,
panther and hippopotamus, and names of people we knew, but
after a while you said that was boring, and it was hard to guess
because of our shirts, so I took off my shirt and lay down on
the sofa, my face in the smell of dust and perfume and cigarette
smoke that lingered in the upholstery from days gone by, and I
felt how your nice finger slowly wrote words we never dared to
say, first a-s-s and then, t-i-t and finally w-h-o-r-e, and while I
whispered the words in a soft voice between the cushions of the
sofa I felt my face burning and my nipples which had just
started to sprout hardening against the velvet.

In the afternoon Grandfather and Grandmother came out
of the bedroom with pink cheeks, twenty years younger, and at
five o'clock on the dot Uncle Alfred came and we never understood exactly how he was related to us, maybe he was one of

Grandmother's distant cousins, and her mouth grew thin as a thread whenever his name was mentioned and Grandfather would roar with rage, Bastard, and we didn't know why they didn't like him, whether it was because he was poor or because he once tried to be an opera singer in Paris or some other reason we couldn't guess, and why they entertained him so nicely in spite of it, and Grandmother served him tea and cake, which he would drink and eat and smack his thick red lips and tell again, his eyes melting with regret, about how he was a student in the Paris Conservatoire and lived in a teeny-tiny attic without a shower and without a toilet in Place de la République, and ate half a baguette-with-butter a day, but at seven in the evening he would put on his only good suit and a bowtie and sprinkle eau-de-cologne on his cheeks and go to the opera, where he would stand under a decorated lighted vault and steal the occasional notes that slipped out through the lattices and caressed the statues of the muses and the cornices of the angels, and in the intermission he would mingle with the audience and go inside, because then they didn't check tickets, and find himself an empty seat in one of the balconies, and so with sobbing heart and damp as a clutched handkerchief he saw the last acts of the most famous operas in the world. And here he would usually stand up, sway like a jack-in-the-box, clasp the back of the armchair with his plump fingers, and burst into an aria from Rigoletto or La Traviata or The Marriage of Figaro, and his voice was frail and fragrant and sweet like the tea he had just drunk, and only at the end did it squeak and break like glass, and Grandmother's thin hands smacked one another in dry applause and Grandfather lowered his eyes to the squares of the carpet and muttered, Bravo, bravo, and we didn't know why Uncle Alfred was thrown out of the Conservatoire one day and didn't become a great singer in the Paris opera, and Grandmother wouldn't tell us, she only clenched her mouth even tighter, as if a huge frog would leap out if she opened it. And Uncle Alfred would sit down and sigh and wipe his reddish nose like a strawberry with a wrinkled handkerchief he pulled out of the left pocket of his jacket, and he would hold out his arms to invite us to ride on both sides of the chair, and hug our waists and tell about the cafes of Montparnasse and Montmartre, which was a meeting place for writers and artists and students, and from his mouth strange names flowed with a wonderful sound I'd never heard before anywhere, like Sartre and Simone de Beauvoir and Cocteau and Satie and Picasso, and then he'd caress your hair and say, You'll be an artist too someday, and stroke your back and say, Or a writer, and press his little white hand on your leg with the short jeans and say, Or a musician, and go on strumming with his fingers on your smooth bare thigh as if he were playing a piano, and he didn't say anything to me. He couldn't know that someday, on a steamy shuddering mid-summer afternoon, we'd be standing in the old cemetery at Carmel Beach, our shamed backs to his tombstone, on which were the words, in gold letters as he requested, of the Chinese poet from Mahler's Lied von der Erde:

When sorrow draws near,
The gardens of the soul lie wasted,
Joy and song wither and die,
Dark is life and so is death.
Now it is time, companions!
Drain your golden goblets to the dregs.

Our backs to his tombstone and our faces to Grandfather wrapped in a sheet, he hurrying to slip into an eternal Schlaffs-tunde next to Grandmother, who died in the winter many years before, but they didn't take us to the funeral because they didn't want us to catch cold and miss school, and our faces to the can-tor, whose closed eyes were turned to the sky as he trilled his *El male rakhamim shokhen bamromim*, and to your father who had turned completely grey, muttering *Yitgadal v'yitkadash sh'me raba*, and to my mother hiding her face in her hands, ripping her shirt, and to the old people responding Amen, their familiar faces mocking me under their wrinkled masks, waving at me sometimes and smiling around the tables in the Balfour Cellar which isn't there anymore, and sometimes dozing off in the chaise longues of the rest home which was closed years ago, and here's Misha, who almost didn't get old but without the visor hat and the smile with the gold tooth, and he's wearing a black kippa and noisily wiping his nose, and my gaze is drawn to the shrivelled sharp face of a stooped little old woman which is stamped on my memory as if it had accompanied me through-out my childhood, though I can't remember where, and I turn to you and seek in your eyes which don't look straight at me, in your worn-out face, in the white threads in your hair, desire in me a sharp wild pain like the whistle of the train now galloping along the shore on its way to the new station at Bat-Galim, but only tatters of memories are pulled from me, connecting to one another with their tails like the coloured handkerchiefs from the box of the magician in the Hungarian circus, and about a week after vacation started you didn't want to join the circus or practise balancing on the tightrope between the pines and you didn't want to play Anne Frank or Emil and the Detectives, you didn't want to play anything with me, you just sat under the big pine tree all day long and read little books with crinkled bindings and you looked worried and sad and full of secret thoughts under your checked cap. At first I tried not to disturb you even though I was insulted, but by the third day I had had enough. I waited until afternoon and when Grandfather and Grandmother went for their Schlaffstunde, I crept up behind you, grabbed the book named The Confession of the Commander's Lover with a picture on the cover of a soldier in a brown uniform with black boots up to his knees aiming a huge pistol at a blonde sprawling in the snow between his legs and wearing only panties and a bra. I hid the book, and said I wouldn't give it back until you told me what was going on. You looked at me strangely through your long light lashes and said, Swear on the black grave of Hitler that you won't tell anyone in the world ever. I swear, I whispered solemnly, and to myself I imagined a deep black hole where the big hairy Hitler of the rest home was standing. Then you told me that recently, ever since you started reading those books, it swelled up in your pants and became so hard you had to rub it with your hand until a kind of white liquid sprayed out of it and that was the most wonderful feeling you ever had in your life, like the explosion of a shooting star, but afterward you were worried because in school they explained to you that women get pregnant from it, and when you wash your hands it goes into the pipes of the sewer along with the water and flows into the sea and a lot of women swim in the sea and it could get into them under their bathing suits, and not all of it would go into the sink either because among millions of little seeds some twenty or thirty were bound to be left on your hand, and sometimes you had to go on the bus afterward or to basketball or scouts, and it could get on the money you paid the driver, and from the driver's hands to the tickets he gives the girls and women of all ages, and then they go back home and go to the bathroom and tear toilet paper and wipe themselves and it gets inside them and they don't even know, and now thousands of women are walking around the streets with babies from you in their swollen bellies, and not only here in Israel, because the sperm can be washed away in the water and even go as far as Europe. An ashamed spark of pride glimmered in your eyes for a moment and died out. I sat silently awhile and thought, chewing on dry pine needles. That was a really serious problem. Meantime you were tossing pine cones, trying to hit the treetrunk opposite, thunk, thunk, thunk. Suddenly I had an idea. I stood up and ran to the kitchen, opened the drawer next to the sink which had all kinds of things you need in a house, matches and bandaids and rubber bands, and took out a few plastic sandwich bags Grandmother used to pack food for the road when we went on a visit Saturday to one of the rest homes, and I ran back and gave it to you and said, Here, do it in this and bury it in the ground. From that day on, the worry and the pride disappeared from your face and we were friends again and played all the old games, and only sometimes did you suddenly stop and give me long pensive looks, and at night I'd creep into the kitchen and count the bags to know how many were missing, and I'd go out barefoot to the fragrant dark grove with gloomy treetops and the sound of rustling and chirping and howling and mysterious hissing, and I'd find the places where dry pine needles were piled up and the earth was loose, and I'd dig with feverish curious hands and panic and bring up the plastic bags from their graves and look at the wonderful liquid in the moonlight for a long time. One day you added the crinkled little books to our treasure and said, I don't need this garbage anymore, I can invent better stories myself, and I said, You'll surely be a writer someday, and I remembered that Uncle Alfred had said it before me. So we tore the pages out of the books and sat down to cut out the words, especially the coarsest ones, and pasted them into scary anonymous threatening letters to the gang of criminals under the supermarket and to Mrs. Bella Blum of the Post Office, and we gorged ourselves on the chocolate we had stolen earlier from Grandmother's kitchen, where she kept it for baking her cakes, and it tasted a little like almond paste, and suddenly you touched my face with your fingertips, as if to wipe off a chocolate moustache, and you went behind me and wrote slowly on my back, word after word, I-love-you, and hugged me tight. You lay on the sofa, and I lay down on top of you, my face in the soft shadow between your shoulder and your neck, a smell of paste and starch from your green shirt, and your damp fingers stroked the back of my neck for a long time, trembled, hovered over my hair. Stuck together without moving, almost without breathing, only our hearts galloping like horses in a mad race, and I slowly stroked your face, as if I were sculpting it anew, your fair curls and your smooth brow and your eyelids and underneath them is a whole world and your little nose that a finger could slide down like a ski to your lips, where a hot draft breathes on my frozen finger, and you pull up my shirt, your cool hand on my back down and up, then up and down to that nice place where if we were cats our tails would grow out of, and I put my mouth on your mouth, taste the stolen chocolate, our tongues met, circle, and push each other like two panicky wrestlers, and I tug the shirt up off your smooth chest and my shirt up off my breasts, to press my nipples hard from the cold against the warm soft skin of your panting belly, and I feel a sweetness between my legs as if honey had spilled and a little of it drops on my panties, and that makes me open them and move back and forth on your thigh, and you hug me tight and suck my lips like lemon drops and you put my hand on the hard bulge in your shorts and your face becomes serious and fragile so in it I can see what no one before me has ever seen, and I breathe fast-fast like a little animal without memories, my melted belly stuck to yours the sweetness in my panties more and more until it hurts until I can't and suddenly those spasms inside me the first time so strong and sharp and long and then shorter and faster like flutterings but I don't shout so they won't wake up and I want it never to end but finally it does end and I fall on you breathless as if I had run the sixty-yard-dash, and I see that you too are half fainted, struggling to swallow air, your face burning, and I get off you and lie beside you and discover a big spot on your pants and, excited, I inhale the sharp smell rising from the two of us, a smell not like any other.

Then you looked at me with flashing green eyes and you smiled and kissed me on my cheek, and you wildly pushed aside the hair stuck to your brow and sat up and took off your shirt in one movement and said, Take off yours too. And I took off mine, and you laid your head on my stomach, and we rested like that awhile, my hand stirring your damp hair, and fingers of sun pierced the chinks in the shutter and spread golden fans on the walls. Then I stroked your back and said your skin was soft as velvet, and you said mine was soft as water, and you kissed my stomach and drew strange forms on it with your lips, and you said, When you lie on your back your breasts are as flat as mine, and you licked my nipples, and your tongue was a little rough like a cat's, and you licked and licked until they got hard as cherry pits, and again I felt sweet and smooth between my legs and I wanted it to go on as before, but Grandmother's voice rose from downstairs, sharp and probing, like the periscope of a submarine, Children, where are you, five o'clock tea and cake. We put on our shirts fast and came down and you went to change your pants, while I looked in the gilded mirror in the vestibule. My eyes sparkled like cups of sky, and the whole world, the furniture in the living room and Grandfather and Grandmother and Uncle Albert looked far away and unreal but sharp and clear, as on a stage.

That night I couldn't sleep because I missed you too much, you were sleeping quietly in the room at the end of the hall and maybe your body was dreaming of me. I wanted so much to come to you in the dark and hug you and hear you breathing, but Grandmother was always strict about you sleeping in your father's old room and me in my mother's room, next to their room, so I controlled myself and thought about tomorrow, about the ceremony we planned down to the smallest detail after dinner, when Uncle Alfred had gone and Grandfather and Grandmother sat down in the living room to watch the Friday night news on television, and we whispered back and forth in the kitchen, and we could hear Menachem Begin the new Prime Minister giving a speech about Auschwitz and the Six Million, and then he announced he was willing to meet in Jerusalem with President Sadat, and Grandfather said, At last that idiot came out with something good, and Grandmother called us, You should see this, important news, but we knew that tomorrow's ceremony was much more important, and especially what would come afterward, and there was no way I could stop the film that kept repeating over and over on the dark screen, the film we starred in. And suddenly, from their room, I heard Grandmother scream in a whisper, Aaron, Aaron, and Grandfather woke up and said gently, Yes, Minna, and Grandmother said she couldn't fall asleep, and she told him quietly, but I could hear every word, that in the morning, as she was walking around in the supermarket with the cart to buy food for the Sabbath, she suddenly felt that her mother was standing next to her, in a black fur coat, the one she wore years ago when they said goodbye at the railroad station, and her face was as pale and terrified as it was then, and she told her something, but Grandmother didn't pay attention because she said to herself, It's summer now, why is Mother wearing a fur coat, and before she could understand, her mother wasn't there anymore. I've been calm ever since, Grandmother went on in a harsh whisper, I'm sure it's something very bad. From her face I know something awful is going to happen. Grandfather didn't say anything, he just sang her something very quiet, a tune of yearning without words, and repeated it over and over until it filled me completely, until I fell asleep.

The next day was the Sabbath. Grandfather and Grandmother woke us early to go with them to visit the rest home in Tiberias, and were surprised when we muttered from under the covers that we were tired and wanted to stay home, but they gave in. I remembered what I had heard at night from their room, and I thought to myself, How can ghosts wander around in our supermarket, and why didn't Grandfather comfort her and tell her it was all her imagination and nothing bad would happen, and suddenly I thought, Maybe that whole conversation didn't happen and I only dreamed it, and I decided not to tell anybody, not even you. Grandmother made hard-boiled egg sandwiches for our lunch, and prepared food to take on the road, and my heart began to pound when I heard the drawer next to the sink open and Grandmother whisper to herself, Funny, I remember there was a whole package here. Finally she wrapped it in waxpaper because Misha was already honking for them outside, and pecked each of us on the cheek and said, We'll be back by seven-thirty tonight, behave yourselves, and they left. As soon as the hum of the motor disappeared around the corner, we leaped out of bed and met in the hall, and we started to do everything exactly according to the plan we concocted last night down to the last detail. First each of us took a long and thorough bath, shampooing our hair and cleaning our ears. Then we wrapped ourselves in our sheets, which we tied at the shoulder like Greek togas, and I put on perfume from all the bottles I found on Grandmother's dressing table, and I smeared my lips and cheeks with a lot of red, and my eyes with blue. Then we cut off the tops of the pink flowers Grandmother had bought for the Sabbath, in the golden vase on the credenza, and we plaited two wreaths for our heads. Then we went into the kitchen but didn't eat breakfast because we couldn't swallow a thing, but from Grandmother's hiding-place for candles, next to the hiding-place for chocolate, we stole six Yahrzeit candles, she always kept it full of them because there was always a Yahrzeit for somebody in her family who had remained over there, and from the sewing box covered with flowered cloth we took a pair of scissors, and from Grandfather's linen drawer we took a white handkerchief,

and from the pantry a glass of wine, and from the library a
small Bible your father got as a Bar-Mitzvah present from his
school, and barefoot we went up to our room in the attic with
all those things. Then we closed the shutter on the day and on
the cemetery and we made it absolutely dark, and we lit the
Yahrzeit candles and put them about the room, which was
filled with the shadows of scary demons dancing on the ceiling
and the walls, and we left one candle on the table, and we put
the Bible next to it, and you asked, You ready, and I whispered,
Yes, and my heart was pounding, and we stood facing each
other, and we put one hand on the Bible and we raised the
other with thumb and pinkie together as in the scouts' oath,
and I looked straight into your eyes where the flames of the
candles were burning and repeated after you slowly, solemnly:

I swear by God and by the black grave of Hitler,
I swear by God and by the black grave of Hitler,
I will never marry another woman,
I will never marry another man,
And I will love only you forever,
And I will love only you forever.

Then we hugged each other and almost couldn't breathe
because we knew that that oath was strong as death and to
make it even stronger we cut the words out of the Bible and
pasted them on a sheet of paper in the light of the candle. The
two Gods we found right away in the creation, and woman in
the story of Adam and Eve, and grave in the part about the cave
of Machpelah. Then we found man and swear and I and of and
you and another and love and the and black and will and never.

The rest of the words, Hitler and marry and forever, we couldn't find, so we pasted them together from separate letters. When it was all ready, you wrapped the glass in the handkerchief, put it on the floor and stamped on it hard with your bare foot. The glass broke and a big spot of blood spread over the cloth. You dipped your finger in it and signed your name under the oath. Now you, you said. I took a deep breath, picked up a piece of glass, and scratched my big toe hard, from the bottom, so nobody would see the cut, squeezed a drop of blood onto my finger and signed a shaky signature next to your name. Then we wrote the date, the regular date and the Hebrew date, and the exact address, Presidents' Boulevard, Mount Carmel, Haifa, Israel, Middle East, Continent of Asia, Earth, Solar System, Galaxy, Cosmos. Now we'll tear the oath in two and each of us will keep the half with the other's signature, I said what we had planned to do, and you were silent for a moment and suddenly you said, No, let's wrap it up and bury it under the big pine tree, someplace where we can always find it. I thought to myself that we were forbidden to change the plan, but I didn't say anything. We folded the paper in the aluminum foil of yesterday's chocolate and put it in an empty matchbox, which we wrapped with more paper and in a plastic bag you had left over from the ones you stole from the drawer, and we went downstairs. We dug a deep pit with our hands next to the trunk and hid our package, more important to us than anything in the world, but when we covered it with earth and tamped it down with our feet and piled pine needles on it, I became very sad all of a sudden, and I didn't know why.

When we got back to the room, the Yahrzeit candles were still burning and the demons kept jumping wildly on the walls.

I knew what was about to happen but I wasn't scared. I thought about Anne Frank and how the Germans caught her before she really had a chance to love her Peter, when she was exactly my age, and I said to myself, I will have a chance. We took off the wreaths and the Greek togas and we spread one sheet on the sofa underneath us, and we lay down, and covered ourselves with the other one, and I caressed your whole body which was warm and breathing fast, and I walked my tongue among hills of light and soft shadows and paths of soap and sweat under the sheet, and suddenly you were over me on all fours and looking at me with sparkling yellow eyes and a savage smile, and I wanted that to happen, and I whispered, Come, and you asked, Does it hurt, and I said, No, and I could hear your heart drumming on my breasts rhythmically I-love-you-I-love-you, and I was filled with tremendous pride.

Then heavy steps grated on the stairs and I whispered, The Germans, and I started trembling, and we held each other tight and clung to the wall, and the door opened, and in the opening in a halo of light stood Uncle Alfred. They apparently forgot to tell him they were going away and that he shouldn't come today for tea. He looked at our sweaty bodies and the handkerchief spotted with blood and the pink flowers scattered over the floor and the Yahrzeit candles, and he rubbed his strawberry nose in embarrassment, and his eyes were fixed on some point on your stomach, maybe your belly button, as he stammered, What's this children, it's forbidden, at your age, you shouldn't, if Grandmother finds out. We covered ourselves with the sheet and looked at him cautiously and silently like cats. He lowered his eyes to the shiny tips of his shoes and went on, Of course I'll have to tell her, who would have thought, children, cousins, and God Forbid there'll be a baby with six fingers on each hand, or two heads, or a little tail like a pig, this is very dangerous, who would have thought. And he wagged his head from the right shoe-tip to the left shoe-tip, as if he were setting up a shiny-shoe contest. Then he looked at you again, and said with no stammering now that he was willing not to tell anybody on condition that you agreed to meet him here, tomorrow afternoon, so he could talk to you and explain what a serious thing it was we had done. Why only him, I burst out to defend you, and Uncle Alfred said he regarded you as responsible and that with your sense and talent he hadn't expected anything like this from you. I agree, you said quietly, and he left. As soon as the door closed behind him we jumped off the couch, stood at the window again, with one hand on the Bible and the other in the air, with thumb and pinkie together, and I repeated after you the oath we composed on the spot:

And even if we have a baby
With six fingers on each hand
Or two heads
Or a little tail like a pig
We will love it as if it was a completely normal baby
With five fingers and one head
And no tail at all.

Then we dressed and cleaned up everything fast before Grandfather and Grandmother got back home. Except the dark red spot, blossoming on the green velvet, that we left as a souvenir. Before I feel asleep, I could hear Grandmother whispering into the golden vase on the sideboard, Funny, I remember buying flowers for the Sabbath, and Grandfather comforting her gently, Well, my memory's not what it used to be either, how could I forget to tell Alfred not to come today for tea.

In the middle of the night I felt horribly nauseous, ran to the bathroom and stuck my finger down my throat and suddenly I felt I was throwing up sand, enormous amounts of wet sand, it filled my mouth and gritted between my teeth, and I spat and threw up, threw up and spat, and then something else was vomited up from me with the sand, and I looked into the toilet. A tiny black dog floating stiffly on his side, his legs spread out, his gums exposed in a creepy smile, watching me with a gaping dead eye. In horror I slammed down the lid. Outside it was beginning to turn light.

I wandered around among the trees with my hands in my pockets, kicking pine cones. You'd been up there for more than half an hour, closed in the room. What did he have to tell you that took so much time. I couldn't control myself anymore. I went up very quietly, opened the door a little, and peered in. The two of you were sitting on the sofa. With big opera gestures Uncle Alfred was explaining something to you that I couldn't hear and from time to time he put his cotton hand on your leg. Then he wrapped his arm around your shoulders and put his face which was always flushed, almost purple, close to your face which was ashen. Suddenly he looked up and saw me. A shadow passed over his eyes. I fled downstairs. I lay under the big pine tree, right over the oath we buried yesterday, and I looked at the green sparkling needles that stabbed the clouds which today were in the shape of a huge white hand. I waited. Time passed, more time, a lot of time passed, and you didn't come down. I remembered the dream I had last night, and I shivered with cold. At last the door opened and Uncle Alfred came out breathing deeply as he went unsteadily down the steps. Grandmother opened the door, said, Hello Alfred, and he went into the house. Then you came running out, you lay down beside me, hid your head against my belly, and muffled your howls of anguish. Your whole body shook. I held you. What happened, what did he tell you, I whispered. We have to kill him, you cried. Your hot tears were absorbed by my shirt. I had never seen you cry like that. But what happened, what did he do, I asked again. We have to kill him we have to kill him, you wailed, your feet kicking the ground. But what did he do, hit you, tell me what he did, I pleaded. You lifted your burning wet face where the tears and the snot were running but you didn't care, and you said quietly, Today I'm going to kill him. I looked into your red eyes, with two black pits in them, and I knew that today Uncle Alfred would die.

Within minutes we had a fatal solution of poison made of shells ground up with two ants, a mashed piece of pine cone, and yellow dog-doo. We mixed it all up with pine tar so the ingredients would stick together. My job was to ask Grandmother if I could make the tea today, and to pour the poison into Uncle Alfred's cup. I chose the big black cup for him so I wouldn't confuse it with another and also because I thought the poison would work better in a black cup. I added five spoons of sugar and stirred it well, trying to hear what they were saying in the living room to make sure he wasn't telling on us in spite of everything. They were talking very quietly and only separate words reached me, Dr. Schmidt, chest X-ray, diagnosis, and Dr. Schmidt again. They were talking about diseases. I calmed down. On the tea cart I also put the special two-layer Schwartzwaldertorte that Grandmother baked and I didn't understand what it was in honour of, maybe it was his birthday today. As soon as I entered with the tray, they shut up. Uncle Alfred said, Thank you, and a sad smile clouded his face. You came in too, your eyes dry now, and we huddled together in the chair, waiting with awful tension to see him drink and die on the spot. First he greedily polished off three pieces of cake. Then he sipped noisily, smacked his lips, faced us, and declared, Now I will sing you the first lied from Mahler's Lied von der Erde. He cleared his throat twice, clasped his hands on his stomach, and started singing in German which we couldn't understand. His voice burst out of his chest as a solemn trumpet blast, rose to a great height both bold and trembling like a tightrope walker, and suddenly it fell and plunged into a dark abyss, where it struggled with fate, pleaded, prayed, shouted like a hollow echo, whimpered, abased itself, the face that of a drowning man, tears flowed from his eyes and from Grandmother's eyes too, she understood the words, and even Grandfather blew his nose a few times, and we looked at each other and knew the poison we mixed was also a magic potion, and we held our breath to see him sink into the carpet in the middle of the song, but Uncle Alfred finished it with a long endless shout and his arms waved to the sides and hit the credenza, and the gold vase teetered a moment in surprise and then slid off and smashed on the floor into sparkling slivers. Uncle Alfred sat down, panting heavily, and whispered, Sorry, and Grandmother said, It's nothing, and she came and kissed him on the cheek and Grandfather didn't look at the squares of the carpet and didn't murmur, Bravo, but shook his hand and looked into his eyes and said, Wonderful, wonderful, and Uncle Alfred took another sip of the poisoned tea, and stood up to go, and said to us, Goodbye, and caressed you with his gaze, but we didn't answer, we only looked at him with hatred, and they accompanied him to the door, and wished him good luck, and Grandfather patted him on the shoulder and said, Be strong, Alfred, and Uncle Alfred said hesitantly, Yes, and the door closed behind him and Grandfather and Grandmother looked at each other a moment, and Grandmother nodded her head and brought a broom and dustpan and swept up the slivers.

At night I woke up to the sound of coughing and an awful screeching laughter and I heard Grandmother telling Grandfather in the kitchen, Now I know what she said, now I know what she wanted to tell me then. And the awful laugh was heard again, as if it weren't Grandmother laughing but some demon inside her. I got up to peer from behind the door, and I saw her sitting at the table, her long hair dishevelled and in her nightgown and her mouth stained with cherry juice and chocolate, a knife clutched in her fist over the ruins of Alfred's two-layer cake, and Grandfather in pyjamas grabbing her wrist and pleading, Enough, enough now, you've already eaten too much, and Grandmother struggled to free her hand and the screeching voice of the demon burst out of her, Just one more little piece, just one more little piece, and Grandfather held her and cried, Don't leave me alone, Minna, please don't leave me alone, I can't make it alone. I ran away from there to your room. Your breathing was heavy, uneven. I got in under your blanket and hugged you and put my head next to yours. The pillow was soaked.

The next day we went with Misha and Grandfather and Grandmother who sat in front, her braid now pinned together, and Misha let them off at Rambam Hospital and took us to the beach at Bat-Galim, and we took off our clothes and had our bathing suits on underneath, and Misha looked like a lifeguard with his visor cap and broad chest, all he needed was a whistle. He sat down in a chaise longue at the edge of the water, and you ran into the sea with a spray splashing colourfully and you plunged into the waves, and I ran in behind you and also plunged because I wanted to feel what you were feeling, and my eyes burned and I swallowed salt water, and when I came back to the shore, you were already standing there and shaking your curls, and we sat down on the sand next to Misha, leaning against his sturdy legs, and we watched the sea and were silent because none of us had anything to say. Then I asked Misha to tell us again how he played for the king of Yugoslavia because I knew how much he liked to tell it, and I thought maybe that would save the situation. He was silent a moment, and suddenly he said quietly, It wasn't I who played for the king, it was another boy, he was also called Misha, and he played better than I did, so they chose him to wear the uniform with gold buttons, and the trumpet sparkled in the sun, and the flag went up to the top of the flagpole, it was so beautiful I'll never forget it, and King Pavel came and patted his head and his mother cried so they had to hold her up, and I stood there in the line with all the children and I cried too. He wiped his nose, and then he went on, as if to himself, But that Misha isn't here anymore, Hitler took him, all of them, all of them, my parents too, my brothers and sisters, I'm the only one alive, the sixth child, the one they didn't want, because Papa and Mama got married very young, they were cousins, but the family decided to marry them off at thirteen, that's how it was done in those days, and every year they had a baby, every year a baby, until Papa said, enough. But then they went for a vacation in Austria and when they came back Mama was pregnant again. Misha fell silent and lit a cigarette, and then he said out of the blue, Your grandfather is a fine man, there aren't many people like him. We quietly watched a young man who finally managed to walk on his hands and a man who threw a stick in the water and his big dog charged in barking and swam and brought the stick out in his mouth and the man patted his head. I took an ice-cream stick and drew a house and a tree and the sun on the wet sand, and the waves came and erased my picture. And the sea slowly turned yellow and we got chilly so we dressed and went to get Grandfather and Grandmother, who were waiting for us at the entrance to the hospital with grey faces and looking suddenly very old.

A few days later Grandmother told us that Uncle Alfred had died in the hospital. She wiped her tears and said, He had a disease in his lungs and the operation didn't succeed. But we knew the real reason, and we didn't dare look at each other as we walked with Grandmother, who was weeping for Alfred and for herself, and with Grandfather, who was weeping for Grandmother, and with our parents and the other three people we didn't know, behind the undertakers busy like angels in white shirtsleeves and sweaty faces, carrying the shrivelled body on a stretcher under a dark dustcloth, the head almost touching the fat black behind of the first gravedigger, the legs dangling in front of the open fly of the second one, and I thought, It could be anyone under the cloth, maybe it's not him, but when we got to the open grave the cantor said his name and a desperate crying burst out of me because I knew you couldn't move time backward. And you stood silently on the other side of the black grave, and I knew that Uncle Alfred would always be between us, and after the funeral your father would take you home, long before the end of summer vacation because Grandmother already didn't feel well, and in a few months, in the winter, she would die too, and Grandfather would close the office on Herzl Street and move to an old people's home, and he would go on talking to her all those years as if she were still beside him, and we would never again be together in our little room under the roof, and only sometimes, before sleep came, you would crouch over me on all fours and look at me with yellow pupils and I would whisper to you, Come, and I would feel your heart drumming on my breasts, until the last flutter. I wipe my tears and go with all the old people to put a little stone on the grave, and now everyone is turning to go, but I stay another moment at Uncle Alfred's yellowed marble, I know you're standing here next to me. Up close you can see that I too have lines at the corner of my mouth and many grey hairs, and the two of us read by heart the lines from the first lied of Das Lied von der Erde, whose words we didn't understand then, and I put a little stone under the words and you put a little stone and then you put your hand on my shoulder and say, Let's go. My mother and your father are walking in front of us, whispering about the city's plan to destroy the old house and dig up the grove to build an expensive apartment building on the site, and I see the ground, which can't still be holding all we buried there, it will split open and the highrise will crack and collapse. Misha comes behind us and sighs and says, If you could only go backward in life, even one minute, and I know exactly what minute he wants to go back to. And at the gate stands the stooped-over old woman whose shrivelled face is so familiar, and she grabs my sleeve with a trembling hand and screeches, Maybe you don't remember me but I remember your grandfather very well, he was a regular customer of mine, in the old Post Office. You're Mrs. Bella Blum from the Post Office, I whisper and my heart turns pale, and for a split-second I see eyeglasses on the end of a sharp nose, grey hair, icy fingers reaching out for the necks of children and triangular stamps, and I remember the anonymous threatening letters, and I glance over at you, but you're looking at your shoes covered with dust and you say, I have to go, we have a meeting at the factory, and once again I touch her soft hand under the purplish straw hat. Suddenly a strong wind comes from the sea and snatches the hat off her head and rolls it down the path, and she runs after it among the tombstones in her fluttering flowery dress, with her rounded belly, with the strips of her chestnut hair, flinging out her full arms to catch it, but the hat mocks her, it flies into the sky like a purple butterfly, and just as it's about to light on the sharp top of the cypress, it changes its mind, flips over twice and lands on the tombstone of Abba Hushi the famous mayor of Haifa, and you and Misha and all the other men volunteer to get it for her and you jump around among the graves, but the hat is already far away from there, crushed and ashamed between Hanoch ben Moshe Gavrieli born in the city of Lodz and Zilla Frumkin model wife and mother, who lie crowded next to each other, and all of you are flushed and sweating, but the hat pulls away again with a splendid somersault and soars, and you chase it, look up and wave your hands, like survivors on a desert island to an airplane, then the hat loses its balance and spins around itself like a dancer with a jumble of purple ribbons and lands with a bang outside the gate and lies on its side and laughs with its round mouth, and she runs to it, heavy and gasping and bends over and picks it up and waves it high in the air and brimming with joy she turns to you with sparkling eyes, I got it, I got it.

KŌNO TAEKO

ANTS SWARM

Japan's classic literature of the eleventh century was largely in the hands of women. Two of the world's masterpieces, Lady Murasaki's Tale of Genji *and Sei Shonagon's* Pillow Book *were written by educated court ladies, confined to certain quarters and not allowed to use the official language. Relegated to the vernacular and deprived of holding public offices, the women created an extraordinary literature that steered away from the traditional models. In our time, writers such as Kōno Taeko have found that their society continues to regard women's writing as a separate category within Japanese culture. Paradoxically, this has given many women writers a constant and large audience of their own and, since they are only reluctantly accepted as part of the "official" culture, it has allowed them a greater degree of experimentation.*

For over thirty years, Kōno Taeko found it almost impossible to write. A weak child who, in later years, contracted tuberculosis, she failed in her attempt to enter the literature department of Osaka Women's College and after studying economics, she accepted a government job. Her first short story wasn't published until 1961, when she was thirty-five. Kōno's literature explores the closed worlds of women and children, worlds in which her heroines must invent for themselves fantasies of fulfilment which ultimately fail. Her erotic stories are sombre and violent, on the threshold of what Kōno calls, ironically, "the deep, free world."

———————

FOR A MOMENt Fumiko had the feeling that she could return to the deep, free world in which she had been until a moment before, but after all she could not go back to sleep any longer. Wanting to get up, she pushed away the light cover with one hand. But she could not shift her position further. She was concerned with the change her body might feel when she moved. Pressed by the warm darkness, she stayed in the same position, lying on her side, bending her body slightly like a bow, and keeping her legs together completely all the way to her toes.

Her husband, Matsuda, continued to breathe strongly in his sleep. The pendulum on the wall clock swayed busily but did not tell the time at all. Lying down in the same position as if forced to do so, she gradually came to feel a sense of pressure on her chest, as if her breathing was being controlled. After remaining immobile in this way out of laziness and hesitation, she finally raised the upper part of her body, supporting herself with one hand. She did not feel any change. Untying her tightly pressed legs and raising her knee, she moved one leg to a cold tatami mat. This time too there was no special feeling. She stepped on the tatami.

Opening the paper door, she found to her surprise that it was not midnight. In the quiet corridor, she could see the shapes of things. The clouded-glass door looked weakly whitened. Since Fumiko's sleep seemed to become deeper toward dawn, it was very rare for her to wake up at this time. Thinking that she must have been worried even in her sleep, she touched the doorknob of the bathroom.

Fumiko's menstruation was already about a week late. This had seldom happened. From her girlhood, her menstruation had been very punctual, to the point of being amusing. Even the time it started, usually in the evening, was the same. Since her marriage to Matsuda, a man a year younger than she was, its punctuality had never changed. The two had meant to avoid having a child and had had no trouble at all.

When it was three days overdue, she told Matsuda about it.

"Hmm" was Matsuda's first word.

"Just as I said – I felt sure that time," Fumiko said.

In their married life, they depended on nothing but the punctuality of Fumiko's menstruation to avoid having a child. Fumiko was working for an American law firm; she left the office promptly and had Saturdays off. Matsuda, on the other hand, was a journalist responsible for political affairs, and his work schedule was irregular. When he was busy there were days when he came home at dawn or did not return home for two days. He was sometimes busy for weeks at a stretch. When he could finally take a breather, it sometimes happened that Fumiko was in a danger period. When that happened, Fumiko felt concerned and had suggested taking some measures other than their usual one. But Matsuda never considered it. He said no and avoided the subject.

"Lions eat at one time and they are free from appetite the rest of the time. I am like them. I don't develop a lingering attachment," he added. Fumiko thought she could understand.

When Matsuda's caresses started, Fumiko's body immediately desired pain. And seeing her desire pain, Matsuda, as if he had been waiting for it, became excited. He tortured her hands and feet, eventually using some tools. Finally, without being aware of it, she would whisper in a hoarse voice, "You love me as much as this." Then responding to the still further heightened effect that was evoked, she would blurt out, demanding crazily yet begging, "Please forgive me, forgive me." Finally, Matsuda finished loving while torturing. It was not unusual for him to want to share the following night in the same way. But when they entered the unsafe period, Matsuda was unbelievably clean. During that time he sometimes made a few scars on Fumiko's body, but he never bothered her more than that. And she loved this aspect of him mixed with his passionate aspect.

One morning, about half a month ago, she was dragged back to bed when she was about to get up. When she reminded him of the unsafe period, he answered irritably that he knew. Fumiko frowned. Even on the safe days, Matsuda would awaken with the sound of many newspapers being placed above his pillow, and after absorbing himself in them, he would fall asleep again. The reason why Fumiko felt miserable may have been because she was used to his usual clean behaviour; since it was very rare for him to act in that way, however, she could not refuse him. Seeing him getting excited hastily and unable to rid himself of his desire, she finally urged him on.

Yet Fumiko's unpleasant feeling remained. Although that fleeting feeling she had of not caring gave her a sense of release, the fear of pregnancy was always with her. She had to leave for the office soon. Besides, it was love-making which omitted pain, and all the more for that reason she could not be immersed in it.

Getting up and making herself ready quickly, Fumiko felt even worse. Turning back she saw Matsuda under the covers, only his head showing.

"I feel I conceived a child. It felt different from usual," she said to him deliberately.

"Is that right?" Matsuda answered from under the quilt. She smiled bitterly. But at the time she was struck by the feeling that her words were true. She stopped her hand while drawing up the zipper of her skirt. When she had gathered all her impressions, she felt sure that there was a special feeling, despite the fact that she had been unable to lose herself.

When the usual time for her menstruation approached, she became more restless. And finally when the day came and it did not start then or on the day after, she was annoyed and nodded to herself, yes it was true. It may be true that there cannot be a feeling of conception. But she thought she must have felt it as if by some presentiment. She thought it was not only because of her fear that she had felt sure at the time.

It was not that there was no tone of resentment in her

telling him about the lateness of her menstruation and touching upon that day.

"What are we going to do?" she said.

"What shall we do? We're in trouble." So saying, Matsuda held his knees in his arms.

"Yes, we're truly in trouble."

"But it's funny to say I'm sorry between husband and wife." Fumiko felt that she was being scolded for her tone of voice.

"Yes, that time, I too felt as if I were under some evil influence," she said. "But we must think about it. The time is the problem."

They were supposed to go to the United States in July to study for a year. Matsuda had received a Fulbright fellowship and was to attend C University. Since Matsuda had applied early, she too was to enter the university. She had already completed the necessary entrance procedures. Since they had to attend the orientation program there before the start of school, they had only about a month before they were to leave for the United States. Fumiko, who had not experienced this before, did not know for certain, but she felt it would be impossible to take care of the fetus and return to her normal self within a month. She had heard that it would be very difficult to take care of it in the United States. Even if it were not, it would not be possible to do such a thing soon after they arrived.

Matsuda listened to Fumiko's words silently and finally said, "But it doesn't mean that it's certain."

"It's been three days. It's never happened before."

"Relax."

"Yes, but if I wasn't mistaken –"

"Yes, that's right." After thinking for a while, Matsuda,

raising his face, said, "Can you give up studying in the U.S.?"

"If it proves difficult to take care of before we leave."

"Will you do that?"

"Although regretfully, I will stay."

Then Matsuda said, "Then you will have the child."

"Do you mean what you said?" It took some time before she asked that.

"Yes. It's not bad to have one."

"What! When did you start thinking like that?" Fumiko gazed at Matsuda. "That morning, was that intentional – ?"

"No, it was not. Absolutely not."

"Yes, I think so too. I believe you. But since when have you been thinking – ?"

Matsuda did not answer.

"It was because I told you about it. Right? Isn't that right?"

"Of course partly because of that –"

"Is that right – I understand." Sighing, she averted her eyes.

Getting married while both were working, they had naturally avoided having a child. But when they gradually realized that they clearly did not like children, they promised each other that they would not have a child.

"There are very few men who want to have children badly. The reason why they make them, after all, while declaring that they will not have any, is because they are begged by their wives. I know at least two couples among my friends. If it's okay with you, it's fine with me."

When Matsuda said so repeatedly, she felt no resistance and would even take the initiative in swearing that she would not have a child. Recently they had become so used to their plan that they did not have to remind themselves of it.

Fumiko loved to hear Matsuda talk of his childhood days. "When my grandmother was dying, I couldn't be found anywhere. I was up on the roof shooting pigeons with an air gun. People in the house did not hear the sound of the gun, for they were out of their minds in that situation." He recounted, "Now I am middle-sized, but I was very small when I was in elementary school. When I entered school, I was the second from the front. Line up, the teacher would say and there was only one in front of me. I was very sad. I hated line-up." Saying this, he would stand up and stretch his arms straight out in front of him as the children were taught to do when lining up. At these moments she was attracted to him very strongly. When he was anxious to take off her dress in bed, he would suddenly become obedient, and putting his head on her chest like a child, put the button ripped forcibly off her dress next to her pillow, saying, "*Hai*" [here]. She could not help bursting out laughing with happiness.

Yet Fumiko had never wanted to have a child. Just to think of bearing the child and having to raise it disgusted her. This time too, when her menstruation was late, she was fearful, held a grudge against Matsuda, and was concerned only with finding a solution; she never had any real hope. Therefore she found Matsuda's words extremely shocking. She felt betrayed and jealous when she thought that Matsuda, while she remained oblivious, had come to think of a child and experience a parental emotion which she would never have, despite the fact that they had promised each other so emphatically. She also thought of Matsuda's childlike character which used to please her so much. Then, together with the feeling of betrayal, she felt that he was not grown-up enough to have a child of his own, forgetting the fact that although a year younger than she, he was thirty years old. This made her even more irritated.

Despite all this, when she said "not yet" after laying the mattress as he told her to and returning from the bathroom, she was surprised by her own obedient tone. Besides, since the day when she told Matsuda about being overdue, she went to the bathroom more frequently. It was not much different at work, but at home she felt like going to the bathroom quite often. Coming back from the bathroom she always reported to Matsuda whenever he was at home. He had never asked, but she knew well his tension when resisting the desire to ask her. She reported to him tenderly.

This did not mean, however, that she had already made up her mind to have a child in case she was pregnant. In her mind, she was thinking that if it did not start within a few days, she would investigate ways to take care of it. If everything could be taken care of before the beginning of the term, then of course she would go abroad. In that case, even Matsuda would agree to give up the child. But what if it could not be taken care of before that time? Then she would have no choice but to remain here; even then she did not imagine that she could come to want to bear the child. Despite these thoughts, the way she reported to Matsuda became more tender each time. To Matsuda, it meant that he had almost obtained her consent.

Fumiko came to notice that Matsuda's face shone each time she told him that it had not yet started. Then he would say,

"The tiny one is there, isn't it? It must be like a dot now. Or is it like a sesame seed? The sesame child, we must take good care of it."

Influenced by his manner, the words which Fumiko used in reporting changed to "It's still all right."

"Are you happy?" she even added sometimes, unconsciously.

"Of course I'm happy," Matsuda answered.

"You want me to bear it," Fumiko said as if appealing to him, but Matsuda only nodded two or three times, burying his face in her chest. When Matsuda made such a gesture, like a child expressing a heartfelt desire with constraint and worrying about her response, she felt that she could not win. Yet since it was covered up in playfulness, it was easier for her to give him a response which was different from what she really felt.

"Do you want me to have the child?" she said. She wanted to see Matsuda's childish gesture again. Each time Matsuda would nod while burying his head.

"All right, then I will bear him for you," she answered each time.

It was only a matter of days, but Matsuda's fantasies about the child became inflated. Because Fumiko's attitude was such, Matsuda did not hesitate to share them with her.

Seeing Matsuda like this, Fumiko could not but wonder. Her wish that her period would start had never completely vanished from her heart. It was not only because of their study abroad. It was because she did not want to have a child. It was because she thought of the helpless feeling of conceiving a child which she did not want, and having to bear and raise it. She was stunned when she thought of herself letting Matsuda dream of a child and then letting his dream immediately become so overly inflated.

In spite of this, Fumiko did not dislike hearing Matsuda talk about a child. She even encouraged him to do so, thereby compounding her crime.

"The child will have been born by this time next year," she said.

"That's right. But I feel really sorry that I can't be with you when you are in labour. I wish I could pull it out from between your fingers," Matsuda said.

"I'll be fine, you don't have to worry. By the time you return –"

"A little one will be waiting for me. It really will be nice. I will love him. I will buy many things for him."

"What kind of things?" Asking, she pulled out a cigarette. But noticing Matsuda's worried face, she put it down.

"Dolls, tricycles – Then I will take the child to the zoo. Is there a book of tickets for the zoo?"

"A book of tickets?"

"I will buy a book of tickets to take him to the zoo. When he grows up, I will arrange it so that he can charge all the drinks he wants anywhere. If he does not drink much I will be worried."

"Oh dear! You really are an indulgent father."

"Yes, indeed I am," said Matsuda. "I will attend PTA meetings."

"Yes, please do. It will save me the bother."

"I may have to bow as deeply as this when I meet his teachers." So saying, he bowed his head so deeply as to hit the dining table. "– But if a teacher complains about my child, I will beat him up." She could not stop laughing. While laughing she thought she would like to see Matsuda play a father's role. She did not want to bear a child. Nor did she have the broadmindedness to allow Matsuda to have a woman other than herself. Yet a desire to see Matsuda play father welled up in her strongly.

Fumiko knew that her period had started. First she felt relieved. Then she thought it had been late because her fear and tension had been so strong since that morning. She thought again that there was nothing to worry about for a while. The matter of going to study abroad came back to her as before.

But when coming out of the bathroom to return to the bedroom, she stopped suddenly, looking down the quiet corridor at dawn. She looked around. There was a wash basin at the side. On the shelf were two or three razor blades which Matsuda had used and left there. The door to the kitchen a few meters away was open and she could see a cupboard there. At the end of the corridor was the entrance to the house. At the entrance, a short, dark, Japanese-style curtain was hung; it was for winter use, but had been left hanging for a few months now. The platform where the stairs started, the paper door to the bedroom, and the door to the western room – More than a year had passed since the two had moved to this rented house. They had already become accustomed to the place. Yet their life there in the past week had been completely different from before. It was particularly so since Fumiko confessed to Matsuda about the delay of her period.

Fumiko reflected deeply on the past several days. At night Matsuda's footsteps had sounded different. While she was preparing evening snacks for him, he had been eager to talk about the child. Since Matsuda usually had fallen asleep again when she was ready to leave the house for the office, she was accustomed to saying good-bye to him casually, but it had been different these days. Whenever I opened and closed this door – thinking of it she looked back at the bathroom door. She realized that she could not dismiss this incident as a foolish experience. She realized that the familiar curtain, corridor, wooden door, wall, and pillar had all been imbued with a certain richness during these days, but that the richness was now diminishing rapidly.

As she brought her body into the bed in the pitch dark, Fumiko thought of the disappointment Matsuda would feel when he learned that it was a mistake, and thought she might keep it from him for a few days. Yet raising her head which was almost sinking into her pillow, she moved closer to Matsuda. His breathing in sleep stopped, and murmuring something while half-asleep, he responded at last as if only his arms were awake. His cheek was warm. She embraced his head again, pushing her nose strongly against it and inhaling the smell of his ears which she deeply loved.

"It was a mistake," she said away from his ear a little. Suddenly she started sobbing. Realizing that Matsuda had raised his body sharply, she said again weeping, "It was a mistake."

"Is that right?" Matsuda's voice showed disappointment. "But it's all right. It's all right. Wait a second." The light was turned on, making a "*pachin*" sound.

"Oh, don't turn the light on."

"All right, I'll turn it off." So saying, he pulled the cord once again.

"I should have kept silent from the start. I talked too early," Fumiko said on the pillow which Matsuda let her share and cried again. She felt that she was like a barren woman who had been longing for a child and who had to face the bitter fact once again. Yet the tears flowed spontaneously.

"No, it was nice that you told me. It was good that we could have a rehearsal," Matsuda said.

"You were so delighted."

"Why not truly make me happy next time. First we will go

to America together and then it will be fine when we come back."

"I will do it before it is very late," Fumiko said, and it was a truthful voice. She felt that she would like to let Matsuda have his child. "Although I do not like children."

"You will change. I too did not like children before."

"What if I don't change? What if the child is born and still I don't like him?"

"It wouldn't matter. I'd change the diapers."

"You must be an indulgent father. But I'll be different. It will not be so extreme if it's a boy, but to a girl I will be very strict. Since you will be exceptionally sweet and I will be extremely strict, other people will think I am a stepmother." So saying, she felt a strong feeling toward her stepchild-like child arise in her heart. It was certain that the incident had affected her. Yet she was released from the worry of the past several days. For this reason, the feelings about the child they had experienced stimulated her imagination extravagantly.

"If it is a girl," Fumiko said, "I will not let her have much education."

"I agree," Matsuda answered. "School education will surely do no good."

"I might let her go through compulsory education."

"No, that compulsory education is the worst. Let's go with tutors."

"Such a luxury! I'll never agree to that," Fumiko said. "It is more than enough for her to go to a local school. After she graduates from junior high school I will make her stay at home and use her as a maid. Yes, by this time of day she'd be forced to get up to prepare breakfast. I'll be here with you like this."

"That will be good."

"Do you like it? Then I'll make her do it when she enters elementary school."

"Can a first-grader cook rice?"

"I'll make her do it."

"What a poor child our child will be."

"But it will be good for the child. It's for the child."

"That's true too."

"I hate a girl who thinks of all sorts of things. Let's raise her to be a girl who never talks back. It won't do if she just restrains herself from talking back. She ought to be a child who is incapable of criticism, a child who has no opinion of her own. A child who can automatically do what she is told – an idiot-like child – even her face must look like an idiot's."

"You mean a child like a doll."

"Yes, like a Chinese girl in olden times; we'll let her learn only domestic matters from an early age, and soon after she graduates from junior high school, I'll marry her off."

"I'll visit her often to see how she is. I'll bring her some of the sugar we receive without your knowing."

"No!"

"But you never cook with sugar. There's lots of unused sugar."

"Is that so? Okay then, you can bring it."

"I'll go to her every Sunday."

"You'll be disliked by your son-in-law."

"No matter. He'll be a nice husband. I'll find her a nice, gentle one."

"It won't work that way. I'll urge him to be a bad husband, to be dissipated. You too must encourage him to be dissipated.

Even if you find beautiful women, I know you will give them up. Bring them to your daughter's husband, as many as possible, like you bring sugar."

Fumiko continued, "I will not listen even if she comes to me to complain. I'll show her my body and tell her that her father is such a cruel man, but that her mother endures it. I'll tell her that she must bear it too."

The clock on the pillar struck. It had stopped after one.

"What time is it?" Matsuda asked.

"It must be six-thirty."

"Go look. It must be seven-thirty. You'll be late."

"That's all right."

Fumiko did not want their delightful conversation to be interrupted further. She was eager to resume it as soon as possible. But Matsuda got up, and making a noise as he unlocked the glass door, opened the outside rain door slightly.

"It is six-thirty, as I thought," Fumiko said, looking at the clock from the pillow. Matsuda closed the glass doors where the outer wooden doors were opened and drew the curtain again, just as Fumiko had often done for Matsuda, who used to stay in bed until after breakfast. Then he walked out into the corridor.

Today Matsuda brought the newspapers in by himself, and sitting cross-legged on the tatami in his pyjamas, started to open them one after another. Fumiko could not complain, considering his profession. Yet seeing after a while that his eyes were wandering, she called to him from the bed,

"There's nothing, is there? It's okay, isn't it?" It was all right. Matsuda left the newspapers and returned to the bed, asking,

"Do you have time – is it still all right?"

"Yes," Fumiko answered, but already more than twenty minutes had passed. She certainly had to get up now.

"It is nice."

"I am envious that you can go late." While saying this she remembered suddenly that she had run out of butter for breakfast. She said,

"Is it all right if we don't have butter this morning? There isn't any left. I forgot to buy some."

"We have jam, don't we?"

"Yes, and cheese too."

"Then that's enough," said Matsuda. Through the opening left where Matsuda had failed to close the door completely, Fumiko caught a glimpse of the pleats of a skirt fluttering. It was the daughter she and Matsuda had created, a daughter whom strangers might think a stepdaughter.

"If our child forgets to buy butter, I will never forgive her," Fumiko said to Matsuda. "I am very strict with girls. Very strict. You will not be able to take it. Although you can do anything to me. You may hide in a closet and hold your ears with your hands."

The paper door opened. A short, pleated skirt came in. Fumiko pretended to be asleep.

"Mother," said her daughter, who was around seven or eight. Making the pause as long as possible, Fumiko said with her eyes closed, "I did not hear the sound of the door closing. You were scolded before for not closing the door tightly."

"But father does the same," the daughter said.

"Are you the same as father?" So saying, she jumped up and attacked the daughter.

"Do you mean to talk back?" With all the strength in her

fingers, Fumiko pinched both sides of her daughter's mouth. The daughter tried to escape, but since she was pinched tightly from the right and left she couldn't move.

"Please forgive me, forgive me," she begged. They were the same words which Fumiko uttered at night in her frenzy when begging Matsuda for more pain.

"I cannot forgive you," Fumiko said. "It's not only talking back. Think of all the bad things you have done. To talk to your mother standing – who taught you such a thing? Also, when you came in here, you came in without saying anything. You must say something before you come in."

At the same time, Fumiko's fingers continued to torture her. Not only the short, pleated skirt, but also her blouse and undergarments, she took off everything and pinched her all over her body. Still she could torture her further about the butter. When she realized that, Fumiko brought the daughter to the kitchen, still torturing her.

"Is there butter?"

"We ran out. I was going to buy some, so in order to receive money –"

"You forgot to buy butter."

"Yes." As soon as she answered she crouched beside the gas range as if hiding and lowered her face. There were several red scars on her back. They looked like scars left by cigarette burns.

"Go and buy butter," Fumiko said. Butter in a yellow paper box slid down from the ceiling and onto her palm, feeling cold and heavy. Fumiko peeled off the thin, unwrinkled paper attached to it and scooping some out with a spoon, brought it to the gas flame. If it melts completely it will be very hot. Looking down at the back of the daughter who was squatting at her feet, Fumiko gazed at the butter in the spoon. A yellow lump melting smoothly from its edges –

"You'll be late," Matsuda said. The hands of the clock had already passed seven and were hanging down.

"Yes, I'll be late," Fumiko said, as if it concerned someone else.

"You must have been tired out. Because of this, since that time," Matsuda said. "Will you stay home? I'll call the office for you."

"Since I have never stayed away from the office –" Fumiko showed her decision to stay ambiguously.

"It's all right, now and then." Answering so, Matsuda's hands groped for her breasts. Being excited herself, Fumiko could not, like the other morning, think him despicable.

"When should I have a baby?"

"After we return from America."

"When after?"

"Any time."

"Isn't earlier better for you? Really, I would like to let you have a baby. But –" Fumiko felt Matsuda's fingers holding one nipple tightly. It was being pulled inward and the little finger of the same hand groped for the other nipple. The neck of the little finger missed the nipple two or three times. When it was finally caught, she felt severe pain in both nipples, as if they were being torn out. Yet Matsuda pulled them harder, with all his might, as if raising a heavy bucket. As they were pulled she gasped with pain and pushed her face against his shoulder, but this withdrew her chest further, increasing the pain and the pleasure.

"I would like very much to bear a baby for you, but as you

know I don't like babies," she said as soon as she was able to breathe. "So please order me. Any time will be fine. If not, I will not –" Just then, her breath was cut short. Trembling all over her body with the pleasure of the pain and scarcely able to breathe, she said,

"Please, order me – please force me."

"I will. At the right time I will order you. 'Bear a baby even if you die,'" Matsuda said, strengthening his grip.

"I will bear a baby even if I die. So when I give birth to the baby stay with me darling," she continued to say, panting.

"Of course I'll be with you."

"To be with me is not enough. I may struggle because of the pain. You must tie me. That may not be enough. If not, will you hit me? It will be so wonderful to bear a child while being tied and hit. If it is such a childbirth, I would like to experience it soon – Please be quick."

Matsuda jumped up. Fumiko realized a strip of light was reflected on the curtain. But when she heard Matsuda open the closet and take out the fishing rods which were placed there although neither of them ever fished, she could not care about people knowing.

———————

At the doorway, Matsuda, who had already put on his shoes, received the bottle of milk from Fumiko and brought it to his mouth.

"Are you all right?" he asked, taking the bottle from his lips a little. Fumiko smiled silently.

"When you become pregnant we cannot do what we did

this morning for a while. I'll have to treat you with discretion. Be prepared for it, all right?"

"But when you can do it for me again, there'll be a child."

"Don't worry." So saying, Matsuda emptied the bottle, pushing his head back. "I'll make a soundproof room. Even now we need one. If it's going to be like this morning –" Handing the milk bottle to Fumiko, Matsuda said,

"I'll call your office." He left.

The bed was not yet made. The outer rain doors were all open. There was a little pause in the rainy season and the early summer sun was shining and the wind was blowing.

Fumiko sat down near the open corridor. She indulged herself in the sense of her body. Everywhere on her body, the hotness turned to pain and the pain turned to hotness while both gradually diminished. She liked the feeling – as if her body were rippling under the touch of the early summer breeze. Since they had used up their time and Matsuda had left without breakfast, she did not have breakfast. It was not that she was not hungry, but she continued to sit in this way, and gradually she became sleepy. She lay down in her clothes on the unmade bed and closed her eyes. She felt again that it was a pleasant, early summer breeze.

When she realized what time it was, it was already close to two o'clock. I cannot let my child see me this way, she suddenly felt. She made the bed and went to the kitchen.

When she was about to open the window, she saw something jet black about the size of her palm on the bay window. It was wriggling. For a moment she could not tell what it was, but on closer examination it turned out to be a chunk of beef on which numerous ants were swarming fiercely. It was in fact lying on the wooden board. It was the meat which Fumiko had earlier put in the nearby refrigerator.

Matsuda had placed one of the pieces before they were infested with the ants on one of Fumiko's scars this morning. Fumiko had had him place them there several times before. Matsuda used to bring the pieces of meat with chopsticks. Seeing them brought dangling to her hip or shoulder, she used to burst out laughing. This morning Matsuda must have forgotten to put the wooden board holding the meat back into the refrigerator.

Numerous ants completely covered the meat. They all swarmed on it eagerly. There were a few ants which were wandering around the wooden board. And strangely, since all the ants had come to the meat, there was no line of ants leading up to it.

Nothing could be done with the meat now, even if she got upset. Since there was no need to chase the ants away quickly, Fumiko looked at them swarming and wriggling as if they were one body. She had not realized that so many ants lived in her house. She had never even seen them. Was it because her family had little to do with sugar? The reason why this family had little to do with sugar was partly because Fumiko was not a domestic woman. Besides the fact that neither husband nor wife liked coffee, and therefore did not need sugar for that, she had never tried to have a baby who would drink milk or a child who would throw away candy wrappers. She herself preferred smoking to eating snacks and she rarely spent time preparing dishes using sugar.

Yet there were so many ants living even in such a house. They must be ants which had forgotten the taste of sugar, or ants which did not know the taste of sugar. There must have been a taste of sweetness in the blood of the beef which, not having been put back in the refrigerator, had become a little sour. It was as might be expected of ants that they did not miss the meat, and came to swarm in such huge numbers.

Fumiko tried to observe the movement of individual ants. They appeared to be trembling rapidly and to be rubbing their heads on the meat eagerly. After a while, however, she could not continue to look at them since there were too many ants swarming too busily, too close to each other. As Fumiko watched them, the ants came to appear to be one black, wriggling thing. The black lump of ants continued to wriggle as if laughing at her, as if encouraging her.

ROBIN METCALFE

THE SHIRT

Sometime in the sixteenth century, the Portuguese merchants who traded with the ancient kingdoms of West Africa brought back to Europe ivory, vanilla pods and religious charms which the sailors called feticos. The charms, exported to England, were translated as "fetishes." Four centuries later, in 1901, the word was used for the first time to describe an object that arouses erotic feelings.

Since our curiosity is boundless, it isn't surprising to discover that the most unexpected things can become arousing. The clothes left behind by Aeneas when he abandoned Queen Dido, Rapunzel's hair which the Prince begs her to let down, the topless herring boxes which served as sandals to My Darling Clementine can, no doubt, send a lover into ecstasy. Less obviously romantic are the collectors of frilly underwear and jockstraps. And yet, in all these examples, what matters to the lover is the evocation of a loved one through one of his or her parts, a portion of the erotic universe which somehow reflects the enormous whole.

Sometimes the loved one has a specific face and name: Cinderella, Beatrice, Christ; sometimes – as in Robin Metcalfe's story – only the objects exist, and the person conjured up is a multitudinous and inexpressible fantasy whose being depends on the shoe, the handkerchief, the shirt.

———————

THE STREET where Randall Zinck has his store is bracketed between busy thoroughfares. A torrent of traffic rushes past on either side of the little neighbourhood. Occasionally a stray car wanders down the street as if lost. In the park across from Randall's store, sunlight settles through the trees like silt in a deep, slow pool. You can just hear the sound of traffic above the rustling of the leaves.

The faded letters on the tall, old-fashioned windows of Randall's store say ZINCK'S ARMY SURPLUS, but one can find all sorts of old clothes, not to mention camping supplies, among the dusty racks. Randall is both the proprietor and the only sales clerk. A tall, thin man on the elderly side of middle age, Randall has the air of a dealer in rare and erotic antiquities, a connoisseur of the most exquisite taste. His smile, while perfectly proper, is also somehow suggestive, as if it harbours an indecent secret. I know what you are looking for, it says, and I am quite certain you will find it here.

It is Randall's preference to deal in used clothing. For all their flashy stylishness, new clothes are cheap and shallow things. They have no history. Used clothing, even the most drab and tattered, is steeped in the past, in that most mysterious kind of history, the personal, the unknown. For what is unknown must be imagined, and how much vaster and more complex is the geography of the imagination compared to the plain streets of daily reality.

The first time I visited Randall's store, I found the jacket of my dreams. An old high school jacket, probably of the fifties or late forties, judging by the quality of the sturdy, navy wool cloth. The white satin lining under the collar was yellowed but still intact, the pockets bordered with white leather piping. And on the shoulder – what joy! – the name Steve, embroidered in silver thread. Who is Steve, what is he? By now, he is probably married, middle-aged, dead. I don't want to know. I can see him bundled in blue wool, during some ancient, innocent winter, going to basketball practice, walking his best friend home along the railway tracks, jerking off in his bedroom surrounded by pennants and Hardy Boy novels. I am in love with him. Every time I put on his jacket I become him, I put on his youth and his unknowing beauty. Strangers, misled by my small deception, address me by his name. Sometimes I correct them, sometimes I do not.

Randall always calls me Steve. He knows my real name, having seen it on my credit card when I made my first purchase. Nevertheless, he calls me Steve, out of respect for my fantasy. It has become our private joke. Since that first visit, he has treated me with a polite familiarity, as if he recognizes in me a kindred spirit. He smiles as the bell tinkles above the wooden door to announce my arrival and leads me to the bin of army-surplus footwear, where a pair of white canvas sneakers is waiting for me. A label sewn neatly to the underside of the tongue says that GAUTHIER, P.L., pulled these onto his sweaty feet more times than he would care to remember. I am enchanted, of course, and wear them home.

Three blocks from Randall's store, across from the army base on Gottingen Street, I crouch on the sidewalk to retie my shoelaces. A young man walks slowly past me, pauses, stops. I look up into the blue eyes of a pretty soldier with curly blond hair. He asks if I am from Windsor Park. Not understanding his question, I grunt noncommittally. He takes this to mean yes, and suddenly smiles at me as if I were a long-lost brother. I am from his regiment, it seems – he recognizes the sneakers. Can he walk with me? (Can he!) Used clothing can be one of the most powerful aphrodisiacs.

———

It is a fine bright day in early summer. Too fine – I know I won't get any work done today. A good day to visit Randall's store.

The air is warm enough to get away with wearing only a T-shirt. Light green, armed-forces issue, with darker green trim at the neck and sleeves. A gift from the pretty blond soldier, who left in the halflight of morning wearing one of mine. I can smell the odour of his golden skin trapped in the soft fabric. My armpits sprout dark hairs from under the sleeves, where his blond hair would have glistened before. And after he left my bed – embarrassment of riches! – I found his jockey shorts, lost between the tangled sheets. The horny god of love smiles on me. I have them on now, beneath my blue jeans. The white cotton that cradled his hard little nuts is wrapped snugly around my balls. They roll inside their hairy sac as the juices stir within. My cock nuzzles against warm cloth.

Randall's street is nearly deserted in the lazy afternoon sun. Two old men doze on a park bench in the little square. The shop is hazy with dust as I open the front door. A tinny aria from *Tosca* drifts up from a portable cassette player propped against the cash register. Randall is bent over a newspaper that is spread out in front of him on the countertop. He looks up to greet me with a genteel nod and returns to his reading. The smoke from his cigarette plays hide-and-seek with the shafts of light that filter through the dirty windows. The air in the store is warm and stale.

Randall always lets me take my time poking through the tumbled bins of clothing. I linger over piles of combat boots, sneakers, T-shirts, dark-green army sweaters peppered with moth holes, military caps with the insignia removed. I try one of these on, but as usual it is far too small. Do soldiers all have tiny heads? Nothing here catches my interest. I move over to the other side of the store, passing over the boxes of manufacturers' rejects and secondhand jackets. The table of used shirts is a circus of colours. I sort absently among garish paisleys and stripes, sniffing for the special find that makes the search worthwhile.

My fingers catch at a patch of dark cloth. I pull out a knit shirt with short sleeves. It is burgundy with fine yellow horizontal stripes. Nothing beautiful, but something about it holds my interest. Stretched and rumpled, it long ago lost its shape – or, rather, it gained a shape, that of the body it once clothed. The ghosts of biceps bulge at the sleeves, swelling pectorals stretch the chest, an invisible neck surges from the open collar.

A faint male odour lingers about the fabric. Some unknown man has left his imprint here for me to snuggle into, as in the morning one might curl into the warm hollow left by a body that has gone on its way.

Ah, I see that one has found you. Randall regards me from behind his counter with that secret smile of his. That shirt is very special. You must try it on. He pauses to extinguish his cigarette with a delicate tap, then walks around the back of the counter and out into the store. Come. I'll open up the dressing room.

I follow Randall down the twisting aisles to the back of the store. The path to the dressing room leads through a rack of World War II greatcoats, looming shaggy and black like old bison. We push through the herd of coats and out into a small back storage room, crowded with dusty boxes. To the left is a familiar cubicle with a curtain stretched across the opening. I move toward it. No, says Randall, not that one. Over here.

Randall turns a key in a lock and pushes open the door to a small room that I have not seen before. He flips on the light and it glares off of white walls and ceiling. Here we are, says Randall. Take as long as you like. I step into the room and pull the door shut behind me.

The bareness of the room is a relief after the musty clutter of the store. It is larger than an ordinary dressing room. A chair upholstered in blue vinyl is positioned against the wall to my left. Across from it stretches a large mirror. And beneath the mirror, a clean white shelf, with a glass bottle, a neatly folded towel, and a book.

I strip off my T-shirt and pause to admire myself in the mirror. I run my fingers lightly over the ripples on my stomach, bought with the agony of many thousands of sit-ups. The burgundy shirt is soft to the touch and tickles my nose as I pull it over my head. It flows like a cool hand across my skin. What man has worn this shirt before? I feel as if I am in contact with him now, through my contact with the shirt. I regard myself in the mirror. I have deliberately let the shirt fall carelessly. The collar is crumpled and crooked, the tail hangs out rumpled over my jeans. My hair is mussed up. I look like a tough. For a moment I experience that delicious sensation of seeing myself as a stranger, someone glimpsed briefly on the street, perhaps a labourer. It's an ugly shirt, and shows its age, the sort of shirt a man would wear to perform heavy physical work. To hoist garbage into a truck, perhaps. I smile at myself, a come-on to the stranger in the mirror. I strike a couple of poses.

My movements bring my eye back to the articles arranged on the shelf. They have been placed there as neatly and carefully as if on an altar. They are Randall's, I tell myself, and private, but my curiosity gets the better of me. I unscrew the cap of the bottle and take a cautious sniff. Ordinary vegetable oil. In a dressing room? I move on. The towel is antiseptically clean, with a chemical odour, its virginity restored by detergent and bleach. If it has any secrets, it will not give them up. At last my hand hovers over the book. It is large with a black cover, a looseleaf binder I now realize, not an ordinary book. Carefully, as if trespassing, I turn back the cover.

The image startles me. For a moment I think I am looking again in the mirror. A dark-haired, muscular man gazes at me, his build as stocky as my own. He is wearing the same burgundy-and-yellow knit shirt that I am wearing now. But he is not me, of course. The man in the polaroid photograph has a ragged moustache; I am clean shaven. His hair is a cluster of playful curls, like that of a Greek faun. Mine is straight. Nevertheless, the resemblance is striking.

The next page holds another surprise. The same man, only now his hand has moved up from his side and reaches in toward the centre, to grasp his cock, which is hard and exposed. The cloth of his jeans is peeled back in a wide V, his balls dangle free like pale fruit, the pink shaft points up toward his navel. More images follow, showing him pushing the shirt up over his chest, squeezing his balls, closing his eyes – and finally, in the last photograph, trailing his fingers through a shiny puddle of white smeared across his belly. I gaze at this last image with rapt attention, my hand pressed against the growing bulge in my jeans, gently kneading the eager flesh.

Did I say the last photograph? I meant the last of him. For the next page begins a new series, this time of a slender young blond man with long lank hair. The burgundy shirt hangs loosely over his flat belly. This one has his pants off entirely, posing with his cock in his hand, smirking at the camera. His eyes remain wide open right through to the final photograph, watching the white liquid come threading out into the air. My own cock is pounding at the tight fabric of my jeans.

The photographs continue. I plunge into them as if deeper into a dream. There must be at least a dozen men. I start to count, but keep losing my concentration. A thin man with close-cut brown hair, as stern and serious as a schoolteacher, his cock a ruler pointing upward. A middle-aged man, grizzled and masculine, thick hair sprouting from his powerful arms and from the open neck of the burgundy shirt. A soldier with a tiny black moustache and a tattoo on the bulge of his upper arm, gazing from the photograph with deep, liquid eyes. His cock aims straight out of the picture like a gun. A dozen men, standing before a white wall, their cocks hard for the camera, jerking off one by one. Eyes open or closed, cocks straight or curved, cut or uncut, all joined in the animal ritual of coming.

The mirror presents me, spotlit in a white room like an actor in the opening scene of a play. The script lies open before me. I examine the mirror more closely. The glass is dark, like the mirrors in police questioning rooms. Not all the light is being reflected. I press my face against the glass and peer into a silver void. I see my own eyes glistening in the shadow of my hand. My reflection steps back and smiles at me. We know what to do next.

I take my time starting, rubbing the hard ridge that has risen in my jeans. Deliberately, with a tantalizing slowness, I open the fly, gingerly lift out the tender balls, the long pink root of my cock. The edge of the shirt brushes against the tip of my cock, a maddening sensation that makes it stiffen and point upward. My hand strokes soothingly up and down. Horniness seems to flow into my groin from the shirt. The mirror turns me into my own porn star, one of a series. Tinker Tailor Soldier Sailor. Me, I'm the Garbage Man. Stick out yer can. I have ceased to be me and have become an ideal type: Man with Hard-on.

My balls are framed by the folded-back flaps of my jeans. The pressure of the underside of my cock is pleasant, but the pants are becoming an encumbrance. I peel them off and feel the sweet freedom of air tingling against my bare ass. My cock waves in the air like a flag. I prance about the room, horny as a goat, grabbing my stiff dick and eyeing myself in the mirror. My cock feels as if a dozen hard cocks were stuffed inside it, the dozen hard-ons of the men who have worn the shirt before me.

The mirror makes the room a closed circuit. There is nowhere to look except at my own reflection. My flickering glance cruises the stranger in the mirror. I am alone with my eyes, my cock, and the burgundy shirt. I leer at myself lustfully, strutting and grinning like a bare-assed satyr. The sticky surface squeaks the word as I wriggle about, whispers it to my cock, which is trembling with frustration, but I won't let it come, not yet.

Ever so slowly, I peel back the soft velvet blanket of my foreskin. The flesh beneath is swollen to a slick, glistening red. My dry fingers are raw against the tender skin. As I reach toward the shelf, I thank my thoughtful benefactor for the provision of the slippery golden oil the bottle contains.

I cannot put it off any longer. As the pressure mounts, I give in to the pounding rhythm of my fist, give myself over to the spirit of Horny Man that inhabits the shirt, that is possessing me as the hot tide rises within me. Even the image in the mirror is squeezed out of consciousness as my eyes close and I am lost to spurting, surging pleasure. In the moment of serene silence that follows I hear only my own heartbeat and a faint mechanical click and whirr from somewhere behind the glass.

––––––––––

Randall is sitting behind the counter when I come out again into the store. He smiles and raises his head from the paper before him. An interesting garment, is it not? I nod and smile in return. Too bad it is not for sale, he sighs – it is part of my personal collection; it would never do to break up the set.

The bell above the door tinkles over my head. The sound of *Tosca* trails after me, out into the sunlit street.

LOURDES ORTIZ

ALICE

On July 4, 1862, the Reverend Charles Ludwidge Dodgson made an expedition up the river from Christ Church to Godstow, taking with him the three daughters of Dean Liddell. To amuse the children, Dodgson began telling them the story of a girl who, bored with sitting on the river bank, follows a white rabbit down a mysterious hole. Upon returning, one of the Liddells made him promise that he would write the story down. The result of that famous excursion was Alice's Adventures Under Ground *or, as it came to be known,* Alice's Adventures in Wonderland. *Much has been written about the friendship between the Reverend Dodgson (who took the name, of course, of Lewis Carroll) and Alice Liddell. "I love all children," Carroll once said, "except boys." His passion for what, years later, Vladimir Nabokov would call nymphets, led him not only to compose stories for his young girl friends but also to take their photographs, an expensive hobby in Victorian England. Photographing young girls became Carroll's obsession and, on at least one occasion, he had one of them, under her mother's supervision, model in the nude. After the poet Alfred Lord Tennyson confessed at a dinner to dreaming long passages of poetry, he turned to Lewis Carroll and said: "And you, I suppose, dream photographs."*

Whether Carroll's relationship with Alice was ever more than an infatuation is a question that has long been debated. The Spanish writer Lourdes Ortiz, reflecting on the question from the point of view of the child Alice, has decided that it was. Whatever the truth might have been, it is certain that after Alice had become a grown woman Carroll lost interest in her and, when she married in 1880, he did not attend the wedding.

I

HE'S NICE but also a nuisance. And he's dreadful at telling stories. You can't ever get him to reach the end. Suddenly he's like dumbstruck, and I have to say, "Go on … the rabbit …" And he mumbles, "the rabbit, the rabbit …" and when the story is starting to become interesting, he begins with all sorts of nonsense that has no rhyme nor reason. He thinks I'm not smart because I'm young. I like ordinary stories about princesses and princes, or about the boy who had to fulfill many tasks, but he says, "Ah, yes! The rabbit!" And then there's the clock … Because time goes by and he's not even aware of it. I'm always wanting to go off and play, but he asks me to wait a little, just one more photograph. What a bother, those photographs! I have to stand still for hours and he starts telling his story, but then he gets distracted and says, "Of course, now I remember!" and skips a part that was just starting to sound exciting, and it seems as if everything he was saying just vanished away … like the bit about the Mad Hatter … What a silly tea-party that was! But he's like that, always spilling his tea outside the cup, pouring it into his saucer, staring at me with his mouth wide open, as if he were going to swallow a fly, because he gets caught in the cobwebs – as my teacher says when I forget to do my homework and my mind's elsewhere … In just the same way, he falls silent and stares me over and over again as if he'd gone crazy … The other day, when he was in that state, I took out of his hand the biscuit he was about to dunk in his cup and I put a pebble in its place, and he dunked the pebble in the tea and put it in his mouth and almost broke a tooth, and I almost split my sides laughing, and he choked and, splash, he spat out the tea as if he were a hose and he went all red in the face, just like Jim when he does something naughty and the teacher catches him, and Jim puts on a face as if he hadn't done anything, but I can guess because his ears turn red, and I know him very well. He is exactly like that, he turns red as a red pepper, and he becomes terribly polite, bowing low, apologizing … That's what I enjoy most: playing at being grown-up. He treats me like a lady and it's very funny to see him bent over, begging me to forgive him like Mr Lauren with Aunt Miller. And I say to him, let's go play princesses, I'll be the queen and he will be my slave bought in a

Turkish market. He loves that and falls on his knees, and then I take a wicker rod, which he gave me as a present, and I whip his ass soundly, and he barks and curls up in a ball at my feet … And then yes, then I have fun because it's much easier to get him to do things than when I play with Matilde: Matilde always wants to be queen, and she's bossy. He, instead, will play dog or cat, will do whatever I want. Today, for instance, I told him he had to lick a cut I had … and at once, just like Pretty, Mrs Cirlot's cat, he went and licked my hand until it was all pins and needles, and I got bored and told him I no longer wanted to play. And then he, instead of standing up again, started to purr like a cat and it seemed as if he were crying. It was strange what he was doing, it sounded almost like snoring, and I got frightened because his face was puffed up, red, just like that of Mrs Lorris's little boy when he caught chicken-pox and had such a high temperature …

II

I've eaten a cupcake with my eyes closed to see whether I'll grow. Like in the story. He says it's enough to close your eyes and, bang, you grow or shrink … The other day we played a really good game. He said "Eat me!" and, bang, it's true, the thing he kept hidden grew: just looking at it seemed to make it grow and…. And then it became tiny, as tiny as the girl in the story who could almost fit inside a bottle. But the magic doesn't work for me. I've spent the morning rubbing my thumb, eyes closed and saying "Eat me!" but nothing happens. Maybe it's true that he's a wizard. Or that you have to do it with the same

seriousness with which you go to Sunday service. Lick me, eat
me, drink me ... Today I tried to play the same game with Larry
but the fool ran away, saying that these are things of the devil,
that they are not done, that it's a sin. That's because the only
game Larry wants to play is pirates, and I seem to enjoy playing
pirates less and less. I like performing miracles and making
things grow or shrink to a tiny, tiny size like Alice in the story,
falling, falling, and almost drowning ... That's fun. When the
moment of the fountain comes, I say "Let's see if it's a big one
today!" because the truth is that it's usually just a very small pool
where a fly would barely drown, but I enjoy seeing him spurting
all of a sudden this stream of white milk that spreads and
splashes me. And I laugh and ask him to do it again, but he
becomes all stern and says, "Enough for today; now we must
have a rest ... We've told quite a few stories." And it makes me
very angry, because it happens exactly when things are becoming interesting. And he quiets down and tells me how she, Alice,
splashed around and was about to drown when all of a sudden
... Those are the best moments, when I'm the least bored. He,
on the other hand, falls asleep and I realize he doesn't feel like
carrying on, but I know that if I curl up by his side he'll keep on
talking and talking. He looks like one of those ventriloquists,
because you can only see his mouth, as if the body weren't there.
I think he becomes transparent, and I told him so, and he told
me the story of the Chesire Cat. So I said to him, "Right, now
you're my Chesire Cat," and then he smiled with that smile of a
cat who has done something naughty, an eerie smile but
friendly. At night I dream of that smile which I can't very well
explain, a smile hanging from the trees, a smile of a cat licking
its chops, a huge satisfied and mischievous cat pursuing me

from the branches. And I told him this, and he said he'd always be my Chesire Cat, watching over me with his two eyes like lanterns so that nothing bad ever happens to me, so that no one will ever hurt me. And then he sings me the song about the cat and the maid, and we play-act. *"Pussy was watching her, ding-dong-dell,"* he sings, *"with greedy eyes and a hey nonny-no."* And I carry on: *"If you scratch me, Pussy, ding-dong-dell, I'll cut off your tail and a hey nonny-no,"* and he goes down on all fours and runs after me. When he catches me he tries to scratch, but he never hurts me, and I have to cut off his tail and he laughs, and squirms because I tickle him, and finally he lets me do it; he rolls on his back with his arms and legs up high – just like Leo, my dog, when he wants me to pat his tummy – and I place a foot on his gut and give a shout, covering and uncovering my mouth with my hand, like Larry when he has captured the fort. And he mews very softly, a sad mew of a defeated cat, and I straddle him just as if he were a pony and say: "Dirty cat, now you can't move. A tailless cat is no cat at all," and I pretend to cut off his nose as well, cut off that smile that hangs from trees. And we stay like that for a long while, he defeated and I lying on him, and then he asks me to forgive him and says: "My Lady, here we are, a maid and her cat without a tail …" and starts telling me an even longer story, and asks me to close my eyes so that I can cross through to the other side of the looking-glass, and I close them and he says: "My little girl is tired, my little girl, just like Alice, wants to sleep under the trees …" and I quietly fall asleep listening to his slow voice, a lulling voice. And it seems to me that the leaves of the trees whirl around in the wind, and in the distance I see again the cat's smile as he winks at me from the roof, while the White Rabbit runs off in a panic because he's late, and the Mad Hatter overturns the teapot, and everywhere are labels that say *"Eat Me," "Drink Me."*

III

Today I got mad with him because I'm tired of posing and posing, and I went off to play with Larry and the other children. But Larry is a fool and quickly bores me, so I went looking for him. First I pretended to be still angry and he went down on his knees and promised me to be good if I would forgive him and give him a kiss on the cheeks, one on each side as if I were knighting him. And he also promised not to become distracted and to tell me a proper story, with a beginning and an end. Because I know it upsets him, I told him that otherwise we wouldn't play the fountain game, nor the Chesire Cat game – we wouldn't play anything at all. And I told him that when I'm older I'll marry Larry, but not yet, because now he's a little boy who only enjoys playing soldiers. And he told me I must never grow up, that little girls like me must never do that. And I, to annoy him, told him that of course I was going to grow up, and that I'd have lots of babies. And he grew even angrier and told me that when women grow up they become horrible witches, and that babies squeal like pigs, unbearable pigs who suck up their mother's milk until they leave them empty, and then the mothers become ugly and dishevelled, dirty and loud, all day among the pots and pans, working away, stained with grease and smelling of fried onions, always busy in the kitchen with their hands chapped and red and covered in blisters, pummelling away at the dough to make bread. And I told him that my mother was not like that, that my mother was beautiful and very elegant, and that she was never dirty, nor smelly. And he said well no, not my mother, but that was what usually happens, is what happened to Alice when she came to the Duchess's house full of women working in the kitchen, and that it was much better for me to stay as I was, smooth as a leaf, so that I wouldn't have to suckle any piglets who'd pull on my breasts and puff them up like balloons, and make them huge and stretched. And I promised him I'd never get married, but that instead I'd become a dancer or something similar, so that I wouldn't have to throw saucepans at anyone's head, or have to scrub away at the washing-board. He says that if I grow up and become fat and ugly, he'll no longer be my friend and won't tell me any more stories. And he showed me photographs of many other girls, and told me he loved me better than all of them, and that he had never told the others as many stories as he told me, nor as long, and that if I paid attention to him he'd teach me to play chess, and that I'd be able to win when I played with Larry and the other children.

IV

What he prefers is apple tart, which I hate. He eats my share almost without noticing it, because I exchange plates with him as he's about to finish, and then he tells me the story of the fight between the Lion and the Unicorn which, he explained, is a fantastic animal, a white donkey with a single horn. And we play at being Alice and the unicorn, and he says that only a little girl can see a unicorn and pat his horn, and then the unicorn rests his head on the girl's lap and falls asleep, while the maiden – as he calls her – caresses him very, very gently, as if she were polishing a silver tray. And the horn

is a miraculous horn, a horn that can cure everything, and if the girl
is daring enough to kiss its tip, it glows happily and weeps a tear, a
little pearl delightful to the tongue because it is nothing less than a
magic potion, warm, useful for guessing all sorts of riddles, a
potion that makes you clever so that after tasting it you can do
tricks with words and even invent new ones, or skip along the
chessboard squares as if you were skipping through the woods. It is
simple: you just close your eyes and take a first step, while his voice
carries on with the story. But then he becomes all muddled up
again, and starts telling a stupid episode about a train and a man
dressed in newspaper and a goat, and I tell him I don't like that,
that I like the one about the playing-cards better, because I too
want to be a Queen of Hearts, or a Red Queen, or whatever. And
then he tells me that if I keep on caressing him, little by little his
ideas become clearer, because it's difficult sometimes to grab hold
of ideas, they keep running away like the objects in the store of the
Knitting Sheep, jumping about and changing places when you try
to pick one up. And I tell him I don't want to be a maiden anymore, that my hand is so tired I can't feel it any longer and that I'm
going off to play with my friends, and that I'll never eat apple tart
again, even if the Queen of Hearts threatens to cut off my head.

V

Something very odd happened today. I was feeling bored and
bothered, lying there with the ridiculous ribbon he'd put in my
hair, and he said, fine, it was enough for one day and that he had
brought with him something he wanted me to see. It was one of
those pipes, a hookah, the kind the Caterpillar smoked sitting

crosslegged on top of the mushroom. He lit the pipe and a strange white smoke poured out of it, and he began to puff deeply, his hand wrapped around the stem in order – he said – to capture the genii of the pipe who carry you off to the world of dreams. Then he lay back, reclining against the pillows – those same pillows against which he has me lean when he's taking my photograph. He lay back like a Roman, propped up on an elbow, and I took off my blue satin ribbon and made him a turban with it so that he'd look even more like the Caterpillar, and then I sat on the floor by his side, legs crossed as if I were his servant, and while he smoked I broke off little pieces of pie and popped them in his mouth, just as if he were a baby. That put him in the best of moods, better than ever, so much so that he no longer seemed himself. He said he was now Humpty Dumpty and that if I gave him a little push he'd fall to the floor and break into a thousand pieces, so I started pushing him playfully and he laughed out loud, so loud that I thought he'd gone mad, like the Hatter. He told me that Nobody was to see this pipe and I told him that Nobody *had* seen the pipe, and that Nobody would see it again. And he said that if Nobody had seen it, Nobody might go out and tell others about it. "Nobody can tell anyone because Nobody has seen it," I insisted, and he rolled around with laughter. "Let Nobody know that if he tells anyone, I'll make him pay dearly for his indiscretion."

VI

It was one of those silly days when I wish Larry were with me, because afterwards he doesn't believe it when I tell him what happened. For instance, when he told me that he'd had a lovely dream in which a girl once again called Alice, entered a garden in which the gardeners were painting the roses red. Then, in the dream, Alice took part in a game of croquet, and when she grabbed the stick to hit the ball, the stick became soft, very soft, like a flamingo's neck or like the neck of a swan … "A long white swan's neck," he said and laughed, and then he told me he'd love me to be his Leda and that we'd play croquet together or whatever else I liked. "You," he said, "would hold the stick to hit the ball," he laughed, "and how disgusted you'd feel when you found it to be as soft as a long, long neck!". And then my head started spinning, like when Alice falls down the hole and everything is upside-down, and it felt light and good as in the story. I felt like a leaf, like a page in a book carried away by the wind, and it seemed to me that I was weightless, that I was made out of thin cardboard like one of the playing-cards. And he, the Caterpillar, never stopped laughing, and blew white smoke rings at me, rings that looked like the letters of the alphabet. And I too started laughing, everything seemed to tickle me, and he kept changing his shape, and his smile was no longer like that of the Chesire Cat. Instead, he looked more and more like an enormous egg, like Humpty Dumpty sitting on the wall, and I kept pushing him as if he were a balancing toy, rocking backwards and forwards, and suddenly he opened his mouth like the enormous mouth of the Red King, and everything felt as soft and damp as a lawn, and I was playing croquet. And the ball seemed all at once huge and hairy, as if a forest had grown all over it, a furry thicket, and he hummed all the while something about delicate dancing oysters coming out of the sea and being eaten up by the Walrus and the Carpenter … delicious oysters ... just about to be devoured by a Walrus with big whiskers. And he said I-don't-know-what about closed petals, that I was a flower of closed white petals – I think that's what it was, the same as what the flowers tell Alice in the garden – and it felt good, soft like the afternoon breeze when my hair hangs loose and it seems as if it will blow away. And then I saw the Chesire Cat smile again, and stick out an enormous tongue and slowly lick me all over, especially my back and my small breasts, just like Kitty, Alice's cat, washing her babies. And I was unable to move. I felt trapped and I pushed my arms out of the windows of the house, but I was not afraid because I knew that if I bit into the cake or drank from the bottle, I'd shrink again. And then the brook reached me, the fountain that never stopped flowing, and I was covered in water, drowning with my mouth full. And then I must have fallen asleep and when I was there, in the land of dreams, I heard him repeat from far away, almost as far as the stars: "Nobody must know about our games, not even Larry. Nobody." And I, in my dreams, I think I answered: "But if Nobody knows, Nobody will be able to tell ..." And he said: "He might tell, he might indeed; but if I ever catch Nobody, I'll cut off his head." And the Chesire Cat showed me his gigantic white teeth, mockingly, tamely, slippery, almost frightening, while Humpty Dumpty, fat and proud like a huge croquet ball fell asleep by my side, and not the King's horses nor the King's men would have been able to lift him.

ALEJANDRA PIZARNIK

THE BLOODY COUNTESS

In 1614, the Transylvanian Countess Elizabeth Bathory, niece of the King of Poland, died immured in a room of her castle. She had been kept prisoner as a punishment for torturing and murdering hundreds of young girls in the belief that their blood would grant her eternal youth. The Countess had her predecessors: The Roman Emperor Tiberius sacrificed children at his tempestuous orgies and the French Marshall Gilles de Rais, who rode by the side of Joan of Arc, killed hundreds of young boys for his pleasure and preserved the most beautiful heads in his study as a memorial. In these bloody characters, the Argentinian poet Alejandra Pizarnik saw ambiguous examples of what she called "the absolute freedom of the human creature." She thought that they carried the quest for erotic sensations beyond the body itself, as if they believed that in the destruction of the flesh and in the sensuality of pain they would be able to discover "a species of immortality, something dark and dangerous and still forbidden."

431

"Fools will object that they were monsters," wrote the Marquis de Sade, comparing himself to the Countess and her kin. "My answer is, yes, but only according to our customs and our manner of thinking. In relation to Nature's views on us, they were merely the instruments of her design. It was only to fulfill her laws that she bestowed upon them such ferocious and bloodthirsty characters."

———————————

The criminal does not make beauty;
he himself is the authentic beauty.
JEAN-PAUL SARTRE

THERE IS A BOOK by Valentine Penrose which documents the life of a real and unusual character: the Countess Bathory, murderer of more than six hundred young girls. The Countess Bathory's sexual perversion and her madness are so obvious that Valentine Penrose disregards them and concentrates instead on the convulsive beauty of the character.

It is not easy to show this sort of beauty. Valentine Penrose, however, succeeded because she played admirably with the aesthetic value of this lugubrious story. She inscribes the underground kingdom of Erzebet Bathory within the walls of her torture chamber, and the chamber within her medieval castle. Here the sinister beauty of nocturnal creatures is summed up in this silent lady of legendary paleness, mad eyes, and hair the sumptuous colour of ravens.

A well-known philosopher includes cries in the category of silence – cries, moans, curses, form "a silent substance." The substance of this underworld is evil. Sitting on her throne, the Countess watches the tortures and listens to the cries. Her old and horrible maids are wordless figures that bring in fire, knives, needles, irons; they torture the girls, and later bury them. With their iron and knives, these two old women are themselves the instruments of a possession. This dark ceremony has a single silent spectator.

I. The Iron Maiden

… among red laughter of glistening lips and
monstrous gestures of mechanical women.
RENÉ DAUMAL

There was once in Nuremberg a famous automaton known as the Iron Maiden. The Countess Bathory bought a copy for her torture chamber in Csejthe Castle. This clockwork doll was of the size and colour of a human creature. Naked, painted, covered in jewels, with blond hair that reached down to the ground, it had a mechanical device that allowed it to curve its lips into a smile, and to move its eyes.

The Countess, sitting on her throne, watches.

For the Maiden to spring into action it is necessary to touch some of the precious stones in its necklace. It responds immediately with horrible creaking sounds and very slowly lifts its white arms which close in a perfect embrace around whatever happens to be next to it – in this case, a girl. The automaton holds her in its arms and now no one will be able to uncouple the living body from the body of iron, both equally beautiful. Suddenly the painted breasts of the Iron Maiden open, and five daggers appear that pierce her struggling companion whose hair is as long as its own.

Once the sacrifice is over another stone in the necklace is touched: the arms drop, the smile and the eyes fall shut, and the murderess becomes once again the Maiden, motionless in its coffin.

II.   Death by Water

He is standing. And he is standing as
absolutely and definitely as if he were sitting.
WITOLD GOMBROWICZ

The road is covered in snow and, inside the coach, the sombre lady wrapped in furs feels bored. Suddenly she calls out the name of one of the girls in her train. The girl is brought to her: the Countess bites her frantically and sticks needles in her flesh. A while later the procession abandons the wounded girl in the snow. The girl tries to run away. She is pursued, captured and pulled back into the coach. A little further along the road they halt: the Countess has ordered cold water. Now the girl is naked, standing in the snow. Night has fallen. A circle of torches surrounds her, held out by impassive footmen. They pour water over the body and the water turns to ice. (The Countess observes this from inside the coach.) The girl attempts one last slight gesture, trying to move closer to the torches – the only source of warmth. More water is poured over her, and there she remains, for ever standing, upright, dead.

III.   The Lethal Cage

... scarlet and black wounds burst
upon the splendid flesh.
ARTHUR RIMBAUD

Lined with knives and adorned with sharp iron blades, it can hold one human body, and can be lifted by means of a pulley. The ceremony of the cage takes place in this manner:

Dorko the maid drags in by the hair a naked young girl, shuts her up in the cage and lifts it high into the air. The Lady of These Ruins appears, a sleepwalker in white. Slowly and silently she sits upon a footstool placed underneath the contraption.

A red-hot poker in her hand, Dorko taunts the prisoner who, drawing back (and this is the ingenuity of the cage) stabs herself against the sharp irons while her blood falls upon the pale woman who dispassionately receives it, her eyes fixed on nothing, as in a daze. When the lady recovers from the trance, she slowly leaves the room. There have been two transformations: her white dress is now red, and where a girl once stood a corpse now lies.

IV. Classical Torture

> Unblemished fruit, untouched by worm
> or frost, whose firm, polished skin
> cries out to be bitten!
> BAUDELAIRE

Except for a few baroque refinements – like the Iron Maiden, death by water, or the cage – the Countess restricted herself to a monotonously classic style of torture that can be summed up as follows:

Several tall, beautiful, strong girls were selected – their ages had to be between 12 and 18 – and dragged into the torture chamber where, dressed in white upon her throne, the Countess awaited them. After binding their hands, the servants would whip the girls until the skin of their bodies ripped and they became a mass of swollen wounds; then the servants would burn them with red-hot pokers; cut their fingers with scissors or shears; pierce their wounds; stab them with daggers (if the Countess grew tired of hearing the cries they would sew their mouths up; if one of the girls fainted too soon they would revive her by burning paper soaked in oil between her legs). The blood spurted like fountains and the white dress of the nocturnal lady would turn red. So red, that she would have to go up to her room and change (what would she think about during this brief intermission?). The walls and the ceiling of the chamber would also turn red.

Not always would the lady remain idle while the others busied themselves around her. Sometimes she would lend a hand, and then, impetuously, tear at the flesh – in the most sensitive places – with tiny silver pincers; or she would stick needles, cut the skin between the fingers, press red-hot spoons and irons against the soles of the feet, use the whip (once, during one of her excursions, she ordered her servants to hold up a girl who had just died and kept on whipping her even though she was dead); she also murdered several by means of icy water (using a method invented by Darvulia, the witch; it consisted of plunging a girl into freezing water and leaving her there overnight). Finally, when she was sick, she would have the girls brought to her bedside and she would bite them.

During her erotic seizures she would hurl blasphemous insults at her victims. Blasphemous insults and cries like the baying of a she-wolf were her means of expression as she stalked, in a passion, the gloomy rooms. But nothing was more ghastly than her laugh. (I recapitulate: the medieval castle, the torture chamber, the tender young girls, the old and horrible servants, the beautiful madwoman laughing in a wicked ecstasy provoked by the suffering of others.) Her last words, before letting herself fall into a final faint, would be: "More, ever more, harder, harder!"

Not always was the day innocent, the night guilty. During the morning or the afternoon, young seamstresses would bring dresses for the Countess, and this would lead to innumerable scenes of cruelty. Without exception, Dorko would find mistakes in the sewing and would select two or three guilty victims (at this point the Countess's doleful eyes would glisten). The punishment of the seamstresses – and of the young maids in general – would vary. If the Countess happened to be in one of her rare good moods, Dorko would simply strip the victims who would continue to work, naked, under the Countess's eyes, in large rooms full of black cats. The girls bore this painless punishment in agonizing amazement, because they never believed it to be possible. Darkly, they must have felt terribly humiliated because their nakedness forced them into a kind of animal world, a feeling heightened by the fully clothed "human" presence of the Countess, watching them. This scene led me to think of Death – Death as in old allegories, as in the Dance of Death. To strip naked is a prerogative of Death; another is the incessant watching over the creatures it has dispossessed. But there is more: sexual climax forces us into death-like gestures and expressions (gasping and writhing as in agony, cries and moans of paroxysm). If the sexual act implies a sort of death, Erzebet Bathory needed the visible, elementary, coarse death, to succeed in dying that other phantom death we call orgasm. But, who is Death? A figure that harrows and wastes wherever and however it pleases. This is also a possible description of the Countess Bathory. Never did anyone wish so hard not to grow old; I mean, to die. That is why, perhaps, she acted and played the role of Death. Because, how can Death possibly die?

Let us return to the seamstresses and the maids. If Erzebet woke up wrothful, she would not be satisfied with her *tableaux vivants*, but:

To the one who had stolen a coin she would repay with the same coin … red-hot, which the girl had to hold tight in her hand.

To the one who had talked during working hours, the Countess herself would sew her mouth shut, or otherwise would open her mouth and stretch it until the lips tore.

She also used the poker with which she would indiscriminately burn cheeks, breasts, tongues....

When the punishments took place in Erzebet's chamber, at nighttime, it was necessary to spread large quantities of ashes around her bed, to allow the noble lady to cross without difficulties the vast pools of blood.

V.   On the Strength of a Name

And cold madness wandered aimlessly
about the house.

MILOSZ

The name of Bathory – in the power of which Erzebet believed, as if it were an extraordinary talisman – was an illustrious one from the very early days of the Hungarian Empire. It was not by chance that the family coat-of-arms displayed the teeth of a wolf, because the Bathory were cruel, fearless and lustful. The many marriages that took place between blood relations contributed, perhaps, to the hereditary aberrations and diseases: epilepsy, gout, lust. It is not at all unlikely that Erzebet herself was an epileptic: she seemed possessed by seizures as unexpected as her terrible migraines and pains in the eyes (which she conjured away by placing a wounded pigeon, still alive, on her forehead).

The Countess's family was not unworthy of its ancestral fame. Her uncle Istvan, for instance, was so utterly mad that he would mistake summer for winter, and would have himself drawn in a sleigh along the burning sands that were, in his mind, roads covered with snow. Or consider her cousin Gabor, whose incestuous passion was reciprocated by his sister's. But the most charming of all was the celebrated aunt Klara. She had four husbands (the first two perished by her hand) and died a melodramatic death: she was caught in the arms of a casual acquaintance by her lover, a Turkish Pasha: the intruder was roasted on a spit and aunt Klara was raped (if this verb may be used in her respect) by the entire Turkish garrison. This however did not cause her death: on the contrary, her rapists – tired perhaps of having their way with her – finally had to stab her. She used to pick up her lovers along the Hungarian roads, and would not mind sprawling on a bed where she had previously slaughtered one of her female attendants.

By the time the Countess reached the age of forty, the Bathory had diminished or consumed themselves either through madness or through death. They became almost sensible, thereby losing the interest they had until then provoked in Erzebet.

VI.   A Warrior Bridegroom

When the warrior took me in his arms
I felt the fire of pleasure ...
THE ANGLO-SAXON ELEGY (VIII CEN.)

In 1575, at the age of fifteen, Erzebet married Ferencz Nadasdy, a soldier of great courage. This simple soul never found out that the lady who inspired him with a certain love tinged by fear was in fact a monster. He would come to her in the brief

respites between battles, drenched in horse-sweat and blood –
the norms of hygiene had not yet been firmly established – and
this probably stirred the emotions of the delicate Erzebet,
always dressed in rich cloths and perfumed with costly scents.

One day, walking through the castle gardens, Nadasdy saw a
naked girl tied to a tree. She was covered in honey: flies and ants
crawled all over her, and she was sobbing. The Countess
explained that the girl was purging the sin of having stolen some
fruit. Nadasdy laughed candidly, as if she had told him a joke.

The soldier would not allow anyone to bother him with
stories about his wife, stories of bites, needles, etc. A serious
mistake: even as a newly-wed, during those crises whose
formula was the Bathory's secret, Erzebet would prick her
servants with long needles; and when, felled by her terrible
migraines, she was forced to lie in bed, she would gnaw their
shoulders and chew on the bits of flesh she had been able to
extract. As if by magic, the girl's shrieks would soothe her pain.

But all this is child's play – a young girl's play. During her
husband's life she never committed murder.

VII.   The Melancholy Mirror

Everything is mirror!
OCTAVIO PAZ

The Countess would spend her days in front of her large dark
mirror a famous mirror she had designed herself. It was so comfortable that it even had supports on which to lean one's arms,
so as to be able to stand for many hours in front of it without

feeling tired. We can suppose that while believing she had designed a mirror, Erzebet had in fact designed the plans for her lair. And now we can understand why only the most grippingly sad music of her gypsy orchestra, or dangerous hunting parties, or the violent perfume of the magic herbs in the witch's hut or – above all – the cellars flooded with human blood, could spark something resembling life in her perfect face. Because no one has more thirst for earth, for blood, and for ferocious sexuality than the creatures who inhabit cold mirrors. And on the subject of mirrors: the rumours concerning her alleged homosexuality were never confirmed. Was this allegation unconscious, or, on the contrary, did she accept it naturally, as simply another right to which she was entitled? Essentially she lived deep within an exclusively female world. There were only women during her nights of crime. And a few details are obviously revealing: for instance, in the torture chamber, during the moments of greatest tension, she herself used to plunge a burning candle into the sex of her victim. There are also testimonies which speak of less solitary pleasures. One of the servants said during the trial that an aristocratic and mysterious lady dressed as a young man would visit the Countess. On one occasion she saw them together, torturing a girl. But we do not know whether they shared any pleasures other than the sadistic ones.

More on the theme of the mirror: even though we are not concerned with *explaining* this sinister figure, it is necessary to dwell on the fact that she suffered from that sixteenth-century sickness: melancholia.

An unchangeable colour rules over the melancholic: his dwelling is a space the colour of mourning. Nothing happens in it. No one intrudes. It is a bare stage where the inert *I* is assisted by the *I* suffering from that inertia. The latter wishes to free the former, but all efforts fail, as Theseus would have failed had he been not only himself, but also the Minotaur; to kill him then, he would have had to kill himself. But there are fleeting remedies: sexual pleasures, for instance, can, for a brief moment, obliterate the silent gallery of echoes and mirrors that constitutes the melancholic soul. Even more: they can illuminate the funeral chamber and transform it into a sort of musical box with gaily-coloured figurines that sing and dance deliciously. Afterwards, when the music winds down, the soul will return to immobility and silence. The music box is not a gratuitous comparison. Melancholia is, I believe, a musical problem: a dissonance, a change in rhythm. While on the *outside* everything happens with the vertiginous rhythm of a cataract, on the *inside* is the exhausted *adagio* of drops of water falling from time to tired time. For this reason the *outside*, seen from the melancholic *inside*, appears absurd and unreal, and constitutes "the farce we must all play." But for an instant – because of a wild music, or a drug, or the sexual act carried to its climax – the very slow rhythm of the melancholic soul does not only rise to that of the outside world: it overtakes it with an ineffably blissful exorbitance, and the soul then thrills animated by delirious new energies.

The melancholic soul sees Time as suspended before and after the fatally ephemeral violence. And yet the truth is that time is never suspended, but it grows as slowly as the fingernails of the dead. Between two silences or two deaths, the prodigious, brief moment of speed takes on the various forms of lust: from an innocent intoxication to sexual perversions and even murder.

I think of Erzebet Bathory and her nights whose rhythms

are measured by the cries of adolescent girls. I see a portrait of the Countess: the sombre and beautiful lady resembles the allegories of Melancholia represented in old engravings. I also recall that in her time, a melancholic person was a person possessed by the Devil.

VIII.   *Black Magic*

... who kills the sun in order to install
the reign of darkest night.
ANTONIN ARTAUD

Erzebet's greatest obsession had always been to keep old age at bay, at any cost. Her total devotion to the arts of black magic was aimed at preserving – intact for all eternity – the "sweet bird" of her youth. The magical herbs, the incantations, the amulets, even the blood baths had, in her eyes, a medicinal function: to immobilize her beauty in order to become, for ever and ever, *a dream of stone.* She always lived surrounded by talismans. In her years of crime she chose one single talisman which contained an ancient and filthy parchment on which was written in special ink, a prayer for her own personal use. She carried it close to her heart, underneath her costly dresses, and in the midst of a celebration, she would touch it surreptitiously. I translate the prayer:

Help me, oh Isten; and you also, all-powerful cloud. Protect me, Erzebet, and grant me long life. Oh cloud, I am in danger. Send me ninety cats, for you are the supreme mistress of cats. Order them to assemble here from all their dwelling-places: from the mountains, from the waters, from the rivers, from the gutters and from the oceans. Tell them to come quickly and bite the heart of —— and also the heart of —— and of ——. And to also bite and rip the heart of Megyery, the Red. And keep Erzebet from all evil.

The blanks were to be filled with the names of those whose hearts she wanted bitten.

In 1604 Erzebet became a widow and met Darvulia. Darvulia was exactly like the woodland witch who frightens us in children's tales. Very old, irascible, always surrounded by black cats, Darvulia fully responded to Erzebet's fascination: within the Countess's eyes the witch found a new version of the evil powers buried in the poisons of the forest and in the coldness of the moon. Darvulia's black magic wrought itself in the Countess's black silence. She initiated her to even crueller games; she taught her to look upon death, and the *meaning* of looking upon death. She incited her to seek death and blood in a literal sense: that is, to love them for their own sake, without fear.

IX. Blood Baths

If you go bathing, Juanilla,
tell me to what baths you go.
CANCIONERO OF UPSALA

This rumour existed: since the arrival of Darvulia, the Countess, in order to preserve her comeliness, took baths of human blood. True: Darvulia, being a witch, believed in the invigorating powers of the "human fluid." She proclaimed the merits of young girls' blood – especially if they were virgins – to vanquish the demon of senility, and the Countess accepted the treatment as meekly as if it had been a salt bath. Therefore, in the torture chamber, Dorko applied herself to slicing veins and arteries; the blood was collected in pitchers and, when the victims were bled dry, Dorko would pour the red warm liquid over the body of the waiting Countess – ever so quiet, ever so white, ever so erect, ever so silent.

In spite of her unchangeable beauty, Time inflicted upon her some of the vulgar signs of its passing. Towards 1610 Darvulia mysteriously disappeared and Erzebet, almost fifty, complained to her new witch about the uselessness of the blood baths. In fact, more than complain, she threatened to kill her if she did not stop at once the encroaching and execrable signs of old age. The witch argued that Darvulia's method had not worked because plebeian blood had been used. She assured – or prophesied – that changing the colour of the blood, using blue blood instead of red, would ensure the fast retreat of old age. Here began the hunt for the daughters of gentlemen. To attract them, Erzebet's minions would argue that the Lady of Csejthe, alone in her lonely castle, could not resign herself to her solitude. And how to banish solitude? Filling the dark halls with young girls of good families who, in exchange for happy company, would receive lessons in fine manners and learn how to behave exquisitely in society. A fortnight later, of the twenty-five "pupils" who had hurried to become aristocrats, only two were left: one died some time later, bled white; the other managed to take her life.

X.　*The Castle of Csejthe*

The stone walk is paved with dark cries.
PIERRE-JEAN JOUVE

A castle of grey stones, few windows, square towers, underground mazes; a castle high upon a cliff, a hillside of dry wind-
blown weeds, of woods full of white beasts in winter and dark
beasts in summer; a castle that Erzebet Bathory loved for the
doleful silence of its walls which muffled every cry.

The Countess's room, cold and badly lit by a lamp of
jasmine oil, reeked of blood, and the cellars reeked of dead
bodies. Had she wanted to, she could have carried out her
work in broad daylight and murdered the girls under the sun,
but she was fascinated by the gloom of her dungeon. The
gloom which matched so keenly her terrible eroticism of stone,
snow and walls. She loved her maze-shaped dungeon, the
archetypal hell of our fears; the viscous, insecure space where
we are unprotected and can get lost.

What did she do with all of her days and nights, there, in
the loneliness of Csejthe? Of her nights we know something.
During the day, the Countess would not leave the side of her
two old servants, two creatures escaped from a painting by
Goya: the dirty, malodorous, incredibly ugly and perverse
Dorko and Jo Ilona. They would try to amuse her with
domestic tales to which she paid no attention, and yet she
needed the continuous and abominable chatter. Another way
of passing time was to contemplate her jewels, to look at herself
in her famous mirror, to change her dresses fifteen times a day.

Gifted with a great practical sense, she saw to it that the underground cellars were always well supplied; she also concerned
herself with her daughters' future – her daughters who always
lived so far away from her; she administered her fortune with
intelligence, and she occupied herself with all the little details
that rule the profane order of our lives.

XI.   Severe Measures

> … the law, cold and aloof by its very nature,
>   has no access to the passions that might
>   justify the cruel act of murder.
>
> SADE

For six years the Countess murdered with impunity. During
those years there had been countless rumours about her. But
the name of Bathory, not only illustrious but also diligently
protected by the Hapsburgs, frightened her possible accusers.

Towards 1610 the king had in his hands the most sinister
reports – together with proofs – concerning the Countess.
After much hesitation he decided to act. He ordered the
powerful Thurzo, Count Palatine, to investigate the tragic
events at Csejthe and to punish the guilty parties.

At the head of a contingent of armed men, Thurzo arrived
unannounced at the castle. In the cellar, cluttered with the
remains of the previous night's bloody ceremony, he found a
beautiful mangled corpse and two young girls who lay dying.
But that was not all. He smelt the smell of the dead; he saw the
walls splattered with blood; he saw the Iron Maiden, the cage,

the instruments of torture, bowls of dried blood, the cells – and in one of them a group of girls who were waiting their turn to die and who told him that after many days of fasting they had been served roast flesh that had once belonged to the bodies of their companions.

The Countess, without denying Thurzo's accusations, declared that these acts were all within her rights as a noble woman of ancient lineage. To which the Count Palatine replied: "Countess, I condemn you to life imprisonment within your castle walls."

Deep in his heart, Thurzo must have told himself that the Countess should be beheaded, but such an exemplary punishment would have been frowned upon, because it affected not only the Bathory family, but also the nobility in general. In the meantime, a notebook was found in the Countess's room, filled with the names and descriptions of her 610 victims in her handwriting. The followers of Erzebet, when brought before the judge, confessed to unthinkable deeds, and perished on the stake.

Around her the prison grew. The doors and windows of her room were walled up; only a small opening was left in one of the walls to allow her to receive her food. And when everything was ready, four gallows were erected on the four corners of the castle to indicate that within those walls lived a creature condemned to death.

In this way she lived for three years, almost wasting away with cold and hunger. She never showed the slightest sign of repentance. She never understood why she had been condemned. On August 21, 1614, a contemporary historian wrote: "She died at dawn, abandoned by everyone."

She was never afraid, she never trembled. And no compassion, no sympathy or admiration may be felt for her. Only a certain astonishment at the enormity of the horror, a fascination with a white dress that turns red, with the idea of total laceration, with the imagination of a silence starred with cries in which everything reflects an unacceptable beauty.

Like Sade in his writings, and Gilles de Rais in his crimes, the Countess Bathory reached beyond all limits the uttermost pit of unfettered passions. She is yet another proof that the absolute freedom of the human creature is horrible.

Translated by
Alberto Manguel

JAMES PURDY

LILY'S PARTY

To celebrate Christmas in the year 1492, at the castle of the Duke of Alba, the Spanish writer Juan del Enzina composed a religious drama with comic overtones which he called, A Nativity Farce. *Over the years, Del Enzina wrote several other Christmas farces that became increasingly popular, losing at the same time much of their religious content and increasing their profane and humorous elements. By the year 1550, the Spanish farce was closer to slapstick than to drama, and had acquired many of the characters also found in the popular theatre of Italy and France: the unfaithful wife, the wily lover, the cuckolded or resourceful husband.*

James Purdy, a master of what has become known as American Gothic, has revised and transformed the elements of the classic European farce. The same characters appear in the same improbable plots – as in his novels Narrow Rooms *or* Eustace Chisholm and the Works *– but they are now embodiments of censored sexual passions. In "Lily's Party," for instance, the wife is replaced by an obsessed spinster; the* *lover, by a brutish priest; the husband, by a lustful voyeur. Kirkegaard accused Christianity of having introduced sexuality into the world as a separate concept by setting it aside under the label of "sin." This makes Purdy's characters, for whom sexuality is the driving force, not merely the participants in a grotesque farce, but the outcasts of conventional society.*

———————

As HOBART came through the door of Crawford's Home Dinette, his eyes fell direct on Lily sitting alone at one of the big back tables, eating a piece of pie.

"Lily! Don't tell me! You're supposed to be in Chicago!" he ejaculated.

"Who supposed I was to be?" Lily retorted, letting her fork cut quickly into the pie.

"Well, I'll damn me if –" he began to speak in a humming sort of way while pulling out a chair from under her table, and sitting down unbidden. "Why, everybody thought you went up there to be with Edward."

"Edward! He's the last person on this earth I would go anywhere to be with. And I think you know that!" Lily never showed anger openly, and if she was angry now at least she didn't let it stop her from enjoying her pie.

"Well, Lily, we just naturally figured you had gone to Chicago when you weren't around."

"I gave your brother Edward two of the best years of my life," Lily spoke with the dry accent of someone testifying in court for a second time. "And I'm not about to go find him for more of what he gave me. Maybe you don't remember what I got from him, but I do …"

"But where were you, Lily … We all missed you!" Hobart harped on her absence.

"I was right here all the time, Hobart, for your information." As she said this, she studied his mouth somewhat absent-mindedly. "But as to your brother, Edward Starr," she continued, and then paused as she kept studying his mouth as if she found a particular defect there which had somehow escaped scrutiny hitherto, "As to Edward," she began again, and then stopped, struck her fork gingerly against the plate, "he was a number-one poor excuse for a husband, let me tell you. He left me for another woman, if you care to recall, and it was because of his neglect that my little boy passed away…. So let's say I don't look back on Edward, and am not going to any Chicago to freshen up on my recollections of him…."

She quit studying his mouth, and looked out the large front window through which the full October moon was beginning its evening climb.

"At first I will admit I was lonesome and with my little boy lying out there in the cemetery, I even missed as poor an excuse for a man as Edward Starr, but believe you me, that soon passed."

She put down her fork now that she had eaten all the pie, laid down some change on the bare white ash wood of the table, and then closing her purse, sighed, and softly rose.

"I only know," Lily began, working the clasp on her purse,

"that I have begun to find peace now…. Reverend McGilead, as you may be aware, has helped me toward the light…."

"I have heard of Reverend McGilead," Hobart said in a voice so sharp she looked up at him while he held the screen door open for her.

"I am sure you have heard nothing but good then," she shot back in a voice that was now if not deeply angry, certainly unsteady.

"I will accompany you home, Lily."

"You'll do no such thing, Hobart … Thank you, and good evening."

He noticed that she was wearing no lipstick, and that she did not have on her wedding ring. She also looked younger than when she had been Edward Starr's wife.

"You say you have found peace with this new preacher," Hobart spoke after her retreating figure. "But under this peace, you hate Edward Starr," he persisted. "All you said to me tonight was fraught with hate."

She turned briefly and looked at him, this time in the eyes. "I will find my way, you can rest assured, despite your brother and you."

He stayed in front of the door of the dinette and watched her walk down the moonlit-white road toward her house that lay in deep woods. His heart beat violently. All about where he stood were fields and crops and high trees, and the sailing queen of heaven was the only real illumination after one went beyond the dinette. No one came down this small road with the exception of lovers who occasionally used it for their lane.

Well, Lily is a sort of mystery woman, he had to admit to himself. And where, then, did the rumour arise that she had been to Chicago. And now he felt she had lied to him, that she had been in Chicago after all and had just got back.

Then without planning to do so, hardly knowing indeed he was doing so, he began following after her from a conveniently long distance down the moonlit road. After a few minutes of pursuing her, he saw someone come out from one of the ploughed fields. The newcomer was a tall still youthful man with the carriage of an athlete rather than that of a farmer. He almost ran toward Lily. Then they both stopped for a moment, and after he had touched her gently on the shoulder they went on together. Hobart's heart beat furiously, his temple throbbed, a kind of film formed over his lips from his mouth rushing with fresh saliva. Instead of following them directly down the road, he now edged into the fields and pursued them more obliquely. Sometimes the two ahead of him would pause, and there was some indication the stranger was about to leave Lily, but then from something they said to one another, the couple continued on together. Hobart would have liked to get closer to them so that he might hear what they were saying, but he feared discovery. At any rate, he could be sure of one thing, the man walking with her was not Edward, and also he was sure that whoever he was he was her lover. Only lovers walked that way together, too far apart at one time, too weaving and close together another time: their very breathing appeared uneven and heavy the way their bodies swayed. Yes, Hobart realized, he was about to see love being made, and it made him walk unsteadily, almost to stumble. He only hoped he could keep a rein on his feelings and would not make his presence known to them.

When he saw them at last turn in to her cottage he longed for the strength to leave them, to go back home to forget Lily, forget his brother Edward, whom he was certain Lily had been "cheating" all through their marriage (even *he* had been intimate once with Lily when Edward was away on a trip, so that he had always wondered if the child she bore him in this marriage might not have been after all his, but since it was dead, he would not think of it again).

Her cottage had a certain fame. There were no other houses about, and the windows of her living room faced the thick forest. Here she could have done nearly whatever she liked and nobody would have been the wiser, for unless one had stood directly before the great window which covered almost the entire width of her room, any glimpse within was shut out by foliage, and sometimes by heavy mist.

Hobart knew that this man, whoever he was, had not come tonight for the purpose of imparting Jesus' love to her but his own. He had heard things about the young preacher, Reverend McGilead, he had been brief on his "special" prayer meetings, and had got the implication the man of the cloth had an excess of unburned energy in his make-up. He shouted too loud during his sermons, people said, and the veins in his neck were ready to burst with the excess of blood that ran through him.

From Hobart's point of observation, in the protection of a large spruce tree, nothing to his surprise he saw whom he believed to be the young preacher take her in his arms. But then what happened was unforeseen, undreamed of indeed, for with the rapidity of a professional gymnast, the preacher stripped off his clothing in a trice, and stood in the clear illumination of her room not covered by so much as a stitch or thread. Lily herself looked paralyzed, as rodents are at the sudden appearance of a serpent. Her eyes were unfocused on anything about her, and she made no attempt to assist him as he partially undressed her. But from the casual way he acted, it was clear they had done this before. Yes, Hobart confessed to himself, in the protective dark of the tree under which he stood, one would have expected certainly something more gradual from lovers. He would have thought that the young preacher would have talked to her for at least a quarter of an hour, that he would have finally taken her hand, then perhaps kissed her, and then oh so slowly and excitingly, for Hobart at least, would have undressed her, and taken her to himself.

But this gymnast's performance quite nonplussed the observer by the spruce tree. For one thing the gross size of the preacher's sex, its bulging veins and unusual angry redness reminded him of sights seen by him when he had worked on a farm. It also recalled a surgical operation he had witnessed performed by necessity in a doctor's small overcrowded office. The preacher now had pushed Lily against the wall, and worked vigorously at, and then through her. His eyes rolled like those of a man being drawn unwillingly into some kind of suction machine, and saliva suddenly poured out of his mouth in great copiousness so that he resembled someone blowing up an enormous balloon. His neck and throat were twisted convulsively, and his nipples tightened as if they were being given over to rank torture.

At this moment, Hobart, without realizing he was doing so, came out from his hiding place, and strode up to the window, where he began waving his arms back and forth in the manner of a man flagging a truck. (Indeed Lily later was to believe that she thought she had seen a man with two white flags in his hands signalling for help.)

Lily's screams at being discovered broke the peace of the neighbourhood, and many watchdogs from about the immediate vicinity began barking in roused alarm.

"We are watched!" she was finally able to get out. Then she gave out three uncadenced weak cries. But the preacher, his back to the window, like a man in the throes of some grave physical malady, could only concentrate on what his body dictated to him, and though Lily now struggled to be free of him, this only secured him the more tightly to her. Her cries now rose in volume until they reached the same pitch as that of the watchdogs.

Even Hobart, who had become as disoriented perhaps as the couple exhibited before him, began making soft outcries, and he continued to wave his arms fruitlessly.

"No, no, and no!" Lily managed now to form and speak these words. "Whoever you are out there, go, go away at once!"

Hobart now came directly up to the window. He had quit waving his arms, and he pressed his nose and mouth against the pane.

"It's me," he cried reassuringly. "Hobart, Edward Starr's brother! Can't you see?" He was, he managed to realize, confused as to what he now should do or say, but he thought that since he had frightened them so badly and so seriously disturbed their pleasure, he had best identify himself, and let them know he meant no harm. But his calling to them only terrified Lily the more, and caused her young partner to behave like someone struggling in deep water.

"Hobart Starr here!" the onlooker called to them, thinking they may have mistook him for a housebreaker.

"Oh merciful Lord," Lily moaned. "If it is you Hobart

Starr, please go away. Have that much decency –" she tried to finish the sentence through her heavy breathing.

The preacher at this moment tore off the upper part of Lily's dress, and her breasts and nipples looked out from the light into the darkness at Hobart like the troubled faces of children.

"I'm coming into the house to explain!" Hobart called to them inside.

"You'll do no such thing! No, no, Hobart!" Lily vociferated back to him, but the intruder dashed away from the window, stumbling over some low-lying bushes, and then presently entered the living room where the preacher was now moaning deeply and beginning even at times to scream a little.

"What on earth possessed you," Lily was beginning to speak when all at once the preacher's mouth fell over hers, and he let out a great smothered roar, punctuated by drumlike rumblings from, apparently, his stomach.

Hobart took a seat near the standing couple.

The preacher was now free of Lily's body at last, and he had slumped down on the floor, near where Hobart was sitting, and was crying out some word and then he began making sounds vaguely akin to weeping. Lily remained with her back and buttocks pressed against the wall, and was breathing hard, gasping indeed for breath. After her partner had quit his peculiar sobbing, he got up and put on his clothes, and walked out unsteadily into the kitchen. On the long kitchen table, the kind of table one would expect in a large school cafeteria, Hobart, from his chair, could spy at least fifteen pies of different kinds, all "homemade" by Lily expressly for the church social which was tomorrow.

He could see the preacher sit down at the big table, and cut himself a piece of Dutch apple pie. His chewing sounds at last alerted Lily to what was happening, and she managed to hurry out to the kitchen in an attempt to halt him.

"One piece of pie isn't going to wreck the church picnic. Go back there and entertain your new boyfriend, why don't you," the preacher snapped at her attempt to prevent him eating the piece of pie.

"He's Edward Starr's brother, I'd have you know, and he's not my boyfriend, smarty!"

The preacher chewed on. "This pie," he said, moving his tongue over his lips cautiously, "is very heavy on the sugar, isn't it?"

"Oh, I declare, hear him!" Lily let the words out peevishly, and she rushed on back into the living room. There she gazed wide-eyed, her mouth trying to move for speech, for facing her stood Hobart, folding his shorts neatly, and stark naked.

"You will not!" Lily managed to protest.

"Who says I don't!" Hobart replied nastily.

"Hobart Starr, you go home at once," Lily ordered him. "This is all something that can be explained."

He made a kind of dive at her as his reply, and pinioned her to the wall. She tried to grab his penis, clawing at it, but he had perhaps already foreseen she might do this, and he caught her by the hand, and then slapped her. Then he inserted his member quickly into her body, and covered her face with his freely flowing saliva. She let out perfunctory cries of expected rather than felt pain as one does under the hand of a nervous intern.

At a motion from her, some moments later, he worked her body about the room, so that she could see what the preacher was doing. He had consumed the Dutch apple pie, and was beginning on the rhubarb lattice.

"Will you be more comfortable watching him, or shall we return to the wall?" Hobart inquired.

"Oh, Hobart, for pity's sake," she begged him. "Let me go, oh please let me go." At this he pushed himself more deeply upwards, hurting her, to judge by her grimace.

"I am a very slow comer, as you will remember, Lily. I'm slow but I'm the one in the end who cares for you most. Tonight is my biggest windfall. After all the others, you see, it is me who was meant for you…. You're so cosy too, Lily."

As he said this, she writhed, and attempted to pull out from him, but he kissed her hard, working into her hard.

"Oh this is all so damned unfair!" She seemed to cough out, not speak, these words. "Ralph," she directed her voice to the kitchen, "come in here and restore order…."

As he reached culmination, Hobart screamed so loud the preacher did come out of the kitchen. He was swallowing very hard, so that he did remind Hobart of a man in a pie-eating contest. He looked critically at the two engaged in coitus.

A few minutes later, finished with Lily, Hobart began putting on his clothes, yawning convulsively, and shaking his head, while Ralph began doggedly and methodically to remove his clothing again, like a substitute or second in some grilling contest.

"Nothing more, no, I say no!" Lily shouted when she saw Ralph's naked body advancing on her. "I will no longer co-operate here."

He had already taken her, however, and secured her more firmly than the last time against the wall.

Hobart meanwhile was standing unsteadily on the threshold of the kitchen. He saw at once that the preacher had eaten two pies. He felt understandably both hungry and nauseous, and these two sensations kept him weaving giddily about the kitchen table now. At last he sat down before a chocolate meringue pie, and then very slowly, finickly, cut himself a small piece.

As he ate daintily he thought that he had not enjoyed intercourse with Lily, despite his seeming gusto. It had been all mostly exertion and effort, somehow, though he felt he had done well, but no feeling in a supreme sense of release had come. He was not surprised now that Edward Starr had left her. She was not a satisfier.

Hobart had finished about half the chocolate meringue when he reckoned the other two must be reaching culmination by now for he heard very strenuous breathing out there, and then there came to his ears as before the preacher's intense war whoop of release. Lily also screamed and appealed as if to the mountain outside, *I perish! Oh, perishing!* And a bit later, she hysterically supplicated to some unknown person or thing *I cannot give myself up like this, oh!* Then a second or so later he heard his own name called, and her demand that he save her.

Hobart wiped his mouth on the tablecloth and came out to have a look at them. They were both, Lily and Ralph, weeping and holding loosely to one another, and then they both slipped and fell to the floor, still sexually connected.

"Gosh all get out!" Hobart said with disgust.

He turned away. There was a pie at the very end of the table which looked most inviting. It had a very brown crust with golden juice spilling from fancily, formally cut little air holes as in magazine advertising. He plunged the knife into it, and tasted a tiny bit. It was of such wonderful flavour that even though he felt a bit queasy he could not resist cutting himself a slice, and he began to chew solemnly on it. It was an apricot, or perhaps peach pie, but final identification eluded him.

Lily now came out into the kitchen and hovered over the big table. She was dressed, and had fixed her hair differently, so that it looked as if it had been cut and set, though there were some loose strands in the back which were not too becoming, yet they emphasized her white neck.

"Why, you have eaten half the pies for the church social!" she cried, with some exaggeration in her observation of course. "After all that backbreaking work of mine! What on earth will I tell the preacher when he comes to pick them up!"

"But isn't this the preacher here tonight?" Hobart waving his fork in the direction of the other room motioned to the man called Ralph.

"Why, Hobart, of course not.... He's no preacher, and I should think you could tell ..."

"How did I come to think he was?" Hobart stuttered out, while Lily sat down at the table and was beginning to bawl.

"Of all the inconsiderate selfish thoughtless pups in the world," she managed to get out between sobs. "I would have to meet up with you two, just when I was beginning to have some sort of settled purpose."

Ralph, standing now on the threshold of the kitchen, still stark naked, laughed.

"I have a good notion to call the sheriff!" Lily threatened. "And do you know what I'm going to do in the morning? I'm going back to Edward Starr in Chicago. Yes siree. I realize now that he loved me more than I was aware of at the time."

The two men were silent, and looked cautiously at one another, while Lily cried on and on.

"Oh, Lily, even if you do go see Edward you'll come home again to us here. You know you can't get the good loving in Chicago that we give you, now don't you?"

Lily wept on and on repeating many times how she would never be able to explain to the church people about not having enough pies on hand for her contribution to the big social.

After drying her tears on a handkerchief which Hobart lent her, she took the knife and with methodical fierce energy and spiteful speed cut herself a serving from one of the still untouched pies.

She showed by the way she moved her tongue in and out of her mouth that she thought her piece was excellent.

"I'm going to Chicago and I'm never coming back!" As she delivered this statement she began to cry again.

The "preacher," for that is how Hobart still thought of him, came over to where Lily was chewing and weeping, and put his hand between the hollow of her breasts.

"No don't get started again, Ralph … No!" she flared up. "No, no, no."

"I need it all over again," Ralph appealed to her. "Your good cooking has charged me up again."

"Those pies *are* too damned good for a church," she finally said with a sort of moody weird craftiness, and Ralph knew when she said this that she would let him have her again.

"Hobart," Lily turned to Edward's brother, "why don't you go home. Ralph and I are old childhood friends from way back. And I was nice to you. But I am in love with Ralph."

"It's my turn," Hobart protested.

"No, no," Lily began her weeping again, "I love Ralph."

"Oh hell, let him just this once more, Lily," the "preacher" said. Ralph walked away and began toying again with another of the uncut pies. "Say, who taught you to cook, Lily," he inquired sleepily.

"I want you to send Hobart home, Ralph. I want you to myself. In a bed. This wall stuff is an outrage. Ralph, you send Hobart home now."

"Oh why don't you let the fellow have you once more. Then I'll really do you upstairs." Meanwhile, he went on chewing and swallowing loudly.

"Damn you, Ralph," Lily moaned. "Double damn you."

She walked over to the big table and took up one of the pies nearest her and threw it straight at the "preacher."

The "preacher's" eyes, looking out from the mess she had made of his face, truly frightened her. She went over to Hobart, and waited there.

"All right for you, Lily," the "preacher" said.

"Oh, don't hurt her," Hobart pleaded, frightened too at the "preacher's" changed demeanour.

The first pie the "preacher" threw hit Hobart instead of Lily. He let out a little gasp, more perhaps of surprised pleasure than hurt.

"Oh now stop this. We must stop this," Lily exhorted. "We are grown-up people after all." She began to sob, but very put-on like, the men felt. "Look at my kitchen." She tried to put some emphasis into her appeal to them.

The "preacher" took off his jockey shorts, which he had put on a few moments earlier. He took first one pie and then another, mashing them all over his body, including his hair. Lily began to whimper and weep in earnest now, and sat down as if to give herself over to her grief. Suddenly one of the pies hit her, and she began to scream, then she became silent.

There was a queer silence in the whole room. When she looked up, Hobart had also stripped completely, and the "preacher" was softly slowly mashing pies over his thin, tightly muscled torso. Then slowly, inexorably, Hobart began eating pieces of pie from off the body of the smeared "preacher." The "preacher" returned this favour, and ate pieces of pie from Hobart, making gobbling sounds like a wild animal. Then they hugged one another and began eating the pies all over again from their bare bodies.

"Where do you get that stuff in my house!" Lily rose, roaring at them. "You low curs, where do you …"

But the "preacher" had thrown one of the few remaining pies at her, which struck her squarely in the breast and blew itself red all over her face and body so that she resembled a person struck by a bomb.

Ralph hugged Hobart very tenderly now, and dutifully ate small tidbits from his body, and Hobart seemed to nestle against Ralph's body, and ate selected various pieces of the pie from the latter.

Then Lily ran out the front door and began screaming *Help! I will perish! Help me!*

The dogs began to bark violently all around the neighbourhood.

In just a short time she returned. The two men were still closely together, eating a piece here and there from their "massacred" bodies.

Sitting down at the table, weeping perfunctorily and almost inaudibly, Lily raised her fork, and began eating a piece of her still unfinished apple pie.

DIANE SCHOEMPERLEN

LOVE IN THE TIME OF CLICHÉS

*"There are a number of difficulties with dirty words," says
the American novelist William Gass, "the first of which is
that there aren't nearly enough of them; the second is that the
people who use them are normally numskulls and prudes;
the third is that in general they're not at all sexy; and the
main reason is that no one loves them enough." The relationship between the erotic experience and the words used to
describe it is a long and painful one. We require words to
understand our sensations, we use words to enhance or guide
us through lovemaking, we construct fantastical sensual
encounters out of words and yet our languages have little or
no erotic vocabulary. Because to name the erotic would be to
embrace it, we sternly condemn our pleasures to the pedantic
jargon of medicine or to the "dirty" words of the playground.*

*Lovers who want to speak to one another have to borrow
words from the mystic poets (ecstasy, dying, transport), from
landscape artists (hills, gardens, hollows), from cooks (nibbling, stirring, eating, and drinking), from butchers (flanks,*

*loins, rump). Or from book-lovers: "I want to pick you up
and caress your spine," says a character in Aloyse Debordes's
novel* Blue of the Night. *"I want to open you and flip
through your pages, and slide my finger down your lines
looking for that one word or phrase that will burn in my
mind like fire. I want to read you carefully, silently, or out
loud, like a poem. I want to carry you with me, in my
breast-pocket, and then, at night, take you to bed." Or, as in
Diane Schoemperlen's story, lovers have to find their experience retold in the clichés of Hallmark cards and the banalities of romantic songs.*

… it was love at first sight …

SHORTLY AFTER Carmen falls irretrievably in love with
Abraham, she notices that she is often at a loss for words.
This is unusual for Carmen, who has been told many times
that she's been blessed with the gift of the gab. She supposes
that she inherited or appropriated this gift from her mother,
Maureen. Most of Carmen's childhood memories feature the
sound of Maureen's lilting voice running as an undercurrent
through everything, the melodious background music to their
daily lives.

There, for instance, was Carmen, already a devoutly practising insomniac at an early age, tossing and turning in her

narrow bed till the sheets were twisted like seaweed round her ankles. She could hear her mother in the living room, talking to her father, Frank, who never said much in reply, who was in fact probably stretched out on the couch half-asleep, not even listening, but Maureen didn't seem to notice or mind much. Carmen was on the tip of being a teenager then and often coaxed herself to sleep with fantasies of what it would be like to have a man, a full-grown, not-too-hairy man beside her in the bed, a man who would sleep all night long with his arm around her waist, his hand between her legs, not caressing, just cradling and holding her close, quietly.

It was not until Carmen took on the surly self-absorbed silence of adolescence that she began to wish Maureen would just SHUT UP. She never had anything important to say anyway, Carmen fumed silently. Especially first thing in the morning, Maureen was just like a magpie: yack, yack, yack. She just loved the sound of her own voice, Carmen thought, and closed her long-suffering eyes while her oatmeal congealed.

It was almost ten years later, long after Carmen had surfaced from beneath the iceberg of adolescence, had finished university, moved away from home, and settled into her own eventual adult life, that she understood how her mother's sometimes manic loquaciousness might actually have been compensation for the fact that she *knew* she had nothing important to say or, if she did, for the fact that she was afraid to say it.

Now Carmen finds she can afford to be sympathetic and doesn't mind admitting that, in terms of volubility anyway, she is her mother's daughter. It is an inheritance which serves Carmen well, both in her teaching job and in her personal life.

She is often admired for her ability to talk to anyone about anything. She can talk to her students about their families (who don't understand them), their boyfriends (who are collectively uncooperative and afraid of commitment), their wardrobes (which must look stylish but not too studied), their hair (which must be easy to take care of and yet look perfect at all times). She can talk to her fellow English teachers about the existential commitment in *Macbeth*, the symbol of the green light in *The Great Gatsby*, and the passage of time in the novels of Virginia Woolf. She can even talk to people she doesn't particularly like about things she isn't the least bit interested in. She talks to the jocks about football, to the math teachers about sine, cosine, and tangent, to the cashier in the cafeteria about the occupational hazard of breaking your fingernails on the cash register drawer, and to the foreign students about the price of tea in China. She is seldom stuck for a snappy answer to anything.

She works hard during the week and goes to lots of parties on weekends. Usually the first to arrive and the last to leave, she can dance and dance and never get tired, drink and drink and never pass out or throw up. She is the legendary life of the party. Her friends marvel at her stamina, her energy, her irrepressible love of life. She is, someone once said admiringly, the kind of person you cannot ever imagine asleep.

They don't know the half of it. They don't know about the insomnia, Carmen waking up in a sweat (hot or cold or an indescribable combination of both) at 3:14 a.m., her heart pounding so hard she can see it trembling beneath her nightgown, and then she can't go back to sleep even though she has to get up for work at six-thirty, so she lies there worrying about anything and everything that crosses her mind, watching the red numbers on the digital clock click inexorably over until morning.

Her friends don't know how she sits by herself for hours on end not doing anything, not listening to music or looking out the window or anything, but just sitting there, brooding and stewing and travelling further and further inside herself, trying to catch a glimpse of what is really in there.

They don't know how she often plays a game with herself when walking down the street: looking closely at total strangers and trying to imagine them making love – not necessarily to her, but to anyone. That woman there in the purple shorts, the one with the snotty-nosed toddler on a leash and the prune-faced baby screaming in the stroller. That man there in the three-piece suit with his neck bulging over his perfectly-knotted tie, his hair combed forward over his bald spot, a chunky gold wedding band on his third left finger. Could they ever really have been laughing and snuggling, naked and happy in their lovers' arms? There are, Carmen has discovered, a great many people who, despite all evidence to the contrary, cannot be imagined into love in any position. She is afraid that she has become one of them.

Carmen has had lovers, of course – lots of them, in fact. Too many lovers, some people (her mother) might say. But nothing has ever worked out. With the twenty/twenty hindsight acquired somewhere around her thirtieth birthday, Carmen can see these men now as a long and relatively listless line of losers. Not one of them, she sees now, could have changed her life even if she'd wanted them to. Once, in a fit of foolishness precipitated by a six-month dry spell and a bottle of wine, she sat down to make a list of them (in order of appearance, not importance). When she got halfway through, when she got to the veterinarian who, in his exuberance to get her into his waterbed, knocked over the hamster cage on the night stand, killing the stupid smelly little thing, when she discovered that she couldn't even remember his name (Kevin? Karl? Keith?), she was so appalled and depressed that she went to bed, where, of course, she couldn't sleep for a long time anyway and then all of her dreams were dotted with furry little dead things.

Her friend, Lorraine, a woman with a similarly chequered and disappointing past, once sent Carmen a cute card that said: "A question every woman asks herself … Is it possible that I deserve the kind of men I attract?" So Carmen smiled wryly, said, "Yes, well, yes," and kept on wondering, kept on trying to convince herself that none of it mattered anyway, that she preferred to be alone anyway, that sex wasn't what it was cracked up to be anyway, was definitely not one of the basic human needs like food, water, and shelter. And what was all the fuss about anyway when there were so many more important things to be considered?

And sometimes she even manages to look fondly forward to spending the rest of her life alone. Sometimes, when she can embrace it from just the right angle, she is able to conjure an image of herself as very tall, very thin, standing very straight, wearing something white and willowy, feeling stoic and serene, untouched by human hands and so, unsullied, uncomplicated, and clean.

Carmen's friends misinterpret her liveliness as the result of a natural ebullient energy, when really it is the result of a persistent low-grade anxiety which escalates according to the situation at hand. Knowing that she has a party to go to on Friday night is enough to keep her going all week long. By Friday morning she is so keyed-up that all day at work she is thinking of it: of what she will wear (does she need a new shirt? a black one? new pants? a new hairdo?), of what she will say (did she tell that story about the hamster last week or what about the guy who told her she was pretty well-preserved for her age and then couldn't understand why she dumped him?), of what she will drink (beer makes her sloppy but affectionate and gregarious, Scotch leaves her lucid but brave), of who else might be there, of the music, the dancing, the sky going dark outside the windows and then maybe coming light again too, pinkish and pale, and she won't have to sleep (or try to) all night long.

Nobody knows that she is the first to arrive because, by that time, she can't take the anticipation a minute longer and has to swing into action before she explodes. And that she is the last to leave because, by that time, she can't bear to admit that the party is over and nothing has happened. (She is never quite sure what she is expecting to happen but she *is* sure that if it ever does, she'll know. This is akin to what her mother told her years ago when Carmen asked her how you know when you're really in love, and Maureen said, mysteriously, maddeningly, as all mothers do, "Oh, you'll know, you'll just *know*.")

So it is at a party, naturally enough, that Carmen first meets Abraham. A party thrown for no good reason other than that they are all mired in the backwater of mid-February and they just need to let loose. Carmen is wearing her tightest black jeans, her baggy hot-pink sweatshirt, and silver hoop earrings the size of saucers. Her hair, for once, has turned out just right and her black leather jacket, she thinks, adds just the right hint or promise of danger.

She has never seen Abraham before in her life (he is new in town, working in the English Department at the university, so she's been told) but as she watches him browsing through the tape collection, selecting one and then plugging it into the machine, she suddenly thinks, Now there's a man I'd like to have around all the time.

For about a minute and a half the fact that he has chosen her own favourite tape seems merely coincidental. Emmylou Harris sings, *I would walk all the way/From Boulder to Birmingham/If I thought I could see/I could see your face.*

When Abraham asks Carmen to dance and takes her in his arms, it all makes perfect and sudden sense.

... love makes the world go round ...

It is exactly two weeks later that Carmen notices she is more and more often at a loss for words. Her friends are concerned at first. They think she is depressed. When they realize that she is just in love, they take to teasing her gently while she smiles stupidly (they call it "mooning") with the realization that Abraham is the only person in the whole world she wants to talk or listen to anyway. Sometimes her friends complain that she's just no fun anymore.

She can feel herself beginning to shed the cynicism with which she has protected herself for years. It comes peeling off her in ragged sheets like sunburned skin. Sometimes it is embarrassing, like when she does get talkative and catches herself quite unconsciously running off at the mouth about a beautiful sunset, a perfect tree, or the precious light of a misty morning. Her friends take to rolling their eyes impatiently whenever she begins to wax poetic about how WONDERFUL everything is. They don't understand how loving Abraham is like getting new glasses which amplify and intensify everything so that even the colour of the clouds, the sound of the rain, and the taste of her chicken salad sandwich at lunch are magnificent and miraculous.

Abraham usually picks Carmen up after work and, as they drive through the familiar city streets, they joyfully point out landmarks and points of interest to each other. There is their favourite house on the corner of Dundas and Tait, the vine-covered brick one with the verandah, the dormers, the bay window through which they can see a stone fireplace, floor-to-ceiling bookshelves, and hanging plants everywhere. They are both thinking, Someday we'll have a house like that. Even though they see it every day, it never ceases to amaze them.

They comment happily on sleepy cats curled on porches or window ledges, frisky black squirrels, bright-eyed and bushy-tailed, chasing each other from branch to branch, rosy-cheeked children in pink snowsuits and bunny hats, plump lumpy snowmen with carrot noses and corn-cob pipes. The whole neighbourhood strikes them as happy and handsome, resplendent and promising, tangible proof of the power of love.

When they see a young couple kissing on the corner, the girl's face tilting up to meet the boy's lips, her naked throat an offering, tantalizing with trust, Carmen and Abraham feel tender and empowered and Carmen lays her head on his shoulder while they wait for the light to change and the boy on the corner buries his face in the girl's cold hair.

On Fridays they stop at The Brunswick Bar for a drink on

the way home. At The Brunswick they hold hands across the table and share a plate of nachos with cheese.

One Friday afternoon in the car when both of them are singing along with the Top 40 AM radio love songs (*I had the time of my life/And I owe it all to you*), they notice that, much as this music used to seem sappy and naïve, it has lately become poignant and perceptive.

Suddenly they simultaneously realize that most of what has been coming out of their mouths these days is one massive love-soaked starry-eyed cliché.

They go directly to The Brunswick to talk it over. The bar, as usual on Friday afternoon, is crowded with other hard-working people celebrating the end of another busy week. Everyone feels exuberant: they're buying drinks for each other as fast as they can, laughing uproariously, taking off their jackets and ties, letting their hair down for a few happy hours. Abraham and Carmen are lucky enough to get their favourite table and they smile and nod at familiar faces as they make their way to the back corner by the window. It's a cold dark day with snow clouds piled like blankets in the northern sky. The fireplace is lit and the room closes cosily in around the orange-tinted light, the smell of wood smoke, the sound of jazz music.

They are disgruntled at first by their unsettling revelation. They have always thought of themselves as creative, original, sophisticated, and very amusing people. They look cautiously around The Brunswick wondering if anyone has noticed the change in them but been too polite to mention it. Today they consciously resist the urge to feed nachos to each other.

No wonder they can only talk to each other these days! How could they say such things to their friends, to their conscientious politically-correct friends who are all wrapped up in the larger issues: the environment, the Third World, the nuclear arms race, poverty, pornography, abortion, AIDS, and injustice. Certainly their friends have their love lives too, but they seem to look upon these liaisons with practical, matter-of-fact eyes. They are careful never to neglect their work, their other friends, or their social consciences in favour of their loves and/or their lusts. They are mature, independent, self-sufficient, self-controlled, meticulously realistic people who would never let love get in the way of anything.

Before she fell in love with Abraham, Carmen was just like them. Not since one misguided juvenile moment in Grade Ten has she turned down an evening with her female friends in favour of staying home and waiting for the phone to ring. She once laughed out loud at a woman who kept a snapshot of her lover on the dashboard of her car when he was away travelling and thought it probably served this woman right when she ran out of gas because the picture was over the gas gauge. She used to sneer churlishly at couples who kissed on corners. She had, a scant six weeks ago, turned down a date with a man she had been interested in for ages because he invited her to go and see a band called The High Heels whose lyrics were notoriously sexist and, besides, there was a rally that same night for animal rights.

Abraham too admits that he once broke a hot date with a gorgeous lustful woman because he wanted to stay home and reread *Madame Bovary*. And that he had once ended a fairly serious relationship with a woman named Wanda because she said nuclear war was inevitable so what was the point in getting all worked up about it?

Now Carmen and Abraham, by comparison both to their friends and to their former selves, are either iconoclastic or insipid lovebirds.

They order more beer and consider the nature of clichés.

Carmen recalls an incident from Grade Eleven English class when, in a short essay on Dickens' *Great Expectations*, she used the phrase "the eyes are the windows of the soul" and referred to it as "that old cliché." Her teacher, Miss Crocker, had put a question mark in the margin and a comment saying she'd never heard that saying before. Even then Carmen was aghast and never trusted Miss Crocker again.

Abraham suggests that the reason clichés become clichés in the first place is because they are true and that's why they come so easily to mind. "So yes," he says, "there must be a great many people in the world who have skin white as snow, hair black as night, lips red as cherries, voices clear as bells, and eyes just like diamonds or stars."

Carmen frowns into her half-empty glass.

Abraham elaborates on his theory: "Certainly, all over the world there must be thousands, if not millions, of people who are smart as whips, quick as winks, busy as bees –"

Carmen catches the spirit and they trade clichés across the table like playing cards:

"– right as rain," she offers. "Nervous as cats, quiet as mice, happy as clams –"

"– wicked as witches, thick as bricks, crazy as loons, strong as bulls, big as houses –"

"– mad as hatters, sick as dogs, cold as ice –"

"– wise as owls, bald as billiard balls, weak as kittens, naked as jaybirds –"

"– hot as blazes –"

"– nutty as fruitcakes –"

"– slow as molasses in January –"

"– pretty as pictures –"

"– ugly as sin –"

"– as old as the hills."

"So what's wrong with that?" asks Abraham.

"And drunk as skunks too," Carmen adds, taking another sip. She is not quite convinced that clichés might actually be acceptable currency in intelligent conversation. "When was the last time you saw a drunk skunk?" she counters skeptically. She also points out that people who sleep like babies have obviously never had one. And those who insist they are happy as larks know next to nothing about the real secret lives of birds, about the pressures they're under, trying to get that nest built out of thin air, laying those eggs and then sitting on them for God knows how long, hatching the babies, feeding them, teaching them how to fly – and having to keep on singing the whole time too.

"But what about love?" Abraham asks. "What about 'I love you'? What about 'I love you like there's no tomorrow'?"

Their sheepish chagrin is replaced quickly enough by an amused relief at finding themselves finally able to indulge their nascent romanticism, a tendency they had convinced themselves was a shameful weakness to be forever monitored, suppressed, and camouflaged for their higher-minded friends, indeed for the entire modern world. They marvel now at their ability to say romantic things to each other without feeling embarrassed or self-conscious, without having to make fun of themselves for being in love. They congratulate themselves on their new-found ability to say such things over and over again with a straight face and without gagging.

"Next thing you know," Carmen warns, "we'll be reading romance novels. Our hearts will be pounding, our breasts will be heaving, our hands will be quivering. Even the tips of our fingers will be tingling and electrified. We will be throbbing all over the place."

They say to hell with the cynical high-minded modern world. They have been tempted (or trying) to fall in love like this all their lives. They have nothing to hide, they can wear their passion everywhere. They are immaculate lovers, shameless. They will never be ordinary people again.

… you are always on my mind …

Abraham is coming over for a special dinner to celebrate their first-month anniversary. Carmen spends the whole day, Saturday, getting ready while Abraham puts in a few hours of work at the university. She gets up early and reads cookbooks. Then she goes downtown to gather the ingredients for the meal, which will be a nourishing feast fit for a king. Abraham is a man who loves to eat and Carmen loves to cook.

At the A&P, Carmen hums along with the muzak (*… the girl from Ipanema goes walking …*) and grins when they play a mutilated instrumental version of "You Light Up My Life." She makes her way slowly up and down the aisles, instead of tearing through the whole store in ten minutes like she usually does. She reads labels and considers prices carefully, instead of grabbing items off the shelves with one hand while still pushing the cart with the other so that it never stops moving. She waits patiently behind an elderly woman who has left her cart blocking the cereal aisle and smiles sympathetically as the woman tries to decide between regular oatmeal and the new quick-cooking kind. (She is not happy to recall the time an innocent but unsteady old man tried to shuffle past her in the produce section and banged into her cart with his and she told him to fuck off.) She lovingly selects the zucchini, the onions, the green peppers, weighs them gently in each hand, caresses them intimately, then lays them down in the cart as if they were alive. She hand-picks the mushrooms from the bulk bin instead of buying a pre-packaged plastic tub. She imagines them slippery and flavourful in Abraham's mouth. She is patient with the cashier who is new on the job and doesn't have the hang of the electronic scanner yet. She loves every minute of it.

On her way into the seafood store, she bumps into her friend Debbie from school. Debbie teaches Health. Debbie says she just read an article in *Popular Psychology* which said that over 75% of any given person's thoughts on any given day are about either food or sex. The article also said that the average person has seven sexual fantasies per day.

Carmen thinks, What? Is that all? Only seven?

Debbie says, "I don't believe it. Nobody has that many! I've never had that many. I must be one of those people who fantasize about hot fudge sundaes instead!" She heads for the Dairy Queen, chuckling.

In the seafood store, Carmen buys a whole pound of fresh jumbo shrimp with the shells still on. While the man behind the counter wraps them up, she tells him she's making a special dinner tonight for her lover and they'll just have to see if it's true what they say about seafood being an aphrodisiac. She isn't even embarrassed when the man stares at her as if she's gone straight out of her mind.

At a gift store, she buys two pale blue candles and two white porcelain candle holders. She imagines Abraham's tender face touched by their elegant light. At the flower shop, she buys a bouquet of dusty pink astermaria, arranged with graceful green ferns and white Baby's Breath. She imagines Abraham pressing his face close into them and sighing deeply. At the liquor store, she buys a bottle of brandy. She imagines Abraham lifting the glass to his full moist lips, tasting the wine as thoroughly as he will afterwards taste her nipples and the back of her neck.

She spends the whole afternoon chopping, slicing, and dicing, singing along with Emmylou: *I don't want to hear a sad story/Full of heartbreak and desire.* She puts together the zucchini and barley casserole, then the cold lentil salad. She has to consult *The Joy of Cooking* about how to clean the shrimp. The cookbook has instructions and a diagram: "Shelling is easy – a slight tug releases the body shell from the tail. De-vein using a small pointed knife or the end of a toothpick, as sketched. This is essential." In the diagram, two disembodied female hands lay a small black knife upon a plump shrimp that looks like a fat peapod. The procedure may be essential but it's not easy and it takes Carmen a long time to master this tugging and hacking, so that the blue veins come snapping out of the meat like elastic bands. She marinates the shrimp in olive oil, parsley, basil, wine, and garlic. There is garlic in everything because they love garlic and the smell of it in the warm kitchen is pungent.

Finally content with her efforts, she sits down to read the

newspaper and wait for Abraham. She recognizes that, short of an apron and bare feet, the whole scene is a cliché. *The way to a man's heart ...*

"The way to a man's heart," she used to like to quip for her friends, "is an unmarked minefield." Or: is a barbed wire fence, an electric one at that. Is a shot in the dark. Is a roller-coaster ride to hell. At the time she thought she was vastly amusing. Now she feels sorry for her former self.

"Contentment," she used to say, "is for cows."

"Patience," she used to say, "is a virgin."

In the newspaper, she reads the story of two lovers reunited finally and forever after seventeen years and her eyes mist over lightly with sweet warm tears.

And so it is in the power of true love to liberate all emotions unequivocally and without restraint. It is no longer necessary to deny your emotional excesses. No longer necessary to pretend you have something in your eye when you cry at the long-distance commercials on television. No longer necessary to try and convince anyone, not even yourself, that you stopped believing in "happily ever after" around the same time you got smart about Santa Claus and the Easter Bunny. It is no longer necessary to keep your heart in check and your passion under control. You can be as flagrant and ecstatic as you have always wanted to be.

Abraham arrives with more flowers, white wine, and a chocolate cheesecake for dessert. They kiss for a long time in the doorway, stranded on the stairs.

"My lover," Carmen says, "my lover." The mere sound of the word lets loose a voluptuous leaping in her heart, her stomach, or some hitherto unknown, unexercised internal organ. The other beautiful feast will just have to wait.

... I can't live if living is without you ...

In the morning they make love again. Carmen is above him, her hands on his shoulders, his tongue licking her breasts, his hands squeezing her buttocks as she moves on him in small circles, his long thin fingers sliding in and out of all her moist places, beads of sweat and her long hair falling into her eyes, into his, and when she comes he says, "I love you, I love you." He says he loves the way she looks right at him when she comes, the way she comes *into* him rather than away, the way she doesn't go off to some other planet where he can no longer reach her. And he is right, she is not transported; rather, she is transformed. In his innocent arms she becomes the person she has always hoped to be.

Everywhere their bodies are like mouths, slippery and warm, brimming with nerve endings and succulent taste buds.

Abraham holds her there on top of him. She rests her wet face on his wet chest and she can feel his heart beating against her forehead like a pulse in her own brain. When he says, "I want to hold you like this forever," she can feel the words as much as hear them. Even if she were deaf, she would know what he was saying. They stretch out side by side face-down on the big bed and take turns tracing words with their fingertips on each other's bare backs and then trying to guess what they are. They make words like "hope," "love," "forever," "hearts," "sweethearts." Even if they were blind, they would dwell in the language of love.

Abraham says it's his turn to make breakfast. Carmen gets to luxuriate in her own laziness, lolling around in the messy bed, the smell of their lovemaking still on the sheets, the smell of his hair still on the pillow. While Abraham clatters around in the kitchen, she tries smelling her own skin, her arms, the crook of her elbow, tries to catch that smell of herself which Abraham is always saying he loves so much. Except for a possible hint of garlic from last night's meal still on her hands, she cannot smell anything special. This is akin, she supposes, to not being able to tickle yourself – why can't you?

If she sprawls crossways on the bed and leans over the edge, she can just see Abraham in the kitchen at the stove. The sight of him stirring and tasting, bare-chested in his blue jeans, leaves her weak-kneed with pleasure.

She comes into the kitchen in her pink chenille housecoat which makes her feel like an irresistible if slightly dissolute movie queen from the fifties. Dishing up their hot porridge, Abraham tells her that she looks glamorous. The sash of the housecoat comes loose as she sits down at the table. Abraham smiles at her brown nipples which look like another pair of eyes, blinking with surprise at the light.

"There is," he says, laughing, "a fine line between sordid and glamorous."

Porridge is something that Carmen would never make for herself (if only because it would remind her of those mornings when she was busy hating her mother, Maureen, who was rambling on about the virtues of a hot breakfast while

Carmen's oatmeal turned to concrete in her bowl). But cooked up now by Abraham, it is the best thing she has ever eaten. And when he expounds on the virtues of a hot breakfast, she is touched by his loving concern for her health.

From the kitchen window, they watch the empty Sunday morning street. It has rained heavily all night and now the temperature is dropping quickly, freezing the rain as it falls, forming a skin of ice on everything in sight. It is springtime, or it should be. (Carmen thinks again of Maureen who, whenever the weather was unusual, said it was because of those damned Russians out in space always shooting at the moon.) An occasional car slides past the house, windshield wipers flapping ineffectually, ferrying intrepid men in rumpled suits and devout women in subdued hats to worship at the churches of their choice. They laugh, but not unkindly, at the woman from next door making her way down the treacherous sidewalk with a box of salt in her hand, sprinkling it on the ice in front of her as she inches along.

They decide it is a good day to be decadent. They close up all the curtains again, put a little brandy in their coffee, and carry their cups into the living room. They've got classical music on the stereo, Beethoven's "Ode to Joy": *O friends, no more these sounds!/let us sing more cheerful songs,/more full of joy!*

They're curled up on the chesterfield like luxurious cats and the hanging lamp in the corner drops a circle of yellow light down around them like a tent. They take turns reading poetry to each other.

The day unravels in slow motion around them and they know in their hearts how beautiful they truly are.

By mid-afternoon it is still raining and they are still nestled there in each other's arms. Abraham is dozing and Carmen is suspended somewhere between thinking and dreaming, all of her borders blurred. Now that she has at last learned how to love, she worries sometimes about how much now she has to lose.

As if from a great snow-covered stony height, she feels Abraham's fingers go limp and fall away from hers. Her eyes snap open.

To look into the future and not see them together is like going blind.

In his sleep, Abraham tucks his hand between her legs where it is furry and moist and he sighs.

... wish you were here ...

In August, Carmen goes home to visit her parents for two weeks. Abraham drives her to the airport where they re-enact the time-honoured scene, hugging and promising while Carmen hides her teary eyes in his neck. At the last minute, Abraham tucks the Emmylou Harris tape into her purse, and says, "Reinforcements."

The small plane gaining altitude after take-off fishtails like a car skidding on the ice in slow motion. Carmen, who does not like flying at the best of times, is praying silently at the top of her lungs, praying to a God she is not sure she believes in but whom she is not averse to invoking when she thinks it might help, praying, Please don't let me die now, not now, not now when I'm in love. But then, sinking back into her seat, she thinks, Oh well, all right then, go ahead, at least I won't have died without learning how to love.

But of course she doesn't die. She smiles gratefully at the calm competent stewardess and tries to enjoy the flight. The man in the seat beside her is headfirst in his briefcase, avoiding her glance, clearly not interested in making conversation. She looks out the window.

The sight of the familiar countryside falling away from her at odd angles as the plane continues to climb is mesmerizing. She is already writing a letter to Abraham in her head. She must remember to tell him about these lakes like the little mirrors on that embroidered Indian bag she used to carry, about these trees like broccoli, too green to be true, about this highway like an artery, these country roads like veins. She relaxes and closes her eyes. The two women in front of her are gossiping in shrill but thrilled voices, using words like "odious," "flagrant," "screaming," and "wild-eyed." Over the drone of the plane, nothing they are saying connects. There is another voice, a pretty voice in her own head, running as the soothing undercurrent through everything. It takes her a minute to realize it is the voice of Emmylou, singing.

As Carmen drifts further away, the voice in her head becomes that of Maureen superimposed upon a picture of Carmen in her sandbox, mucking around with a yellow plastic shovel and a little red pail while her mother leaned against the white picket fence, chatting with the neighbour lady, Mrs. Lutz, who smiled and nodded knowingly as Maureen considered at length the possibilities of the weather, the problems of the old wringer washing machine (which once got a good grip on her left hand and flattened all four fingers), and what would become of the Watson house now that the Widow Watson had finally passed on, poor old thing? Mrs. Lutz was poking around in her big garden while they talked, handing Maureen vegetables over the fence: waxy green cucumbers, plump red tomatoes, crisp orange carrots with the dirt still on them. Maureen carried them into the house cradled in her apron as if they were alive. Carmen didn't mind being left alone in the yard. Not until she heard the sound of a train on the track at the end of the street and as it bore down on her, she ran the whole length of the yard screaming, banged the screen door open and flew into her mother's safe arms in the safe yellow kitchen.

Maureen and Frank are waiting at the airport and Carmen is surprised at the lump which rises in her throat when Maureen takes her in her arms. For a minute, Carmen thinks Maureen is wearing little white gloves, wrist-length, the kind she would have been wearing twenty years ago with her white feathered hat with the veil. But no, it's just that Maureen's skin is so white that her hands look disembodied, as if hung from the sleeves of her fancy black blouse. Her father, Frank, pats her gently on the back.

Maureen talks all the way home in the car, while Frank drives smiling, and Carmen marvels, as she does every year, at how nothing and everything has changed: how the street looks the same but wider and the houses look the same too but smaller and cleaner.

Maureen's kitchen hasn't changed either: there is the same flooring (white with gold swirls), the same arborite kitchenette set (blue with black specks), Maureen's collection of little ceramic animals and birds gathered from boxes of Red Rose tea and arranged on the windowsill above the sink, Carmen's Grade Twelve school picture still stuck to the fridge with an owl magnet.

But this year, Carmen finds she does not immediately turn back into a seething sixteen-year-old the minute she steps into the house. This time, as she lays her suitcase down on her old bed, she is still a grown woman with a good job. She is still a happy woman with a photograph of Abraham in the gold locket at her throat. It is an antique locket which Maureen gave her when she left home and so it is engraved in delicate curling script with Maureen's initials instead of her own. She has never worn it before and now, with Abraham's picture inside, the locket is a potent talisman which will protect her from all sadness, all evil, despair. Abraham's spirit will not desert her. Whenever the ache of loneliness surges up into her throat so that she can feel it like a second pulse, she rubs the gold locket between her thumb and forefinger until it is warm, warm as his hands on her cheeks when he kisses her closed eyelids, warm as the sound of his voice in the dark.

This time, too, Maureen and Frank seem to sense the change in her and, indeed, they treat her like an adult instead of like a seething sixteen-year-old. She finds she can even afford this time to remember scenes from those tortured adolescent years with a nostalgic fondness for her own plaintive perpetual whining ("Stop treating me like a child!") and for Maureen's condescending triumphant reasoning ("Then stop acting like one!")

She can sit there at the table eating a pressed ham and Kraft processed cheese sandwich on white bread, drinking Lone Star beer right out of the can, skimming through Frank's *National Enquirer* and Maureen's *True Romances*, listening to Frank suck his teeth while Maureen complains about the new people next door who never mow their grass and what will become of this neighbourhood anyway? She can sit there calmly without hating them at all. She can think with amusement: Ah, the life I left behind!

She can even look at the fake fireplace in the living room (plaster of Paris painted like bricks which Maureen was always touching up with a piece of grey chalk when the paint got chipped and there is a revolving orange lightbulb below the metal grate which is filled with charcoal briquets) without cringing or wishing she could take a sledgehammer to the damn thing.

She can think of Abraham's face between her naked trembling thighs and she can hear him whispering her name when she comes. For once in her life, she does not feel guilty about anything, least of all about growing up.

> And so the lovers, the true lovers, may become at long last generous and genuine, capable of expanding in all directions at once without ever losing track of themselves. All memories are bearable, all dreams are possible, and the future feels like a very fine thing full of truth and spirit and tender power.

... *the minutes pass like hours* ...

On the third day of her visit, Carmen goes to bed early because the time will not pass. She has always had a problem with time. As a child, she was always trying to coax or trick the hours into hurrying up because there was always something she could hardly wait for and Maureen was always warning her, "Girl, you're wishing your life away."

Now she lies awake in the half-dark watching the numbers on the digital clock and listening to the Emmylou Harris tape. She can hear her mother in the kitchen, talking on the phone to her sister, Giselle.

Carmen can picture Maureen perched on the stool by the phone, twirling the coiled cord with one hand and doodling all over the phone book with the other. Maureen and Giselle are having the same conversation they had twenty years ago while Carmen struggled with her math homework and eaves-dropped. They would talk on about shopping, cooking, their respective aches and pains, some program they'd both watched on TV and hated or loved.

Often they would reminisce about giving birth: Giselle to her two boys and Maureen to Carmen, who is an only child. Childbirth, Carmen discovered while eavesdropping, is some-thing that mothers never tire of talking about, no matter how many years have by then intervened. They love to tell each other the numbers again and again, slipping them back and forth like the balls on an abacus: hours in labour, hours in the delivery room, minutes between contractions, how many pushes before the head popped out like a pumpkin. It is a competition of sorts to see who has suffered the most pain and indignity and survived. It is also proof that those who say you won't remember the pain are lying.

Sometimes they talked about their own childhoods and how they hated each other when they were kids: "Do you remember when you broke the teapot over my head? Do you remember when I tried to stick your head down the hole in the outhouse?" It was a wonder they hadn't killed each other. They laughed and laughed and left red lipstick all over their respective receivers.

When Maureen hung up, she looked flushed and girlish again.

Tonight, after she hangs up, she taps on Carmen's door and slips into the dark room. "That's pretty music," she says and curls up on the bed with Carmen. She is wearing her chenille housecoat which falls half-open to reveal a shiny white slip with spaghetti straps and Carmen can see just the top of her mother's breasts which are beautiful and luminous like the inside of seashells.

They wiggle around on the bed until they are both sitting propped against the headboard with the pillows behind them. Carmen lays her head against her mother's shoulder and tells her all about Abraham. She tells her how he is kind, sensitive, intelligent, funny, warm, wise, healthy, peaceful, passionate, serious, generous, gentle, beautiful, and strong. How he is the man she'd almost given up hoping to meet, how he is the man she has had in her heart all along. She shows Maureen his picture in the locket.

Her father seems to have graciously accepted the fact that he can inhabit only the fringes of this moment and she can hear him paddling around in the kitchen in his slippers, humming and making cocoa and toast.

As she talks, Carmen feels like she has been doing this all her life. But the truth is she has not told her mother anything important since the time Mickey Roach kissed her on the mouth at recess and Carmen punched him in the nose.

Years later, there was the time Reg Henderson took her out to the airport parking lot where all the would-be lovers used to go and she let him touch her small breasts under her sweater and there was a tickling between her legs and she wanted him to touch her there but then she pushed him off her and felt sick to her stomach with loving it and hating it. She was crying when she got home and her hair was a mess and of course Maureen was waiting up for her but when she tried to talk to her, Maureen said, "I don't want to hear about it," and then she went to bed, leaving Carmen alone in the dark living room, trying to make sense of herself.

Years later still, there was the time Carmen called home long-distance and she was telling Maureen about the trip to Toronto she'd made that weekend with her boyfriend, Terry, and how their hotel room was so elegant, an oak four-poster bed with curtains and everything, and Maureen said, "I don't want to hear about it," and Carmen, in a flash of futile anger, said, "What the hell do you think I do out here – knit?" But Maureen was already talking about the new wallpaper they'd hung in the bathroom and Carmen couldn't get another word in edgewise.

Now Carmen tells her mother that Abraham is the best lover she has ever had and Maureen doesn't even flinch. She doesn't laugh or change the subject either. She is silent and then she says, "Yes," and her voice is smiling.

They talk about Abraham for two hours straight and the time passes so slowly that missing him is exquisite.

... I'm so lonesome I could cry ...

Long after Maureen and Frank have gone to bed, Carmen is still awake. Listening to her parents giggling and whispering in bed, it occurs to her for the first time that they are in love, still in love.

When the phone on the night table rings, it is Abraham.

"I miss you," he says and his voice is rich.

"When you get home," he says, "I want to make love to you until you pass out."

"I've been reading about lions," he says, "who have been known to make love eighty times a day, and this," he says, "is something to strive for."

The sound of his voice in the dark makes her wet.

After Carmen hangs up, she thinks about a summer evening at Black Bridge Falls when they had been swimming, were sitting afterwards on the high grassy bank in their bathing suits, just watching the river flow. Carmen pushed him gently back onto the grass, pulled down his bathing suit, and took him into her mouth and he moaned and arched up towards her.

In the dark bedroom now, she pretends the cool sheets against her naked body are his skin against hers and she strokes her breasts until the nipples grow hard and she touches herself just the way he touches her and she imagines him watching her as she slides her own fingers in and out slowly, so slowly. But when she comes, she cries.

Falling asleep finally, she realizes that the man in the original memory was not Abraham at all, but Jason Campbell whom she dated ten years ago. And in real life, when she tugged at the waist of his bathing suit, Jason brushed her hand away as if it were an insect and said, "Don't do that. Someone will see. Are you crazy?"

And so it is in the power of true love to alter everyone and everything that has gone before. All of your former lovers, it seems, are reduced to stand-ins, replaced now in your memories by the figure of the beloved. All of their lips have become his. All of their lips were his all along.

The thought of Abraham is so much with her that often she can't tell whether she's thinking of him or not. She knows this sounds crazy. But he is so much inside of her, that even when she is consciously thinking of other things, she is always aware too of his presence, or now of his absence, which is everywhere. She thinks of all the places they can touch each other when she gets home. They can turn each other inside out.

... I love you like October ...

Autumn is their favourite season, when the sky is cool blue and the air is a tonic, sharp and invigorating after the humid muzzle of the summer heat. On Saturday, they go walking through the neighbourhood just at that hour when the lights have been lit but the curtains are still open and all the houses are emitting snug squares of yellow light into the deepening afternoon. Carmen knows that half the people inside those houses may well be bored to tears or hollering at each other but they look so contented from the outside that, when she walked like this before she met Abraham, she would be enveloped by a sickening liquid envy running through her like vinegar and, at the sight of lovers walking hand in hand, she would be swamped by a self-pity so caustic that it left her clenching her fists in pure rage, white-knuckled.

Now she and Abraham walk down to the park at the corner which has been abandoned these cool days by all but the faithful: a woman in a camel-hair coat walking her Cocker Spaniel, a group of half-grown boys in rubber boots and too-small sweaters playing hockey with a ball where the rink will be, another pair of lovers on a green wooden bench eating chocolate doughnuts with their mittens on.

Carmen and Abraham leave the paved pathways and shuffle through the fallen leaves piled so high in places that they are up to their knees and the colours fall away in front of them like noisy surf. They lie down together and the crispy leaves envelop them. As they put their arms around each other, a woman alone walks past, stares, and then averts her eyes. Carmen recognizes this woman as her own former self, fighting her way through another serious Saturday, jamming her fists into her pockets and heading home still alone, with the waste-land of another Sunday yet to come.

On the way home, they gather leaves, carefully selecting the best ones from among the millions under their feet: red, orange, yellow, one maple leaf gone so dark it looks black. At home, Carmen arranges the leaves on lengths of wax paper, places them between sheets of old newspaper, and then presses the whole package beneath the thick volumes of the Encyclopedia Britannica.

Abraham, in the living room, is putting on a tape: *The last time I felt like this/I was in the wilderness/And the canyon was on fire/And I stood on the mountain/In the night/And I watched it burn/I watched it burn/I watched it burn.*

As Carmen watches him from the doorway, he turns for a moment back into the stranger she met at the party, the man she knew nothing about, the man who could change her life if she let him.

At such a moment, unknowingly observed, the beloved becomes a singular distant miracle, a transcendent untouchable star. At such a moment, the lover is illuminated by the impossibility of love and of loss, galvanized by the immutable possibility of both. At this moment, the lovers may believe they are immortal.

Carmen goes up behind him and drapes her arm around his shoulders, nuzzling her face into his neck. "You smell like the leaves," she says. "You smell like October." He says this is the nicest thing anyone has ever said to him.

... I love you like a child ...

In the dream, Carmen and Abraham are standing naked face to face but when she reaches out to stroke his neck, the rise of his breastbone, the curve of his hips, he feels like a blank wall covered with glossy white paint.

In the dream, Carmen is pregnant, her round belly slick with sweat and luminous, the way Maureen's breasts were luminous, glistening like mother-of-pearl.

In the dream, Maureen is dead, laid out in a glass coffin covered with flowers and pendulous fruit. The funeral parlour is filled with singing strangers. Maureen says, "Listen. Can you hear me? Listen. Can you hear the sound of my eyes closing, the sound of my breath in your body, the sound of your head coming out from between my legs? Can you hear the singing? Can you hear the celebration?"

When Carmen wakes up sobbing, Abraham takes her in his arms and he says, "Cry, just cry. It's all right to cry."

In his arms like a child, she must give over her fear, all fear all grieving all trust all power, and she must deliver it there into his purified arms. And here is all the faith in the world, all the trust in tomorrow, and the possibility of finding and losing everything, and the rocking of a soul, these souls ecstatic in such sorrow such joy the attainment of all and every extraordinary life.

She is lying facedown on the big bed and he rubs her neck her shoulders, his hands drawing wordless circles into the small of her back, his tongue on her buttocks and the backs of her thighs.

She moves beneath him slowly so slowly and the sweetness runs out of her over his long fingers between her legs between her opening legs inside of her aching where she is aching and he slides in and slides in and slides in moving together sweating and he rubs his wet chest against her trembling back his teeth are on her neck and they are silent so silent they have never loved before in such excellent silence only breath and breathing they are only breathing the room is full of them and she can feel the hot liquid spurting into her and they are blossoms opening in an instant in what could be forever flowers unfurling the petals like pale skin encompassing all time and they are opening each other opening themselves to the world and there is room enough inside at last for everything room enough for all life new life and the serious suddenness of love and there can be no word for this or if there is a word and if they ever find it there will be nothing left to say and they are moaning and laughing and they will never be ordinary people again.

MARILYN SIDES

THE ISLAND OF THE MAPMAKER'S WIFE

During a serious illness in the year 1635, the mystical poet John Donne imagined himself in cartographical terms:

> "Whilst my physicians by their love are grown
> Cosmographers, and I their map, who lie
> Flat on this bed, that by them may be shown."

Images sometimes reflect back: if the body can become a map, to be traced and studied, then a map can be seen as a sort of body. The ancient cartographers who so meticulously worked over their sheets of parchment or silk, translating into colours and shapes the vision of mountains and seas that others had seen and described, established with their creations an intimate, amorous relationship. "I worked on this map until my fingers were numb, my eyes grew dark, my head felt like stone, but it was a labour of love and I am glad," *reads a Latin annotation on a sixteenth-century map preserved at the Royal Library of Toledo, in Spain. Sometimes the map becomes the actual depiction of an amorous state: in the several-volume-long seventeenth-century novel* Clélie, *the author, Mademoiselle de Scudéry drew a map of love and courtship which came to be known as the* Carte de Tendre *and which set out the locations of the cities of Constancy and Tenderness, the Sea of Unfaithfulness, the Vale of Caress, and many other sensuous geographical sites.*

In Marilyn Sides's story the erotic relationship between maps and lovers is made explicit. The map is not only an object to be loved; it also hides within itself the clue to a secret passion, the chart of a hidden desire.

S HE TRADES in antique maps. Her small shop is on Congress Street, three blocks from Boston Harbour. Full of history, tourists drop in from Bunker Hill, Beacon Hill and exclaim in surprise, "You're the owner?" They wonder, often aloud, why does this rather young woman, with only a few glinting silver threads in her hair, why does she spend her time behind the tarnished letters *C.M. Descotes* on the dusty window? What makes her hand linger so on the ancient sea-charts as she smooths out their creases? An unnatural woman, they think, never out loud, to care about latitude and longitude.

The old map-dealers, retired military men and historians in

worn tweeds, know better, point out that Descotes is only too predictably a woman. For all her expert abilities – which they admit with grudging respect – to date any map, to attribute it to its designer, to price it for the market, Descotes betrays herself by her specialty. Her passion, the map she knows best and collects for herself, is the frivolous picture map so prized three hundred years ago by fat Dutch wives for their homes.

"Descotes," the dealers reproach her in dismal tones, "merely interior decoration, you know." But it pleases her to think of thin light coming from a window, watery light falling on a white wall spread with a gaily coloured map of Europe, Africa – it makes no difference, any annihilation of vast seas and continents to a rectangle will do – bleak light falling further on a table spread with a rich red Turkey carpet, one corner lifted back like a raised skirt. Pure light falling on the woman reading there.

"Ah, Descotes, most unscientific, those maps. Truth? Progress?" But, like her mapmasters, Descotes would sink a newly discovered Alaska for a mermaid billowing her breast on a wave. Descotes would shrink Siberia for a long-whiskered sea monster rolling at the sea-queen's side.

Among the map-dealers, only one indulges her taste without raising an eyebrow. William taught her everything he knew about maps. She learned to love them as much as she loved to pore over his old skin lined and loose until the day, years ago, he decided that he was "Too old for you" and rolled himself up and away from her as she lay still in bed. Between them now there is the cool comfort of shop talk. One afternoon in January, William telephones her from his shop in Salem, a shop with something for people with all sorts of specialties: Indian medicine bags, Chinese chess sets, embroidered chasubles, grass masks with little saucer ears, and maps.

"Two of *your* maps are coming on the market, sweetheart. In Amsterdam, number 4, Prinsengracht. Very fine maps, I hear. Now the dealer's a strange bird, likes to talk out a sale. Won't deal over the telephone. Doesn't care if he loses the business. You're going to have to get up and go there, this time."

"But it's so inconvenient for me to go, right now. I'm expecting offers. You don't have his number, do you? Maybe he'll talk to *me*, I'm good on the phone, you know."

"Sweetheart, not a chance. My friend there says he doesn't even have a number. So, I've said you're on your way and reserved you a seat on the plane for tonight at nine-thirty."

"The maps are good ones, you say, excellent ones? Very good, your friend says? *My* maps, you're sure?"

"Beautiful maps. You won't be disappointed. Good-bye, sweetheart. Good luck."

On a card she writes "Closed 'til Saturday" and tapes it right above her name on the front window. Three days, she tells her answering service. Three days should be enough. No need to loiter once the map is hers. There's nothing else in the world that interests her anymore. For several years, after losing William, before opening her shop, she travelled, cheap drugstore map in hand, to Italy, Mexico, India, anywhere, for months at a time, every chance she had, wide-eyed, ready to snap a picture, ready to exclaim "how strange, how beautiful" to the man next to her whether it was Stephen, Mark, or Bill, willing to stroke the flesh of Stephen, Bill, or Mark lit up by a tropical moon or the northern lights. One morning, however, New Delhi seemed like Paris, like Tokyo, all the same red square on the Michelin maps, the hotels the same black blotches. Bill was as thin, dry, and dark with tiny criss-crossing sentences as Stephen or Mark.

Back in Boston, she "retired," as she likes to put it, and opened her map store. Using her typewriter and her telephone, she manages to find the maps she wants without leaving the city, much less the country. A quiet day spent stroking the downy surface of the thick map paper, then a long walk puffed up and down the shore by fat-cheeked winds, and at last home alone with mad continents of colour on the walls – this is a day filled with enough earthly glory for her.

That night the plane cabin seems a prison and a hell. It is drab and smelly, the plastic forks and the passengers make an empty clatter. As the plane rushes past the last lighthouses on the coast and into the blind, shapeless night, she sweats with a fear that, bound to her seat, she can't walk off. She never used to be afraid to fly, what has made her fear to die now? When her mind strays towards the black nothing outside the window – sleep is just as dark, just as much a dense dark fog – she tries to guide it home by sketching out on the airline napkins her favourite maps, so bright, so brimming with ships and flowers and the walls of perfect cities. She makes herself imagine the maps in Amsterdam, very fine maps, William says, very good maps, lovely maps to gaze upon.

———

In Amsterdam at last, exhausted, she takes a short nap in the hotel room before going to look at the maps. But, she sleeps too long. Waking up in the dark, she angrily reminds herself that there is no time to waste on this trip, and now the shop will be closed. All she can do tonight is walk to the dealer's shop and make sure she knows the way. A good decision, she congratulates herself an hour later, as after several wrong turns in the maze of canals – it has been years since she used a map to find something, the small map is awkward in her hand, the tiny print a strain – she circles towards the shop.

Along Prinsengracht, tall, narrow houses stand stiffly up into the night, the light from their upper rooms blurred by drawn lace curtains in a hundred starry patterns. The maps had better be good, to get her away from home, where she, too, could be behind her curtains in a soft light. Number 4 is a house narrower and darker than all the others. Yet downstairs in the tiny ground-floor chamber there glows a heavily shaded lamp. No one comes, however, when she taps, and taps again louder on the cold glass, a sound too loud in the empty street, a neighbour may look out the window and think she is a thief. The door is locked. Pressed against the window, she makes out the quite good things risked in the window – Renaissance globes, Islamic sextants – the maps will be fine ones. Startling her, a face looms up before her eyes, that of a huge cat, dusky yellow with a white tufted bib, who stretches out between an astrolabe and an ancient tome. The cat shakes his head officiously like an old clerk, as if to say, "Closed. Go away."

A cold winter wind turns through the canals. She has to move on. Walking back down the street, she enters into a pub for some dinner. The customers, mostly men, raise their heads to stare at her, but out of habit she looks only at the waiter, nods to him, and follows him to a small table near the central stove that heats up the dark-panelled room. She orders and soon the food comes, promptly and properly hot. As the waiter sets the plate before her, she thinks how long it took to acquire the ability – self-taught – to enjoy eating alone. To make herself served well and courteously, to eat slowly, enjoying her meal, thinking her own thoughts.

A shout of laughter bursts from a group of men standing behind her in one corner. Startled, she looks over at them and a big, tall man, obviously the teller of the joke, catches her eye with his bright, curious glance. Of course, the laugh was raised to make her turn around; it always provokes men, as men, to see a woman alone, making her way without one of them. She must still be quite exhausted to have fallen for that; she knows better. Yet at one time, she suddenly recalls and it's like finding an old dress and thinking instantly of a certain night, at one time, when she used to travel, she would have looked back at this man with a long look and a smile, she would have let him join her for a drink. But now, it's a quiet triumph to have only business on her mind – the maps, her maps, fine maps – once they are in hand she can go home, stay at home. She turns back around, finishes her dinner, pays, and nods good night to the waiter.

———

In widening circles, squinting at her map over and over, she returns to her hotel and goes to bed. However, having slept too long that afternoon, she sleeps fitfully. Finally falling asleep, she sleeps heavily and wakes up late, again. Rushing through her breakfast, hurrying past canals, she arrives at number 4 by eleven only to find a note saying "back at eleven-thirty" in Dutch and English. Forced into unwilling tourism, she idles

along the canal glancing at the shop windows. But she finds a
little pleasure after all. In one window a painting with a map in
it, her kind of map, is displayed. A sign she will be successful,
she tells herself, and begins to be more cheerful. In the picture
only the back of a painter, elegant in a slitted doublet, is visible
as he sits before his easel. At the far right corner of the room,
placed between a casement window and a heavily carved table,
stands a model bedecked with pearls, ostrich plumes, and blue
silk brocade. Her face turns slightly away from the artist's gaze.
The rival-beauty of the painting is a map of Spain, bordered
with panoramic views of the principal cities, which takes up
almost all of the back wall. The artist has spent his best efforts
on where the light falls from the leaded window – the shirt
shining through the doublet on the painter's wide back, the
averted cheek of the woman, the gleaming emptiness of sea on
the map. These glow in the gloom of the room.

The picture keeps her standing so long enthralled before it
that Descotes has attracted the attention of another idler. He
has been strolling up and down the street, looking at windows,
watching her. She has felt him there, behind her, she realizes.
Now he moves closer, in a moment – she remembers how it
goes – he will be so close that they will have to say something
about the painting, then the weather, then comes an invitation
to coffee, to dinner, to bed, if only she keeps standing still for a
few more seconds.

But her maps. With a quick glance at her watch she sees it's
time for the shop to be open. She turns away as he takes the last
step towards her. She used to smile a polite, apologetic smile at
moments like these. The practice comes back to her an instant
too late now. The man frowns after her.

At number 4, the shop door opens with a grating rumble and shuts with a loud click. The room is as empty as last night, except for the big cat, who rises, stretches, and jumps to her feet. By running at her ankles, he steers her to the desk at the back where the lamp still burns. From the ceiling to the wainscoting are shelves of calf-bound books whose spines glimmer with gold lettering, beneath the shelves wide cabinets of polished drawers, map drawers she knows. A large table blackened with age takes up the rest of the room.

Steps come thumping down some hidden stairs. A big head topped with a shock of red hair ducks through the low door to the left, the heavy body that follows blocks up the doorway. How this body must fill up this thin, narrow house, how it almost looks at this moment that he is some great hermit crab, carrying his fragile shell house on his back.

———

Then she sees it is the joketeller from the pub. He recognizes her right away, a grin splits his wide round face. She can see how he could make people laugh, to look at him would make anyone laugh. His brown corduroy suit hangs flabbily around his thick body. His rumpled white shirt sticks out between the waistband of his pants and the thin belt he has hitched up too high and too tight. Part of his shirttail is even caught in his fly, the tuft of it sticks out like a gay white sail before him. She remembers the quick eyes, she sees they are a rich chestnut, curious and direct. His long thin nose along with these eyes gives him the look of a courtly bird. A very funny man, except, it strikes her sharply, for the lips. They are almost too thin, too severe, the lips of an exacting man. Between the upper part of this face and these lips there must run some invisible fault line, along which the two characters, the clown and the master, strain together unevenly.

She hands him her card. "You were told to expect me, I believe."

Throwing up his hands in exaggerated surprise, he exclaims, "Ah, the map-lover. I should have guessed it was you last night. Loitering around the shop, hoping for even one glimpse, a little lovesick already, no? That's a good sign for the dealer, yes? He can charge what he likes. He knows the customer must have the map."

So she's to be paid back for her coolness in the pub.

"I must say that it is rare to encounter a young woman – oh yes, my dear, to a dilapidated, insomniac, old carcass like myself, I'm broken beyond my forty years – yes, yes, you are young, very young – rare to meet a young someone as fervent as you about their trade. Lingering in the cold night simply to be near the maps." He pauses, notes her annoyance with delight, and then turns mock-professional. "All right, let's be very serious, let's have a look at the maps, the all-important maps."

He bustles over to the locked drawers, at the same time pulling a ring of keys from his pocket. The ring comes out, and along with it an ink pen, a crumpled handkerchief, and a leather change purse that falls to the floor spilling coins all around. "You see how clumsy I am – the customer says to herself, 'The dealer is nervous, the advantage is mine.'" He stops and bends over to pick up the coins. As he stoops over with his back to her, his jacket pulls up, his shirt pulls out of his trousers, and he is exposed almost down to the cleavage of his buttocks. Surprised, she thinks "how ridiculous" and at the same time she wants to place her hand there on that skin, it is so fine-grained, smooth, firm almost luminous as if the whiteness were some sheen of silver melted into gold. She'd like to run her fingers down the ridge of the spine to where it ends, she'd like to feel under her palm the muscles playing there so smoothly and powerfully. This must be the centre of power for the big body.

———

Her body starts to tighten up, her thighs, her belly – it has been a long time since she has longed so sharply to touch someone's flesh, to have the feel of it in her fingertips at that moment, knowing it will linger there like a soothing shock for days. Just as she becomes afraid that her hand will go out of its own accord, he straightens up, the clothes covering him in a clumsy bunching of fabric.

In relief she allows herself to smile, she shouldn't let such a silly thing distract her. The maps are all that counts, the maps and going home. Luckily, he has noticed nothing and, unlocking the drawer, has drawn out a roll and pulled the desk lamp over to the big table. He unfurls the map and with a click turns up the power of the lamp to illuminate a beautiful – William was right – beautiful piece of work.

And with one look at the map she is completely back in her mapworld. Here the Netherlands of 1652 have been painted in as a blue heraldic lion rampant on the northern coast of Europe. She almost laughs, for the lion – in spite of his gold crown and elegant tufted tail – looks like a fat blue cat standing on his hind legs to bat at a fly. He could be the royal cousin of the yellow cat gazing at her from the desk. Turning professional, she admires the colouring, a fine wash of blue bice, names the probable date of the map and the map-making firm. Impressed, the dealer cries, "Oh, very good, very good, absolutely right. I shall sigh when you're gone. I see only pretentious amateurs and tourists all day long."

She could maybe afford it at what she estimates its price to be. The map of the Battle of Waterloo that she has been holding on to as the price climbed, she could let that go for this. Finishing the thought, she straightens up. He takes the hint, rolls up the map, and then going back to the drawer he produces the second map.

Before her are every fanciful figure of the East, quaint and funny as in a children's book. Ruling the Mongolian plain, the great Khan twirls his moustaches in front of his golden-tasselled tent. Further south Mandarins bow beside their pagodas. A cannibal couple of Borneo, modest in their grass skirts, look shyly at each other over the human elbows they nibble. In the reaches of the sea, fretted calligraphy, like a handwritten letter home, details the terrible marvels of the world.

As she looks the map over, she almost hums; it's good, it's what she had hoped to see. Her explorer's map of the Belgian Congo, she knows a small, rich museum that covets it. To the dealer, again, she names the date and the mapmaker. He is delighted, of course, she is right. Now to business, she thinks and prepares her offers in her mind.

However, he has one more map to show her. "A special

map. It's not for sale, but if you don't mind, I'd like you to see it. It will give me great pleasure to have you appreciate it, oh, not give it a price, simply see how beautiful it is. I'm rather proud of it and like to show off my good taste." While putting back the second map and bringing back the new map, he tells her that the circumstances of the map's purchase were curious. One day, an old woman had summoned him to come look at a map she had for sale. The map was kept in a locked cabinet in her room. Descotes should imagine a big, tall white-haired woman with the smallest of keys on a blue scrap of ribbon, leading him to her bedroom, shutting the door behind them. The map, she told him, was a gift she had made to herself years ago, with some money left to her by her grandmother, a gift she had kept all to herself all these years, until now when she needed the money to, as she laughed, bury herself. When he saw it, he thought how well she had rewarded herself all those years of her life. "Another mapmistress, she was," he grins at Descotes, "though of only this one map." In fact, he felt very humble in front of her, as if she knew the map better than he, an expert, did. After one look at it, he bought it.

Descotes is immediately wary; declaring the map not for sale, telling the odd story of its former owner – he must be setting her up for the map he really wants to sell her today. She prepares herself to give a cold eye to the map.

But when he lays the map before her, she finds it impossible to do anything but gaze upon it with absolute abandonment to pleasure. This map of South America would have seemed to anyone else a very plain map compared with the first two – but she sees right away it is as lavish, even more so in its own way. She has to admit to herself it is the best of the three maps, truly a superb map beyond comparison. The work could only have been done by the best illuminator of maps in the seventeenth century, Margarethe Blau, the wife of the master printer Theodor Blau. The long spine of the Andes, Frau Blau has rendered in the finest golden tincture of myrrh with the western slope reflecting the setting sun in a delicate pink wash of cochineal. Several stands of trees, in a thousand varying shades of green, play the vast rain forest of Brazil. Rivers have been threaded through the continent in indigo banded with magenta. The southern pampas wave their bluish leaves and the golden stalks. Red lead, the colour of dried blood, shadows the double cathedral towers of Spanish settlements. Surrounding the land, showing off its gentle brightness, the sea is stippled like shot silk in dark indigo and a wash of lighter blue bice.

As she examines it, what suddenly strikes Descotes about the map is that its very perfection wants to be saying something, like a child perfectly composed at high tension in order to get the attention of its mother. Taking her magnifying glass from her purse, she works down the western coast, around the Horn, and up the eastern coast to the Caribbean. Everything, every inlet and spit of land, every island, is absolutely correct, and Margarethe Blau has blessed her husband's perfect outlines with her rare colours.

No, here is an island, just off the coast of Venezuela, an island out of place, no, not out of place, for it belongs nowhere else. An imaginary island, drawn in with quick strokes of a pen, not printed. This is what the map's perfection silently strains to tell – the error, the gratuitous island.

The dealer sees Descotes staring at the island and laughs in delight. "So, you've discovered the secret of the map. Frau Blau has sketched in her own paradise: 'Let there be an island and an island appeared on the bosom of the sea.'"

The island *is* a lovely Eden, all for oneself. There are minute patches of greenish gold furze, tiny trees toss in a breeze, tender hillocks – and then Descotes gasps, looks again, narrows her eyes. She can hardly believe it, this exquisitely detailed landscape, its contours, take on the breathtakingly precise outline of a woman embracing a man. That faultless drawing of the upper coast, the taut single line is the woman's exposed neck, her back, the curve of her buttocks, the sweep of her legs superbly clean down to the graceful feet tapering off into the ocean. The arched lower coast is the lover's long back, stretched out afloat on the Caribbean waves. He presses up against her breast and belly and thighs, his thighs and legs flail. His arms are outstretched above his head, grasped by her hands. The good Frau must have found it unbearable to show them – her and her lover, some sailor? – crying out in pleasure, golden hair falls over the woman's face, the lover's face, it flows into the sea, curling and rushing like foam against the rocky shore.

Staring at the island, Descotes feels her own breasts ache, her face must glisten, again a sharp and sudden excitement makes her almost tremble. It isn't fair to be taken so unexpectedly with longing.

"Quite wonderful, no?"

Of course, he knows! He has set up this scene like a voyeur, forcing this upon her, so he could watch her, shock her. Angry, she cannot look at him, she won't give him the satisfaction.

"You don't find the island delightful? Oh, you must, I would be so disappointed!" He seems genuinely puzzled by her silence, his voice innocent of any smile.

Descotes can hardly believe he cannot see, truly see the island. It is so alive, so terrible a picture of possession. He sees only an island, an idiosyncratic island, not a seizure, a conquest, an establishing of rights. It is as if he were an amateur and hadn't recognized the signature or the distinguishing stamp that would make a valuable map in fact priceless. Would she be dishonest if she doesn't point out the true nature of the island to him? But she cannot bear to, it would be like making him aware of her own body pressing, it seems to, against the very walls of the room. Why should she tell him, if he can't see it himself? "Forgive me. I'm sorry, I was lost in it. It's beautiful." Trying to control the tremor in her voice, she adds, "It's so beautiful I'd like to buy it. Would you sell it to me?"

———————

He laughs in triumph. "I knew you would love it. But, as I said, it's not for sale, I simply wanted you to admire it. Now that your immense expertise has confirmed my judgement, I'm very happy. I shall not regret the enormous sum I paid for it."

Descotes, thinking she hears him working up the price, almost smiles and bites her lips. She sings to herself, he's going to sell, he's going to sell.

"We all," he continues, "must allow ourselves an extravagance once in a while, isn't that right? And this is so beautiful?" He looks back down at the map with unfeigned pleasure.

"It's a masterpiece, I agree. Name your price."

Surprised by her insistence, he gives her a long look. Then he laughs, "Oh, forgive me, you must think I'm bargaining with you. No, no, I don't make deals that way. With me, business is always very straightforward. I'm sorry, the map is not for sale. I tell you very honestly, I bought it for myself. It called out for someone who would admire it as much as the old woman."

"But it may be that I admire it more than you and as much as she did. Then, by rights, it should be mine."

He stares at her for several moments. Then, as if testing her, he names a price. It is an immense sum. Almost humiliated to show him what the map means to her – but then he doesn't know what she knows – she swallows and says she can raise the sum, if he will sell the map to her.

His silence is rather cruel, since he must know now that he has her, that she would probably give anything to have the map. When he finally speaks, it is in a serious, friendly tone, a tone that strikes her as only too much like that which William uses with her. "I'm older than you, let me protect you from yourself. Take one of the other maps. They are masterpieces, too, albeit gaudy compared to this one. I'll give you a very good deal on them. For this map, I'll make you beggar yourself."

"That's my affair. I know the business as well as you. I still would like to buy the map. All you have to do, it seems to me, is decide to sell it."

He looks down at the map again, stares at it intently, questioning it, searching it for some answer to her. "It is a fine map, very fine, not another like it, so quiet and calm in its mastery, so happy with its lovely island. Is it really worth so much to you? Why, I must ask myself?"

She manages a crooked smile. "You know women, we have our fancies, our cravings, mine is your map, that's all."

"A woman's weakness? You're that kind of woman, then? Not a map-dealer?" Rolling up the map (oh, my island, gone, she thinks in pain), he puts her off. "Go back to your hotel and think about it. Can you really get the money? I'll see you again at ten o'clock tomorrow. I have to think about it too."

He has to sell to her, he has to give her his word *now*. She wants to argue on, badger him, but she reminds herself, with difficulty, that she has already passed the limit of what is considered civil bargaining among dealers; she consoles herself, with difficulty, that at least she's made him consider selling. Forcing herself to nod, smile, she hurries back to the hotel and there she places her calls as if she were raising a ransom – quick, a matter of life and death. She lies to the manager of her bank and gets a loan. From William, she demands money. She tells him that it is an invaluable map, that she has to have it. When he argues that it is too expensive for her business, she argues back that if he hadn't taught her to prize maps she wouldn't be in the business at all anyway. For the first time in all these years, she makes him feel he owes her something for making her go away, he has to pay her off with the map. He promises her the money and then with a cool good-bye hangs up.

But she doesn't pause an instant to feel ashamed of herself. Adding up the figures, she finds she has the dealer's price. At first she's elated, in the next second frightened at the thought that she is going to throw all this money away for one map. She hastily promises herself she'll work extra hard this spring, she'll move maps round, she'll deal in ways she's refused to before. She's already thinking how she can strip her favourite maps from her own walls, maps she used to treasure as if they were her children; now, she'll sell them down the river – heartless.

At dinner, she starts to worry again. Is the map worth so much? She sketches and resketches the map on a scrap of paper.

But her island comes out merely as an island every time. If the island was really that man bound to that woman, he would have seen it. It is only an island, only an island. But, she argues back to her own doubts, the old woman knew it, she kept it secret in her cabinet, an exquisite torment. That was the clue, wasn't it?

She packs, there will not be much time tomorrow to close the deal – he has to sell it! – and make her flight. Trying to sleep, she finds her mind too busy. She is either adding up columns of figures, or sorting out the maps she will have to sell, or attempting to conjure up the island – but it is always only an island. That makes her despair more than she ever has in her life, the very thought of that island being only an island, merely an island.

Only an island – she gets out of bed, gets dressed, she has to go back and look at the island, tonight, she has to know.

Once more, she winds in and in to the shop, by now she has found her footing, she knows every landmark, every bridge, every house along the way. Prinsengracht, number 4, cat, lamplight. The door is open, but at the loud click of its closing no one comes. She goes to the back of the shop and in through the small door. Off to one side is a dark kitchen and on the other nothing but a narrow screw of white stairs. Up and up she goes, up into this whelk. At the top is a large room, most of it in the dark except for a light on the table where he sits in a bag chair. His jacket is off, the shirtsleeves rolled up over massive forearms, with gilt hairs glinting. He stares at the map, her map. She walks in and over to the table. Looking down at the map, she sees instantly that she was right, yes, the two bodies taut as one still arch in that sea.

"I have the money. I raised it." She has barely any voice.

His eyes are sharp and black, his lips tightened up, as he looks up into her face as if he would read it. "What do you see in my map?"

Her face is made as smooth, as white as thick paper, her eyes almost closed into thin brushstrokes of black lashes. Provoked by her silence, he pushes his chair back, stands up and steps over to her, watching her closely. "Tell me about my map."

She stays perfectly still and says nothing. If she just waits and stays still he'll have to give her the map, she says to herself over and over, stay still, just wait, let him find his way to giving her the map, it is inevitable that he will give her the map.

"I won't sell it to you."

Oh, mere defiance easily brushed aside, brushed aside with her hands, reaching out, brushing against that big chest, over across the shoulders, down the arms to take the thick forearms in her hands, to steady herself, to grasp the thick forearms, brushed with gold in the light, to steady him, to keep him on course. She holds fast to them, at the wrists, she wants to know the sinews, the bone, the muscle, to feel the grace of flesh – her hands had almost forgotten such grace – she wants to promise herself with this grip, to make a claim with this grip, that she will close her lips over his, she will unbutton his shirt and push him back to the bed she sees over his shoulder, there she will free him from that belt, pants, socks and shoes, she will lay him out on that bed, his fine white legs, the knees knotted intricately like silk cording, the thighs, white and firm as ivory, furzed red-gold, she will smooth him out and then raise up with her hand the long thick spit of land from his bristling thicket of gold, raise it up very long and high, then mount it, as the dawn whirls in and in the canals after her, the light falling on her as she mounts him and holds the wrists down, hard, as she leans over to watch his face in exquisite dread, as she pulls herself up on him, then crashes back down, as he cries out sharp and hard against the white walls of that room, as she washes up gasping in the billowed sheets, the cat lolling in the shallows by their side.

MICHEL TOURNIER

THE RED DWARF

The Germans coined a word, Schadenfreude, *to describe the joy we shamefully feel at someone else's misfortune. Around this gloating, there are some who construct their whole life and feed like vampires off that which fortune has decreed will not happen to them. Catherine the Great of Russia had her ministers describe to her in detail the most atrocious miseries of her subjects, so that she could retire each evening thanking God that she had been spared these sufferings. The painter Toulouse Lautrec, dwarfish and deformed, said that the sight of squalor allowed him to bear his own plight with less anger at his unjust creator.*

Michel Tournier's characters come from the fringes of what society calls normal: giants, magical twins, and dwarfs populate his literature, mingling fables with historical narrative, always tempting the reader with a hidden moral. Sometimes, as in the case of the young German giant, who has to find his own identity in Nazi Germany, in Tournier's novel The Ogre, *characters achieve salvation through sacrifice; other times, as in "The Red Dwarf," they assume the monstrous quality with which society has endowed them and end up taking their place amongst its freaks and horrors.*

"A fable," Tournier says, "has its moral spelled out in black and white; the short story à la Maupassant or Chekhov contains a message that there isn't any message, that the world is meaningless. I prefer tales, which include elements of both fable and short story. In a tale the precise meaning is hidden; it's like dipping into muddy water looking for fish. The reader has to do half the work."

WHEN LUCIEN GAGNERO reached the age of twenty-five he had to give up, with a broken heart, all hope of ever becoming any taller than the four feet one he had already reached eight years before. All he could do now was resort to special shoes whose platform soles gave him the extra four inches that elevated him from dwarf status to that of small man. As the years went by, his vanishing adolescence and youth left him exposed as a stunted adult who inspired mockery and scorn in the worst moments, pity in the less bad ones, but never respect or fear, in spite of the enviable position he occupied in the office of an important Paris lawyer.

His specialty was divorce and, not being able to dream of marriage for himself, he applied himself with avenging ardour to the task of destroying the marriages of other people. This was why he one day received a visit from Mrs. Edith Watson. A first marriage to an American had left this former opera singer extremely wealthy, and she had then married a lifeguard from Nice who was much younger than she. It was this second union that she now wished to dissolve and, through the numerous and confused grievances she had against her Bob, Lucien scented secrets and humiliations that more than interested him. He felt personally concerned in the wreck of this couple, even more so, perhaps, after he had had a chance to see Bob. The young man was a colossus, with a sweet, naïve face – like an athletic girl, Lucien thought – a beautiful, golden, pulpy fruit on the beach, designed to arouse all kinds of appetites.

Lucien prided himself on his literary talents and was most meticulous in refining the style of the insulting letters which, according to French law, couples have to exchange in order to achieve an amicable separation. This time he surpassed himself, and Bob was horrified by the vulgarity and violence of the letters which, over several months, he dictated to him and got him to sign. They even included unqualified death threats.

Some time later, Lucien went to visit his client, who lived in a luxurious duplex apartment on the borders of the Bois de Boulogne, to get her signature to some documents. A spiral staircase joined the upper apartment, where Bob was still living, to the lower one, which was enhanced by a vast terrace. That was where he found Edith Watson, practically naked on a chaise longue, surrounded by refreshments. The radiance of that big, golden body, with its violent odour of woman and suntan lotion, intoxicated Lucien – and it seemed to intoxicate

Edith herself, for she didn't care a fig about her visitor, and answered his questions in an absent-minded, far-off voice. The heat was stifling, and Lucien was extremely uncomfortable in his dark, thick, notary's clerk's clothes, and all the more so since the ice-cold beer Edith had offered him on his arrival had immediately drenched him in sweat. The last straw was that it had also made him want to urinate, and he was twisting and turning like a woodlouse in the hollow of the big deckchair he had coiled up in. Finally, in an embarrassed voice, he asked where the lavatory was, and Edith answered with a vague gesture towards the interior, and mumbled a few words, the only one of which he caught was "bathroom."

The room seemed immense to Lucien. It was all black marble, with a bath-tub sunk into the floor. There were various silver-plated appliances, spotlights, bathroom scales, and above all a profusion of mirrors which sent his image back to him at most unusual angles. He pissed, and then began to luxuriate in this cool spot. The bath-tub, which looked like something between a pitfall, a tomb, and a snake pit, didn't attract him in the least, but he was fascinated by the shower, which was surrounded by frosted glass. A whole battery of jets converged in it, and it seemed that you could spray yourself with water not only from above but also from the front, from the back, from the sides, and also vertically from below. There was a complicated set of taps to regulate these jets.

Lucien undressed and began to switch on the various sprinklers; their direction, violence, and temperature surprised him, like aggressive practical jokes. Then he smeared himself in a light, perfumed lather which he sprayed on with an aerosol, and remained in the multiple shower for quite a while. He was enjoying himself. For the first time he saw his body as something other than a shameful, repulsive object. When he jumped out of the shower onto the rubber mat he discovered that he was immediately surrounded by a whole crowd of Luciens imitating his movements in a labyrinth of mirrors. Then they stood still and looked at one another. Their face had an indisputable air of rather majestic gravity – sovereign was the word that occurred to Lucien – with a wide, rectangular forehead, a steady, imperious gaze, a fleshy, sensual mouth, and it even displayed that slight touch of flabbiness in the lower part of the face which suggested incipient jowls of impressive nobility. After that, everything began to deteriorate, for the neck was disproportionately long, the torso as round as a ball, the legs short and bandy, like those of a gorilla, and the enormous penis cascaded in black and purple waves down to the knees.

But it was time to think of getting dressed. Lucien glanced in disgust at the dark, sweaty pile of his clothes, then he noticed a huge crimson bathrobe hanging from a chrome peg. He took it down, draped it around him until he was completely hidden within its folds, and then, with the aid of the mirrors, he devised a dignified, casual bearing. He wondered whether he would put his shoes on. This was a crucial question, for if he relinquished the four inches of his platform shoes he would be confessing, and even proclaiming, to Edith Watson that he was a dwarf and not merely a small man. The discovery of an elegant pair of Turkish slippers under a stool decided him. When he made his entrance onto the terrace, the long train formed by the outsize bathrobe gave him an imperial air.

The big sunglasses concealing Edith's face made it impossible for him to see what she was thinking, and only her sudden immobility betrayed her stupefaction when the majestic little personage appeared and with a kind of weasel leap buried himself in the depths of a canopied deckchair. The notary's clerk had disappeared and given place to a comical, disquieting creature of overwhelming, bewitching ugliness – to a fabulous monster, whose comic aspect added a negative, acid, destructive component.

"That's Bob's bathrobe," she murmured, just for something to say, in a tone that was half protest, half simple observation.

"I can easily do without it," Lucien replied insolently.

Throwing off the bathrobe, he slid down onto the floor like a caterpillar emerging from a flower, and in the same movement climbed up onto Edith's chaise longue.

Lucien was a virgin. His awareness of his infirmity had stifled the cries of his nascent puberty. But he discovered love that day, and the rejection of his clerk's clothing and especially of his built-up shoes, and the acceptance of his dwarf status, were in his mind inseparable from this dazzling revelation. As for Edith – who was only getting divorced because of the inadequacy of her too-handsome husband – she was enchanted to discover that such a small, misshapen body should be so fantastically equipped, and so delightfully efficacious.

This was the beginning of a liaison whose passion was entirely physical and to which Lucien's infirmity added a slightly shameful, sophisticated piquancy, for her, and a pathetic tension mixed with anguish for him. They were both agreed to throw a veil of absolute secrecy over their relationship. Apart from the fact that Edith wouldn't have had the courage to display such a strange lover to the world, he had explained to her that it was of paramount importance to her divorce for her conduct to appear irreproachable until the case came to court.

From then on, Lucien led a double life. Outwardly he was still a small man, dressed in dark clothes and built-up shoes, whom his colleagues saw pen-pushing every day at his big desk; but at certain irregular, capricious hours – determined by coded telephone messages – he disappeared into the block by the Bois de Boulogne, let himself into the duplex apartment with his own key and there, metamorphosed into an imperial dwarf, wilful, swaggering, desirous and desired, he subjected the big blonde with the sophisticated accent, whose drug he was, to the law of pleasure. His embrace sent her into ecstasies, and her love song, which usually began with guttural trills, rapturous flourishes, and vocalizes extending over three octaves, always culminated in a volley of affectionate, obscene abuse. She would call her lover my plaything, my lover boy, my arse-scratcher, my dildo ... After the storm she would make a speech from which it emerged that he was nothing but a penis with organs around it, a walking penis, and, now calling him my pendant, my lubricity belt, she played a game of going about her business in the house while carrying him around, clinging to her flank, the way female monkeys carry their young.

He let her say and do what she liked, and, while being bounced up and down by his "dwarf-carrier" as he called her in retaliation, he would amuse himself watching her breasts wobbling above his head like a pair of tethered balloons. Yet he was terrified of losing her, and it was with anguish that he wondered whether the pleasure he gave her was great enough to make up for the satisfactions of the social life that he could not offer her. His long experience of divorce cases had taught him that women are more social beings than men, and that they can only really blossom in an atmosphere that contains plenty of human relationships. Wouldn't she one day abandon him for some prestigious – or at least presentable – lover?

Suddenly there was a period of inexplicable silence. He had been trained not to go to the Bois de Boulogne unless Edith telephoned him. For a whole, long week, she gave no sign of life. He fretted in silence, then began to vent his feelings in violent outbursts of aggression against the office juniors. Never had the letters of rupture he dictated to his clients been so venomous. Finally he simply had to find out, and went to visit his mistress on his own initiative. He did find out, and without delay. Silently opening the door with his key, he stole into the vestibule. He heard voices. He had no difficulty in recognizing them as those of Edith and Bob, who seemed to be on the best of terms – the most affectionate of terms, even.

The blow was all the more severe in that it was totally unexpected. Had the couple become reconciled? Was there now some doubt about the divorce? This reversion made Lucien feel not only that he had been rejected by his mistress, but that he was being thrust back into his former life and deprived of the marvellous metamorphosis that had changed his destiny. He was overwhelmed with murderous hatred, and it took a violent effort to force himself to hide under a shelf when Edith and Bob came out of the bedroom, laughing, and made for the door. When the sound of the lift had died away, Lucien came out of his hiding place and almost automatically went over to the bathroom. He undressed, had a shower, and then, draped in Bob's big crimson bathrobe, sat down on a stool where, stock-still, he waited.

Three hours later the door banged and Edith came in alone, humming. She called out something up the inner stairway, which indicated Bob's presence on the upper floor. Suddenly, she went into the bathroom without switching on the light. Lucien had let the bathrobe slip down off his shoulders. In one bound he was on her, clutching her flank as usual, but his two hands, powerful as a bulldog's jaws, had closed round her throat. Edith staggered, then rallied, and, weighed down by her mortal burden, took a few tottering steps.

Finally she halted, swayed, and collapsed. While she was in her death throes Lucien possessed her for the last time.

None of this was premeditated, and yet from that moment his acts followed one another as if they were part of a long matured plan. He dressed, and rushed back to his office. Then he returned to the apartment with the insulting, threatening letters he had dictated to Bob and put them in Edith's chest of drawers. Finally he went home and immediately dialled Bob's number. The telephone rang for a long time. At last a grumpy, sleepy voice answered.

"Murderer! You've strangled your wife!" was all that Lucien said, in a disguised voice. Then he repeated this accusation three times, for Bob was showing the most obtuse lack of understanding.

Two days later the papers carried this news item and went on to say that the number one suspect – the victim's husband, whose letters found at the scene of the crime left no doubt about his intentions – had taken flight, but that his arrest was no doubt imminent.

Lucien disguised himself within the character of the ill-favoured clerk, a suffering, mocked little man, but the memory

of the superman he had been through renouncing the extra
four inches his special shoes added to his height, haunted him
day and night. Because he had finally had the courage of his
own monstrosity, he had seduced a woman. She had deceived
him. He had killed her, and his rival, the husband, doubling as
a ridiculously tall man, was everywhere being hunted by the
police! His life was a masterpiece, and there were moments
when he was overwhelmed with breathtaking joy at the
thought that he only had to take his shoes off to become immediately what he really was, a man apart, superior to the gigantic
riffraff, an irresistible seducer and infallible killer! All the
misery of the past years was due to his having refused the fearsome choice that was his destiny. In cowardly fashion he had
shrunk from crossing the Rubicon into dwarfism, as he might
have hesitated at the threshold of a temple. But he had finally
dared to take the step. The slight quantitative difference that
he had accepted in deciding to reject his platform shoes in
Edith's bathroom had brought about a radical qualitative metamorphosis. The horrible equality of dwarfism had infiltrated
him and turned him into a fabulous monster. In the greyness of
the lawyer's office where he spent his days he was haunted by
dreams of despotism. By chance, he had read a document
about Ravensbrück and Birkenau, the Nazi concentration
camps reserved for women. He saw himself as the Komman-
dant, the governor, controlling with his huge whip vast troops
of naked, wounded women – and on several occasions the
typists were surprised to hear him let out a roar.

But the secret of his new dignity lay heavy on him. He
would have liked to adopt it in the face of the whole world. He
dreamed of a conspicuous, public, devastating proclamation in

front of an ecstatic crowd. He went to his tailor and ordered a dark red leotard that emphasized the curves of his muscles and genitals. Back in his office he shed the livery of the little clerk, had a shower, and put on what he privately called his evening clothes, to which he added a mauve silk scarf tied tightly around his long neck, like the old style apaches. Then, wearing moccasins with thin, pliant soles, he slipped out. He had discovered the superior comfort his height afforded him. He could pass under the lowest doorways with his head held high. He could stand upright in the smallest cars. Every seat was a spacious nest for him. The glasses and plates in bistros and restaurants offered him ogres' portions. He was surrounded by abundance in all circumstances. Soon he became aware of the colossal strength accumulated in his muscles. He quickly became known in various nightclubs, where the habitués would invite him to drink with them. He would jump up and perch on a high stool at the counter, and he could stand on his hands with his short legs crossed in the air, like arms. One night, a customer who had had too much to drink insulted him. Lucien threw him to the floor and twisted his ankle, then started jumping up and down on his face with a rage that terrified the onlookers. The same day a prostitute offered herself to him for nothing, out of curiosity, because the sight of his strength had excited her. From then on men were afraid of the red dwarf, and women submitted to the obscure fascination that emanated from him. His vision of society began to change. He was the unshakeable centre of a crowd of feeble, cowardly, stilt-walkers who were unsteady on their limbs and had nothing to offer their women but the genitals of a marmoset.

But this limited renown was to be merely a prelude. One

evening, in a bar in Pigalle, after he had just won a bet by tearing in half a pack of fifty-two cards, he was accosted by a man with a swarthy face and black, curly hair, whose hands were adorned with diamonds. He introduced himself: Signor Silvio d'Urbino, the owner of the Urbino Circus, whose big top was at the Porte Dorée for a week. Would the red dwarf agree to join his troupe? Lucien grabbed a glass carafe, intending to smash it into smithereens on the head of the insolent fellow. Then he had second thoughts. His imagination had just shown him a vast crater in which the spectators' heads were squeezed together like granules of caviar, rising up in terraces around a harshly lit ring. From this crater a mighty, continuous, and interminable ovation burst over the head of a minuscule individual dressed in red, standing alone in the centre of the ring. He accepted.

For the first months Lucien was content to liven up the interludes between the acts. He would run along the circular platform round the ring, get entangled in the apparatus, run away with shrill cries when threatened by one of the exasperated men in the ring. Finally he would allow himself to be caught in the folds of the acrobats' big mats and the men would carry him off unceremoniously, a large hump in the middle of the rolled-up sheet.

The laughter he aroused in the audience elated him rather than hurt him. It was no longer the concrete, savage, individual laughter that had terrorized him before his metamorphosis. It was a stylized, aesthetic, ceremonial, collective laughter, a veritable declaration of love, expressing the deference of the female crowd to the artiste who subjugates her. And in any case, this laughter turned into applause whenever Lucien reappeared in the ring, as the alchemist's lead turns into gold in the depths of his crucible.

But Lucien wearied of this petty buffoonery, which was nothing but exercises and experiments. One day his comrades saw him wriggling into something that looked like a pair of pink plastic dungarees shaped like a giant hand. Five fingers, ending in nails, corresponded to his head, his two arms and his two legs. His torso was its palm, and sticking out behind was the stump of a truncated wrist. This enormous, terrifying organ revolved by supporting itself successively on each of its fingers, it sat on its wrist, it contracted when facing the spotlights, ran with nightmare speed, and even climbed up ladders and rotated around a pole or a trapeze, hanging on by one finger. The children roared with laughter and the women had a catch in their throats at the approach of this enormous pink-fleshed spider. The press of the entire world spoke of the "giant hand act."

But Lucien was still not completely satisfied by this fame. He felt there was something lacking, something was incomplete. He was waiting – not impatiently, but confidently – for something, perhaps, though more probably for someone.

The Urbino Circus had already been on tour for five months when it pitched its tents in Nice. It was to stay there for a week, and then cross the frontier back to its native Italy. The evening performance of the third day had been brilliant, and the giant hand act had been a sensation. Lucien had removed his make-up and was relaxing in the luxurious caravan he had been promoted to since his great success, when he heard a soft knock at a window. He put the light out and went over to the looped curtains framing a pallid rectangle. A tall, massive silhouette was outlined against the phosphorescent sky. Lucien half-opened the window.

"Who is it?"

"I'd like to speak to M. Gagnero."

"But who *is* it?"

"It's me, Bob."

Lucien was so overcome by emotion that he had to sit down. He knew now what he'd been waiting for, whom he had come to look for in Nice. He had been keeping a kind of rendezvous, a rendezvous with Edith Watson. He let Bob in, and the lifeguard's awkward mass immediately filled all the space of the narrow abode in which Lucien was perfectly at his ease. Once again he despised stilt-walkers, who are nowhere in their right place.

Bob explained his situation in a whisper. Ever since Edith's death he had led a hunted existence in sunbaked attics or dank cellars, fed like an animal by his mother and a friend. He was obsessed with the temptation to give himself up to the police, but just the very idea of being held in custody terrified him, and, worse still, there were those accursed letters of rupture, full of threats to kill her, which made his case look even blacker. But Lucien could testify that it was he who had dictated these letters to Bob for the purposes of his divorce, and that the threats they contained were fictitious – purely conventional.

Lucien savoured his omnipotence over this giant with the girlish face. Curled up in the hollow of a nest of cushions, his only regret was that he didn't smoke – a pipe, in particular – for then, before replying, he would have taken infinite time in cleaning it, filling it, and finally lighting it, according to all the rules of the art. For want of a pipe, he closed his eyes and allowed himself a good minute of voluptuous, smiling, Buddhist reflection.

"The police are looking for you," he finally said. "It is really my duty to denounce you. I'll give some thought to what I can do for you. But I need proof that you have total, blind confidence in me. Well, it's very simple. Go back to your hiding place. Come back tomorrow at the same time. There won't be any trap. That will prove that you have confidence in me. Then we shall be united in a pact. You're quite free not to come back."

The next day, Bob was there.

"I can't promise that I will give evidence about the letters," Lucien told him. "But I have something better to offer you. The day after tomorrow we'll be crossing the frontier into Italy. I'll take you with me."

Bob fell on his knees in the caravan and kissed his hands.

It was child's play for Lucien to smuggle him over the frontier by hiding him in his bed. He insisted that he should stay hidden during the circus's stops at San Remo, Imperia, and Savone. He waited until Genoa to introduce him to Signor d'Urbino as a friend met by chance in the crowd, with whom he intended to stage a new act. They started work right away.

The enormous difference in their height in itself suggested several classic mime numbers. One was the battle of David and Goliath, to which Lucien added a finale of his own invention. After the giant had fallen to the ground, his conqueror blew him up with a bicycle pump. From then on he was an obese, docile, flabby pachyderm, rolling from one side of the arena to the other at the mercy of the dwarf who handled and manhandled him. He put him to various personal uses: as a pneumatic mattress to take a nap on, as a trampoline to leap up into the apparatus, as a punching bag. And the colossus was always ridiculed and trounced by his minuscule adversary. Finally Lucien perched himself astride his neck and put on an enormous overcoat that covered Bob right down to his ankles. And they perambulated in this fashion, having become a single man eight feet two tall, Bob blinded and obliterated by the coat, Lucien perched on high, imperious and wrathful.

It was when they reverted to the great tradition of the whiteface clown and the Auguste that their entrance took on its definitive form and crowned Lucien's triumph. The whiteface clown, made up, titivated, wearing pumps, his calves bulging in silk stockings, had formerly had the ring to himself and dazzled the audience with his wit and elegance. But he had been foolish enough to want to find a foil, to set off his beauty and éclat; and the hilarious, vulgar Auguste, with his tippler's face – invented for this purpose – had gradually supplanted him. Lucien extended this development by turning his over-refined partner into his thing, his whipping boy. And yet nothing was too splendid for Bob. The dwarf dressed him in a platinum wig, he added cascades of ribbons, embroidery, lace, swansdown, to his costume. Finally, carried away by the logic of his number, he imagined the grotesque marriage, to the strains of Mendelssohn's Wedding March, of this enormous girl decked out in snowy white, to the minute red toad who kept jumping up at her dress, croaking. At the end of the number he leaped up like a dog, circled his partner's waist with his short legs, and in this fashion she carried him off into the wings, to thunderous applause.

This final leap disturbed Lucien deeply, because it

reminded him painfully and voluptuously of the stranglehold that had killed Edith Watson. Were not Bob and he united by their love for the former singer? Lucien used to speak of her to Bob in the evenings, and then, obsessed by her memory, he finally confused her with his companion. And as it was even more important to him to subjugate and humiliate the stilt-walkers than to take their wives away from them, it happened one night, then every night, that he climbed into the side-berth in which his former rival slept, and possessed him like a female.

Later, the imperial theme, first sketched out in Bob's crimson bathrobe, once again took possession of him. Nothing was more in keeping with the clown tradition than to develop the Auguste – the name itself suggested it – into a parody of a Roman emperor. Lucien draped himself in a red tunic that left his crooked, muscular thighs naked. He wore a necklet, and a crown of roses. He was no longer the Auguste, he was Nero, gag-Nero, as he was one day called by d'Urbino, who was always on the look-out for slogans and texts for his playbills. As for Bob, he quite naturally became Agrippina. The fact that Nero had had his mother murdered, after having taken her as his first mistress, seemed a good omen to Lucien (Lucius Nero) who, not having found his place among decent, everyday models, was always willing to find inspiration in the grandiose turpitudes of Antiquity. It pleased him that his life should have taken the form of a caricature of stilt-walkers' morals, highly coloured, and spattered with blood and sperm.

"The one thing that bothers me," he said one night as he left Bob to go back to his own little bed, "is that, whatever we do, we shall never have a child."

This thought was certainly charged with its weight of brutal cynicism, but it was nonetheless secretly inspired by a recent discovery that was to mark a new turning point in his destiny. He had noticed that while the adulation of the ordinary public had no noticeable influence on the ball of hatred that weighed hard and heavy in his breast, a warm, springlike breath did sometimes seem to reach him from the audience, and particularly from the very top of the tiers, from the last benches hidden in the shadows of the big top. From then on he waited passionately for this breath which touched, moved and blessed him, and tried to discover in which of the performances it manifested itself. Now it was always during the matinées, and on Thursdays rather than on Sundays, Thursday being at that time the day when children didn't go to school.

"I'd like it," he said to d'Urbino one evening, "if once a week at least the circus refused to admit anyone over the age of twelve."

The director showed extreme surprise at this demand, but he respected the whims of the stars whose inventive genius had led to profitable and spectacular innovations.

"We could start on December the twenty-fourth, Christmas Eve," the dwarf added.

The date was so close and the danger of losing money so clear, that d'Urbino began to worry.

"But why, my dear Maestro, what an idea! Under the age of twelve, what does that mean?"

Once again Lucien felt himself in the grip of his old, malevolent wrath, and he advanced menacingly on the director.

"It means that for once I shall have an audience of my own size! Can't you understand? I don't want any stilt-walkers – not a single one!"

"But, but, but," d'Urbino stammered, "if we refuse to admit adults and adolescents it'll cost us an enormous amount of money!"

Lucien's reply rooted him to the spot – Lucien who was always so prodigiously gasping.

"I'll pay!" he announced dogmatically. "We'll get the cashier to work out how much you'll lose and you can deduct it from my pay. And in any case, for the matinée on December the twenty-fourth it's very simple – I'll buy all the seats. Entrance will be free ... for children."

This Christmas performance was to remain memorable in the history of the Circus. Children flocked in from several leagues around, whole coachloads of them in some cases, because schools, reformatories, and orphanages had been notified. Some mothers who were refused entry had the idea of tying their children together so that they shouldn't get lost, and roped parties of five, six, and even seven brothers and sisters were to be seen climbing up onto the tiers.

What act the red dwarf performed that day no one will ever know, because it was witnessed by no one but children, and he swore them to secrecy. At the end of the show they gave him a tremendous ovation and he, standing squarely in the sawdust on his immovable legs, his eyes closed with bliss – he allowed himself to be submerged in this storm of tenderness, this tempest of sweetness, which cleansed him of his bitterness, justified him, illuminated him. Then, children in their thousands surged into the ring, surrounded him in a tumultuous, caressing flood-tide, and carried him off in triumph and in song.

Behind the red and gold curtains leading to the stables, the riders, the tamer, the Chinese conjurers, the flying trapeze artiste, the Nepalese jugglers, and behind them the tall, grotesque silhouette of Agrippina, all retreated, effaced themselves, amazed by this savage hymn.

"Let him be," said d'Urbino. "He's with his own kind, he's being fêted by his own people. For the first time in his life, maybe, he is no longer alone. As for me, I have my slogan: Lucius Gag-Nero, Emperor of Children! I can already see my playbill: the Red Dwarf in a toga with his sword and crown, and with the crowd, the immense crowd of little people, not one of whom is a fraction of an inch taller than him! But what a matinée, my friends, what a matinée!"

DUBRAVKA UGREŠIĆ

A HOT DOG IN A WARM BUN

*The Greeks worshipped the phallus in the person of the god
Priapus, son of Dionysus and Aphrodite, and made him the
guardian of fields and herds. Horticulture, vine-growing,
goat and sheep-breeding, bee-keeping and even fishing were
supposed to come under his protection. Wooden phalluses
painted red were set up in orchards and gardens, and the
first fruits of the harvest were offered to these exuberant
altars. The vulva too, was worshipped in certain places, but
it was the phallus – carved in ivory, minted in coins, sometimes adorned with wings – that became, in the Hellenistic
patriarchal imagination and until the advent of the Christian Church, an independent part of the male body, a
powerful creature with a life and will of its own.*

*The phallus has not, however, been a popular literary
subject. Only one novel that I can think of has a phallus in
the protagonist's role: Alberto Moravia's* You and I. *The
notion of writing a story around the holy attribute of
Priapus occurred to Dubravka Ugrešić as a variation on*

Gogol's story "The Nose." Before settling on the final version, however, Ugrešić considered retelling a story she knew in reality, but was inhibited by too close a relationship of life to literature. "A person of the male gender," Ugrešić recalled, "suffered for a whole year from a very awkward and unusual fixation: the person of the male gender in question walked around the whole of that time with a handkerchief pressed to his nose, convinced that instead of a nose he had a you-know-what and, presumably, instead of a you-know-what, a nose. Fortunately, the person of the male gender was successfully cured."

I

ON THE TWENTY-FIFTH OF MARCH a truly unbelievable thing took place in Zagreb. Nada Matić, a young doctor specializing in plastic surgery, awoke in her room and looked at the clock. It was 6:15. Nada jumped out of bed, jumped into the shower, squatted under the stream of water, then, lighting a cigarette, jumped into a terrycloth robe. It was 6:25. She pulled on her grey spring suit, daubed some rouge on her cheeks, and grabbed her bag. It was half past six. She locked the door, finished the cigarette in the elevator, and hurried off to catch her tram.

By the time Nada Matić stepped off the tram, it was ten to

seven. And just then, right in the middle of the square, Nada Matić was overcome by a sudden, unusually intense hunger. She rushed over to the Skyscraper Cafeteria, which served hot dogs in warm buns, nervously called out to the waitress, "More mustard, please!" greedily grabbed the hot dog, and impatiently threw away the napkin. (This is what Nada Matić did. This is what I do too: I always dispose of those unnecessary and shamefully tiny scraps of paper waitresses use to wrap hot dogs.)

Then she set off across the square. She was about to bring the hot dog to her lips, when – was it some dark sense of foreboding or a ray of the March morning sun alighting on the object in question, illuminating it with its own special radiance? In either case, to make a long story short – she glanced down at the fresh pink hot dog and her face convulsed in horror. For what did she see peering through the longish bun and ocherish mustard foam but a genuine, bona fide ...! Nada came to a complete and utter halt. No, there could be no doubt. *Glans, corpus, radix, corpora cavernosa, corpora spongiosa, praeputium, frenulum, scrotum,* our heroine, Nada Matić, thought, running through her totally useless anatomy class knowledge and still not believing her eyes. No, that thing in the bun was most definitely not a hot dog!

Utterly shaken, Nada resumed her journey to the Municipal Hospital at a much slower pace. It had all come together in a single moment: the anatomy lesson, plastic surgery, the desire to specialize in aesthetic prosthetics – it had all flashed before her eyes like a mystical sign, a warning, the finger of fate, a finger that, if we may be forgiven the crudeness of our metaphor, peered out of the bun in so tangible, firm, fresh, and pink a state as to be anything but an illusion.

Nada Matić decided to give the "hot dog" issue top priority. Taking the "hot dog" to the laboratory and dropping it in a bottle of Formalin would have been the simplest solution, of course, but what would her colleagues have said? Nada looked here and there for a litter basket; there were none in sight. As she'd thrown the napkin away and had no paper tissues, she tried to hide the "hot dog" by coaxing it into the bun with her finger, but smooth, slippery, and springy as it was, it kept sliding out, the head gleaming almost maliciously in Nada's direction.

It then occurred to Nada that she might drop into a cafe and just happen to leave the "hot dog" on the lower shelf of one of the tables she often stood beside – she had said goodbye to three umbrellas that way – but in the end she lost her nerve. For the first time in her life Nada felt what it was like to be a criminal.

Oh, before I forget, I ought to tell you a few things about our heroine. Nada Matić is the kind of shortish, plumpish blonde that men find attractive. But her generous, amicable, amorous character kept getting in her way, and men disappeared from her life, poor thing, without her ever quite understanding why. Abandoned by no fault of her own, she naturally and periodically found herself involved in hot and heavy escapades with married medical personnel of the male sex.

Suddenly Nada felt terribly sorry for herself: her whole life seemed to have shrunk into that grotesque symbol of bun-*cum*-relay-race-baton. No, she'd better take care of it at once. She gave the bun an unconscious squeeze and the hot dog peeked out at her again, turning her self-pity to despair. And just as she noticed a broken basement window and was about to toss it away, bun and all, who should pass by with a cold nod but one of the surgeons, Otto Waldinger. Quick as lightning, Nada stuffed the "hot dog" into her pocket, smearing gooey mustard all over her fingers. The bastard! Scarcely even acknowledging her, while not so long ago …!

And then she spied a mercifully open drain. She removed the "hot dog" from her pocket with great care and flung it into the orifice. It got stuck in the grating. She nudged it with her foot, but it refused to budge. It was too fat.

At that point up sauntered a young, good-looking policeman.

"Identity papers, please."

"What for?" Nada mumbled.

"Jaywalking."

"Oh," said Nada, rummaging frenetically through her bag.

"What's the matter?" asked the policeman, looking down at the grating. "Lost your appetite?" A good inch and a half of the "hot dog" was sticking out of the bun. Nada Matić went pale.

But at this point everything becomes so enveloped in mist that we cannot tell what happened next.

II

Mato Kovalić , a writer (or, to be more specific, a novelist and short story writer), awoke rather early and smacked his lips, which he always did when he awoke though he could not for the life of him explain why. Kovalić stretched, moved his hand along the floor next to the bed until it found his cigarettes, lit one, inhaled, and settled back. There was a full-length mirror on the opposite wall, and Kovalić could see his bloated grey face in it.

During his habitual morning wallow in bed he was wont to run through the events of the previous day. The thought of the evening's activities and Maja, that she-devil of an invoice clerk, called forth a blissful smile on his face, and his hand willy-nilly slid under the covers …. Unbelievable! No, absolutely impossible!

Kovalić flung back the blanket and leaped up as if scalded. *There* he felt only a perfectly smooth surface. Kovalić rushed over to the mirror. He was right. *There* he saw only an empty, smooth space. He looked like one of those naked, plastic dummies in the shop windows. He pinched and pulled at himself several times; he slapped his face to see whether he was awake; he jumped in place once or twice; and again he placed his hand on the spot where only the night before there had been a bulge…. No, *it* was gone!

But here we must say a few words about Kovalić and show the reader what sort of man our hero is. We shall not go into his character, because the moment one says something about a writer all other writers take offense. And to point out that Kovalić was a writer who divided all prose into two categories, prose *with balls* and prose *without* (he was for the former), would be quite out of place in these circumstances and might even prompt the reader to give a completely erroneous and vulgar interpretation to the whole incident. Let us therefore say instead that Kovalić greatly valued – and wished to write – novels that were true to life, down to earth. What he despised more than anything were symbols, metaphors, allusions, ambiguities, literary frills; what he admired was authenticity, a razor-edged quality where every word meant what it meant and not God knows what else! He was especially put off by intellectualizing, attitudinizing, high-blown flights of fancy, genres of all kinds (life is too varied and unpredictable to be forced into prefabricated molds, damn it!), and – naturally – critics! Who but critics, force-fed on the pap of theory, turned works of literature into paper monsters teeming with hidden meanings?

Kovalić happened to be working on a book of stories called *Meat*, the kingpin of which was going to be about his neighbour, a retired butcher positively in love with his trade. Kovalić went on frequent drinking bouts with the man for the purpose of gathering material: nouns (brisket, chuck, flank, knuckle, round, rump, saddle, shank, loin; weinerwurst, weisswurst, liverwurst, bratwurst, blood pudding, etc.), verbs (pound, hack, gash, slash, gut, etc.), and whole sentences: "You shoulda seen me go through them – the slaughterhouse ain't got nothing on me!" "A beautiful way to live a life – and earn a pile!" "My knives go with me to the grave." Kovalić intended to use the latter, which the old man would say with great pathos, to end the story with a wallop.

We might add that Kovalić was a good-looking man and much loved by women, about which he had no qualms whatsoever.

Well, now the reader can judge for himself the state our hero was in when instead of his far from ugly bulge he found a smooth, even space.

Looking in the mirror, Kovalić saw a broken man. God, he thought, why me? And why not my arms or legs? Why not my ears or nose, unbearable as it would have been…. What good am I now…? Good for the dump, that's what! If somebody had chopped it off, I wouldn't have made a peep. But to up and disappear on me, vanish into thin air…? No, it's impossible! I must be dreaming, hallucinating. And in his despair he started pinching the empty space again.

Suddenly, as if recalling something important, Kovalić pulled on his shoes and ran out into the street. It was a sunny day, and he soon slowed his pace and began to stroll. In the street he saw a child peeling a banana, in a bar he saw a man pouring beer from a bottle down his gullet, in a doorway he saw a boy with a plastic pistol in his hand come running straight at him; he saw a jet cross the sky, a fountain in a park start to spurt, a blue tram come round a bend, some workers block traffic dragging long rubber pipes across the road, two men walking toward him, one of whom was saying to the other, "But for that you really need balls…."

God! thought Kovalić, compulsively eyeing the man's trousers. Can't life be cruel!

Queer! the cocky trousers sneered, brushing past him.

I must, I really must do something, thought Kovalić, sinking even deeper into despair. And then he had a lifesaver of a thought … Lidija! Of course! He'd go and see Lidija.

III

You never know what's going to happen next, thought Vinko K., the young, good-looking policeman, as he jaywalked across the square. Pausing in front of a shop window, he saw the outline of his lean figure and the shadow of the truncheon dangling at his side. Through the glass he saw a young woman

with dark, shining eyes making hot dogs. First she pierced one
half of a long roll with a heated metal stake and twisted it
several times; then she poured some mustard into the hollow
and stuffed a pink hot dog into it. Vinko K. was much taken
with her dexterity. He went in and pretended to be waiting his
turn, while in fact he was watching the girl's pudgy hands and
absentmindedly twirling his billy.

"Next!" her voice rang out.

"Me? Oh, then I might as well have one," said a flustered
Vinko K., "as long as ..."

"Twenty!" her voice rang out like a cash register.

Vinko K. moved over to the side. He subjected the bun to a
close inspection: it contained a fresh hot dog. Meanwhile, two
more girls had come out of a small door, and soon all three
were busy piercing rolls and filling them with mustard and hot
dogs.

Vinko K. finished off his hot dog with obvious relish and
then walked over to the girls.

"Care to take a little break, girls?" he said in a low voice.
"Can we move over here?" he added, even more softly. "Yes,
this is fine...."

Squeezed together between cases of beverages and boxes of
hot dogs, a sink, a bin, and a broom, Vinko K. and the waitresses could scarcely breathe.

"I want you to show me all the hot dogs you have on the
premises," said a calm Vinko K.

The girl opened all the hot dog boxes without a murmur.
The hot dogs were neatly packed in cellophane wrappers.

"Hm!" said Vinko K. "Tell me, are they all vacuum-
packed?"

"Oh, yes!" all three voices rang out as a team. "They're all vacuum-packed!"

A long, uncomfortable silence ensued. Vinko K. was thinking. You never knew what would happen next in his line. You could never tell what human nature had in store.

Meanwhile the girls just stood there, huddled together like hot dogs in a cellophane wrapper. All at once Vinko K.'s fingers broke into a resolute riff on one of the cardboard boxes and, taking a deep breath, he said, as if giving a password, "Fellatio?"

"Aaaaah?!" the girls replied, shaking their heads, and though they did not seem to have understood the question they kept up a soft titter.

"Never heard of it?" asked Vinko K.

"Teehee! Teehee! Teehee!" they tittered on.

"Slurp, slurp?" Vinko K. tried, sounding them out as best he could.

"Teehee! Teehee! Teehee!" they laughed, pleasantly, like the Chinese.

Vinko K. was momentarily nonplussed. He thought of using another word with the same meaning, but it was so rude he decided against it.

"Hm!" he said instead.

"Hm!" said the girls, rolling their eyes and bobbing their heads.

Vinko K. realized his case was lost. He sighed. The girls sighed compassionately back.

By this time there was quite a crowd waiting for hot dogs. Vinko K. went outside. He stole one last glance at the first girl. She glanced back, tittered, and licked her lips. Vinko K. smiled and unconsciously bobbed his billy. She, too, smiled and vaguely nodded. Then she took a roll and resolutely rammed it onto the metal stake.

But at this point everything becomes so enveloped in mist again that we cannot tell what happened next.

IV

"Entrez!" Lidija called out unaffectedly, and Kovalić collapsed into her enormous, commodious armchair with a sigh of relief.

Lidija was Kovalić's best friend; she was completely, unhesitatingly devoted to him. Oh, he went to bed with her all right, but out of friendship; she went to bed with *him* out of friendship too. They didn't do it often, but they had stuck with it for ages – ten years by now. Kovalić knew everything there was to know about Lidija; Lidija knew everything there was to know about Kovalić. And they were never jealous. But Kovalić the writer – much as he valued sincerity in life and prose – refused to admit to himself that he had once seen their kind of relationship in a film and found it highly appealing, an example (or so he thought) of a new, more humane type of rapport between a man and a woman. It was in the name of this ideal that he gave his all to her in bed even when he was not particularly up to it.

They had not seen each other for quite some time, and Lidija started in blithely about all the things that had happened since their last meeting. She had a tendency to end each sentence with a puff, as if what she had just produced was less a sentence than a hot potato.

Lidija had soon trotted out the relevant items from the pantry of her daily life, and following a short silence – and a silent signal they had hit upon long before – the two of them began to undress.

"Christ!" cried Lidija, who in other circumstances was a translator to and from the French.

"Yesterday …" said Kovalić, crestfallen, apologetic. "Completely disappeared …"

For a while Lidija simply stood there, staring wide-eyed at Kovalić's empty space; then she assumed a serious and energetic expression, went over to her bookcase, and took down the encyclopedia.

"Why bother?" asked Kovalić as she riffled the pages. "Castration, castration complex, coital trophy – it's all beside the point! It's just disappeared, understand? Dis-appeared!"

"Bon Dieu de Bon Dieu!" Lidija muttered. "And what are you going to do now?"

"I don't know," Kovalić whimpered.

"Who were you with last?"

"Girl named Maja … But that's every bit as much beside the point."

"Just wondering," said Lidija, and said no more.

As a literary person in her own right, Lidija had often cheered Kovalić up and on with her gift for the apt image. But now her sugar-sweet sugar beet, her pickle in the middle, her poor withered mushroom, her very own Tom Thumb, her fig behind the leaf, her tingaling dingaling, her Jack-in-the-box had given way to – a blank space!

All of a sudden Lidija had a divine inspiration. She threw herself on Kovalić and for all the insulted, humiliated, oppressed, for all the ugly, impotent, and sterile, for all the poor in body, hunched in back, and ill in health – for every last one she gave him her tenderest treatment, polishing, honing him like a recalcitrant translation, fondling, caressing, her tongue as adroit as a keypunch, kneading his skin with her long, skilful fingers, moving lower and lower, seeking out her Jack's mislaid cudgel, picking and pecking at the empty space, fully expecting the firm little rod to pop out and give her cheek a love tap. Kovalić was a bit stunned by Lidija's abrupt show of passion, and even after he began to feel signs of arousal he remained prostrate, keeping close tabs on the pulsations within as they proceeded from pitapat to rat-tat-tat to boomety-boom, waiting for his Jack to pump, his rubber-gloved Tom to thump, he didn't care who, as long as he came out into the open!

Kovalić held his breath. He felt the blank space ticking off the seconds like an infernal machine; felt it about to erupt like a geyser, a volcano, an oil well; felt himself swelling like soaked peas, like a tulip bulb, like a cocoon; felt it coming, any time now, any second now, any – pow! boo-oo-oom! cra-a-a-sh-sh-sh!

Moaning with pleasure, Kovalić climaxed, climaxed to his great surprise – in the big toe of his left foot!

Utterly shaken, Kovalić gave Lidija a slight shove and peered down at his foot. Then, still refusing to believe that what happened had happened, he fingered the toe. It gave him a combination of pleasure and mild pain – and just sat there, potatolike, indifferent. Kovalić stared at it, mildly offended by its lack of response.

"Idiot!" said Lidija with a French intonation, and stood up, stalked out, and slammed the door.

Kovalić stretched. The smooth space was still hideously smooth. He wiggled his left toe, then his right. The left one struck him as perceptibly fatter and longer.

It did happen, thought Kovalić. There's no doubt about it. It actually happened. Suddenly he felt grateful to Lidija. The only thing was, did he really climax in his toe or was his mind playing tricks on him? Kovalić leaned over and felt the toe again, then went back to the smooth space, and finally, heaving a worried sigh, lit a cigarette.

"Anyone for a nice homemade sausage?" asked a conciliatory Lidija, peeking in from the kitchen.

Kovalić felt all the air go out of him: Lidija's proposition was like a blow to the solar plexus; it turned him into the butt of a dirty joke.

Kovalić was especially sensitive to clichés; he avoided them in both literature and life. And now he was terribly upset. By some absurd concatenation of events his life had assumed the contours of a well-established genre (a joke of which he was the punch line). How could life, which he had always thought of as vast – no, boundless – how could life give in to the laws of a genre? And with nary a deviation! Kovalić was so distressed he felt tears welling in his eyes. How he loved – literature! It was so much better, more humane, less predictable, more fanciful. In a well-written story Lidija would have offered him nothing less than a veal cutlet; in the low genre of life, Lidija, she gives him – a sausage!

Suddenly Kovalić felt hungry.

V

On Saturday, the seventh of April, Nada Matić awoke from a nightmare she had had for many nights. She would dream she

was working in her office at Plastic Surgery. It was crammed
with anatomical sketches, plaster molds, and plastic models –
all of "hot dogs" of the most varied dimensions. Suddenly, in
trooped a band of students who tore them all to pieces, laughing
and pointing at her all the while. Nada thought she would die of
shame, and to make matters worse she felt something sprouting
on her nose – an honest-to-goodness sausage! At that point the
scene would shift to the operating room, where she – Nada –
and Dr. Waldinger were performing a complex procedure. But
there was a round hole in the white sheet covering the patient,
and she couldn't stop staring through it at his hideous smooth
space. Then the scene would shift again, and she and Otto
Waldinger were in a field pulling out a gigantic beet. She was
holding Otto around the waist when suddenly she was attacked
by a gigantic mouse! She could feel its claws on her thighs.

Nada Matić was drinking her morning coffee, smoking a
cigarette, and leafing through the evening paper. She would
seem to have acquired the fine habit of perusing the Saturday
classifieds. Suddenly an item in the "Lost and Found" column
caught her eye. She did a double take, stunned by a wild but
logical thought: If someone were to lose something like that, it
would only be natural for him to try to find it!

> On the twenty-fifth of March, I left a collapsible
> umbrella in the Skyscraper Cafeteria. Would the finder
> please return it. No questions asked. Phone xyz and ask
> for Milan.

Nada jumped out of her seat. The ad was perfectly clear!
The umbrella was obviously a respectable substitution for *that*.

The fact that it was collapsible made the whole thing absolutely unambiguous!

Nada grabbed the telephone and dialled the number. The conversation was to the point: That's right. Five o'clock. See you there. Good-bye.

At five o'clock that afternoon Nada Matić rang the doorbell of a Dalmatinska Street apartment. A dark man of about thirty opened the door.

He could well be the one, thought Nada and said, "Hello, my name is Nada Matić."

"And mine is Milan Miško. Come in."

"Are you the one who lost his umbrella?"

"That's right."

"At the cafeteria?"

"The Skyscraper."

"Collapsible?"

"Yes, yes," said Milan Miško, the owner of the lost umbrella, in an amiable voice. "Do come in." Nada went in.

They sat down. The owner of the collapsible umbrella brought out a bottle of wine and two glasses.

"So, you're the one who lost it," Nada said tellingly and took a sip of the wine.

"That's right."

"God, how thick can he be?" thought Nada, beginning to feel annoyed. She took a long look at *that* place, but could make nothing out. She had to put it into words! But how?

"It must have been hard for you …" she said, trying a more direct approach.

"With all the spring showers, you mean? I'd have picked up another one, but you do get attached to your own …"

"What was it like? Your umbrella, I mean," she asked its owner nonchalantly.

"Oh, nothing special…. You mean, what colour, how long?"

"Yes," said Nada, swallowing hard, "how long…?"

"Oh, standard size," he said, as calm as could be. "You know – collapsible." And he looked over at Nada serenely. "The kind that goes in and out."

Now there could be no doubt. Nada resolved to take the plunge and call a spade a spade, even if it meant humiliating herself. After all, she had played her own bitter part in the affair. So she took the sort of deep breath she would have taken before a dive, half-shut her eyes, stretched out her arms in a sleepwalker's pose, and – jumped! I'm wrong, she thought as she flew mentally through the air, terribly, shamefully wrong. But it was too late to retreat.

And though at this point everything becomes enveloped in mist again, we can guess exactly what happened.

VI

The waitress switched off the light and shut the door after the other girls. For some reason she didn't feel like going with them. She sat down for a short rest and looked through the window at the passersby and the brand names atop the buildings. As she bent over to take off the slippers she wore at work, her hand happened to graze her knee. She let her hand rest on the knee and froze in that position as if listening for something. Then, heaven knows why, she thought of the dark handsome guy who'd left his umbrella in the cafeteria a week or so before and that young, good-looking policeman with the funny, kinky questions – both of them so attractive and somehow connected…. Or had she noticed them and had they registered with her mainly because they had – of that she was sure – noticed *her*?

Sheltered by the darkness, the cartons, and the glass, the girl sat with her legs slightly parted, relaxed, peering out of the window at the passersby, when suddenly her hands reached by themselves for one of the cardboard boxes, pulled out a few packages of hot dogs, and started tugging feverishly at the cellophane wrappers. God, what was she doing? What was she doing? What if somebody saw her? Nobody saw her.

She slowly brought a raw hot dog to her lips and quickly stuffed it into her mouth. The hot dog slid down her throat, leaving practically no taste behind. She grabbed a second and quickly chewed it up. Then a third, a fourth, a fifth …

There in the heart of the city, enslaved by the darkness, the cartons, and the glass, sat a waitress with her legs slightly parted and her dark, shining eyes peering out at the passersby while she greedily downed hot dog after hot dog. At one point the image of a gigantic, ravenous female mouse flashed through her mind, but she immediately forgot it. She was following the movements of her jaws and listening in on her gullet.

VII

In the afternoon of the seventh of April there was a nervous ring at Kovalić's door. Kovalić was a bit taken aback to see a young, good-looking policeman carrying an unusual-looking bundle.

"Are you Mato Kovalić the writer? Or, rather, the novelist and short story writer?"

"I am," said Kovalić with a tremor in his voice.

"Well, this is yours. Sign here."

"But …" Kovalić muttered.

"Good-bye," said the policeman and, with a knowing wink, added, "and good luck!"

"But officer…!" Kovalić cried out. It was too late. The policeman had disappeared into the elevator.

Kovalić unwrapped the bundle with trembling hands. Out of the paper fell a bottle filled with a clear liquid, and floating in that liquid was his very own…! Unbelievable! Kovalić was beside himself. For several moment he stood stock-still; then he went back and cautiously removed the object from the bottle and started inspecting it.

That's it, all right – the real thing! Kovalić thought aloud. He'd have recognized it anywhere! And he jumped for joy – though carefully grasping it in his hands.

Since, however, it is a well-known fact that nothing on this earth lasts for very long, our hero suddenly frowned. He had had a terrifying thought. What if it wouldn't go back on?

With indescribable terror in his heart Kovalić walked over to the mirror. His hands were trembling. He carefully returned the object to its former place. Panic! It refused to stick! He brought it up to his lips, warmed it with his breath, and tried again. No luck!

"Come on, damn you!" Kovalić grumbled. "Stick! Stick, you stupid fool!" But the object fell to the floor with a strange, dull, corklike thud. "Why won't it take?" Kovalić wondered nervously. And though he tried again and again, his efforts were in vain.

Crushed, Kovalić was left holding his own, his very own and now very useless part. And much as Kovalić stared at it, it clearly remained indifferent to his despair and lay there in his hand like a dead fish.

"Ba-a-a-a-astard!" Kovalić screamed in a bloodcurdling voice and flung the object into a corner and himself onto his bed. "No, I'm not dreaming," Kovalić whispered into his pillow. "This can't be a dream. This is madness, lunacy ..." And with that he fell asleep.

VIII

Lidija typed out the word *maladie* and paused. She was still on page one. The translation of the report was due on Monday morning at the Department of Veterinary Medicine.

She stood up, stretched, and switched on the light. She glanced out of the window. It was still day, but the street was grey and empty and smooth from the rain.

Lidija went into the kitchen and opened the refrigerator door out of habit. She peered in without interest and slammed it shut.

Then she went into the bathroom, turned on the tap, and put her wrist under a jet of cold water. It felt good. She glanced up at the mirror. All at once she felt like licking it. She moved in close to its smooth surface. Her face with tongue hanging out flashed into sight. She drew back slowly. A smooth and empty gesture. Like her life. "Smooth, empty, empty, smooth ..." she murmured on her way back to the kitchen.

On the kitchen table Lidija noticed a few dried-out bits of bread. She touched them. She liked the way dry crumbs pricked the pulp of her fingers. She moistened her finger with saliva, gathered up the crumbs, and went into the combined bedroom and living room. Again she looked out at the street, preoccupied, nibbling on the crumbs from her finger and on the finger itself. The street was empty.

And then she noticed a young, good-looking policeman. He had a limber way about him and was crossing the smooth street, or so it seemed to Lidija, as if it were water. Suddenly she opened the window, breathed deeply, pursed her lips for a whistle, and stopped. What was she doing, for heaven's sake? What had gotten into her?

The policeman looked up. In a well-lit window he saw an unusual-looking woman standing stock-still and staring at him. His glance came to rest on her full, slightly parted lips. He noticed a crumb on the lower one. Or was he just imagining it? Suddenly he had a desire to remove that real or imagined crumb with his own lips.

"What if she really ..." flashed through his mind as he noiselessly slipped into the main door. But what happened next we really have no idea.

IX

Kovalić awoke with a vague premonition. His head felt fuzzy, his body leaden. He lay completely motionless for a while when all at once he felt an odd throbbing sensation. He tore off the blanket, and lo and behold! – *it* was back in place.

Kovalić couldn't believe his eyes. He reached down and fingered it – yes, it was his, all right! He gave it a tug just to make sure – yes, it popped out of his hand, straight, taut, elastic. Kovalić jumped for joy and leapt out of bed, rushing over to the mirror for a look. No doubt about it: there it stood, rosy, shiny, and erect – and just where it had been before. Kovalić cast a worried glance at the bottle. He saw a little black catfish swimming about as merrily as you please. Intent on engineering clever turns within its narrow confines, it paid him no heed.

"Oh!" Kovalić cried out in amazement.

Then he looked back down below. Situation normal: stiff and erect! Trembling with excitement, Kovalić raced to the phone.

At this point, however, the events are temporarily misted over by censorship, and the reader will have to deduce what happened from the following lines.

Exhausted and depressed, her eyes circled in black, her mouth dry, Maja the invoice clerk lay on her back apathetically staring at that horrid black fish. It was making its two-thousand-one-hundred-and-fifty-first turn in the bottle. At last she picked herself up slowly and started gathering her clothes the way an animal licks its wounds. Suddenly her eyes lit on a slip of paper lying next to her left shoe. The paper contained a list of names in Kovalić's handwriting. *Vesna, Branka, Iris, Goga, Ljerka, Višnja, Maja, Lidija.* All the names but Lidija's (hers too!) had lines through them.

"Monster!" she said in a hoarse, weary voice, and slammed the door.

Kovalić stared apathetically at the lower half of his body. *It* was in place, sprightly, and erect as ever. He flew into a rage, bounded out of bed, bolted to the bottle, and smashed it to the floor. The catfish flipped and flopped for a while, then calmed down. Kovalić gleefully watched the gill contractions subside. But *it* was still erect.

"Down, monster!" Kovalić shouted and gave it a mean thwack. It swayed and reddened, but then spryly, with a rubberlike elasticity, sprang back into place and raised its head at Kovalić almost sheepishly.

"Off with you, beast!" Kovalić screamed. The object refused to budge.

"I'll strangle you!" Kovalić bellowed. The object stared straight ahead, curtly indifferent.

"I wish you'd never been found," Kovalić whimpered, and flung himself onto the bed in despair. "You bastard, you! I'll get you yet!" And he burst into sobs, mumbling incoherent threats into the pillow. Then, wiping his tears, he raised his fist into the air, heaven knows why, and muttered, "I'll put you through the meat grinder!" And all of a sudden the old butcher's saying went off like an alarm in his brain: *My knives go with me to the grave!*

And the fear and trembling caused by this new piece of data sent Kovalić reeling – and into a dead faint.

X

Well, dear readers, now you see the sort of thing that happens in our city! And only now, after much reflection, do I realize how much in it is unbelievable – starting from the alienation of the object in question from its rightful owner. Nor is it believable that authors should choose such things to write stories about. First, they are of no use either to literature or to the population, and second, they are of no use … well, either. And yet, when all is said and done, there is hardly a place you won't find similar incongruities. No, say what you will, these things do happen – rarely, but they do.

For my part, I have a clear conscience. I have stuck to the plot. Had I given myself free rein, well, I don't know where things would have ended! And even so, what happened to Nada Matić? Who is Milan Miško? What became of Vinko K.? And Lidija and the waitress and the butcher? To say nothing of our hero Mato Kovalić? Is he doomed to spend his life getting it – down?

But I repeat: I have stuck to the plot. Though if the truth be told, I did insert two nightmares from my own childhood, to wit: 1) the sausage dream ("Watch out or a sausage will sprout on your nose," my grandfather used to say when he got angry with me), and 2) the beet dream (I can recall no more terrifying story from my childhood than the one in which a whole family gathered to pull out a big, beautiful, and completely innocent beet!).

In connection with said plot may I suggest the following points as worthy of further consideration:

1. How did the object alienated from its owner, Mato Kovalić, find its way into the bun?
2. How did Vinko K. discover its owner?
3. Miscellaneous.

All that is merely by-the-by, of course, in passing. I myself have no intention of taking things any further.... But if you, honoured readers, decide to do so, I wish you a merry time of it and a hearty appetite!

Translated by
Michael Henry Heim

JOHN UPDIKE

WIFE-WOOING

What do we see, what do we fail to recognize in the loved one? A medieval Arab fable tells of the following: A man bought a girl for four thousand dinars. One day he looked at her and burst into tears. The girl asked him why he was crying. He answered: "You have such beautiful eyes that I forgot to adore God." When she was left alone, the girl tore out her eyes. The man saw her then and was heartbroken. "Why did you do such violence to yourself? You have diminished your worth." She answered: "I do not wish anything in me to keep you from adoring God." That night, the man heard a voice in a dream saying to him: "The girl diminished her worth for you, but she increased it for us and we have taken her from you." On waking, he found four thousand dinars under his pillow. The girl was dead.

John Updike has made his the stormy province of marriage and charted its many dangers: habit, boredom, forgetfulness, infidelity. Here, it seems, each partner must conjure up, over and over again, as if they were both magicians,

569

what is valuable, what is surprising and marvellous about the other, the renewed source of desire, the gift of attraction. At the end of one of the chapters in Couples, *perhaps Updike's most eloquent defense of the marital state, a husband caresses his wife's back as she sleeps, causing her to dream that she is a pool of water and that lions come down to drink from her. In "Wife-wooing," the act of magic is through words, through the transformation, in naming it, of everyday acts into erotic moments of wonder.*

———————————

O H   M Y   L O V E . Yes. Here we sit, on warm broad floor-boards, before a fire, the children between us, in a crescent, eating. The girl and I share one half-pint of French fried potatoes; you and the boy share another; and in the centre, sharing nothing, making simple reflections within himself like a jewel, the baby, mounted in an Easybaby, sucks at his bottle with frowning mastery, his selfish, contemplative eyes stealing glitter from the centre of the flames. And you. You. You allow your skirt, the same black skirt in which this morning you with woman's soft bravery mounted a bicycle and sallied forth to play hymns in difficult keys on the Sunday school's old piano – you allow this black skirt to slide off your raised knees down your thighs, slide *up* your thighs in your body's absolute geography, so the parallel whiteness of their undersides is exposed to the fire's warmth and to my sight. Oh. There is a line of

Joyce. I try to recover it from the legendary, imperfectly explored grottoes of *Ulysses*: a garter snapped, to please Blazes Boylan, in a deep Dublin den. What? Smackwarm. That was the crucial word. Smacked smackwarm on her smackable warm woman's thigh. Something like that. A splendid man, to feel that. Smackwarm woman's. Splendid also to feel the curious and potent, inexplicable and irrefutably magical life language leads within itself. What soul took thought and knew that adding "wo" to man would make a woman? The difference exactly. The wide w, the receptive o. Womb. In our crescent the children for all their size seem to come out of you toward me, wet fingers and eyes, tinted bronze. Three children, five persons, seven years. Seven years since I wed wide warm woman, white-thighed. Wooed and wed. Wife. A knife of a word that for all its final bite did not end the wooing. To my wonderment.

We eat meat, meat I wrestled warm from the raw hands of the hamburger girl in the diner a mile away, a ferocious place, slick with savagery, wild with chrome; young predators snarling dirty jokes menaced me, old men reached for me with coffee-warmed paws; I wielded my wallet, and won my way back. The fat brown bag of buns was warm beside me in the cold car; the smaller bag holding the two tiny cartons of French-fries emitted an even more urgent heat. Back through the black winter air to the fire, the intimate cave, where halloos and hurrahs greeted me, the deer, mouth agape and its cotton throat gushing, stretched dead across my shoulders. And now you, beside the white O of the plate upon which the children discarded with squeals of disgust the rings of translucent onion that came squeezed into the hamburgers – you push your toes an inch closer to the blaze, and the ashy white of the inside of your deep thigh is lazily laid bare, and the eternally elastic garter snaps smackwarm against my hidden heart.

Who would have thought, wide wife, back there in the white tremble of the ceremony (in the corner of my eye I held, despite the distracting hail of ominous vows, the vibration of the cluster of stephanotis clutched against your waist), that seven years would bring us no distance, through all those warm beds, to the same trembling point, of beginning? The cells change every seven years and down in the atom, apparently, there is a strange discontinuity; as if God wills the universe anew every instant. (Ah God, dear God, tall friend of my childhood, I will never forget you, though they say dreadful things. They say rose windows in cathedrals are vaginal symbols.) Your legs, exposed as fully as by a bathing suit, yearn deeper into the amber wash of heat. Well: begin. A green jet of flame spits out sideways from a pocket of resin in a log, crying, and the orange shadows on the ceiling sway with fresh life. Begin.

"Remember, on our honeymoon, how the top of the kerosene heater made a great big rose window on the ceiling?"

"Vnn." Your chin goes to your knees, your shins draw in, all is retracted. Not much to remember, perhaps, for you; blood badly spilled, clumsiness of all sorts. "It was cold for June."

"Mommy, what was cold? What did you say?" the girl asks, enunciating angrily, determined not to let language slip on her tongue and tumble her so that we laugh.

"A house where Daddy and I stayed one time."

"I don't like dat," the boy says, and throws a half bun painted with chartreuse mustard onto the floor.

You pick it up and with beautiful sombre musing ask, "Isn't

that funny? Did any of the others have mustard on them?"

"I *hate* dat," the boy insists; he is two. Language is to him thick vague handles swirling by; he grabs what he can.

"Here. He can have mine. Give me his." I pass my hamburger over, you take it, he takes it from you, there is nowhere a ripple of gratitude. There is no more praise of my heroism in fetching Sunday supper, saving you labour. Cunning, you sense, and sense that I sense your knowledge, that I had hoped to hoard your energy toward a more ecstatic spending. We sense everything between us, every ripple, existent and nonexistent; it is tiring. Courting a wife takes tenfold the strength of winning an ignorant girl. The fire shifts, shattering fragments of newspaper that carry in lighter grey the ghost of the ink of their message. You huddle your legs and bring the skirt back over them. With a sizzling noise like the sighs of the exhausted logs, the baby sucks the last from his bottle, drops it to the floor with its distasteful hoax of vacant suds, and begins to cry. His egotist's mouth opens; the delicate membrane of his satisfaction tears. You pick him up and stand. You love the baby more than me.

Who would have thought, blood once spilled, that no barrier would be broken, that you would be each time healed into a virgin again? Tall, fair, obscure, remote, and courteous.

We put the children to bed, one by one, in reverse order of birth. I am limitlessly patient, paternal, good. Yet you know. We watch the paper bags and cartons ignite on the breathing pillow of embers, read, watch television, eat crackers, it does not matter. Eleven comes. For a tingling moment you stand on the bedroom rug in your underpants, untangling your nightie; oh, fat white sweet fat fatness. In bed you read. About Richard Nixon. He fascinates you; you hate him. You know how he defeated Jerry Voorhis, martyred Mrs. Douglas, how he played poker in the Navy despite being a Quaker, every fiendish trick, every low adaptation. Oh my Lord. Let's let the poor man go to bed. We're none of us perfect. "Hey let's turn out the light."

"Wait. He's just about to get Hiss convicted. It's very strange. It says he acted honourably."

"I'm sure he did." I reach for the switch.

"No. Wait. Just till I finish this chapter. I'm sure there'll be something at the end."

"Honey, Hiss was guilty. We're all guilty. Conceived in concupiscence, we die unrepentant." Once my ornate words wooed you.

I lie against your filmy convex back. You read sideways, a sleepy trick. I see the page through the fringe of your hair, sharp and white as a wedge of crystal. Suddenly it slips. The book has slipped from your hand. You are asleep. Oh cunning trick, cunning. In the darkness I consider. Cunning. The head-lights of cars accidentally slide fanning slits of light around our walls and ceiling. The great rose window was projected upward through the petal-shaped perforations in the top of the black kerosene stove, which we stood in the centre of the floor. As the flame on the circular wick flickered, the wide soft star of inter-locked penumbrae moved and waved as if it were printed on a silk cloth being gently tugged or slowly blown. Its colour soft blurred blood. We pay dear in blood for our peaceful homes.

———

In the morning, to my relief, you are ugly. Monday's wan breakfast light bleaches you blotchily, drains the goodness from your thickness, makes the bathrobe a limp stained tube flapping disconsolately, exposing sallow décolletage. The skin between your breasts a sad yellow. I feast with the coffee on your drabness. Every wrinkle and sickly tint a relief and a revenge. The children yammer. The toaster sticks. Seven years have worn this woman.

The man, he arrows off to work, jousting for right-of-way, veering on the thin hard edge of the legal speed limit. Out of domestic muddle, softness, pallor, flaccidity: into the city. Stone is his province. The winning of coin. The manoeuvering of abstractions. Making heartless things run. Oh the inanimate, adamant joys of job!

I return with my head enmeshed in a machine. A technicality it would take weeks to explain to you snags my brain; I fiddle with phrases and numbers all the blind evening. You serve me supper as a waitress – as less than a waitress, for I have known you. The children touch me timidly, as they would a steep girder bolted into a framework whose height they don't understand. They drift into sleep securely. We survive their passing in calm parallelity. My thoughts rework in chronic right angles the same snagging circuits on the same professional grid. You rustle the book about Nixon; vanish upstairs into the plumbing; the bathtub pipes cry. In my head I seem to have found the stuck switch at last: I push at it; it jams; I push; it is jammed. I grow dizzy, churning with cigarettes. I circle the room aimlessly.

So I am taken by surprise at a turning when at the meaningful hour of ten you come with a kiss of toothpaste to me moist and girlish and quick; the momentous moral of this story being, An expected gift is not worth giving.

ALICE
WALKER

PORN

*"All the imbeciles of the bourgeoisie, who never cease to
utter the words 'immoral,' 'immorality,' 'the morality of art'
and other such idiocies," fumed Baudelaire, "remind me of
Louise Villedieu, a five-franc whore, who, accompanying
me to the Louvre one day, where she had never been before,
blushed with shame, covered her face with her hands, and
pulling at my sleeve asked me again and again, in front of
deathless paintings and statues, how it was possible to show
publicly such indecencies." What is decent and what indecent, what belongs to art and what to pornography apparently lies in the hands of the reader, the listener, the viewer.
There are those who, like Louise Villedieu, will look at the
Venus of Milo with disgust, and others who discover in X-
rated films profound aesthetic stimulation.*

*The couple in Alice Walker's "Porn" struggle to define
not only the material labelled "pornographic," but themselves. They inhabit a tired world in which everything, it
seems, must be renamed in order to make it vital once*

again. Walker has described herself as a medium through which her characters can find a voice. "I do feel visited," she explains. "All of the characters are absolutely there in the house with me, and I often think about what one or the other would say about something, or how something would look to them, or what would make them laugh or what would make them cry." And Walker respectfully allows them to speak their mind, without guidance or comment, even when they're headed for destruction.

———————

LIKE MANY thoughtful women of the seventies, she had decided women were far more interesting than men. But, again like most thoughtful women, she rarely admitted this aloud. Besides, again like her contemporaries, she maintained a close connection with a man.

It was a sexual connection.

They had met in Tanzania when it was still Tanganyika; she was with an international group of students interested in health care in socialist African countries; he with an American group intent upon building schools. They met. Liked each other. Wrote five or six letters over the next seven years. Married other people. Had children. Lived in different cities. Divorced. Met again to discover they now shared a city and lived barely three miles apart.

A strong bond between them was that they respected their

former spouses and supported their children. They had each arranged a joint custody settlement and many of their favourite outings were amid a clash of children. Still, her primary interest in him was sexual. It was not that she did not respect his mind; she did. It was a fine mind. More scientific than hers, more given to abstractions. But also a mind curious about nature and the hidden workings of things (it was probably this, she thought, that made him such a good lover) and she enjoyed following his thoughts about the distances of stars and whole galaxies from the earth, the difference between low clouds and high fog, and the complex survival mechanisms of the snail.

But sex together was incredibly good: like conversation with her women friends, who were never abstract, rarely distant enough from nature to be critical in their appraisal of it, and whose own mechanisms for survival were hauled out in discussion for all to see. The touch of his fingers – sensitive, wise, exploring the furthest reaches of sensation – were like the tongues of women, talking, questing, searching for the *true* place, the place which, when touched, has no choice but to respond.

She was aflame with desire for him.

On those evenings when all the children were with their other parents, he would arrive at the apartment at seven. They would walk hand in hand to a Chinese restaurant a mile away. They would laugh and drink and eat and touch hands and knees over and under the table. They would come home. Smoke a joint. He would put music on. She would run water in the tub with lots of bubbles. In the bath they would lick and suck each other, in blissful delight. They would admire the rich candle glow on their wet, delectably earth-toned skins. Sniff the incense – the odour of sandal and redwood. He would carry her in to bed.

> *Music. Emotion. Sensation. Presence.*
> *Satisfaction like rivers*
> *flowing and silver.*

On the basis of their sexual passion they built the friendship that sustained them through the outings with their collective children, through his loss of a job (temporarily), through her writer's block (she worked as a free-lance journalist), through her bouts of frustration and boredom when she perceived that, in conversation, he could only *be* scientific, only *be* abstract, and she was, because of her intrepid, garrulous women friends – whom she continued frequently, and often in desperation, to see – used to so much more.

In short, they had devised an almost perfect arrangement.

One morning at six o'clock they were making "morning love." "Morning love" was relaxed, clearheaded. Fresh. No music but the birds and cars starting. No dope.

They came within seconds of each other.

This inspired him. He thought they could come together.

She was sated, indifferent, didn't wish to think about the strain.

But then he said: "Did I ever show you [he knew he hadn't] my porn collection?"

"What could it be?" she inevitably wondered. Hooked.

———————

His hands are cupping her ass. His fingers like warm grass or warm and supple vines. One thumb – she fancies she feels the whorled print – makes a circle in the wetness of her anus. She shivers. His tongue gently laps her vulva as it enters her, his top lip caressing the clitoris. For five minutes she is moving along as usual. Blissed *out*, she thinks to herself. Then she stops.

"What have you got?" she has asked him.

"This," he replied. "And this."

———————

A gorgeous black woman who looks like her friend Fannie has a good friend (white boy from her hometown down South) who is basically gay. Though –. "Fannie" and let us call him "Fred" pick up a hick tourist in a bar. They both dig him, the caption says. He is not gorgeous. He is short, pasty, dirty blond. Slightly cross-eyed. In fact, looks retarded. Fred looks very much the same. "Fannie" invites them to her place where without holding hands or eating or bathing or putting on music, they strip and begin to fondle each other. "Fannie" looks amused as they take turns licking and sucking her. She smiles benignly as they do the same things to each other....

———————

"And this."

A young blonde girl from Minnesota [probably kidnapped, she thinks, reading] *is far from home in New York, lonely and very horny. She is befriended by two of the blackest men on the East Coast. (They had been fighting outside a bar and she had stopped them by flinging her naive white self into the fray.) In their gratitude for her peacemaking they take her to their place and do everything they can think of to her. She grinning liberally the whole time. Finally they make a sandwich of her: one filling the anus and the other the vagina, so that all that is visible of her body between them is a sliver of white thighs.* [And we see that these two pugilists have finally come together on something.]

———

She is sitting with her back against the headboard of the bed so that her breasts hang down. This increases sensation in her already very aroused nipples. He crawls up to her on all fours like a gentle but ravenous bear and begins to nuzzle her. He nuzzles and nuzzles until her nipples virtually aim themselves at him. He takes one into his mouth. She begins to flow.

But the flow stops.

Once he said to her: "I could be turned on by bondage." No, he said "by 'a little *light* bondage.'" She had told him of a fantasy in which she lay helpless, bound, waiting for the pleasure worse than death.

———

There is no plot this time. No story of an improbable friendship down South, no goldilocks from the Midwestern plains. Just page after page of women: yellow, red, white, brown, black [she had let him tie her up very loosely once; it was not like her fantasy at all. She had wanted to hold him, caress him, snuggle and cuddle] *bound, often gagged. Their legs open. Forced to their knees.*

———

He is massaging the back of her neck, her shoulders. Her buttocks. The backs of her thighs. She has bent over a hot typewriter all day and is tired. She sinks into the feeling of being desired and pampered. Valued. Loved. Soon she is completely restored. Alert. She decides to make love to him. She turns over. She cradles his head in her arms. Kisses his forehead. His eyes. Massages his scalp with her fingers. Buries her nose in his neck. Kisses his neck. Caresses his chest. Flicks his nipples, back and forth, with her tongue. Slowly she moves down his body. His penis (which he thinks should not be called "penis" – "a white boy's word"; he prefers "cock") is standing. She takes it – she is on her knees – into her mouth.

She gags.

———

The long-term accommodation that protects marriage and other such relationships is, she knows, forgetfulness. She will forget what turns him on.

"No, no," he says, very sorry he has shown her his collection; in fact, vowing passionately to throw it away. "The point is for *you* to be turned on by it *too!*"

She thinks of the lovely black girl – whom she actually thinks of as her friend Fannie – and is horrified. What is Fannie doing in such company? she wonders. She panics as he is entering her. Wait! she says, and races to the phone.

The phone rings and rings.

Her friend Fannie is an out-of-work saleswoman. She is also a lesbian. She proceeds to write in her head a real story about Fannie based on what she knows. Her lover at work on her body the whole time.

———

Fannie and Laura share a tiny loft apartment. They almost never make love. Not because they are not loving – they do a lot of caressing and soothing – but they are so guilty about what they feel that sexuality has more or less dried up. [She feels her own juices drying up at this thought.]

They have both been out of work for a long time. Laura's mother is sick. Fannie's younger brother has entered Howard University. There is only Fannie to send him money for books, clothes and entertainment. Fannie is very pretty but basically unskilled in anything but selling, and salespersons by the thousands have been laid off in the recession. Unemployment is not enough.

But Fannie is really very beautiful. Men stop her on the street all the time to tell her so. It is the way they chose to tell her so, when she was barely pubescent, that makes her return curses for "compliments" even today.

But these men would still stop her on the street, offer her money "for a few hours' work." ...

By now she has faked all kinds of things, and exhausted her lover. He is sound asleep. She races to Fannie and Laura's apartment. Sits waiting for them on the stoop. Finally they come home from seeing a Woody Allen movie. They are in high spirits, and besides, because she shares part of her life with a man, care much less for her than she does for them. They yawn loudly, kiss her matronizingly on both cheeks, and send her home again.

———

Now, when he makes love to her, she tries to fit herself into the white-woman, two-black-men story. But who will she be? The men look like her brothers, Bobo and Charlie. She is disgusted, and worse, bored, by Bobo and Charlie. The white woman is like the young girl who, according to the *Times, was* seduced off a farm in Minnesota by a black pimp and turned out on 42nd Street. She cannot stop herself from thinking: *Poor: Ignorant: Sleazy: Depressing.* This does not excite or stimulate.

———

He watches her face as he makes expert love to her. He knows his technique is virtually flawless, but he thinks perhaps it can be improved. Is she moving less rhythmically under him? Does she seem distracted? There seems to be a separate activity in her body, to which she is attentive, and which is not connected to the current he is sending through his fingertips. He notices the fluttering at the corners of her eyelids. Her eyes could fly open at any moment, he thinks, and look objectively at him. He shudders. Holds her tight.

He thinks frantically of what she might be thinking of him. Realizes he is moving in her *desperately*, as if he is climbing the walls of a closed building. As if she reads his mind, she moans encouragingly. But it is a distracted moan – that offends him.

He bites the pillow over her head: Where *is* she? he thinks. Is she into fantasy or not?

He must be.

He slips her into the role of "Fannie" with some hope. But nothing develops. As "Fannie" she refuses even to leave her Southern town. Won't speak to, much less go down on, either of the two gays.

He races back and forth between an image of her bound and on her knees, to two black men and a white woman becoming acquainted outside a bar.

This does not help.

Besides, she is involved in the activity inside herself and holding him – nostalgically.

He feels himself sliding down the wall that is her body, and expelled from inside her.

DENTON WELCH

ALEX FAIRBURN

Since we're attracted to the unknown, to the hidden, to the dangerously undiscovered, we tend to find erotic attraction in what we perceive as our opposite. The young, white Desdemona is attracted to the older, darker Moor; the aristocratic Lady Chatterly falls in love with her rustic gamekeeper; Beauty falls in love with the Beast, King Kong with Fay Wray. The Duke of Wellington, apparently, fell in love with Lady Georgina Fane whom her contemporaries called "wild, hideous and half-cracked." People wondered at the strange attachment of the handsome duke to this ungainly lady. "He has always had one or two women whom he liked to talk to and to be intimate with, and very often odd women too," wrote Lord Greville in his diary on July 25, 1851, "but the strangest of all his fancies was this tiresome, troublesome, crazy old maid."

Denton Welch, a brilliant young English writer, crippled after a bicycle accident when he was only in his twenties, describes in his semi-autobiographical fiction his quest for that shadow image of himself: the adventurer he couldn't be, the rough, coarse male his genteel upbringing would have scorned, the Dionysian lover whom he would never meet. Praising Welch's writing, the poet Edith Sitwell spoke of "the extraordinary paradox" of finding, under the surface of an elegant, delicate text, deep currents of sensual desire, memorably disturbing.

A<small>LEX FAIRBURN</small> bent her fair head nearer to her work and counted the stitches of her petit-point. The fire stretched and yawned at her feet and through the thick curtains she heard the bell-like trickle of the water in the drain pipes. It was seven o'clock on an autumn evening and she was alone.

She had spent most of her time alone since she had left Jack. The thought of him twisted something inside her. It was not hate or fear that she felt but just shame – to have made such a mess of their marriage from the very start. She could not bear to think of it. They were both so stubborn, nobody but a fool would have imagined that they could live together. But at twenty-one she had been a fool and now two years later she realized just how large a one. She thought of Jack with his thin pointed eyes and mouse-soft polished hair, the smallness of his bones and the egoism of his face in repose (the sort of face Little Lord Fauntleroy might be expected to have in the days when his goodness had begun to wear thin), the queer smell of his feet when he took off his socks and the sparkle of his nonsense at a party. Then she thought of her resistance to his will, her foolishness, the beauty of her face and the wealth which made her independent of him. Everyone told me not to marry him, she thought. Daddy said he hadn't enough money and Mother just said don't, but I did and then made everything much worse by behaving so stupidly when I found out my mistake. As if drinking too much could ever make you forget that you had married someone so like yourself that he was unbearable.

When Alex had left her husband she had gone to a psychologist and been analyzed. There had been the endless journeys to the little upstairs room in Wimpole Street and the tense sound of her own voice answering questions and saying whatever came into her head. It had all been so formless and floundering and yet the psychologist seemed to have a pigeonhole for everything. She left halfway through the course and then she found religion.

She went to stay with a friend in a country town where the Oxford Group had sent a mission and one night at a friend's house she met some of the young men and women from Oxford and suddenly became very enthusiastic. She read her Bible daily, applied only the minimum of make-up to her face, and settled in a cottage in the country, near the sea.

The petit-point work was all part of the scheme and of course there was no drink in the house.

Her family thought it peculiar but they were so encased in their wealth and the selfishness which it bred that nothing really got through to them from the outside world. They came once or twice to the country cottage and thought it "very jolly," but wanted to know if she was not very lonely there. Alex replied that she was not, with brittle overemphasis.

She could indeed scream with boredom at times. She had

asked all the friends she could think of to come down and spend a few days with her, but had so overpowered them with her conviction of the meaning of life and had bullied them so with the confidence that this conviction had given her, that they all in turn had left before their time was up and now she was left alone. Even the Belgian maid had gone that very day.

Now that it was autumn, things seemed even drearier and she didn't know what she would do next.

The needle darted in and out of the canvas, never had anyone been so savage about doing petit-point before. Alex thought of the pattern which she had bought ready painted in the shop opposite Harrod's. "It may not be creative," she said to herself, "but at least it's work. What would I do without it?"

The click of the garden gate broke through her concentration and she looked up, hands on the work in her lap, waiting for the bell to ring. It did not, but she heard the thud of feet walking along the wet path to the back door, then there was a knock and she went to open it. The beads of rain were dropping from the low eaves and through their strings she saw a dripping figure, young and grey in the evening light.

"Excuse me, miss, but could I put up in your barn tonight? I'm on the road and it's that wet."

Alex looked at the speaker again quickly. He had tow-coloured hair and a thick-square mouth. His ragged jacket and grey flannels were heavy with rain and Alex caught the gleam of newspaper through the cracks in his squelching shoes.

"Come in," she said hurriedly, acting on impulse. She stepped back into the kitchen and held the door open for him. He followed her sheepishly, hanging his head and fingering the straps of the greasy knapsack on his back. "Won't you take off your wet coat and dry it by the fire? Of course you can stay here tonight." Alex went over to the boiler and stoked it. It was still on, luckily. She opened the door and arranged the clothes horse in front of it.

The young man, still tongue-tied, was easing the knapsack off his back, his eyes glazed and unmeaning.

When Alex turned from the fire she saw him standing there by the kitchen table. He had taken off his coat and it was hanging from his lowered arms and dripping steadily onto the tiled floor.

She realized with a shock that he wore no shirt, only a dirty sweat-stained singlet such as stokers wear and she saw the pale hair on his chest over the low semicircle of its neck.

His whole attitude was so shamefaced and dejected that she hardly dared to look at him. She took the coat gently from his hands and arranged it across the horse. A thin steam rose from it carrying the smells of the man and his tobacco with it.

"Would you like a hot bath?" she said suddenly; then feeling she had been tactless she added, "You've got so wet, I should think you need warming up." A wan smile lit his face, making it look quite weak, and he replied, "All right, if yer like."

"Come on then, I'll show you the way." Alex was bustling now. She led the way up to the landing and fumbled in the dark linen cupboard for a clean towel. Her hands fastened on its rough comfort and she drew it out. She smiled self-consciously when she saw its colour by the bathroom light. It was pale lilac and monogrammed with her initials – a part of one of her wedding presents. She turned on the taps and poured the Russian pine essence into the bath from the great green bottle that stood on the mirrored shelf.

The little room was filled with its scent and the clammy steam which frosted the taps and shining tiles.

Now that she had no excuse for staying longer she went to the door and turning, said, "Don't put your wet things on again after your bath, I'll find you something else." He gave a half-grudging obedient nod and she shut the door.

Outside in the dry warm and darkness of the landing, Alex's mind raced. This new Samaritan feeling had entirely seized her and she did not stop to analyze it. She felt her way to her bedroom and went in. The lamp by the bed glowed under its peach shade and by its dim light she searched in the bottom of the chest of drawers for the sailor's trousers she had bought in Gravesend and worn once or twice on the beach in the garden.

She found them and held them up. She had had to buy them large as otherwise her feminine hips, slight as they were, would not get in the tight top part of the trousers. She hoped he would be able to wear them. She looked amongst her jerseys and found the largest. It was thick with a high polo collar and she had worn it for riding.

When Alex had done all that she went quickly to the dressing table, adjusted her hair and touched up her light make-up with lipstick and powder; then she went to the bathroom door and said, loudly so that he could hear through his splashing, "I've got some clothes here for you. Will you give me your own to dry?"

She heard him get out of the bath and walk towards the door, then the door opened slightly, and his hand and forearm with the golden hairs glistening on the pink flesh were thrust forward, holding the sopping clothes and shoes. She took them with an involuntary fastidiousness and walked down the stairs.

In the kitchen she put them with the coat in front of the boiler and went to the larder. The smell of cold and fat was disagreeable, but there was a dish of spaghetti which the maid had prepared that morning and also several tins of soup and fruit.

The milkman had left the regular quantity of cream she had every day and Alex felt that she had almost enough to make a meal.

She turned on the electric stove and put the spaghetti in the oven and the soup in a saucepan on the hotplate. Then she hastily laid the table in the kitchen and poured the tinned loganberries and the cream over a sponge sandwich which she had found uncut in a tin.

She looked at the table and felt that she had done all she could. The sight of the tumblers made her realize that there was nothing in the house to drink but water. Her scruples were quite gone by now and she wished she had something to offer him. Then she remembered the bottle of whiskey she had bought last month when her white Alsatian was dying and the vet had told her to feed it on whiskey and white of egg. She had been so distracted at the time that she had rushed to the nearest pub and bought a whole bottle. Her dog had only lived two days after this and so there it was still almost full.

She had put it out in the garage to get it out of the house and now she ran out to get it. It was still there in the corner, covered with a few cobwebs.

She brought it in and wiped its neck and stood it on the table. There was no soda water, so she stood the water jug next to it. She could hear him fumbling on the landing upstairs so she called out, "There's no light up there, can you find your way down?" She could not quite hear his low answer but in a few moments she saw him standing in the doorway, still red from his bath, wearing the sailor trousers and her jersey. He had combed his hair with his fingers and it coiled in rough order on his head. The gold stubble was still on his cheeks and chin but the dirt had gone and as he moved forward she caught the glint of his bleached eyelashes as they shone in the light.

The steam from the wet clothes was filling the room and as they sat down to eat, drifts of the warm human air blew between them. He ate gingerly at first, then gaining confidence he applied himself with concentration and Alex ate methodically too to keep him company. She saw that his hands which moved so steadily were still mooned with black at the tip of each fingernail.

"Would you like some whiskey?" she asked when the soup had been finished. "Thank you," he said looking at his plate with the embarrassed grin playing round his mouth and his eyelids.

He did not wait to watch what instrument she used for the spaghetti but said, simply, "I'm afraid I don't know which tool to use."

Hurriedly Alex replied, "I should use any one you like." Then, feeling this unhelpful if polite, she added, "I'm going to use a knife and fork." She quickly picked up the knife she had not intended to use and began eating.

Every now and then he took drinks from the glass of whiskey and when it was empty she filled it again without asking him.

She noticed that the food and drink were heating him. A light dew of sweat made his face shine. The atmosphere in the room was warm and steaming, like a laundry.

When they had finished the loganberries she said, "You go into the other room and make up the fire, while I heat the coffee." She showed him the door across the landing and then went back to the electric stove. She could hear him banking up the fire and then the stillness when he had finished. The coffee and milk which she had mixed in the saucepan frothed up to the brim and she snatched it away before it should bubble over.

She placed it as it was with the cups and sugar on a tray and went with it across the landing. When she opened the sitting room door she saw him standing in front of the fireplace just staring at the picture above it. It was a Dutch flower piece – not stimulating – and his whole body seemed so hopeless that she guessed he was not looking at the picture but quite through it.

He turned when he heard her, but did not offer to help her. He just hung his head.

Alex drew the little table in front of the sofa, the only really comfortable piece of furniture in the room, and then fetched the cigarettes and chocolates from the desk.

"You must be so tired; won't you sit down?" she asked, indicating the sofa.

He leaned back stiffly in one corner as she poured out the coffee. She passed it to him with the sugar. The cup slipped in the saucer and she saw his face give a start and lurch.

When they had both taken cigarettes he quite surprisingly leaned forward and struck a match for her. The light from it gave his impassive face a false animated glow – as the rose lights in butchers' shops enhance the colour of the meat.

He breathed rather deeply after his meal and she saw that he was getting hotter than ever in the heavy sweater. Feeling that conversation was impossible she got up and went to the wireless and turned it on softly.

As she sat down again, she noticed that his eyes had a more unfocused, less staring look. The muscles of his face were less tense and his long legs in the wide sailor's trousers seemed more relaxed.

The music was formless and unmoving, it was difficult to know who would appreciate it, but looking at him again, she realized, with sudden alarm, that his lips and nostrils were twitching and that his chin was thrust forward stubbornly. "Oh Lord, don't let him break down," Alex prayed swiftly to herself. "What shall I do?" Then she sprang up and went into the kitchen to fetch the whiskey. She brought it back with the tumbler of water and two glasses on a tray. She could feel the heat and the trembling of his body through the wool. "Cheer up, let's have a drink." She spoke harshly and brightly and she could see him stirring and contracting as if he were gathering himself together. He gave her a low sound of acknowledgement and nodded his head.

She moved nearer to him on the sofa so that she could pour out the whiskey from the little table in front of him. She put a lot into his glass and only a little into hers. She did not like the taste. She hoped it would cheer him up. As he put the glass to his lips she heard it ring against his teeth. He was trembling. He drank it in large gulps so that he would not have to go on holding the glass. Then he began to choke. This was too much for him. He gasped, choked, and wept all at once. Alex prosaically knelt on the sofa and thumped his back. He was breathing with great sighing gulps now, his body lying open, arms thrown out and legs straddled, exhausted by the paroxysm.

Something caught at Alex as she saw him lying stretched in the corner of the sofa. She leaned across him, her long neck arched, and bent her lips down to his cheek. He made a movement with his face away from her. She lay against him and heard his heavy heartbeats, then slowly she stretched her hand out over his head and switched off the reading lamp. The light from the fire played on the ceiling and walls and shook light from every polished object that it caught. There was no noise but the rain, the hissing of the damp wood and his deep breathing.

She put her arms carefully round his neck and lay on his chest. The weight of their two bodies together made the sofa sag. They slipped to the ground, narrowly missing the table with the whiskey tray, and lay together there on the bearskin rug in front of the fire. He put his big arms round her drowsily and she felt the heat from his body eating into hers. His face was glistening with sweat. Alex knelt up by his side and pulled the thick sweater up from his waist. At last she got it over his head and only his arms lay imprisoned in it, stretched out above him. She looked down at his face and he smiled, his eyes half closed. He drew his hands out of the sweater and holding them up, drew her down so that her cheek was against his chest. It felt to her skin like fine grass scattered on satin. She closed her eyes and whenever she opened them she saw the light of the flames gilding the white top of his body.

They did not go to bed that night but lay in front of the fire on the bearskin, dozing and waking. Alex got cushions and rugs and banked up the fire.

Towards dawn she went soundly to sleep and woke two hours later to see him standing over her and looking down. He

had changed into his own clothes and the straps of the knapsack were across his shoulders.

"I must be going," he said and shifted his feet nervously.
Alex jumped up, the whole of the memory of last night
returning to her. "Don't go, don't go yet. You must have some
breakfast." She sped into the kitchen and found two kippers
and began making toast and coffee.

He stood in the doorway, watching her and not saying a
word. Sometimes he looked at the kitchen clock. They ate their
meal in silence, then he got up and went to the door. "Good-
bye," he said. Alex couldn't stop him or say anything, she could
only stare. She watched him go out and heard him walking
down the path and opening the gate into the road; then she
came to life and ran after him. When she got to the gate he was
already a little way down the road; he turned and gave her a
rather clumsy, distant wave. It stopped her from going further.
She slowly turned back into the house and sat down again at
the breakfast table, leaning her head down on it with her arms
curved round. She shut her eyes and felt the smell of kippers
and butter and coffee piercing through her thoughts. She lay
some time like this, then resolutely she sat up and brushed her
hair back. She looked at the congealing fat on the plates and
the mahogany skin of the eaten kippers, the dregs in the coffee
cups and the smears of butter and marmalade on the small
plates.

She cleaned it all into the sink and began washing up.
When she had finished she stoked the boiler, then went into
the other room. The rugs and cushions lay on the floor in front
of the fire which was out and there were her jersey and sailor's
trousers which he had worn. She looked at them and did not

move, then swiftly she bent forward and gathering them up, she held them close to her face and smelled them. The smell of his body clung to them still. She folded them and put them down on the sofa, then she cleaned away the rugs and the whiskey and the coffee cups. When the room was tidy, she switched on the electric fire as she had not remade the open one and, fetching her Bible, she sat down to read. When she had finished her chapter she sighed, and taking up her petit-point made the needle dart in and out of the canvas. She worked faster and faster, trying not to think at all, but she kept on saying to herself in endless repetition as the stitches grew: "I didn't even give him sixpence, I didn't even give him sixpence."

JOHN EDGAR WIDEMAN

THE STATUE OF LIBERTY

Lovers close their eyes when they kiss so as better to feel the presence of the other. Sight, they know, is an intrusive sense, and it must be excluded from the erotic act if the other senses are to have their play. In the medieval French myth, the fairy Melusine demands that her royal bridegroom meet her only in the dark and escapes when he tries to see her. She wants to remain unknown, but also, perhaps, she wishes to enjoy fully his scent, his sighs and whispers, the salty taste of his skin unhampered by the beauty of his appearance.

A voyeur (we have borrowed from the French much of our erotic vocabulary in English) is someone who favours sight over the other senses. In one of the apocryphal books of the Bible, the lovely Susanna is watched by two old men as she takes off her clothes to step into her bath: these two curious elders, immortalized in countless paintings, are among the first voyeurs in history.

Voyeurs are punished: the two old men were condemned by the wise Daniel, and Peeping Tom of Coventry, who watched the beautiful Lady Godiva ride by naked, was struck blind for his impudence. However, in John Edgar Wideman's story, the voyeur and the voyeur's quarry act out together an erotic game of mutual pleasure in which the eyes are rewarded but also the body that offers itself to the eyes.

———————

O NE OF THE PLEASURES of jogging in the country is seeing those houses your route takes you past each day and wondering who lives in them. Some sit a good distance from the road, small, secluded by trees, tucked in a fold of land where they've been sheltered thousands of years from the worst things that happen to people. A little old couple lives in this kind. They've raised many children and lost some to the city but the family name's on mailboxes scattered up and down the road, kids and grandkids in houses like their folks', farmers like them, like more generations than you'd care to count back to England and cottages that probably resemble these, Capes, with roofs pulled down almost to the ground the way the old man stuffs on a wool cap bitter February days to haul in firewood from the shed. There are majestic hilltop-sitters with immaculate outbuildings and leaded glass and fine combed lawns sloping in every direction, landmarks you can measure your progress by as you reel in the countryside step by step jogging. I like best those ramshackle outfits – you can tell it's an old farm two young people from the city have taken over with their city dreams and city habits because it's not a real farm anymore, more somebody's idea of what living in the country should be at this day and time. A patched-together look, a corniness and coziness like pictures in a child's book, these city people have a little bit of everything growing on their few acres, and they keep goats, chickens, turkeys, ducks, geese, one cow — a pet zoo, really, and a German shepherd on a chain outside the trailer they've converted to a permanent dwelling. You know they smoke dope and let their kids run around naked as the livestock. They still blast loud city music on a stereo too big for the trailer and watch the stars through a kind of skylight contraption rigged in the tin roof and you envy them the time they first came out from the city, starting out fresh in a different place and nothing better to do than moon up at the night sky and listen to the crickets and make each other feel nice in bed. Those kinds of houses must have been on your jogging route once. You look for them now beneath overloaded clotheslines, beyond rusted-out car stumps, in junk and mess and weeds, you can't tell what all's accumulated in the front yard from where you pass on the road.

A few houses close to the road. Fresh paint and shutters and shrubs, a clean-cut appearance and you think of suburbs, of neat house after house exactly alike, exactly like this one sitting solitary where it doesn't fit into the countryside. Retired people. Two frail old maids on canvas folding chairs in the attached garage with its wizard door rolled up and a puffy, ginger-coloured cat crossing from one lady's stockinged feet to the other lady's stockinged feet like a conversation you can't hear from the road. Taking the air in their gazebo is what they're thinking in that suburban garage with its wide door open.

In the window of another one only a few yards from the road you can't tell if there's a person in the dark looking out because the panes haven't been washed in years. A house wearing sunglasses. You have a feeling someone very very old is still alive inside watching you, watching everything that passes, a face planted there in the dark so long, so patient and silent it scares you for no good reason. A grey, sprawled sooty clapboard swaybacked place a good wind could knock over but that wind hasn't blown through yet, not in all the time it's taken the man and woman who live here to shrivel up and crack and curl like the shingles on their steep roof that looks like a bad job of trying to paint a picture of the ocean, brushstrokes that don't become stormy ocean waves but stay brushstrokes, separate, unconnected, slapped on one after another in a hurry-up, hopeless manner that doesn't fool anyone.

A dim-shouldered, stout woman in a blue housedress with a lacy dirty white collar is who I imagine staring at me when I clomp-clomp-clomp by, straining on the slight grade that carries me beyond this house and barn people stopped painting fifty years ago, where people stopped living at least that long ago but they're too old now to die.

Once I thought of an eye large enough to fill the space inside those weather-beaten walls, under that slapdash roof. Just an eye. Self-sufficient. Enormous. White and veiny. Hidden in there with nothing else to do but watch.

Another way jogging pleasures me is how it lets me turn myself into another person in another place. The city, for instance. I'm small and pale running at night in a section of town I've been warned never to enter alone even in daylight. I run burning with the secret of who I am, what I'm carrying, what I can do, secrets no one would guess just watching me jog past, a smallish, solitary white woman nearly naked on dangerous streets where she has no business being. She's crazy, they think. Or asking for it. But no one knows I can kill instantly, efficiently, with my fingers, toes and teeth. No one can see the tiny deadly weapons I've concealed on my person. In a wristband pouch. Under a Velcro flap in my running shorts. Nor would anyone believe the speed in my legs. No one can catch me unless I want to be caught.

When the huge black man springs from the shadows I let him grapple me to the ground. I tame him with my eyes. Instantly he understands. Nothing he could steal from me, throwing me down on the hard cement, hurting me, stripping me, mounting me with threats and his sweaty hand in my mouth so I won't scream, none of his violence, his rage, his hurry to split me and pound himself into me would bring the pleasure I'm ready to give of my own free will. I tell him with my eyes that I've been running to meet him. I jog along his dangerous streets because I'm prepared for him. He lets me undress him. I'm afraid for a moment his skin will be too black and I'll lose him in this dark alley. But my hands swim in the warmth of him. His smell, the damp sheen tells me he's been jogging too. It's peaceful where we are. We understand each other perfectly. Understand how we've been mistaken about each other for longer than we care to admit. Instead of destroying you, I whisper to him, I choose to win you with the gentleness in my eyes. Convert you. Release you. Then we can invent each other this quiet way, breath by breath, limb by limb, as if we have all the time in the world and our bodies are a route we learn jogging leisurely till the route's inside us, imagining us, our bodies carried along by it effortlessly. We stand and trot off shoulder to shoulder. He has Doberman legs. They twirl as if on a spit.

For weeks now they've been going by each morning. Crooker hears them first. Yapping and thrashing, running the length of her chain till it yanks her back to reality. A loud, stupid dog. I think she believes she's going to escape each time she takes a dash at her chain. She barks and snarls at them and I'd like to rubber-band her big mouth shut.

Quiet, Crooker. Hush.

Leave her be, Orland grumps to me. Barking's her job. She gets fed to bark.

We both know Crooker's useless as a watchdog. She growls at her reflection in the French doors. She howls at birds a mile away. A bug can start her yelping. Now she's carrying on as if the Beast from Babylon's slouching down the road to eat us all for breakfast and it's nobody but the joggers she's seen just like I've seen them every morning for a week. Passing by, shading to the other edge of the road because they don't want to aggravate a strange, large country dog into getting so frantic it just might snap its chain.

Nothing but those joggers she's barking at. Shut up, Crooker.

How do you know those people ain't the kind to come back snooping around here at night? Pacify the dog and them or others like them be right up on top of us before we know it.

Orland, please. What in the world are you grumbling about? You're as bad as she is.

I pay her to bark. Let her bark.

She's Crooker because at birth her tail didn't come out right. An accident in the womb. Her tail snagged on something and it's been crook-ended since. Poor creature couldn't even walk through the door of life right. But she was lucky too. Molly must have been spooked by the queerness of that tail. Must have been the humped tail because Molly ate every other pup in that litter. Ate them before we caught on and rescued this crook-tailed one.

When they pass by the window Orland doesn't even glance up. He doesn't know what he's missing. Usually he's gone long before they jog past. I forget what kept him late the morning I'm recalling. It's not that he's a hard worker or busy or conscientious. For years now the point's been to rise early and be gone. Gone the important part. Once he's gone he can figure out some excuse for going, some excuse to keep himself away. I think he may have another place where he sleeps. Tucks himself in again after he leaves my bed and dreams half the day away like a baby. Orland misses them. Might as well be a squirrel or moth riling Crooker. If he knew the woman looked as good as she does in her silky running shorts, he'd sure pay attention. If he knew the man was a big black man his stare would follow mine out the window and pay even more attention.

They seem to be about my age more or less. Woman rather short but firm and strong with tight tanned legs from jogging. She packs a bit more weight in the thighs than I do, but I haven't gained an inch anywhere nor a pound since I was a teenager. My face betrays me, but I was blessed with a trim, athletic high school beauty queen's figure. Even after the first two children Orland swore at me once when he pulled off my nightie, Damned Jailbait.

The man's legs from ankle to the fist of muscle before the knee are straight and hard as pipes, bony as dog's legs then flare into wedges of black thigh, round black man's butt. First morning I was with the kids in the front yard he waved. A big hello-how-are-you smiling-celebrity wave the way black men make you think they're movie stars or professional athletes with a big, wide wave, like you should know them if you don't and that momentary toothy spotlight they cast on you is something special from that big world where they're famous. He's waved every morning since. When I've let him see me. I know he looks for me. I wasn't wearing much more than the kids when he saw me in the yard. I know he wonders if I stroll around the house naked or sunbathe in the nude on a recliner behind the house in the fenced yard you can't see from the road. I've waited with my back close enough to the bedroom window so he'd see me if he was trying, a bare white back he could spot even though it's hard to see inside this gloomy house that hour in the morning. A little reward, if he's alert. I shushed Crooker and smiled back at him, up at him the first time, kneeling beside Billy, tying my Billyboy's shoe. We're complete smiling buddies now and the woman greets me too.

No doubt about it he liked what he saw. Three weeks now and they'd missed only two Sundays and an odd Thursday. Three times it had rained. I didn't count those days. Never do. Cooped up in the house with four children under nine you wouldn't waste your time or energy either, counting rainy, locked-in days like that because you need every ounce of patience, every speck of will, just to last to bedtime. Theirs. Which on rainy cooped-up days is followed immediately by yours because you're whipped, fatigued, bone and brain tired living in a child's world of days with no middle, end or beginning, just time like some Silly Putty you're stuck in the belly of. You can't shape it; it shapes you, but the shape is no real shape at all, it's the formlessness of no memory, no sleep that won't let you get a handle on anything, let you be anything but whatever it is twisted, pulled, worried. Three weeks minus three minus days that never count anyway minus one Thursday minus twice they perhaps went to church and that equals what? Equals the days required for us to become acquainted. To get past curiosity into *Hi there.* To follow up his presidential candidate's grin and high-five salute with my cheeriness, my punch-clock punctuality, springing tick-tock from my gingerbread house so I'm in sight, available, when they jog by. Most of the time, apparently. Always, if he takes the trouble to seek me out. As if the two of them, the tall black man and his shortish, tanned white lady companion, were yoked together, pulling the sun around the world and the two of them had been circling the globe forever, in step, in time with each other, round and round like the tiger soup in a Little Black Sambo book I read to my children, achieving a rhythm, a high-stepping pace unbroken and sufficient unto itself but I managed to blend in, to jog beside them invisible till I learned their pace and rhythm, flowing, unobtrusive, even when they both discovered me there, braced with them, running with them, undeniably part of whatever they think they are doing every morning when they pass my house and wave.

He liked what he saw because when they finally did stop and come in for the cool drinks I'd proposed first as a kind of joke, then a standing offer, seriously, no trouble, whenever, if ever, they choose to stop, then on a tray, two actual frosty tumblers of ice water they couldn't refuse without hurting my feelings, he took his and brushed my fingertips in a gesture that wasn't accidental, he wasn't a clumsy man, he took a glass and half my finger with it because he'd truly liked what he saw and admired it more close up.

Sweet sheen gleamed on him like a fresh coat of paint. He was pungent as tar. I could smell her mixed in with him. They'd made love before they jogged. Hadn't bothered to bathe before starting off on their route. She didn't see me remove my halter. He did. I sat him where he'd have to force himself to look away in order not to see me slip the halter over my head. I couldn't help standing, my arms raised like a prisoner of war, letting him take his own good time observing the plump breasts that are the only part of my anatomy below my neck not belonging to a fourteen-year-old girl. She did not see what I'd done till I turned the corner, but she seemed not to notice or not to care. I didn't need to use the line I'd rehearsed in front of the mirror, the line that went with my stripper's curtsy, with my arm stretched like Miss Liberty over my head and my wrist daintily cocked, dangling in my fingers the wisp of halter: We're very casual around here.

Instead, as we sit sipping our ice waters I laugh and say, This weather's too hot for clothes. I tease my lips with the tip of my tongue. I roll the frosted glass on my breasts. This feels so nice. Let me do you. I push up her tank top. Roll the glass on her flat stomach.

You're both so wet. Why don't you get off those damp things and sit out back? Cool off awhile. It's perfectly private.

I'll fetch us more drinks. Not too early for something stronger than water, is it?

They exchange easily deciphered looks. For my benefit, speaking to me as much as to each other. Who is this woman? What the hell have we gotten ourselves into?

I guide her up from the rattan chair. It's printed ruts across the backs of her thighs. My fingers are on her elbow. I slide open the screen door and we step onto the unfinished mess of flagstone, mismatched tile and brick Orland calls a patio. The man lags behind us. He'll see me from the rear as I balance on one leg then the other, stepping out of my shorts.

I point her to one of the lawn chairs.

Make yourself comfortable. Orland and the kids are gone for the day. Just the three of us. No one else for miles. It's glorious. Pull off your clothes, stretch out and relax.

I turn quickly and catch him liking what he sees, all of me naked, but he's wary. A little shocked. All of this too good to be true. I don't allow him time to think overly long about it.

You're joining us, aren't you? No clothes allowed.

After I plop down I watch out of the corner of my eye how she wiggles and kicks out of her shorts, her bikini underwear. Her elasticized top comes off over her head. Arms raised in that gesture of surrender every woman performs shrugging off what's been hiding her body. She's my sister then. I remember myself in the mirror of her. Undressing just a few minutes before, submitting, taking charge.

Crooker howls from the pen where I've stuffed her every morning since the first week. She'd been quiet till his long foot in his fancy striped running shoe touched down on the patio. Her challenge scares him. He freezes, framed a moment in the French doors.

It's OK. She's locked in her pen. All she'd do if she were here is try to lick you to death. C'mon out.

I smile over at the woman. Aren't men silly most of the time? Under that silence, those hard stares, that playacting that's supposed to be a personality, aren't they just chicken-hearted little boys most of the time? She knows exactly what I'm thinking without me saying a word. Men. Her black man no different from the rest.

He slams the screen door three times before it catches in the glides that haven't been right since Orland set them. The man can't wait to see the two of us, sisters again because I've assumed the same stiff posture in my lawn chair as she has in hers, back upright, legs extended straight ahead, ankles crossed. We are as demure as two white ladies can be in broad daylight displayed naked for the eyes of a black man. Her breasts are girlish, thumb nippled. Her bush a fuzzy creature in her lap. I'm as I promised. He'll like what he'll see, can't wait to see, but he's pretending to be in no hurry, undoing his bulky shoes lace by lace instead of kicking them off his long feet. The three chairs are arranged in a Y, foot ends converging. I steered her where I wanted her and took my seat so he'll be in the middle, facing us both, her bare flesh or mine everywhere he turns. With all his heart, every hidden fibre he wants to occupy the spot I've allotted for him, but he believes if he seems in too much of a rush, shows undue haste, he'll embarrass himself, reveal himself for what he is, what he was when Crooker's bark stopped him short.

He manages a gangly nonchalance, settling down, shooting out his legs so the soles of three pairs of feet would kiss if we inched just a wee bit closer to the bull's-eye. His shins gleam like black marble. When he's jogging he flows. Up close I'm aware of joints, angles, hinges, the struts and wires of sinew assembling him, the patchwork of his dark skin, many colours, like hers, like mine, instead of the tar-baby sleekness that trots past my window. His palms, the pale underpads of his feet have no business being the blank, clownish colour they are. She could wear that colour on her hands and feet and he could wear hers and the switch would barely be noticeable.

We're in place now and she closes her eyes, leans back her head and sighs. It is quiet and nice here. So peaceful, she says. This is a wonderful idea, she says, and teaches herself how to recline, levers into prone position and lays back so we're no longer three wooden Indians.

My adjustment is more subtle. I drop one foot on either side of my chair so I'm straddling it, then scoot the chair with me on it a few inches to change the angle the sun strikes my face. An awkward way to move, a lazy, stuttering adjustment useful only because it saves me standing up. And it's less than modest. My knees are spread the width of the lawn chair as I ride it to a new position. If the man has liked what he's seen so far, and I know he has, every morsel, every crumb, then he must certainly be pleased by this view. I let him sink deeper. Raise my feet back to the vinyl strips of the leg rest, but keep my knees open, yawning, draw them towards my chest, hug them, snuggle them. Her tan is browner than mine. Caramel then cream where a bikini shape is saved on her skin. I show him the bottom of me is paler, but not much paler than my thighs, my knees I peer over, knees like two big scoops of coffee ice cream I taste with the tip of my tongue.

I'm daydreaming some of the things I'll let them do to me. Tie my limbs to the bed's four corners. Kneel me, spread the cheeks of my ass. I'll suck him while her fingers ply me. When it's the black man's turn to be bondaged and he's trussed up too tight to grin, Orland bursts through the bedroom door, chain saw cradled across his chest. No reason not to let everything happen. They are clean. In good health. My body's still limber and light as a girl's. They like what they see. She's pretending to nap but I know she can sense his eyes shining, the veins thickening in his rubbery penis as it stirs and arches between his thighs he presses together so it doesn't rear up and stab at me, single me out impolitely when there are two of us, two women he must take his time with and please. We play our exchange of smiles, him on the road, me with Billy and Sarah and Carl and Augie at the edge of our corn patch. I snare his eyes, lead them down slowly to my pearly bottom, observe myself there, finger myself, study what I'm showing him so when I raise my eyes and bring his up with me again, we'll both know beyond a doubt what I've been telling him every morning when he passes is true.

No secrets now. What do you see, you black bastard? My pubic hair is always cropped close and neat, a perfect triangle decorates the fork of the Y, a Y like the one I formed with our lawn chairs. I unclasp my knees, let them droop languorously apart, curl my toes on the tubing that frames my chair. She may be watching too. But it's now or never. We must move past certain kinds of resistance, habits that are nothing more than habits. Get past or be locked like stupid baying animals in a closet forever. My eyes challenge his. Yes those are the leaves of my vagina opening. Different colours inside than outside. Part of what's inside me unfolding, exposed, like the lips of your pouty mouth.

The petals of my vagina are two knuckles spreading of a fist stuck in your face. They are the texture of the softest things you've ever touched. Softer. Better. Fleece bedding them turns subtly damp. A musk rises, gently, magically, like the mist off the oval pond that must be included in your route if you jog very far beyond my window. But you may arrive too late or too early to have noticed. About a half mile from here the road climbs as steeply as it does in this rolling countryside. Ruins of a stone wall, an open field on the right, a ragged screen of pine trees borders the other side and if you peer through them, green of meadow is broken just at the foot of a hill by a black shape difficult to distinguish from dark tree trunks and their shadows, but search hard, it rests like a mirror into which a universe has collapsed. At dawn, at dusk the pond breathes. You can see when the light and air are right, sometime rare squeezed up from the earth's centre, hanging over this pond. I believe a ghost with long, trailing hair is marooned there and if I ever get my courage up, I've promised myself I'll go jogging past at night and listen to her sing.

TENNESSEE WILLIAMS

DESIRE AND THE
BLACK MASSEUR

"What use of Nature, what enjoyment of the world, what taste of the elements is not consumed by the soul through the agency of the flesh?" asked Tertullian in the first years of the third century A.D. But scorn of the material world must also be experienced through the body. To deliberately seek the suffering of one's own flesh is considered a virtue in some religious contexts (Hindu fakirs who walk on shards of glass or burning coals, Christian devouts who wear hair-shirts and punish themselves with steel-tipped whips) or a vice if the purpose is sexual gratification. Since the eighteenth century, the notion of pleasure through pain has been categorized: a lust for flogging was known in France as "le vice anglais" and in England as "receiving French lessons."

For Tennessee Williams, the flesh is the soul's ambassador and also a mirror of the universe. In the body, beautiful or deformed, young or old, he recognizes vast interstellar

designs and subtle links to the world's smallest creatures,
relationships to which his characters are often blind. In
Williams's play Suddenly Last Summer, *the doomed poet*
Sebastian Venables visits the Encantadas – tropical islands
where the sea turtles come to lay their eggs. There he discov-
ers that the painful efforts which the creatures must make to
give birth will end in their offspring's death, when they are
devoured by carnivorous birds that fall on them from the
sky. In this hideous scene, Sebastian sees the hand of a terri-
ble God, but fails to recognize his own image, the fact that
he too, a lover of the body, will suffer a similar end. What
Sebastian, like the quiet hero of "Desire and the Black
Masseur," ultimately seeks through the agency of the body is
the assurance of his own existence, of his place in the uni-
verse, and ultimately, of the existence of the universe itself.

F ROM HIS VERY BEGINNING this person, Anthony Burns,
had betrayed an instinct for being included in things that
swallowed him up. In his family there had been fifteen children
and he the one given least notice, and when he went to work,
after graduating from high school in the largest class on the
records of that institution, he secured his job in the largest wholesale company of the city. Everything absorbed him and swallowed him up, and still he did not feel secure. He felt more secure
at the movies than anywhere else. He loved to sit in the back rows

of the movies where the darkness absorbed him gently so that he was like a particle of food dissolving in a big hot mouth. The cinema licked at his mind with a tender, flickering tongue that all but lulled him to sleep. Yes, a big motherly Nannie of a dog could not have licked him better or given him sweeter repose than the cinema did when he went there after work. His mouth would fall open at the movies and saliva would accumulate in it and dribble out the sides of it and all his being would relax so utterly that all the prickles and tightenings of a whole day's anxiety would be lifted away. He didn't follow the story on the screen but watched the figures. What they said or did was immaterial to him, he cared about only the figures who warmed him as if they were cuddled right next to him in the dark picture house and he loved every one of them but the ones with shrill voices.

The timidest kind of a person was Anthony Burns, always scuttling from one kind of protection to another but none of them ever being durable enough to suit him.

Now at the age of thirty, by virtue of so much protection, he still had in his face and body the unformed look of a child and he moved like a child in the presence of critical elders. In every move of his body and every inflection of speech and cast of expression there was a timid apology going out to the world for the little space that he had been somehow elected to occupy in it. His was not an inquiring type of mind. He only learned what he was required to learn and about himself he learned nothing. He had no idea of what his real desires were. Desire is something that is made to occupy a larger space than that which is afforded by the individual being, and this was especially true in the case of Anthony Burns. His desires, or rather his basic desire, was so much too big for him that it swallowed him up as a coat that should have been cut into ten smaller sizes, or rather there should have been that much more of Burns to make it fit him.

For the sins of the world are really only its partialities, its incompletions, and these are what sufferings must atone for. A wall that has been omitted from a house because the stones were exhausted, a room in a house left unfurnished because the householder's funds were not sufficient – these sorts of incompletions are usually covered up or glossed over by some kind of make-shift arrangement. The nature of man is full of such make-shift arrangements, devised by himself to cover his incompletion. He feels a part of himself to be like a missing wall or a room left unfurnished and he tries as well as he can to make up for it. The use of imagination, resorting to dreams or the loftier purpose of art, is a mask he devises to cover his incompletion. Or violence such as a war, between two men or among a number of nations, is also a blind and senseless compensation for that which is not yet formed in human nature. Then there is still another compensation. This one is found in the principle of atonement, the surrender of self to violent treatment by others with the idea of thereby clearing one's self of his guilt. This last way was the one that Anthony Burns unconsciously had elected.

Now at the age of thirty he was about to discover the instrument of his atonement. Like all other happenings in his life, it came about without intention or effort.

One afternoon, which was a Saturday afternoon in November, he went from his work in the huge wholesale corporation to a place with a red neon sign that said "Turkish Baths and Massage." He had been suffering lately from a vague sort of ache near the base of his spine and somebody else employed at the wholesale corporation had told him that he would be relieved by massage. You would suppose that the mere suggestion of such a thing would frighten him out of his wits, but when desire lives constantly with fear, and no partition between them, desire must become very tricky; it has to become as sly as the adversary, and this was one of those times when desire outwitted the enemy under the roof. At the very mention of the word "massage," the desire woke up and exuded a sort of anesthetizing vapor all through Burns' nerves, catching fear off guard and allowing Burns to slip by. Almost without knowing that he was really going, he went to the baths that Saturday afternoon.

The baths were situated in the basement of a hotel, right at the center of the keyed-up mercantile nerves of the downtown section, and yet the baths were a tiny world of their own. Secrecy was the atmosphere of the place and seemed to be its purpose. The entrance door had an oval of milky glass through which you could only detect a glimmer of light. And even when a patron had been admitted, he found himself standing in labyrinths of partitions, of corridors and cubicles curtained off from each other, of chambers with opaque doors and milky globes over lights and sheathings of vapor. Everywhere were agencies of concealment. The bodies of patrons, divested of their clothing, were swathed in billowing tent-like sheets of white fabric. They trailed barefooted along the moist white tiles, as white and noiseless as ghosts except for their breathing, and their faces all wore a nearly vacant expression. They drifted as if they had no thought to conduct them.

But now and again, across the central hallway, would step a masseur. The masseurs were Negroes. They seemed very dark and positive against the loose white hangings of the baths. They wore no sheets, they had on loose cotton drawers, and they moved about with force and resolution. They alone seemed to have an authority here. Their voices rang out boldly, never whispering in the sort of apologetic way that the patrons had in asking directions of them. This was their own rightful province, and they swept the white hangings aside with great black palms that you felt might just as easily have seized bolts of lightning and thrown them back at the clouds.

Anthony Burns stood more uncertainly than most near the entrance of the bath-house. Once he had gotten through the milky-paned door his fate was decided and no more action or will on his part was called for. He paid two-fifty, which was the price of a bath and massage, and from that moment forward had only to follow directions and submit to care. Within a few moments a Negro masseur came to Burns and propelled him onward and then around a corner where he was led into one of the curtained-compartments.

Take off your clothes, said the Negro.

———

The Negro had already sensed an unusual something about his latest patron and so he did not go out of the canvas-draped cubicle but remained leaning against a wall while Burns obeyed and undressed. The white man turned his face to the wall away from the Negro and fumbled awkwardly with his dark winter clothes. It took him a long time to get the clothes off his body, not because he wilfully lingered about it but because of a dream-like state in which he was deeply falling. A far-away feeling engulfed him and his hands and fingers did not seem to be his own, they were numb and hot as if they were caught in the clasp of someone standing behind him, manipulating their motions. But at last he stood naked, and when he turned slowly about to face the Negro masseur, the black giant's eyes appeared not to see him at all and yet they had a glitter not present before, a liquid brightness suggesting bits of wet coal.

Put this on, he directed and held out to Burns a white sheet.

Gratefully the little man enveloped himself in the enormous coarse fabric and, holding it delicately up from his small-boned, womanish feet, he followed the Negro masseur through another corridor of rustling white curtains to the entrance of an opaque glass enclosure which was the steam-room. There his conductor left him. The blank walls heaved and sighed as steam issued from them. It swirled about Burns' naked figure, enveloping him in a heat and moisture such as the inside of a tremendous mouth, to be drugged and all but dissolved in this burning white vapor which hissed out of unseen walls.

After a time the black masseur returned. With a mumbled command, he led the trembling Burns back into the cubicle where he had left his clothes. A bare white table had been wheeled into the chamber during Burns' absence.

Lie on this, said the Negro.

Burns obeyed. The black masseur poured alcohol on Burns' body, first on his chest and then on his belly and thighs. It ran all over him, biting at him like insects. He gasped a little and crossed his legs over the wild complaint of his groin. Then without any warning the Negro raised up his black palm and brought it down with a terrific whack on the middle of Burns' soft belly. The little man's breath flew out of his mouth in a gasp and for two or three moments he couldn't inhale another.

Immediately after the passing of the first shock, a feeling of pleasure went through him. It swept as a liquid from either end of his body and into the tingling hollow of his groin. He dared not look, but he knew what the Negro must see. The black giant was grinning.

I hope I didn't hit you too hard, he murmured.

No, said Burns.

Turn over, said the Negro.

Burns tried vainly to move but the luxurious tiredness made him unable to. The Negro laughed and gripped the small of his waist and flopped him over as easily as he might have turned a pillow. Then he began to belabour his shoulders and buttocks with blows that increased in violence, and as the violence and the pain increased, the little man grew more and more fiercely hot with his first true satisfaction, until all at once a knot came loose in his loins and released a warm flow.

So by surprise is a man's desire discovered, and once discovered, the only need is surrender, to take what comes and ask no questions about it: and this was something that Burns was expressly made for.

———————

Time and again the white-collar clerk went back to the Negro masseur. The knowledge grew quickly between them of what Burns wanted, that he was in search of atonement, and the black masseur was the natural instrument of it. He hated white-skinned bodies because they abused his pride. He loved to have their white skin prone beneath him, to bring his fist or the palm of his hand down hard on its passive surface. He had barely been able to hold this love in restraint, to control the wish that he felt to pound more fiercely and use the full of his power. But now at long last the suitable person had entered his orbit of passion. In the white-collar clerk he had located all that he longed for.

Those times when the black giant relaxed, when he sat at the rear of the baths and smoked cigarettes or devoured a bar of candy, the image of Burns would loom before his mind, a nude white body with angry red marks on it. The bar of chocolate would stop just short of his lips and the lips would slacken into a dreamy smile. The giant loved Burns, and Burns adored the giant.

Burns had become absent-minded about his work. Right in the middle of typing a factory order, he would lean back at his desk and the giant would swim in the atmosphere before him. Then he would smile and his work-stiffened fingers would loosen and flop on the desk. Sometimes the boss would stop near him and call his name crossly. Burns! Burns! What are you dreaming about?

Throughout the winter the violence of the massage increased by fairly reasonable degrees, but when March came it was suddenly stepped up.

Burns left the baths one day with two broken ribs.

Every morning he hobbled to work more slowly and painfully but the state of his body could still be explained by saying he had rheumatism.

One day his boss asked him what he was doing for it. He told his boss that he was taking massage.

It don't seem to do you any good, said the boss.

Oh, yes, said Burns, I am showing lots of improvement!

That evening came his last visit to the baths.

His right leg was fractured. The blow which had broken the limb was so terrific that Burns had been unable to stifle an outcry. The manager of the bath establishment heard it and came into the compartment.

Burns was vomiting over the edge of the table.

Christ, said the manager, what's been going on here?

The black giant shrugged.

He asked me to hit him harder.

The manager looked over Burns and discovered his many bruises.

What do you think this is? A jungle? he asked the masseur.

Again the black giant shrugged.

Get the hell out of my place! the manager shouted. Take this perverted little monster with you, and neither of you had better show up here again!

The black giant tenderly lifted his drowsy partner and bore him away to a room in the town's Negro section.

There for a week the passion between them continued.

This interval was toward the end of the Lenten season. Across from the room where Burns and the Negro were staying there was a church whose open windows spilled out the mounting exhortations of a preacher. Each afternoon the fiery poem of death on the cross was repeated. The preacher was not fully conscious of what he wanted nor were the listeners, groaning and writhing before him. All of them were involved in a massive atonement.

Now and again some manifestation occurred, a woman stood up to expose a wound in her breast. Another had slashed an artery at her wrist.

Suffer, suffer, suffer! the preacher shouted. Our Lord was

nailed on a cross for the sins of the world! They led him above the town to the place of the skull, they moistened his lips with vinegar on a sponge, they drove five nails through his body, and He was The Rose of the World as He bled on the cross!

The congregation could not remain in the building but tumbled out on the street in a crazed procession with clothes torn open.

The sins of the world are all forgiven! they shouted.

———

All during this celebration of human atonement, the Negro masseur was completing his purpose with Burns.

All the windows were open in the death-chamber.

The curtains blew out like thirsty little white tongues to lick at the street which seemed to reek with an overpowering honey. A house had caught fire on the block in back of the church. The walls collapsed and the cinders floated about in the gold atmosphere. The scarlet engines, the ladders and powerful hoses were useless against the purity of the flame.

The Negro masseur leaned over his still breathing victim.

Burns was whispering something.

The black giant nodded.

You know what you have to do now? the victim asked him. The black giant nodded.

He picked up the body, which barely held together, and placed it gently on a clean-swept table.

The giant began to devour the body of Burns.

It took him twenty-four hours to eat the splintered bones clean.

When he had finished, the sky was serenely blue, the passionate services at the church were finished, the ashes had settled, the scarlet engines had gone and the reek of honey was blown from the atmosphere.

Quiet had returned and there was an air of completion.

Those bare white bones, left over from Burns' atonement, were placed in a sack and borne to the end of a car-line.

There the masseur walked out on a lonely pier and dropped his burden under the lake's quiet surface.

As the giant turned homeward, he mused on his satisfaction.

Yes, it is perfect, he thought, it is now completed!

Then in the sack, in which he had carried the bones, he dropped his belongings, a neat blue suit to conceal his dangerous body, some buttons of pearl and a picture of Anthony Burns as a child of seven.

He moved to another city, obtained employment once more as an expert masseur. And there in a white-curtained place, serenely conscious of fate bringing toward him another, to suffer atonement as it had been suffered by Burns, he stood impassively waiting inside a milky white door for the next to arrive.

And meantime, slowly, with barely a thought of so doing, the earth's whole population twisted and writhed beneath the manipulation of night's black fingers and the white ones of day with skeletons splintered and flesh reduced to pulp, as out of this unlikely problem, the answer, perfection, was slowly evolved through torture.

DAVID WOJNAROWICZ

LOSING THE FORM
IN DARKNESS

"Each painting, film, sculpture or page of writing I make,"
said David Wojnarowicz, "represents to me a particular
moment in the history of my body on this planet, in
America. Therefore each photograph, film, sculpture and
page of writing I make has built into it a particular frame
of mind that only I can be sure of knowing, given that I
have always felt alienated in this country and have lived
with the sensation of being an observer of my own life as it
occurs."

The experience which Wojnarowicz describes in all
those different media is one of exile since, in a society that
rejects him and his homosexuality, he is an alien. One of his
collage-paintings can stand as an example of this sense of
alienation: it depicts a severed head, a man in flames, a boy
with a drum and the comic-book image of a stunned cow
all floating, dismembered, around a central planet Earth to

which they obviously don't belong. A Memoir of Disinte-gration *is the subtitle of Wojnarowicz's book,* Close To The Knives. *For Wojnarowicz, there is no difference "between memory and sight, dream and actual vision," so that the same act can be at different times rebellion or acceptance, erotic or non-erotic, depending on the will of the performer.*

———————

I T'S SO SIMPLE: the man without the eye against a receding wall, the subtle deterioration of weather, of shading, of images engraved in the flaking walls. See the quiet outline of a dog's head in plaster, simple as the splash of a fish in dreaming, and then the hole in the wall farther along, framing a jagged sky swarming with glints of silver and light. So simple, the appear-ance of night in a room full of strangers, the maze of hallways wandered as in films, the fracturing of bodies from darkness into light, sounds of plane engines easing into the distance.

It is the appearance of a portrait, not the immediate vision I love so much: that of the drag queen in the dive waterfront coffee shop turning toward a stranger and giving a coy seduc-tive smile that reveals a mouth of rotted teeth, but the childlike rogue slipped out from the white-sheeted bed of Pasolini; the image of Jean Genet cut loose from the fine lines of fiction, uprooted from age and time and continent, and hung up slowly behind my back against a tin wall. It's the simple sense of turning slowly, feeling the breath of another body in a quiet room, the stillness shattered by the scraping of a fingernail against a collar line. Turning is the motion that disrupts the vision of fine red and blue lines weaving through the western skies. It is the motion that sets into trembling the subtle water movements of shadows, like lines following the disappearance of a man beneath the surface of an abandoned lake.

He was moving in with the gradual withdrawal of light, a passenger on the shadows, heat cording his forehead and arms, passion lining the folds of his shirt. A handsome guy with unruly black hair, one eye like the oceans in fading light, the other a great vacant yawn shadowed black as the image of his leather jacket, all of it moved with mirage shivers over his heavy shoulders. There is a slight red colour like a bruise or a blush to his cheeks, the muscles of his face smoothing into angles: hard jaw and a nose that might have once been broken. I was losing myself in the language of his movements, the slow rise and fall of a cigarette as he lifted it to his lips and brought it back down again, each drag leaving a small spherical haze to dissipate against his face.

Outside the windows the river light turned from blues to greys to flashes of rain. A serious dark veil ran the length of the horizon; there's a texture to it, a seediness like dream darkness you can breathe in or be consumed by. It swept down bringing with it strong waves and water, sending tiny people running for cars or shelter among the warehouse walls. Headlights began appearing, rain swinging through the holes in the roofs, through the windows emptied of glass. Sounds of dull puddles spreading along the floorboards. The stranger turned on his heel in the grey light and passed into other rooms, passing through layers of evening, like a dim memory, faceless for moments, just the movements of his body across the floor, the light of doorway after doorway casting itself across the length of his legs.

The river was dirty and coming toward me in the wind. A sixteen-wheel rig parked idling near the corner of the warehouse. Through the dark windows I could see this cowboy all the way from Wyoming sitting high up in the front seat, a woman with a blond bouffant seated next to him raising a bottle of whiskey to her lips. The refrigeration motor hummed while big gauze-covered bodies of cattle swung from hooks in the interior of the truck. Out along the waterfront asphalt-strip cars were turning and circling around. Headlights like lighthouse beacons drifted over the surface of the river, brief and unobtrusive, then swinging around and illuminating the outlines of men, of strangers, people I might or might not have known because their faces were invisible, just black silhouettes, outlined suddenly as each car passes one after the other, pale interior faces turned toward the windows, then fading into distance.

Sitting in the Silver Dollar restaurant earlier in the afternoon, straddling a shining stool and ordering a small cola, I dropped a black beauty and let the capsule ride the edge of my tongue for a moment, as usual, and then swallowed it. Then the sense of regret washes over me like whenever I drop something, a sudden regret at what might be the disappearance of regular perceptions: the flat drift of sensations gathered from walking and seeing and smelling and all the associations; and that strange tremor like a ticklishness that never quite reaches the point of being unbearable. There's a slow sensation of that type coming into the body, from the temples to the abdomen to the calves, and riding with it in waves, spurred on by containers of coffee, into the marvellousness of light and motion and figures coasting along the streets. Yet somehow that feeling of beauty that comes riding off each surface and movement around me always has a slight trace of falseness about it, a slight sense of regret, felt at the occurring knowledge that it's a substance flowing in my veins that cancels out the lines of thought brought along with time and aging and serious understanding of the self.

So there was that feeling of regret, a sudden impulse to bring the pill back up, a surge of weariness with the self, then the settling back and the wait for the sensations to begin. I smoked a fast cigarette and the door opened bringing with it sunlight and wind.

Restless walks filled with coasting images of sight and sound: cars bucking over cobblestones down the quiet side streets, trucks waiting at corners with swarthy drivers leaning back in the cool shadowy seats and the windows of buildings opening and closing, figures passing within rooms, faraway sounds of voices and cries and horns roll up and funnel in like some secret earphone connecting me with the creaking movements of the living city. Old images race back and forth and I'm gathering a heat in the depths of my belly from them: flashes of a curve of arm, back, the lines of a neck glimpsed among the crowds in the train stations, one that you could write whole poems to. I'm being buoyed by these discrete pleasures, walking the familiar streets and river. The streets were familiar more because of the faraway past than the recent past – streets that I walked in those odd times while living among them in my early teens when in the company of deaf mutes and times square pederasts. These streets are seen through the same eyes but each time with periods of time separating it: each time belonging to yet an older boy until the body smooths out and lines are etched until it is a young man recalling the movements of a complicated past. I can barely remember the senses I had when viewing these streets for the first time. There's a whole change in psyche and yet there are slight traces that cut me with the wounding nature of déjà vu, filled with old senses of desire. Each desire, each memory so small a thing, becomes a small river tracing the outlines and the drift of your arms and bare legs, dark mouth and the spoken words of strangers. All things falling from the earth and sky: small movements of the body on the docks, the moaning down among the boards and the night, car lights slanting across the distance, aeroplanes falling as if in a deep surrender to the rogue embraces. Various smiles spark from the darkening rooms, from behind car windows, and the sounds of the wind-plays along the coast sustained by distance and levelled landscapes, drifting around the bare legs and through doorways and into barrooms. Something silent that is recalled, the sense of age in a familiar place, the emptied heart and light of the eyes, the white bones of street lamps and moving autos, the press of memory turning over and over. Later, sitting over coffee and remembering the cinematic motions as if witnessed from a discreet distance, I lay the senses down one by one, writing in the winds of a red dusk, turning over slowly in sleep.

The tattooed man came through the sheets of rain, and swinging headlights from cars entering the riverside parking lot caught him among the fine slanting lines of wind and water. Late this evening, I was sitting by the dock's edge, sitting in the rain remembering old jersey showers as a kid and the quiet deliciousness of walking through coal-grey streets where trees leaned over and by the fields where nuns in the cool green summers would hitch up their long black skirts and toss a large white medicine ball to each other in a kind of memory slow motion.

Over the jersey coast, seen through the veils of rain, the old Maxwell House coffee cup, a five-storey neon cup of white, tipped over on its magical side with two red neon drops falling from its rim and disappearing into the darkness of the brush-covered cliffs. The tattooed man came up suddenly and sat down beside me in the rain like a ceramic figurine glazed with water running down the smooth colours of his shirtless chest. Huge fish fins were riding his shoulders and tattooed scales of komodo dragons, returned from the wilds of jungular africa, twisting outlines and colours of clawed feet and tails smoothing over his aged biceps and the cool white of his head, shaved to permit tattoos of mythological beasts to lift around his neck like frescoes of faded photographs of samurai warriors: a sudden flash of Mishima's private army standing still as pillars along the sides of the river.

———

He had a tough face. It was square-jawed and barely shaven. Close-cropped hair wiry and black, handsome like some face in old boxer photographs, a cross between an aging boxer and Mayakovsky. He had a nose that might have once been broken in some dark avenue barroom in a distant city invented by some horny young kid. There was a wealth of images in that jawline, slight tension to it and curving down toward a hungry-looking mouth.

Sitting in a parked car by the river's edge, he leaned over and placed the palm of his hand along the curve of my neck and I was surprised how perfectly it fit, stroking me slowly, his arms brown as the skin of his face, like a slight tan quietly receding into a blush. He seemed shy for a moment, maybe because of what he saw in my eyes, but the heart was pumping inside the car and the waves, turned over and over by the coasting winds, barrelled across the surface of the river beneath darkening clouds. Some transvestites circled down from the highway, going from car to car, leaning in the drivers' windows checking for business.

He eases his hands down toward my legs and slides it back up beneath my shirt, saying, "Take it off." I reached down and lifted the sweater and the t-shirt up together and pull them over my head, dropping them to the floor where my pants are straddling my ankles. He pulls off his green naval sweater revealing a t-shirt the colour of ice blue, reaches down and peels that off too. We are looking at each other from opposite sides of the car. He's got a gleaming torso, thick chest with a smooth downy covering of black hair, brick-red nipples buried inside the down. He leans and bends before me licking my body softly down my sides, one hand massaging slowly between my legs, his other hand wetted briefly against his mouth and working his cock up until it is dark and red and hard.

When he lifted away from my chest I saw his eyes, the irises the colour of dark chips of stone, something like the sky at dusk after a clear hot summer day, when the ships are folding down into the distance and jet exhaust trails are uttered from the lips of strangers. The transvestites were back and leaning in the window refusing to go away. We pulled our clothes back on and closed up the car, heading toward one of the abandoned structures.

Inside one of the back ground-floor rooms there are a couple of small offices built into the garagelike space. Paper from old shipping lines scattered all around like bomb blasts among wrecked pieces of furniture; three-legged desks, a naugahyde couch of mint-green turned upside down, and small rectangles of light and wind and river over on the far wall.

I lean toward him, pushing him against the wall, lifting my pale hands up beneath his sweater, finding the edge of his tight t-shirt and peeling it upward. I placed my palms against the hard curve of his abdomen, his chest rolling slightly in plea-sure. Moving back and forth within the tin-covered coffee cubicle, old soggy couch useless on the side, the carpet beneath our shifting feet reveals our steps with slight pools of water. We're moving around, changing positions that allow us to bend and sway and lean forward into each other's arms so that our tongues can meet with nothing more than a shy hesitation. He is sucking and chewing on my neck, pulling my body into his, and over the curve of his shoulder, sunlight is burning through a window emptied of glass. The frame still contains a rusted screen that reduces shapes and colours into tiny dots like a film directed by Seurat. Pushing and smoothing against the tides, this great dark ship with hundreds of portholes entered the film. His head was below my waist, opening his mouth and showing brilliant white teeth; he's unhooking the button at the top of my trousers. I lean down and find the neckline of his sweater and draw it back and away from the nape of his neck which I gently probe with my tongue. In loving him, I saw a cigarette between the fingers of a hand, smoke blowing backwards into the room, and sputtering planes diving low through the clouds. In loving him, I saw men encouraging each other to lay down their arms. In loving him, I saw small-town labourers creating excavations that other men spend their lives trying to fill. In loving him, I saw moving films of stone buildings; I saw a hand in prison dragging snow in from the sill. In loving him, I saw great houses being erected that would soon slide into the waiting and stirring seas. I saw him freeing me from the silences of the interior life.

Stopped in the Silver Dollar just as dusk was rolling in, paid for some takeout coffee, there's a group of ten drag queens standing outside leaning on shining car fenders, applying lipstick and powders out of tiny mirrored compacts. One young man in a tight white t-shirt, hard white arms, no more dreams, heavy beer belly, had fallen on his face moments before. A couple of his teeth having popped out, there were two vermilion streaks running down the sides of his mouth and some cops were standing over him as he lay on his back, his cheekbones glistening and arms flailing like in some stream, backstroking his way out of this world, out of this life, away from this sea of blue uniforms and white boneless faces, away from this sea of city heat and faraway motion of his eyes fluttering behind dark sunglasses. Walked onto the pier and stood with my back to the river and way over the movements of the city was what looked like a falling star, a photographic negative of one in the night: a jet streak short and vertical falling from the sky, like a falling jet with a single illuminated flame tracing the domed curve of the heavens, a scratch in the sky, a blinding light caught in the scratch from the unseen sun, and slowly changing direction and connecting the rooftops of the buildings one after the other.

In the warehouse just before dark, passed along the hallways and photographed the various graffiti on the walls, some of hermaphrodites and others of sharp-faced thugs smoking cigarettes; in passing through a series of rooms, saw this short fat man with a seedy moustache standing in a broken closet filled with old wet newspapers and excrement and piss, standing with his hands locked behind his head and with a hard-on poking out through his trousers from beneath a grimy heavy overcoat: he was doing this strange dance, undulating his hips, sweat rolling down the sides of his face, beneath dark glasses, grimacing and stabbing the air with his cock and saying in a loud whisper: " … come in here … I'll make ya feel so *goood* … *so good* …"

Later, about 3:00 a.m., a terrific storm swept down on the city, the waves rolling like humpbacked whales just beneath the water's surface: whole schools of them riding first toward and then away from the piers. With another coffee I stepped along the walls of the warehouse and ducked beneath the low doorway to get out of the rain. Somewhere in the darkness men stood around. I thought I could hear the shuffle of their feet, the sense of their hearts palpitating in the coolness. Dark cars outside the windows slowly covered in rain, headlights clicking on suddenly, waves slashing at the pier and huge pieces of unhooked tin, torn down by the wind, clanging and crashing against the upper walls. I thought I saw a person in a white jacket disappearing as I reached the upper hallways. Walked around sloshing hot coffee over the rim of the open cup with every few steps. Looked out the side windows into the squall, tiny motions of the wet city. Inside, for as far as the eye could see, there was darkness and waving walls of iron, rusting sounds painful and rampant, crashing sounds of glass from remaining windows, and no sign of people: I realized I was completely alone. The sense of it slightly unnerving in the cavernous space. Street lamps from the westside highway burn in the windows, throwing shadows behind staircases and burying doors and halls. Walked out on the catwalk and watched the terrific gale and tossing waves of the river from one of the side doors. Huge panoramas of factories and water tanks were silhouetted by green roof lights and cars moving down the highway seen only by the red wink of their taillights.

Walking back into the main section of the warehouse I stopped in one of the rooms facing the elevated highway. The rain had slowed down and the streets were burning with a brassai light and texture. I suddenly felt a hand on my crotch in the darkness and turned toward the dark void where the face should be, stepping back as I did so. The hand belonged to a small, dwarfish man, someone out of an old Todd Browning image. I put my hand to his shoulder and said, "Sorry … just walking around…." And as I passed through a series of rooms, he followed from a distance, sliding along the walls and appearing unexpectedly in the doorways ahead of me, the rise and fall of his cigarette describing a clear arc, like a meteorite, then disappearing into the shadows of his face. As I left by the back stairs, he drifted out of a room over to the top of the staircase and stood silently watching me descend from view.

Standing in a waterfront bar, having stopped in for a beer in mid-afternoon: smoky sunlight riding in through the large plate-glass windows and a thumping roll of music beating invisibly in the air. Over by one window and side wall, a group of guys are hanging out playing pool – one of them is this chicano boy, muscular and smooth with a thin cotton shirt of olive green, black cowboy hat pushed down over his head, strong collarbones pressing out, a graceful curve of muscles in his back and a solid chest, his stomach pressed like a slightly curved washboard against the front of his shirt, muscles in the arms rising and falling effortlessly as he gesticulates with one hand, talking with some guy who's leaning into the sunlight of the window; in his other hand the poolstick is balanced against his palm, a cigarette between his fingers. He leans back and takes a drag and blows lazy smoke rings one after the other that pierce the rafts of light and dissolve within the shadows. The guy that he was talking to looked like some faraway character straight from the fields of old skittering wheat and someone I once travelled with by pickup truck with beer cans in the dusty backseat and buzz in the head from summer: dark eyes and a rosy complexion, roughly formed face made of sharp lines and his hair cut short around the sides and back of his neck. Standing there sipping from a green bottle, I could see myself taking the nape of his neck in my teeth as he turned and stared out the window at the rolling lines of traffic for a moment. Light curved around his face and the back of his head, the shaved hair produced sensations that I could feel cross the palm of my hand, my sweating hand, all the way from where I stood on the other side of the room. He looked around after turning away from the windows and set his eyes on me for a moment, studying me for indiscernible reasons, and I felt myself blush: felt the movement of the bass tapping against some chord where the emotions or passions lie, tilted my head back and took another swig from the beer, a humming gathering from my stomach and rising up past my ears.

He turns away and the chicano guy leans over the pool table for a shot, his back curved and taut like a bow, arm drawing back to softly clack the balls on the table: a couple dropping into the side pocket, and for a moment the two of them were lost in the drift of men entering the bar. I move over a few feet to bring them back into view and some sort of joke developed between them. The country boy reaches into the bottom slot of the table and withdraws a shiny black eight-ball and advances toward the chicano, who drew back until his buttocks hit the low sill of the window. He giggles and leans his head back at an angle and lets a hardness come from his eyes. The country boy's face turned a slight shade of red in the light and he reached out with his hands: one hand pulling the top of the chicano's shirt out and the other deftly dropping the eight-ball into the neckline. The ball rolled down and lodged near his belly and the two of them laughed as he reached in, hand sliding down the chest and stomach retrieving the ball. I took a last swig from my beer, overcome with the sensations of touch, of my fingers and palms smoothing along some untouched body in some imagined and silent sun-filled room, overcome with the heat that had been gathering in my belly and now threatened to overpower me with a sense of dizziness. I barely managed to place the bottle upright on the nearby cigarette machine and push open the doors, into the warm avenue winds, push open the doors and release myself from the embrace of the room and the silent pockets of darkness and the illuminating lines of light thinking it was Jacques Prevert who said "why work when you have a pack of cigarettes and sunlight to play with?" and listened to the horns of ships along the river, far behind the fields of buildings and traffic, turned a corner and headed across town.

———————

Passing down a long hallway there were glimpses of frescoes, vagrant frescoes painted with rough hands on the peeling walls, huge murals of nude men painted with beige and brown colours coupling several feet above the floorboards. Some of them with half-animal bodies leaning into the room's darkness with large outlined erections poised for penetration. Other walls contain crayoned buddhas and shining gems floating above their heads in green wax. One wall where a series of black wire-strewn holes pull apart the surface, where crowbars and hammers searched out copper pipes and wires, but still filled with floating faces almost japanese with pink high-boned cheeks and multicoloured eyelids, a stream of hair touched by loving or by winds, small crudely drawn lanterns serving no discernible purpose but to genie these faces from the vague surface of the plaster.

Passing doorways in slow motion, passing through shadowed walls and along hallways, seeing briefly framed in the recesses of a room a series of men in various stages of leaning. Seeing the pale flesh of the frescoes come to life: the smooth turn of hands over bodies, the taut lines of limbs and mouths, the intensity of the energy bringing others down the halls where guided by little or no sounds they pass silently over the charred floors. They appear out of nowhere and line the walls like figurines before firing squads or figures in a breadline in old times pressed into history. Stopping for a moment, I thought of the eternal sleep of statues, of marble eyes and lips and the stone wind-blown hair of the rider's horse, of illuminated arms corded with soft unbreathing veins, of the wounded curve of ancient backs stooped for frozen battles, of the ocean and the eyes in fading light, of the white stone warthog in the forest of crowfoot trees, and of the face beneath the sands of the desert still breathing.

ZHANG XIGUO

THE CONQUERORS

Throughout the centuries, the Chinese developed a complex erotic vocabulary largely made up of euphemisms. "Crossing the Jade Portico," "entering the Seven Alabaster Gates," "losing oneself in the Palace of Lava and Fire," may seem to us outlandish metaphors; in fact, they were banal conventions to describe copulation. Some euphemisms, however, were extraordinarily subtle: in the eighteenth-century Dream of the Red Chamber, *masturbation is described as "looking at oneself in the Mirror of Wind and Moon."*

By the time of the Great Proletarian Cultural Revolution of 1966, political fiction became established as the staple literature of China. Erotic literature, so much a part of the classic Chinese tradition from the earliest novels and stories, was severely criticized and ultimately banned as belonging to bourgeois sensibility and being, therefore, counter-revolutionary. For the past twenty-odd years, most of the erotic literature of China has been written either in Taiwan or abroad, in exile.

Zhang Xiguo is considered the main representative of the

third generation of Chinese writers in exile in America. A computer specialist at the University of Illinois, he has continued to write in Chinese several works of science-fiction, short stories and essays. "The Conquerors," mingling the erotic experience of the present with the memory of a brutal past, uses a stark, factual style rather than the flourishes of the classic Chinese erotic novel.

———————

"LET ME BE ON TOP, okay?"

He lay back flat, both hands caressing her tender breasts. She sighed and closed her eyes.

"Don't force it. Let it go in by itself. Not so hard, you hurt me again."

He felt as if his flesh were burning. She was tired so he dared not use too much force; he stroked her delicate skin. Without her clothes on she did not appear at all thin; his hands moved to her rounded buttocks. She gradually relaxed and he pressed hard on her tailbone, letting himself enter her completely. She collapsed panting on top of him. He hugged her tightly, enjoying his fill of her perfect, sumptuous flesh.

———————

The road had come to an end.

The three of them happened to look back at the same time.

The small path that twisted its way up to the mountain ridge resembled a dead snake, the skin of its white belly turned upward to be baked by the blistering sun. Whiskers irritably drew out his handkerchief and wiped off the perspiration. Fatty lit a cigarette and then threw it down impatiently. Spectacles opened his briefcase and took out a stack of paper money, spreading it out carefully on the ground. Fatty handed him his lighter; and Spectacles pulled a piece of yellow paper from the stack and lit it. The black border around the paper extended its sphere of influence until, within a few seconds, it had devoured the golden circle in the centre. Clutching the lighter, Spectacles looked around uncertainly.

"It's all burned?"

"Yes, yes." Whiskers said, "That's right, it was right here."

The half-burned money danced in the air in all directions like dead leaves. The air on the mountain ridge had grown drier and hotter. Wiping the perspiration from his forehead, Fatty suddenly burst forth:

"My sword drawn, I laugh at Heaven/My life in the balance, two rare friends."

Spectacles fixed his gaze on the curling, struggling paper money on the ground; he could not keep his eyes from tearing. Fifteen years, he silently calculated, fifteen years and they had finally come up the mountain again. But what had been the use?

When he was young he had been a bed wetter, right up until the time he was eleven or twelve years old. At first it was something he had no control over; later on, however, it was because he just didn't feel like getting up and facing the cold. He liked the brief feeling of warmth on the mattress after he wet the bed; afterward he would roll over onto the other side of the bed, the farther away from the trouble spot the better. He would wrap himself tightly in the bedcovers, feeling slightly guilty, but also somewhat pleased with himself. The worst thing was when he would forget what he had done and thoughtlessly run his hand over the clammy patch, thus being forced to get up to wash his hands. The toilet was behind the kitchen; it was an old-fashioned one in which one squatted over a hole in the ground; the only light came from a small lamp in the doorway. Behind the house, on the other side of the rice paddy, was the railroad. Sometimes he would get up in the middle of the night and he would see in the distance a fiery dragon hurtling forward in the darkness. Sometimes that fiery dragon would also come steaming into his dreams and carry him off to some faraway, nameless country. In the daytime, the blue train would appear small and insignificant. But the fiery dragon that appeared in the deep of the night would always make his heart pound. He would stand outside the toilet, often forgetting the cold, waiting for the fiery dragon to make another appearance.

———————

When she was sucking him she would sometimes take it out and lightly rub her cheek against it. When he was about to ejaculate, she would squeeze it tightly at the base, briefly causing him to groan with pain; then she would interrogate him: "Feel good? Do you love me?" He would respond vaguely. Quite unwilling to give up, she would ask him again. He would say in a loud voice that he loved her. All argument would at this point be superfluous and extremely ridiculous. She enjoyed, at the most intense moments of their lovemaking, pressing him to tell her whether or not he loved her. His declarations and her interrogations were equally futile, yet they never tired of the game just the same. Her skill could undoubtedly conquer all men. Her fair, naked image would often appear afterward in his memory, calling to him with open arms.

"It's all yours. We'll do it whatever way you like, okay?"

She would then close her eyes and lie languidly in his embrace as if she were indeed prepared to surrender him everything. When he became aroused, she would hug the pillow and laugh maliciously at his excited member. This was always when he felt the most uncomfortable; it was only at such times that he might wonder who was actually playing with whom. If she were ever to stop loving him, would she drop him without the slightest hesitation just like she would treat some other boyfriend? Perhaps he ought to be the first one to make a move and let her have a taste of rejection for once.

"How come it shrank?" Flinging the pillow aside, she came over and grabbed him. "What are you thinking about now? One spy to another, you tell me a secret and I'll tell you one."

"I don't have any secrets. I told you all of them."

"Don't give me that." She was massaging him, her other hand slowly caressing his glistening chest. "I'm the spy that you love who lives in the little house. Tell me, what other secrets do you have?"

Anaïs Nin, he thought, even when she was making love she didn't forget to show off. He began to get hard again and pushed her down on the bed; she didn't offer any further resistance.

"Tell me, what other secrets do you have?"
"It was Sunday."
"Huh?"
"Yes, it was on Sunday."

———————

It was Sunday; he had laid his cards on the table with Anna Chu. The affair with Lily had long been out in the open; there was no way that Anna Chu did not know about it. This woman really must have loved him if she could put up with it to the very end without getting angry. Although he was somewhat reluctant, he nevertheless had to harden his heart and say everything that needed to be said. They had been together for three long years, or three short years, depending upon which way one looked at it, and had gradually come to understand clearly each other's temperament. He could not possibly marry her; this had been said he didn't know how many times, and it was repeated once more today. If they could not get married, then it was best to separate as soon as possible; this had also been said he didn't know how many times, but today was the first time it had been said in earnest like this. Anna Chu sat on the side of the bed weeping silently as she listened to him. Finally, she said softly, "She could destroy you, Xin; I feel sorry for you."

———————

She was sleeping now, her soft breasts pressed against the mattress, her face half-covered by her long, dishevelled hair. Gazing at her milky white flesh, he became excited again. He never ceased longing to possess her, and his desire was becoming more and more feverish. She was Salomé; she was the Whore of Babylon; she was Ianthe; she was Pan Jinlian; she was lust incarnate; he had to have her. If one could destroy oneself in the flames of desire, then let those flames burn him up! Let the ashes from his bones be sprinkled all over her naked flesh, forever to lightly kiss her soft breasts, her supple skin, and the soft down between her buttocks ... he would never regret it.

Who was it who wanted to scatter his ashes throughout the land of China? Who was it that pledged to fertilize the fields of the motherland with the ashes of his last remains? Who was it? Who was it?

———————

Spectacles finished burning the last stack of paper money and stood up, his legs aching. Fatty tapped him on the shoulder and said, "Let's go, Zhixin."

"You go ahead. I'm going to have another look around."

Fatty and Whiskers walked down from the mountain ridge together. Spectacles stamped out the last burning embers of the paper money. A black leaf stuck to the leg of his trousers; he brushed it with his hand and it turned into black soot, still clinging stubbornly to the trouser leg. He thought of something *Long Long* had said just before he died: if a man loses his faith, what then is left?

But he had lost his faith, and what did he have left?

He wanted to have a good cry. When Ruan Jinlian died, it was a long time before the sound of weeping could be heard in the quiet hills. But he could not cry; he had long since forgotten how to cry.

———————

Her softly crying figure was beautiful, especially when she was naked. Her tender breasts were lightly resting upon her exquisite knees; he had a tremendous urge to reach out and pinch them.

"You're not listening to what I'm saying at all."

"I'm listening, of course I'm listening. Let's go to bed, okay?"

She glared at him and went on: "My mother and my aunt don't like me. My aunt was a heroine; she could fire a gun with either hand. She was really famous in the guerrilla attacks in the Taihang Mountains during the Anti-Japanese War of Resistance."

"I know," he said with patience. "After the victory she served a term as provincial commissioner. It was only after old Yan from Shanxi fell from power that she went to America, right?"

"My uncle was also a celebrity. When Li Zongren was president he wanted for a time to use him for some important job, but my uncle refused. According to my mother, my uncle was an important player in political circles at that time. I don't really understand what it was that he was doing, but anyway, I do know that at that time he was pulled every which way by all kinds of groups."

"The Democratic Alliance." He lay back, exposing the naked lower half of his body to her. Apparently ignoring him, she hugged her knees, seeming to have once again become a girl of fourteen or fifteen. It was no use; he covered himself with the bedclothes.

"Later on, Uncle had some psychological problems and my aunt left him. Uncle stayed in New York and my aunt came back to Taiwan to live for a short time. She went to Hong Kong later on and ran a school. My mother adores her more than anyone else. It's really strange: my mom loathed my dad so much, yet she treats my aunt just like her own sister. Whenever my aunt comes to Taiwan she always comes to stay at our place. But neither one of them likes me."

"How can they not like you when you're the only daughter?" He put out his hand, wanting to pull her over to him. "I like you baby, even if nobody else does."

She pushed him away.

"My mother is a fine pianist, and my aunt is musical too. My mom forced me to play the piano ever since I was a child. We went through I don't know how many teachers, but I just couldn't learn how to play. I couldn't help it, I just hated the piano more than anything. As soon as I sat in front of the piano my hands would go numb."

Wiping the tears from her face, she suddenly asked him:

"Do you really think I sing well?"

"Of course, yours is the only singing I like to listen to," he lied.

"But I know I don't sing well. Helen Ning sings much better than I do. My mom has never really wanted to come and hear me sing. Once when Auntie had just come back to Taiwan, they showed up all of a sudden. I sang terribly that night. I wanted so badly to sing well, but I don't know what happened – it just wasn't right...."

She was crying again and he hugged her close; this time she didn't push him away.

"Don't you feel sorry for your baby?"

He kissed her lightly. "It's all right, I'm here."

———————

"She could destroy you, Xin; I feel sorry for you."

———————

Spectacles pulled open the bottom drawer of the desk and took out several batches of old letters. Some of the letter paper had already yellowed. Already he was unable to remember clearly how many among them he had conquered. The manuscript paper laid out on the table was still blank. After he had read through the old letters, he retired all the bundles and returned them to the drawer. The smell of fried fish wafted in from the neighbouring flat. The few pots of flowers and plants on the window sill appeared to be half-withered already. He had never had the patience to look after them; Anna had always watered them and kept them nice for him. There were two pots that Anna had bought, the other few having been brought over, one after another, by Mrs. Song when she brought Fenfen to see him – Mrs. Song complained that his living quarters were too dull and empty, that there was nothing there except books. Fen-fen had drawn a few crayon pictures for him; it was anyone's guess where he might have stuck them. Of the ornaments that Anna had bought, Lily had given some away and thrown some out. Women are always like that: right after they move in, they single-mindedly root out all traces of their predecessor, as if they could assume control from that point on. The manuscript paper was, as ever, blank; his mind numb, he opened the drawer once more; the letters were still lying there neatly, storing how many dried and withered teardrops? He closed the drawer and locked it with a key. The smell of frying fish still hung in the air; it wasn't until he went over to close the window that he realized that the stain on his trouser leg had still not disappeared.

Her breasts were certainly the softest part of her body. He could suck her breasts forever and never tire of it. Anna's breasts were small and elegantly erect, and their first night, when she had been moved to tears, he whispered solemn promises of love in her ear, holding her firm breasts tightly in his hands. He once thought he would never want to part with Anna's breasts; he now knew that what he worshipped with his whole heart and soul was in fact Lily's soft, serpentine body, and above all her tender white bosom. His entire being was submerged within it, never wanting to come to the surface.

But each time he finished, he could not bear her persistent asking whether or not he really loved her. She would wrap herself around him like a grapevine, not letting him get out of bed.

"That's enough now, I have to get up and do some writing."

She continued to tease him. Sometimes he would become aroused again and the tension would be temporarily relieved. Sometimes he would suddenly feel an immeasurable exasperation; she would unfortunately sense this and choose the occasion to attack his weak point.

"You don't have to put on an act for me, you can't even write good poetry anyway."

He simply could not understand why she was being so cruel. Five minutes before he had been inside her and she had been crying out his name in ecstasy. Now she was sitting at the head of the bed, teasing him like a hunting dog guarding its prey, affording him no chance of escape. At least he had never criticized her poor singing. Magnanimity was not one of her virtues.

"All you know how to do is play around. There are lots of men around the West Gate area, why don't you just go and grab one?"

She shrugged her small shoulders.

"Actually, I couldn't care less. I was doing you a favour. What's wrong with coming up with another excuse for your inability to write poems?"

He fled to the study. Half an hour later she came in, her face covered in tears, and kissed him.

"We mustn't fight anymore, okay? You don't know how much I'm suffering. If you don't care for me, who else will?"

She opened her night clothes and pressed her milk-white breasts tightly against him. He was compelled to open his mouth and to bite down hard on the cherry-like nipples swaying in front of him, knowing full well that it would do no good. In spite of this fact, as long as he could still do it he was secure.

––––––––––

Long Long. Where is your faith? You were only twenty-six when you died; they all said you were gifted. Where is your faith?

When she was willing to listen respectfully and patiently, he would relate to her events from his childhood. He talked about the morning after the explosion at the munitions recycling factory, when he and his classmates ran over to take a look. The warehouse on the riverbank was still spewing out clouds of smoke, and planks and spent cartridges that had been burned black were scattered all over the cobblestones. A light rain had fallen in the early morning, and the smell of sulphur still hung in the air. As they were picking up the empty cartridges, they eventually discovered, in front of the warehouse, a bent, squatting, half-burnt human figure.

"Late at night …" He hesitated, uncertain if he should continue. "Late at night, I would sometimes run outside and watch the fiery dragon come charging out of the darkness."

She was of course no longer willing to listen. She interrupted him and talked about her performance two days hence. She was always concerned only for herself; sometimes he would become extremely angry over this surprising lack of self-confidence of hers. She was constantly asking him about which songs she should sing, or if she should sign the contract Lao Jin wanted her to sign. Anna had never bothered him with such things. But she sensed when he was about to explode and, kicking off the covers, she stood naked in front of him.

"I'll try on my new clothes for you."

She hid behind the door of the clothes closet and seconds later came out wearing a light yellow dress. "Your own private fashion show. Do you like this one?"

He stared greedily at her softly trembling breasts. She flashed him a professional smile and disappeared again. When she again closed the closet door, she had changed into a black *qipao* splashed with bits of flowers. "How about this one?"

"It's split too high up the side."

"You don't like it?" She pouted her small mouth. "If you don't, your baby isn't going to perform any more. Tell me the truth, do you like it or not?"

"Yes, of course I like it."

———

"My uncle's coming to Taibei." She was sitting in front of the dressing table, carefully applying her eye-shadow. "I'm sure you two will get along. Just be careful what you say. Don't upset him."

"How can I avoid upsetting him?"

"Just don't bring up my aunt." She smiled winsomely in the mirror. "Is your baby beautiful?"

He was deeply attracted by the delicate beauty in the mirror. Admiring her from this distance was like appreciating a painting. Not allowing him a moment's respite, she suddenly threw herself into his arms. "Don't go out. Wait for me to come back, okay?"

"What kind of wicked ideas are rolling around in that head of yours now?"

"Look who's talking. Who was it that was finished before he even got it in this morning? Should he be punished or not?" She thought for a moment, then, inclining her head to one side, asked "Does it bother you when I pester you like this?"

"No, of course it doesn't bother me."

———

Spectacles squeezed his way wearily in and out of the crowds outside the airport. Even his shirt was drenched in perspiration when he finally located the old man beside the road. The latter, however, appeared totally unconcerned and was casually looking around, his hands behind his back. Spectacles rushed up, respectfully calling out, "Uncle Ren." The old man narrowed his eyes, saying coldly:

"You're late. Do you know what time the plane got into Taibei?"

"I got to the airport some time ago, but I couldn't find you. Didn't we decide on the phone to meet at the entrance to the terminal?"

"How was I to know which entrance you were talking about? You're so dense. Couldn't you have taken a look on both sides? Why didn't you come around the corner?"

"No way, I just now looked for you on both sides. Have you been standing here waiting the whole time?"

"Pretty much." The old man sniffed, not a trace of guilt in his expression.

"Pretty much?"

"People do have to go to the bathroom, you know. Lily went on in her letters about how clever you are, but I certainly don't see it myself. All right, all right, hurry up and fetch my luggage. Surely you don't want me to stand here all night. It's those two yellow suitcases. There's also a scroll painting. Be careful you don't bend it, it's a gift for someone."

In fact it wasn't just two suitcases at all. Spectacles called a taxi over and, after pleading with the driver, finally managed with great difficulty to stuff the luggage into the car. There were altogether five pieces of varying sizes.

"Five pieces! Are there any more?"

"Of course not." The old man shot him a look. "I'm not moving after all. What would I be bringing so much luggage for?"

By the time Spectacles got into the car he was so tired he wanted to close his eyes. The old man, who was sitting in the back, was not at all ready to let him off the hook.

"Lily says you're doing history of thought? And you like to write poetry?"

"I haven't accomplished anything. I'm just interested, that's all."

"You'll certainly have no future that way," the old man grunted. "If you're going to do research, you'd be better off researching me."

"Yes." Spectacles turned around to discover the old man sizing him up through squinting eyes. "Uncle Ren, after you've had a few days rest, I'll bring my tape recorder over and ask you some questions." There was no reply from the old man. They had almost reached Taibei, and Spectacles turned around once more, wanting to point out for him the magnificent Grand Hotel, when he discovered that the old man had lain back in the seat and fallen asleep.

In October, Germany launched the war in Europe and blitzkrieged across Western Europe; the French army was defeated. In September, Japan's Fifth Division occupied Vietnam; the Headquarters Division and the Taiwanese Brigade were still tenaciously defending Yongning and Qinzhou in Guangxi. In our Fourth Theatre of Operations, as the lines of communication behind enemy lines were stretched thin, their strength had diminished, and I ordered all armies to launch an offensive. The Thirty-first Army lay siege to Longjin; the Forty-sixth Army mopped up the enemy at Mingjiang. On October 26 the enemy in Longzhou began retreating toward Vietnam and my troops retook Longzhou. The Fourth Theatre ordered the Sixteenth Group Army to carry out mop-up operations against the remaining enemy at the eastern end of the Yong-Qin road and to carry out a joint attack on Nanning. It also ordered the Thirty-fifth Group Army to carry out, from the Yong-Bin and Yong-Wu roads, separate sudden attacks on the enemy in Nanning. Another unit was to cross the Yong River, cut off the Yong-Qin road, and carry out a joint attack on the enemy at the north end of the road. Every one of my units attacked bravely; the Sixty-fourth Army took Gaofeng'ai and Santang in Binyang and pressed on to Nanning. The 155th Division crossed the Yong River from Yongheng and attacked the enemy. At the same time the enemy on the north bank of the Yong River retreated toward the Yong-Qin road and on the 30th, our Thirty-fifth Group Army retook Nanning. At this time the total strength of the enemy was around thirty thousand men. Each of our units continued to press their attack, and up to November 17 the enemy suffered flank attacks and rear attacks on all sides until, with naval air cover, they moved out along the Yong-Qin road and beat a retreat by sea; there was already no trace of the enemy in Nanning.

———

She was crying in her sleep again. He woke up with a start; she didn't wake up at all. He wiped the tears from the corners of her eyes. She looked like a child when she was in a deep sleep, completely without guile, her face half-buried in the pillow. He would prefer that she remain in a deep sleep forever; it seemed that this was the only way he could fully possess her. He took her once while she was sound asleep. She woke up, and with her eyes still closed and a smile on her face, she wrapped her legs tightly around him. In that instant he knew he was finished, already beyond salvation.

———————

"She could destroy you, Xin; I feel sorry for you."

———————

The old man sat, arms folded, on the sofa in front of the window. His wrinkled face had no discernible angles; his eyes, on the other hand, appeared to be extraordinarily clear, the grey pupils following Spectacles' movements, their expression belying his mistrust of Spectacles. Spectacles turned on the tape recorder, fixing his attention on the revolving spools.

"Can we talk about your political ideals?"

"You go ahead."

"What?"

"You go ahead." The old man was watching him cunningly. Suddenly feeling uncomfortable all over, Spectacles managed to force himself to reply:

"I don't have anything to say. Uncle Ren, how can we compare with you? Any casual comments you happen to make, they're all oral history, they're all of value...."

"You go ahead. I'll talk after you."

Spectacles could only turn off the tape recorder. He thought of Lily's milk-white, soft breasts swaying in front of him; he opened his mouth, wanting to bite down hard on the cherry-like nipples.

There was already no trace of the enemy in Nanning.
There was already no trace of the enemy in Nanning.
There was already no trace of the enemy in Nanning.

Long Long, where is your faith? Tell me, *please* tell me, where *is* your faith? Or are you just like me, letting maggots breed inside your skull? Please tell me, where is your faith?

―――――――

When he got back home, Lily had already left. She had left a note on the desk: "Gone to Gaoxiong to do a show. Back on the 17th." He found a package of frozen *jiaozi* in the refrigerator and, heating up some water, one by one dropped in the frozen lumps of dough; the water, which had been boiling, immediately became calm. He stirred it with chopsticks to keep the *jiaozi* from sticking to the bottom of the pot. Lily should already be backstage getting made up, hiding her fear under layers of cosmetics. She had said so many times that she did not want to go on singing, but he couldn't think of any other way for her to go either; they both needed the applause of others. The *jiaozi* in the pot suddenly rose to the surface and he rushed to turn off the gas. After the white foam had disappeared, the half-black, half-white *jiaozi* lay on their sides on the surface of the water like so many floating corpses. His appetite completely gone, he forced himself to ladle out a few and, dipping them in soya sauce, ate them. He took out some manuscript paper and spread it out on the dining table. He turned on the tape recorder, and from the machine came the muffled sound of his own voice.

"Can we talk about your political ideals?"

——————

The old man took off his leather shoes and stood on the sofa, regarding Spectacles with a dignified air.

"Do you know what I came to Taibei for this time?"

"Didn't you come back for a meeting?"

The old man laughed contemptuously.

"You young people are really shortsighted. Who do you think I am that somebody could win me over just by inviting me to a meeting? I'll tell you the truth, even if they offer me a special assignment, I won't do it. Take a look, you just take a look for yourself."

The old man pulled out his pocketbook and with great care drew out a letter that had been cut into small squares, handing it to Spectacles.

"Take a look. Whose handwriting is it?"

"Too bad!" Spectacles gave an involuntary gasp of alarm. "Why cut off only the signature? If the letter had been preserved intact, it would be even more valuable."

The old man gave him a scornful look, delicately putting away the square pieces of the letter.

"Lily tells me that you have quite a varied group of friends. I suppose you do have some talent, but isn't it a shame that if a hero doesn't act then he's really just a coward? It would be much better if you were to get a hold of that bunch of friends of yours and join me in a great undertaking. You young people have no prospects at all. If you're going to do something, then you have to do something great."

"Just tell me what you want me to do, Uncle Ren."

His eyes darting every which way, the old man jumped down from the sofa and went to the hotel room door where he listened carefully for a moment before running back up onto the sofa.

"Go and get together a group of people – it doesn't matter what kind of people they are as long as they have guts. We'll fix a code word and you'll move on my order. We are going to carry out a momentous undertaking on a grand scale! When I've gathered my forces, I'll announce it to the world and advance on Southeast Asia. I'll attack Malaya first, because Malaya has always treated its Chinese population poorly. All of Singapore is Chinese so they'll support me for sure. Thailand will support me as well because they want a share in the spoils too. But it has never occurred to them that when I've beaten Malaya, I'll form an alliance with Burma, catch the Thais unawares, and wipe them out. After I've wiped out Thailand, I'll take advantage of the momentum and wipe out Burma. Then I'll lead an army to the south and march on Indonesia. Of course Indonesia will collapse with the first blow. Once I've finished mopping up in Indonesia, I'll launch a major offensive on the Philippines. When all of Southeast Asia is in my grasp, I'll openly declare war on Japan and exact revenge for the millions upon millions of my countrymen, soldiers and civilians, who were sacrificed in the eight-year War of Resistance! After I've conquered Japan I'll broadcast to the whole of China from the Tokyo Tower, telling everyone that the national shame has been wiped away. At that time all of China will naturally be unified. I want no official position; I'll voluntarily 'remove my armour and return to the fields.' Later generations will respect and admire my great contribution. This is an undertaking worthy of real men! I've been planning it for decades, and now the time is ripe. It's time to act!"

Standing on the hotel sofa, the grey-haired old man, stomach bulging, gesticulating wildly, delivered his speech to the imaginary multitudes. As wave after wave of cheering erupted from the rapt crowd, an expression of satisfaction appeared on his face.

———

He shut off the tape recorder. The aroma of leeks wafted over from the kitchen next door, making him feel suddenly hungry. Unable to sit still, he walked restlessly into the study. The letters were still lying neatly in the locked drawer; the top layer was Anna's letters. Not only did he not have to reread them, he could even recite the contents from memory. The best thing was that she had been able to find a new boyfriend. He never thought she would be getting married so soon. All his worries had been unnecessary. Their separation had been without rancour; this was a rare woman. He had never done anything for her, but she did not reproach him. He had never done anything for Lily either, apart from interviewing her slightly mad uncle. A magniloquent megalomaniac, he actually wanted to conquer Southeast Asia and Japan. But there was already no trace of the enemy in Nanning.

———————

Fenfen's report card was on the table. At the end of each term, Mrs. Song would always remember to bring around his daughter's report card for him to look at. All her grades were quite good: an "A" in conduct, "B–" in physical education. He had never done anything for Fenfen. He had never done anything for anyone. But there was already no trace of the enemy in Nanning.

———————

Long Long, it's not my fault that I've become like this; they forced me to become like this. They really owe me so much. *Long Long*, it's lucky for you that you went early; it was the only way that you could keep your faith. It's not my fault, *Long Long*, can you forgive me? I haven't forgotten our pledge; look, the scar from the knife is still there on my wrist. Whiskers, Fatty, and I even went up the mountain to hold a memorial for you and for our old alliance. *Long Long*, can you still forgive me?

———————

Lily's voice on the long-distance call was so weak that it seemed that it could float away at any moment.

"Come and get me, okay? I really can't go on. I'm so upset. Please come and get me?"

"Isn't Xiao Chen with you? What about Lao Jin?"

"They're both here, but when I'm upset you're the only person I think about. It doesn't matter how many people I have around me, they're no help. Come and get me please. I can't live a minute longer if you don't come."

He kept silent, waiting for her to plead once more before he blew up.

"You know very well I have to go to work first thing in the morning. What kind of spoiled brat are you, calling at 4:30 in the morning!"

"Don't yell at me, I haven't slept all night. Don't be mad, okay?"

He maintained his silence, the sound of her intermittent sobs coming over the line. Finally, she said:

"I'm taking the first Far Eastern flight back to Taibei. You can at least meet me at Songshan airport, can't you? Just how do I have to beg you?"

———————

The train sped along in the blackened distance. The world was gradually changing shape; the limitless darkness was being transformed into a delimited vastness. The violet plain was slowly coming into view; the outline of the mountains was becoming distinct; the power lines beyond the window rose and fell, resembling the vibrating strings of a zither. As the train rounded the base of the mountain, a cluster of golden rays was reflected from the surface of a small square pond into the carriage. Moaning in pain, he turned around; the carriage was full of deathly pale, unsympathetic faces.

———————

Spectacles waited at the airport until 8:30 and Lily still had not appeared. He wasn't particularly angry, as this was not the first time she had changed her mind at the last moment. When he arrived home, the old man, who had been there for some time, was standing in the hall outside the door waiting for him. The old man's shirt was not tucked in properly – half of it was hanging outside his trousers, and his stomach was protruding. As soon as he saw Spectacles, the old man grabbed his arm.

"It's terrible, they're coming to kill me."

Spectacles used all his strength but was still unable to break free of the old man's grip.

"Who's coming to kill you? Don't worry, no one wants to kill you."

"It's true. They all sold me out, every one of them ... every one of them. They know all about my plan. Someone informed on me, everyone I know informed on me. I know, they all want to kill me. Every one of them wants to do me in. Where's Lily? Where's Lily?"

"Lily's not here!" Spectacles struggled with the old man for a few moments, finally unable to restrain himself from slapping him across the face. "Who's coming to kill you? Who would want to sell you out? Are you worth selling out?"

Having been struck, the old man was momentarily dumbfounded, his grey pupils betraying a look of fear.

"Now I see. It was you who sold me out. I told you everything and you sold me out. You're damned ruthless!"

Spectacles slapped him across the face again.

"You're right, somebody did sell you out. It was nobody else but yourself. You hear me? You sold yourself out. You brought everything down on yourself, and this is the punishment you deserve. You hear me?"

The old man sobbed briefly but then immediately settled down. Spectacles tucked his shirt in for him; the old man's abdomen was extraordinarily soft, like a baby's belly. He allowed himself to be ordered about by Spectacles, the corners of his mouth turned down, the light in his grey pupils completely extinguished. Spectacles could not believe that this was the same man who had just yesterday been standing on the sofa in his hotel room delivering an impassioned address on how he was going to conquer Southeast Asia. He called a taxi and took the old man back to his hotel, having no difficulty whatsoever duping him into returning to his room. When he was leaving, the old man looked at him expectantly, the corners of his mouth twitching, but in the end said nothing more.

———————

Lily did not call until the late afternoon of the next day. She sounded very cheerful.

"Can you believe it? Somebody's asked me to go to Singapore and Malaysia. All I have to do is perform for a week and they'll give me a house. That's on top of the other benefits."

"Have you decided to go?"

"Of course." After a short pause she said, "That's okay with you, isn't it? The day before yesterday was my fault. I shouldn't have called so early and disturbed you. I realized that afterward and called you again, but you'd already left."

"It doesn't matter. We should bring this to an end, shouldn't we?"

As he expected she would, she started to cry.

"You're really cruel. I had a tough time getting this chance, so why do you have to treat me like this? I'll come back to Taibei right now if you want me to."

"I don't want you to come back. Okay, baby, you go ahead and go to Singapore. We'll talk about it when you get back."

"I'll be back in a week." She said, "Say something sweet."

"Hmm."

"Miss me?"

"Yeah."

"Love me?"

"Yeah."

"Will you wait for your baby to come back?"

"Of course I'll wait."

He was about to hang up when she continued:

"Thanks for taking care of Uncle. Auntie came back yesterday too. His old disorder probably flared up again as soon as he heard Auntie was coming back. It's beyond me why the two of them get along so badly."

"He said somebody sold him out, leaked his plan for conquering Southeast Asia."

"That story's old as the hills. Uncle always wants to become some heroic figure like the Curly-bearded Stranger. I'll call you again when I get to Singapore. Do you know who asked me?"

He thought for a moment and said, "It's okay, I don't want to know."

———————

He boiled the remaining half package of *jiaozi*. Who would Lily be sleeping with right now? And who would she be allowing to caress her soft breasts? He could almost hear the sound of her moaning and was overcome by a powerful jealousy. He heard a roaring sound in his ears: he had let the liquid from the *jiaozi* spill all over the gas stove. He hated her weakness and had every right to refuse to marry her for that reason. When they were first together she had said, "If you really love me, don't let me be away from you for very long." She completely understood her own weakness, but they were both powerless to do anything about it. Anna had never cheated on him; she had even written him a letter when she was about to get married. He knew it was Anna's final hint, but there was no possibility that he would change his mind. In spite of the recriminations, he actually loved Lily. He hated her weakness; he loved her weakness; he loved her soft flesh and her weak soul – if man still had a soul. He could never forgive her; he could always forgive her. Where was she at this moment?

———————

Long Long, I'm just a third-rate poet, so you can't expect anything of me. You don't know how fortunate you are. You'll always be remembered as you were at twenty-six, your crewcut, a copy of *Leaves of Grass* under your arm, so insistent about life it made my heart ache. *Long Long*, it's a wonderful thing to be cherished forever in people's memories. Lily has told me she regrets not meeting me when she was nineteen. She was still a virgin then; maybe she hopes that would make me always remember her, never leave her. *Long Long*, it's not my fault I've become like this. Can you still forgive me?

There was already no trace of the enemy in Nanning.
There was already no trace of the enemy in Nanning.

Whiskers and Fatty were animatedly discussing their plans for publishing the poetry collection. Spectacles made every effort to concentrate on dealing with the pork chop on his plate. Whiskers was saying something to him, but he had not really heard him clearly; when Whiskers repeated what he had said, he couldn't help smiling. They had been at it for so many years, yet Whiskers had not lost his enthusiasm. Yes, this type of cover design is quite good. Romantic black flag, romantic anarchists. Spectacles carefully cut the pork chop into small pieces, slowly putting them into his mouth and chewing them. Across from him, Fatty wore a slightly mournful expression.

"Zhixin, I met Anna Chu the day before yesterday, and she asked how you'd been recently. Did you know she's getting married?"

With few customers about after lunch, the Old Gentleman had a certain peculiarly bleak atmosphere. Spectacles remembered that some years back, when the poetry society was first established, they had also had a dinner party here. Whiskers' and Fatty's present fascination with the poetry collection was nothing more than an attempt to recapture the past.

"Reconsider very carefully, Zhixin. This Anna Chu is pretty good, and it was your good fortune to run into her. That's all I'm going to say, old friend. You think it over."

"You people don't understand," Spectacles said. "You can't possibly imagine what I've been through, so where do you get off criticizing me?"

"I don't understand, I really don't understand. If you were indecisive about other girls I could see it, but to be like that with Anna Chu, I really can't let you get away with it."

As Fatty went on talking, he eventually began getting worked up, Whiskers exhorting him from the sidelines. Listening to them squabble over him – Fatty berating him, Whiskers defending him – he had actually become a spectator. He found this amusing and hoped that they really could struggle on to some kind of resolution. They finally stopped fighting and both looked at him. Spectacles again thought of Lily's body. They needn't have bothered; there was no possibility that he would change his mind.

———

He collapsed, limp, beside her, the perspiration running off him. With surprising tenderness, she dried his sweat-soaked body with a towel.

"Miss me?"

"Yeah … but now I don't."

"Rat!" She punched him lightly. "Were you bad while I was away?"

"Of course not." He hesitated a moment before asking, "What about you?"

"Silly, I love you."

It would never be clear to him whether or not she was being sincere. Every time he thought of what she might be doing behind his back he became extremely jealous.

"We should split up."

"You said it first." She jumped out of bed and quickly put on her nightgown; sitting down on the edge of the bed, she looked at him coldly. "There's somebody that wants me to marry him and be his third concubine."

"Have you agreed?"

"We're still negotiating."

"What about us?"

"It's never going to come to anything anyway."

"That's not fair. I love you."

She suddenly started to cry. "It's no use. What do you want me to do? I can't go on singing my whole life. I know I'm not a good singer."

"I know I'm a third-rate poet, so we make a good pair."

She stopped crying as quickly as she had started and again regarded him coldly.

"Well I can't help you. You should be taking care of me, yet you force me to make all the decisions. Why didn't you stop me from going to Singapore?"

"It was you who wanted to go."

"Forget it. You only know about looking after yourself. Whatever comes up you can always say it wasn't your fault. You can never let go of the past. Your bloody poetry society, all you are is a bunch of hacks. Has any one of you actually written any good poetry?"

"*Long Long* wasn't like that. He was different."

"If he was still alive, he'd probably be just like the rest of you."

He had no reply. She burst out laughing.

"You look so upset. Get a bit critical of *Long Long* and it's like somebody insulted your highest ideal. I'm not going to force you. Anyway, we still have some time together. You want to?"

"Yeah."

———————

But there was already no trace of the enemy in Nanning.

———————

The old problem of headaches and sleeplessness had returned. A weariness that penetrated deep into his bones prevented him from falling asleep. He had never hated the compilation work at the publishing company more than he did now. A totally futile undertaking, it interfered with his creative thought processes. He often sat the whole day in boredom; he had no feeling whatsoever. His sense of touch had lost its keenness; the words and phrases in his memories were like a broken phonograph, playing the same tune over and over. He often thought of Lily's uncle. It was, after all, a wonderful thing for an old man of seventy to be able to dream of conquering Southeast Asia. He was stronger than Lily's uncle in only one respect: he could still make love.

Even though this was the case, it in fact guaranteed nothing. Since she had come back from Singapore, Lily had rarely initiated overtures. And often when he was in the mood, she would plead some excuse. He had always considered her to have a powerful sex drive, but the present situation had proven this to be a great misconception. In spite of this, she was even more lovely. He could not help creeping onto all fours while she was asleep and admiring the soft glow of her flesh. She was so frail yet tremendously powerful. She was thoroughly degenerate, yet it was he who was the real degenerate. She no longer needed him; he would always need her.

———————

"Auntie and Uncle are both leaving on Sunday. I'm going home for a few days so I can spend some time with them. After that I have to go to Hong Kong again. My aunt is inviting us all to Emerald Lake on Friday, so why don't you come too? Auntie does want to thank you for looking after Uncle that time."

He knew this was only a pretext: all her bags had long since been packed. Standing there in front of him, she looked so delicate, so alluring. Perhaps she may have prepared her lines beforehand, but coming from her lips, they still moved him.

"I can never be apart from you. Even though we are separating, I'll always have a part of you within me, and you'll always keep a part of me."

———————

But there was already no trace of the enemy in Nanning.

———————

The roller coaster rumbled up to the highest point and the roar momentarily abated; it suddenly increased several times, becoming even louder than before, as the roller coaster flew screaming by over their heads. Lily's mother and her aunt both wrinkled their brows, while her uncle appeared to be totally oblivious to the roar; hands behind his back, he was completely absorbed in his own measured pace. It was actually the first time Spectacles had seen Lily's aunt. Half a head taller than Lily, she was completely grey while not appearing at all old, her back ramrod straight. In his imagination Spectacles could see her heroic bearing as she fought those guerrilla battles during her years in the Taihang Mountains. Standing side by side, Lily's mother and aunt looked much like twin sisters – the latter was typical of the southerner with northern features. A heroic spirit flowed from her square face. There was actually not the slightest similarity between Lily and her mother. The roller coaster made a brief stop at the end of the line before roaring off once more. Covering her ears, Lily said:

"It's awfully noisy. Let's take the tour bus down the mountain and get something to eat. There really isn't anything here at Emerald Lake Amusement Park – it's all kids' stuff."

"Come and take a look at the view. It's pretty nice." Spectacles pointed down the mountain. The water in the New Market River sparkled, and Taibei, in the distance, was shrouded in mist. The tiny point of a transmission tower poked out of the grey fog. Spectacles could not determine which television or radio station the transmitter belonged to. Lily's aunt and mother walked side by side to the edge of the little mountaintop park and stood tall and erect under the phoenix tree; it seemed so natural for them to be standing there. The roller coaster was circling above them, but they never once turned their heads to look. Lily suddenly cried out: "He's taken off up there. Uncle!" Spectacles looked up and saw Lily's uncle standing behind the railing at the end of the line, muttering to himself. Thinking of the scene that day when the old man stood on the sofa and delivered his speech, he raced in the direction of the roller coaster. When he climbed onto the platform, the roller coaster was just coming to the end of the line. Spectacles grabbed the old man, saying:

"Uncle Ren, let's go back down."

The old man shook his head firmly and struggled free, stepping by himself onto the roller coaster. Spectacles could only pay for the old man's ticket and take the seat behind him. The roller coaster moved out slowly, making a clicking sound. They were the only two people in the cars. The old man looked up toward the sky and raised his arms high in the air. Afraid he was going to stand up, Spectacles hugged the old man around the waist. Laughing wildly, the old man shouted:

"Don't be afraid, the time is fully ripe. It's time to go into action!"

The roller coaster climbed to the highest point, seemed to pause for a second, then shot like an arrow toward the foot of the mountain. Spectacles instinctively wrapped his arms tightly around the old man's soft belly. He managed, amidst the uproar, to glance in the direction of the phoenix tree ahead of the roller coaster. Lily's aunt and her mother were still standing under it, straight as ramrods. As the roller coaster hurtled toward them, Spectacles heard the old man shout:

"Advance! Advance! The time has come!"

The old man's windblown hair momentarily obscured

Spectacles' line of vision. Below, Lily seemed to be calling out his name, and Spectacles heard himself yelling too. Just as the roller coaster was about to careen into the phoenix tree, it made a sudden ninety-degree turn. As the old man's head shifted to one side, Spectacles' field of vision became clear, and he saw an expanse of deep blue sky.

Notes on Contributors

Allison, Dorothy. Born in Greenville County, South Carolina (1949-). Author of *The Women Who Hate Me* (1983), a collection of poetry; *Trash* (1988), a collection of short stories; *Bastard Out of Carolina* (1992), a novel; and *Skin* (1993), a collection of essays.

Ballard, J(ames) G(raham). Born in Shanghai, China (1930-). British novelist and short-story writer. He is the author of novels: *The Day of Creation* (1987), *Running Wild* (1989) and *The Kindness of Women* (1991); and collections of short stories: *Memories of the Space Age* (1988) and *War Fever* (1990).

Barthelme, Frederick. Born in Houston, Texas (1943-). Writer and artist. His novels include: *Tracer* (1985) and *Two Against One* (1985); his short-story collections include: *Rangoon* (1970), *Moon Deluxe* (1983) and *Chroma* (1987).

Bellow, Saul. Born in Lachine, Quebec (1915-). American novelist, playwright and short-story writer, he has been awarded three National Book Awards, the Pulitzer and Nobel Prizes. Among his many books are the novels: *Herzog* (1964), *Humbolt's*

Gift (1975), *The Dean's December* (1982), *More Die of Heartbreak* (1987), *The Bellarosa Connection* (1989) and *A Theft* (1989). Bellow's collections of short stories include: *Mosby's Memoirs, and Other Stories* (1968) and *Him with His Foot in His Mouth, and Other Stories* (1984).

Burnard, Bonnie. Born in Petrolia, Ontario. She is the author of two collections of stories, *Women of Influence* (1988), which won the Commonwealth Best First Book Award, and *Casino and Other Stories* (1994).

Carter, Angela. British novelist and short-story writer (1940-1992). Her books include: *Shadow Dance* (1966), *The Magic Toyshop* (1967), *Several Perceptions* (1969), *The Passion of New Eve* (1977), *The Bloody Chamber* (1979) *The Sadeian Woman: An Exercise in Cultural History* (1979) and *Wise Children* (1991).

Cheever, John. Born in Quincy, Massachusetts. Novelist and short-story writer (1912-1982). Cheever is considered among the finest American writers, a master of the short story. In 1979, *The Stories of John Cheever* was awarded the Pulitzer Prize in fiction. Among his novels are: *The Wapshot Chronicle* (1957), *Falconer* (1977), *Bullet Park* (1969) and *Oh, What a Paradise It Seems* (1982).

Colette, (Sidonie-Gabrielle). Novelist, playwright, and short-story writer (1873-1954). One of the most important figures in early twentieth-century French literature. Her books include: *Claudine at School* (1900) and its sequels, *Retreat From Love* (1907), *The Tendrils of the Vine* (1908), *The Vagabond* (1910), *Ripening Seed* (1923) and *Morning Glory* (1928).

Cortázar, Julio. Argentine writer born in Brussels (1914-). He achieved notoriety with his novel *Hopscotch* (1965). His collections of short stories include: *End of Game* (1964), *The Secret Arms* (1964), *Bestiary* (1951), *All Fires the Fire* (1966), *Cronopios and Famas* (1962). Cortázar translated Poe and Marguerite Yourcenar into Spanish.

Dubus, Andre. Born in Lake Charles, Louisiana (1936-). He is the author of the novel, *The Lieutenant* (1986) and several short story collections, including *Land Where My Fathers Died* (1984) and *The Last Worthless Evening* (1986).

Gaitskill, Mary. Born in Lexington, Kentucky (1954-). Novelist and short-story writer. Her principal works are *Bad Behavior* (1988), a collection of short stories, and *Two Girls, Fat and Thin* (1991), a novel.

Garner, Helen. Born in Geelong, Victoria (1942-). Garner's first novel, *Monkey Grip* (1977) won an Australian National Book Award and was adapted into a widely acclaimed film. Her subsequent works include two novels, *Honour, and Other People's Children* (1982) and *The Children's Bach* (1984); and a collection of stories, *Postcards From Surfers* (1985).

Gurganus, Allan. Born in Rocky Mount, North Carolina (1947-). His books include: *Breathing Lessons* (1981), *Good Help* (1988), *Oldest Living Confederate Widow Tells All* (1989), *Blessed Assurance: A Moral Tale* (1990) and *White People: Stories and Novellas*, which won the 1991 *Los Angeles Times* Book Prize for the best work of American fiction.

Heighton, Steven. Born in Toronto, Ontario (1961-). Poet and short-story writer. Heighton's work has appeared in many magazines and anthologies in Canada, the United States, Britain, France, and Australia. His most recent book, a collection of stories, is *The Flight Paths of the Emperor* (1992). Heighton's next collection of stories, *On Earth as it is*, will be published in spring, 1995.

House, Amelia. Born and raised in South Africa, House emigrated to the United States in 1972. She has published poetry, critical essays and short stories in the United States, South Africa and France.

Huggan, Isabel. Born in Kitchener, Ontario (1943-). She is the author of two collections of short stories, *The Elizabeth Stories* (1984) and *You Never Know* (1993). Her stories have appeared in many magazines and anthologies, including *Grain*, *Quarry*, and *83: Best Canadian Stories*.

Jordan, Neil. Born in Sligo, Ireland (1950-). Film director, screenwriter, novelist and short-story writer. Although he is most renowned for his films, Jordan had produced an award-winning story collection, *Nights in Tunisia and Other Stories*, by the age of twenty-five. He went on to write two novels, *The Past* (1980) and *The Dream of a Beast* (1983), as well as many screenplays.

Katzir, Yehudit. Born in Haifa (1963-). Katzir belongs to a new generation of Israeli writers. Her debut work, *Closing the Sea* (1992), a collection of four novellas, including the one that appears in this anthology, received international critical acclaim.

Kōno, Taeko. Born in Osaka, Japan (1926-). Novelist, literary critic and playwright. Among her major works are: *Saigo no toki* (The Last Moment, 1966), *Chi to kaigara* (Blood and Shells, 1975) and *Miira Tori: Ryokitan* (Mummy Haunting: A Story of the Grotesque).

Metcalfe, Robin. Born in Chester, Nova Scotia (1954-). Poet, short-story writer, curator and critic. Metcalfe's essays, fiction and poetry has been published internationally in more than fifty periodicals and in several anthologies, including *Flesh and the Word: An Anthology of Erotic Writing* and *Hometowns: Gay Men Write About Where They Belong.*

Ortiz, Lourdes. Born in Madrid (1943-). She is the author of numerous collections of short stories and several novels. Amongst her latest books are: *Urraca* (1982), *Arcángeles* (Archangels, 1986), *Motivos de Circe* (The Motives of Circe, 1988) and the erotic novel *Camas* (Beds, 1989).

Pizarnik, Alejandra. Argentine poet, translator and writer (1936-1972). While living in Paris between 1960 and 1964, Pizarnik translated the work of Antonin Artaud, Henri Michaux, Aimé Cesairé, and Yves Bonnefoy. Following her return to Buenos Aires she published several volumes of poetry, including *Works and Nights* (1965), *Extraction of the Stone Folly* (1988) and *The Musical Hell* (1972).

Purdy, James. Born in Ohio (1923-). Poet, playwright, short-story writer and interpreter. Purdy has contributed to over fifty books and magazines including *Mademoiselle, New Yorker* and

Commentary. His novels include: 63: *Dream Palace* (1956), *Malcolm* (1959), *The Nephew* (1961), *Cabot Wright Begins* (1964), *Eustace Chisholm and the Works* (1967), *In a Shallow Grave* (1976), *Narrow Rooms* (1978), *In the Hollow of His Hand* (1986). His short story collections include: *Color of Darkness: Eleven Stories and a Novella* (1957) and *Children Is All* (1962).

Schoemperlen, Diane. Born in Thunder Bay, Ontario (1954-). She is the author of *Man of My Dreams* (1990), a collection of short stories, and *In the Language of Love* (1994), a novel. Her work has appeared in many magazines and anthologies, including *Saturday Night, The Malahat Review, 87: Best Canadian Stories* and *90: Best Canadian Stories.*

Sides, Marilyn. Born in Birmingham, Alabama (1952-). Author of the forthcoming collection of short stories, *The Island of the Mapmaker's Wife and Other Stories.* Her stories have appeared in the *O. Henry Collection, Kenyon Review* and *Yellow Silk Journal.*

Tournier, Michel. Born in Paris (1924-). French writer, producer and director. Among his many books are: *The Ogre* (1972), *The Fetishist and Other Stories* (1984), *The Golden Droplet* (1987) and *The Midnight Love Feast* (1991). Tournier is also the translator of many German novels, including the works of Erich Maria Remarque.

Ugrešić, Dubravka. Born in Zagreb, Yugoslavia (1949-). Literary scholar, novelist and short-story writer, she has also written screenplays for television, including a treatment of her own work, *Jaws of Life*, winner of the best Yugoslav film award of 1984.

Updike, John. Born in Shillington, Pennsylvania (1932-). Hailed by critics as one of America's greatest novelists, he is said to have won virtually every American literary award. Updike's most recent novels are: *The Witches of Eastwick* (1984), *Roger's Version* (1986), *S.* (1988) and *Rabbit at Rest* (1990).

Walker, Alice. Born in Eatonton, Georgia (1944-). Poet, novelist and short-story writer. Her most recent novels include: *The Color Purple* (1982), which won the 1982 Pulitzer Prize and 1983 American Book Award, *Beloved* (1987), which received a Nobel Prize for Literature, and *The Temple of My Familiar* (1989).

Welch, Denton. English novelist and short-story writer (1915-1948). Author of the novels *Maiden Voyage* and *Youth Is Pleasure*, the prose and poetry collections *Brave and Cruel* and *A Last Sheaf*, and his *Journals*. Welch died at the age of thirty-three. Only two of his books were published in his lifetime.

Wideman, John Edgar. Born in Washington, DC (1941-). Novelist and short-story writer. Among his books are: *Philadelphia Fire* (1990), *All Stories Are True* (1992), and *The Stories of John Edgar Wideman* (1992). Wideman's novel *Sent for You Yesterday* won the 1984 PEN/Faulkner Award.

Wojnarowicz, David. American writer, film maker, artist and sculptor of extraordinary talent (1954-1992). Wojnarowicz's fictional biography, *Close to the Knoves: A Memoir of Disintigration*, was published in 1991.

Williams, Tennessee. (pseud. of Thomas Lanier Williams). American playwright and short-story writer (1914-83). His first success came with *The Glass Menagerie* (1945). Other plays include: *A Streetcar Named Desire* (1947), *Summer and Smoke* (1948), *The Rose Tattoo* (1951), *Cat on a Hot Tin Roof* (1955), *Orpheus Descending* (1957), *Sweet Bird of Youth* (1959). Among his novels and collections of short stories are: *The Roman Spring of Mrs. Stone* (1950), *Hard Candy* (1954), *Three Players of a Summer Game* (1960). *In The Winter of Cities* (1956) is a collection of poems.

Zhang Xiguo. Chinese writer (1944-) whose works include *Qi wang* (The Chess Master), *Zuori zhi nu* (Yesterday's Anger), and *Buxiuzhe* (The Immortals). He earned a degree in electrical engineering from the University of California at Berkeley and has taught for many years at the Illinois Institute of Technology.

Sources

Allison, Dorothy, "Monkeybites," from *Trash: Stories by Dorothy Allison*, copyright © 1988 by Dorothy Allison. Reprinted by permission of Firebrand Books, Ithica, New York.

Ballard, J.G., "Love in a Colder Climate," from *War Fever* by J.G. Ballard, copyright © 1990 by J.G. Ballard. Reprinted by permission of HarperCollins Publishers Ltd., London.

Barthelme, Frederick, "Cut Glass," from *Chroma* by Frederick Barthelme, copyright © 1987 by Frederick Barthelme. Reprinted by permission of Simon & Schuster Inc., New York, and Wylie, Aitken & Stone Inc., New York.

Bellow, Saul, "Something to Remember Me By," from *Something to Remember Me By: Three Tales* by Saul Bellow, copyright © 1990 by Saul Bellow. Reprinted by permission of Viking Penguin, New York.

Burnard, Bonnie, "Nipple Man," from *Casino and Other Stories* by Bonnie Burnard, copyright © 1994 by Bonnie Burnard. Reprinted by permission of HarperCollins Publishers Ltd., Toronto.

Carter, Angela, "Black Venus," from *Black Venus* by Angela Carter, copyright © 1985 by Angela Carter. Reprinted by permission of Chatto & Windus, The Hogarth Press, London.

*This book is set in Garamond, a typeface
designed in 1545 by Claude Garamont, a punch
cutter in Paris. Garamond gained popularity in
the early seventeenth century. It is light in colour,
delicate in design, and yet smoothly legible.
It is one of the finest old styles ever cut.*

Book design by Gordon Robertson